Image Processing Using FPGAs

Image Processing Using FPGAs

Special Issue Editor

Donald G. Bailey

MDPI • Basel • Beijing • Wuhan • Barcelona • Belgrade

MDPI

Special Issue Editor
Donald G. Bailey
Massey University
New Zealand

Editorial Office
MDPI
St. Alban-Anlage 66
4052 Basel, Switzerland

This is a reprint of articles from the Special Issue published online in the open access journal *Journal of Imaging* (ISSN 2313-433X) from 2018 to 2019 (available at: https://www.mdpi.com/journal/jimaging/special_issues/Image_FPGAs).

For citation purposes, cite each article independently as indicated on the article page online and as indicated below:

LastName, A.A.; LastName, B.B.; LastName, C.C. Article Title. *Journal Name* **Year**, *Article Number*, Page Range.

ISBN 978-3-03897-918-0 (Pbk)
ISBN 978-3-03897-919-7 (PDF)

Contents

About the Special Issue Editor

Donald G. Bailey received his Bachelor of Engineering (Honours) degree in Electrical Engineering in 1982, and Ph.D. degree in Electrical and Electronic Engineering from the University of Canterbury, New Zealand, in 1985. From 1985 to 1987, he applied image analysis to the wool and paper industries of New Zealand. From 1987 to 1989, he was a Visiting Research Engineer at University of California, Santa Barbara. Prof. Bailey joined Massey University in Palmerston North, New Zealand, as Director of the Image Analysis Unit in November 1989. He was a Visiting Researcher at the University of Wales, Cardiff, in 1996; University of California, Santa Barbara, in 2001–2002; and Imperial College London in 2008. He is currently Professor of Imaging Systems in the Department of Mechanical and Electrical Engineering in the School of Food and Advanced Technology at Massey University, where he is Leader of the Centre for Research in Image and Signal Processing. Prof. Bailey has spent over 35 years applying image processing to a range of industrial, machine vision, and robot vision applications. For the last 18 years, one area of particular focus has been exploring different aspects of using FPGAs for implementing and accelerating image processing algorithms. He is the author of many publications in this field, including the book "Design for Embedded Image Processing on FPGAs", published by Wiley/IEEE Press. He is a Senior Member of the IEEE, and is active in the New Zealand Central Section.

Preface to "Image Processing Using FPGAs"

Over the last 20 years, FPGAs have moved from glue logic through to computing platforms. They effectively provide a reconfigurable hardware platform for implementing logic and algorithms. Being fine-grained hardware, FPGAs are able to exploit the parallelism inherent within a hardware design while at the same time maintaining the reconfigurability and programmability of software. This has led to FPGAs being used as a platform for accelerating computationally intensive tasks. This is particularly seen in the field of image processing, where the FPGA-based acceleration of imaging algorithms has become mainstream. This is even more so within an embedded environment, where the power and computational resources of conventional processors are not up to the task of managing the data throughput and computational requirements of real-time imaging applications.

Unfortunately, the fine-grained nature of FPGAs also makes them difficult to programme effectively. Conventional processors have a fixed computational architecture, which is able to provide a high level of abstraction. By contrast, on an FPGA, it is necessary to design not only the algorithm but also the computational architecture, which leads to an explosion in the design space complexity. This, coupled with the complexities of managing the concurrency of a highly parallel design and the bandwidth issues associated with the high volume of data associated with images and video, has led to a wide range of approaches and architectures used for realising FPGA-based image processing systems. This Special Issue provides an opportunity for researchers in this area to present some of their latest results and designs. The diversity of presented techniques and applications reflects the nature and current state of FPGA-based design for image processing.

Donald G. Bailey
Special Issue Editor

Journal of
Imaging

MDPI

Editorial
Image Processing Using FPGAs

Donald G. Bailey

Department of Mechanical and Electrical Engineering, School of Food and Advanced Technology,
Massey University, Palmerston North 4442, New Zealand; D.G.Bailey@massey.ac.nz

Received: 6 May 2019; Accepted: 7 May 2019; Published: 10 May 2019

Abstract: Nine articles have been published in this Special Issue on image processing using field programmable gate arrays (FPGAs). The papers address a diverse range of topics relating to the application of FPGA technology to accelerate image processing tasks. The range includes: Custom processor design to reduce the programming burden; memory management for full frames, line buffers, and image border management; image segmentation through background modelling, online K-means clustering, and generalised Laplacian of Gaussian filtering; connected components analysis; and visually lossless image compression.

Keywords: field programmable gate arrays (FPGA); image processing; hardware/software co-design; memory management; segmentation; image analysis; compression

1. Introduction to This Special Issue

Field programmable gate arrays (FPGAs) are increasingly being used for the implementation of image processing applications. This is especially the case for real-time embedded applications, where latency and power are important considerations. An FPGA embedded in a smart camera is able to perform much of the image processing directly as the image is streamed from the sensor, with the camera providing a processed output data stream, rather than a sequence of images. The parallelism of hardware is able to exploit the spatial (data level) and temporal (task level) parallelism implicit within many image processing tasks. Unfortunately, simply porting a software algorithm onto an FPGA often gives disappointing results, because many image processing algorithms have been optimised for a serial processor. It is usually necessary to transform the algorithm to efficiently exploit the parallelism and resources available on an FPGA. This can lead to novel algorithms and hardware computational architectures, both at the image processing operation level and also at the application level.

The aim of this Special Issue is to present and highlight novel algorithms, architectures, techniques, and applications of FPGAs for image processing. A total of 20 submissions were received for the Special Issue, with nine papers being selected for final publication.

2. Contributions

Programming an FPGA to accelerate complex algorithms is difficult, with one of four approaches commonly used [1]:

- Custom hardware design of the algorithm using a hardware description language, optimised for performance and resources;
- implementing the algorithm by instantiating a set of application-specific intellectual property cores (from a library);
- using high-level synthesis to convert a C-based representation of the algorithm to synthesisable hardware; or
- mapping the algorithm onto a parallel set of programmable soft-core processors.

The article by Siddiqui et al. [1] took this last approach, and describes the design of an efficient 16-bit integer soft-core processor, IPPro, capable of operating at 337 MHz, specifically targetting the dataflow seen in complex image processing algorithms. The presented architecture uses dedicated stream access instructions on the input and output, with a 32-element local memory for storing pixels and intermediate results, and a separate 32-element kernel memory for storing filter coefficients and other parameters and constants. The exploitation of both data-level parallelism and task-level parallelism is demonstrated through the mapping of a K-means clustering algorithm onto the architecture, showing good scalability of processing speed with multiple cores. A second case study of traffic sign recognition is partitioned between the IPPro cores and an ARM processor, with the colour conversion and morphological filtering stages mapped to the IPPro. Again, the use of parallel IPPro cores can significantly accelerate these tasks, compared to conventional software, without having to resort to the tedious effort of custom hardware design.

Garcia et al. [2] worked on the thesis that the image processing operations which require random access to the whole frame (including iterative algorithms) are particularly difficult to realise in FPGAs. They investigate the mapping of a frame buffer onto the memory resources of an FPGA, and explore the optimal mapping onto combinations of configurable on-chip memory blocks. They demonstrate that, for many image sizes, the default mapping by the synthesis tools results in poor utilisation, and is also inefficient in terms of power requirements. A procedure is described that determines the best memory configuration, based on balancing resource utilisation and power requirements. The mapping scheme is demonstrated with optical flow and mean shift tracking algorithms.

On the other hand, local operations (such as filters) only need part of the image to produce an output, and operate efficiently in stream processing mode, using line buffers to cache data for scanning a local window through the image. This works well when the image size is fixed, and is known in advance. Two situations where this approach is less effective [3] are in the region of interest processing, where only a small region of the image is processed (usually determined from the image contents at run-time), and cloud processing of user-uploaded images (which may be of arbitrary size). This is complicated further in high-speed systems, where the real-time requirements demand processing multiple pixels in every clock cycle, because, if the line width is not a multiple of the number of pixels processed each cycle, then it is necessary to assemble the output window pixels from more than one memory block. Shi et al. [3], in their paper, extend their earlier work on assembling the output window to allow arbitrary image widths. The resulting line buffer must be configurable at run-time, which is achieved through a series of "instructions", which control the assembly of the output processing window when the required data spans two memory blocks. Re-configuration only takes a few clock cycles (to load the instructions), rather than conventional approach of reconfiguring the FPGA each time the image width changes. The results demonstrate better resource utilisation, higher throughput, and lower power than their earlier approach.

When applying window operations to an image, the size of the output image is smaller than the input because data is not valid when the window extends beyond the image border. If necessary, this may be mitigated by extending the input image to provide data to allow such border pixels to be calculated. Prior work only considered border management using direct form filter structures, because the window formation and filter function can be kept independent. However, in some applications, transpose-form filter structures are desirable because the corresponding filter function is automatically pipelined, leading to fewer resources and faster clock frequencies. Bailey and Ambikumar [4] provide a design methodology for border management using transpose filter structures, and show that the resource requirements are similar to those for direct-form border management.

An important task in computer vision is segmenting objects from a complex background. While there are many background modelling algorithms, the complexity of robust algorithms make them difficult to realise on an FPGA, especially for larger image sizes. Chen et al. [5] address scalability issues with increasing image size by using super-pixels—small blocks of adjacent pixels that are treated as a single unit. As each super-pixel is considered to be either object or background, this means that fewer models need to be maintained (less memory) and fewer elements need to be classified (reduced computation time). Using hardware/software co-design, they accelerated the computationally expensive steps of Gaussian filtering and calculating the mean and variance within each super-pixel with hardware, with the rest of the algorithm being realised on the on-chip CPU. The resulting system gave close to state-of-the-art classification accuracy.

A related paper, by Badawi and Bilal [6], used K-means clustering to segment objects within video sequences. Rather than taking the conventional iterative approach to K-means clustering, they rely on the temporal coherence of video streams and use the cluster centres from the previous frame as initialisation for the current frame. Additionally, rather than waiting until the complete frame has been accumulated before updating the cluster centres, an online algorithm is used, with the clusters updated for each pixel. To reduce the computational requirements, the centres are updated using a weighted average. They demonstrate that, for typical video streams, this gives similar performance to conventional K-means algorithms, but with far less computation and power.

In another segmentation paper, Zhou et al. [7] describe the use of a generalised Laplacian of Gaussian (LoG) filter for detecting cell nuclei for a histopathology application. The LoG filters detect elliptical blobs at a range of scales and orientations. Local maxima of the responses are used as candidate seeds for cell centres, and mean-shift clustering is used to combine multiple detections from different scales and orientations. Their FPGA design gave modest acceleration over a software implementation on a high-end computer.

Given a segmented image, a common task is to measure feature vectors of each connected component for analysis. Bailey and Klaiber [8] present a new single-pass connected components analysis algorithm, which does this with minimum latency and relatively few resources. The key novelty of this paper is the use of a zig-zag based scan, rather than a conventional raster scan. This eliminates the end-of-row processing for label resolution by integrating it directly within the reverse scan. The result is true single-pixel-per-clock-cycle processing, with no overheads at the end of each row or frame.

An important real-time application of image processing is embedded online image compression for reducing the data bandwidth for image transmission. In the final paper within this Special Issue, Wang et al. [9] defined a new image compression codec which works efficiently with a streamed image, and minimises the perceptual distortion within the reconstructed images. Through small local filters, each pixel is classified as either an edge, a smooth region, or a textured region. These relate to a perceptual model of contrast masking, allowing just noticeable distortion (JND) thresholds to be defined. The image is compressed by downsampling; however, if the error in any of the contributing pixels exceeds the visibility thresholds, the 2×2 block is considered a region of interest, with the 4 pixels coded separately. In both cases, the pixel values are predicted using a 2-dimensional predictor, and the prediction residuals are quantised and entropy-encoded. Results typically give a visually lossless 4:1 compression, which is significantly better than other visually lossless codecs.

3. Conclusions

Overall, this collection of papers reflects the diversity of approaches taken to applying FPGAs to image processing applications. From one end, using the programmable logic to design lightweight custom processors to enable parallelism, through overcoming some of the limitations of current high-level synthesis tools, to the other end with the design of custom hardware designs at the register-transfer level.

The range of image processing techniques include filtering, segmentation, clustering, and compression. Applications include traffic sign recognition for autonomous driving, histopathology, and video compression.

Funding: This research received no external funding.

Acknowledgments: The Guest Editor would like to acknowledge the time and contributions of the authors (both successful and unsuccessful) who prepared papers for this Special Issue. Special thanks go to all the reviewers who provided constructive reviews of the papers in a timely manner; your analysis and feedback has ensured the quality of the papers selected. It is also necessary to acknowledge the assistance given by the MDPI editorial team, in particular Managing Editors Alicia Wang and Veronica Wang, who made my task as Guest Editor much easier.

Conflicts of Interest: The author declares no conflict of interest.

References

1. Siddiqui, F.; Amiri, S.; Minhas, U.I.; Deng, T.; Woods, R.; Rafferty, K.; Crookes, D. FPGA-based processor acceleration for image processing applications. *J. Imaging* **2019**, *5*, 16. [CrossRef]
2. Garcia, P.; Bhowmik, D.; Stewart, R.; Michaelson, G.; Wallace, A. Optimized memory allocation and power minimization for FPGA-based image processing. *J. Imaging* **2019**, *5*, 7. [CrossRef]
3. Shi, R.; Wong, J.S.; So, H.K.H. High-throughput line buffer microarchitecture for arbitrary sized streaming image processing. *J. Imaging* **2019**, *5*, 34. [CrossRef]
4. Bailey, D.G.; Ambikumar, A.S. Border handling for 2D transpose filter structures on an FPGA. *J. Imaging* **2018**, *4*, 138. [CrossRef]
5. Chen, A.T.Y.; Gupta, R.; Borzenko, A.; Wang, K.I.K.; Biglari-Abhari, M. Accelerating SuperBE with hardware/software co-design. *J. Imaging* **2018**, *4*, 122. [CrossRef]
6. Badawi, A.; Bilal, M. High-level synthesis of online K-Means clustering hardware for a real-time image processing pipeline. *J. Imaging* **2019**, *5*, 38. [CrossRef]
7. Zhou, H.; Machupalli, R.; Mandal, M. Efficient FPGA implementation of automatic nuclei detection in histopathology images. *J. Imaging* **2019**, *5*, 21. [CrossRef]
8. Bailey, D.G.; Klaiber, M.J. Zig-zag based single pass connected components analysis. *J. Imaging* **2019**, *5*, 45. [CrossRef]
9. Wang, Z.; Tran, T.H.; Muthappa, P.K.; Simon, S. A JND-based pixel-domain algorithm and hardware architecture for perceptual image coding. *J. Imaging* **2019**, *5*, 50. [CrossRef]

Journal of
Imaging

MDPI

Article

FPGA-Based Processor Acceleration for Image Processing Applications

Fahad Siddiqui [1,†] , Sam Amiri [2,†], Umar Ibrahim Minhas [1] , Tiantai Deng [1], Roger Woods [1,*] ,
Karen Rafferty [1] and Daniel Crookes [1]

1 School of Electronics, Electrical Engineering and Computer Science, Queen's University Belfast,
Belfast BT7 1NN, UK; f.siddiqui@qub.ac.uk (F.S.); u.minhas@qub.ac.uk (U.I.M.); tdeng01@qub.ac.uk (T.D.);
k.rafferty@qub.ac.uk (K.R.); d.crookes@qub.ac.uk (D.C.)
2 School of Computing, Electronics and Maths, Coventry University, Coventry CV1 5FB, UK;
ad0246@coventry.ac.uk
* Correspondence: r.woods@qub.ac.uk; Tel.: +44-289-097-4081
† These authors contributed equally to this work.

Received: 27 November 2018; Accepted: 7 January 2019; Published: 13 January 2019

Abstract: FPGA-based embedded image processing systems offer considerable computing resources
but present programming challenges when compared to software systems. The paper describes an
approach based on an FPGA-based soft processor called *Image Processing Processor* (IPPro) which can
operate up to 337 MHz on a high-end Xilinx FPGA family and gives details of the dataflow-based
programming environment. The approach is demonstrated for a k-means clustering operation and
a traffic sign recognition application, both of which have been prototyped on an Avnet Zedboard
that has Xilinx Zynq-7000 system-on-chip (SoC). A number of parallel dataflow mapping options
were explored giving a speed-up of 8 times for the k-means clustering using 16 IPPro cores, and a
speed-up of 9.6 times for the morphology filter operation of the traffic sign recognition using
16 IPPro cores compared to their equivalent ARM-based software implementations. We show that for
k-means clustering, the 16 IPPro cores implementation is 57, 28 and 1.7 times more power efficient
(fps/W) than ARM Cortex-A7 CPU, nVIDIA GeForce GTX980 GPU and ARM Mali-T628 embedded
GPU respectively.

Keywords: FPGA; hardware acceleration; processor architectures; image processing;
heterogeneous computing

1. Introduction

With improved sensor technology, there has been a considerable growth in the amount of data
being generated by security cameras. In many remote environments with limited communication
bandwidth, there is a clear need to overcome this by employing remote functionality in the system such
as employing motion estimation in smart cameras [1]. As security requirements grow, the processing
needs will only need to increase.

New forms of computing architectures are needed. In late 70's, Lamport [2] laid the foundation
of parallel architectures exploiting data-level parallelism (DLP) using work load vectorisation and
shared memory parallelisation, used extensively in Graphical Processing Units (GPUs). Current energy
requirements and limitations of Dennard scaling have acted to limit clock scaling and thus reduce
future processing capabilities of GPUs or multi-core architectures [3]. Recent field programmable gate
array (FPGA) architectures represent an attractive alternative for acceleration as they comprise ARM
processors and programmable logic for accelerating computing intensive operations.

FPGAs are proven computing platforms that offer reconfigurability, concurrency and pipelining,
but have not been accepted as a mainstream computing platform. The primary inhibitor is the need to

use specialist programming tools, describing algorithms in *hardware description language* (HDL), although this has been alleviated by the introduction of high-level programming tools such as Xilinx's Vivado High-level Synthesis (HLS) and Intel's (Altera's) compiler for OpenCL. While the level of abstraction has been raised, a gap still exists between adaptability, performance and efficient utilisation of FPGA resources. Nevertheless, the FPGA design flow still requires design *synthesis* and *place-and-route* that can be time-consuming depending on the complexity and size of the design [4,5]. This FPGA design flow is alien to software/algorithm developers and inhibits wider use of the technology.

One way to approach this research problem is to develop adaptable FPGA hardware architecture that enables *edit-compile-run* flow familiar to software and algorithm developers instead of hardware *synthesis* and *place-and-route*. This can be achieved by populating FPGA logic with a number of efficient soft core processors used for programmable hardware acceleration. This underlying architecture will be adaptable and can be programmed using conventional software development approaches. However, the challenge is to build an FPGA solution that is more easily programmed whilst still providing high performance. Whilst FPGA-based processor architectures exist such as Xilinx's MicroBlaze, Altera's NIOS and others [6–9], we propose an *Image Processing Processor* (IPPro) processor [10] tailored to accelerate image processing operations, thereby providing an excellent mapping between FPGA resources, speed and programming efficiency. The main purpose of the paper is to give insights into the multi-core processor architecture built using the IPPro architecture, its programming environment and outline its applications to two image processing applications. Our main contributions are:

- Creation of an efficient, FPGA-based multicore processor which advances previous work [10], [11] and an associated dataflow-based compiler environment for programming a heterogeneous FPGA resource comprising it and ARM processors.
- Exploration of mapping the functionality for a *k*-means clustering function, resulting in a possible speedup of up to 8 times that is 57, 28 and 1.7 times more power efficient (fps/W) than ARM Cortex-A7 CPU, nVIDIA GeForce GTX980 GPU and ARM Mali-T628 embedded GPU.
- Acceleration of colour and morphology operations of traffic sign recognition application, resulting in a speedup of 4.5 and 9.6 times respectively on a Zedboard.

The rest of paper is organized as follows: Section 2 outlines the various image processing requirements and outlines how these can be matched to FPGA; relevant research is also reviewed. System requirements are outlined in Section 3 and the soft core processor architecture is also briefly reviewed in Section 4. The system architecture is outlined in Section 5. Experiments to accelerate a *k*-means clustering algorithm and a traffic sign recognition example, are presented in Sections 6 and 7 respectively. Conclusions and future work are described in Section 8.

2. Background

Traditionally, vision systems have been created in a centralized manner where video from multiple cameras is sent to a central back-end computing unit to extract significant features. However, with increasing number of nodes and wireless communications, this approach becomes increasingly limited, particularly with higher resolution cameras [12]. A distributed processing approach can be employed where data-intensive, front-end preprocessing such as sharpening, object detection etc. can be deployed remotely, thus avoiding the need to transmit high data, video streams back to the server.

2.1. Accelerating Image Processing Algorithms

Nugteren et al. has characterized image processing operations based on the computation and communication patterns [13] as highlighted in Table 1. The vision processing architecture can be composed of general and special purpose processors, FPGAs or combinations thereof. FPGAs offer opportunities to exploit the fine/coarse grained parallelism that most of the image processing applications exhibit at front-end processing. Heterogeneous architectures comprising CPUs and FPGA fabrics thus offer a good balance in terms of performance, cost and energy efficiency.

Brodtkorb et al. has compared architectural and programming language properties of heterogeneous architectures comprising CPU, GPU and FPGA [14] showing that FPGAs deliver a better performance/W ratio for fixed-point operations; however, they are difficult to program. Different design approaches have been adopted by the research community to build FPGA-based hardware accelerators. These include:

- **Customised hardware accelerator designs in HDLs** which require long development times but can be optimised in terms of performance and area.
- **Application specific hardware accelerators** which are generally optimized for a single function, non-programmable and created using IP cores.
- Designs created using **high-level synthesis tools** such as Xilinx's Vivado HLS tool and Altera's OpenCL compiler which convert a C-based specification into an RTL implementation synthesizable code [15] allowing pipelining and parallelization to be explored.
- **Programmable hardware accelerator** in the form of vendor specific soft processors such as Xilinx's Microblaze and Altera's NIOS II processors and customized hard/soft processors.

Table 1. Categorisation of image processing operations based on their memory and execution patterns [13] allow features of compute and memory patterns to be highlighted and therefore identifying what can be mapped into FPGA.

Operation Type	Domain	Output Depends on	Memory Pattern	Execution Pattern	Examples
Point and Line	Spatial	Single input pixel	Pipelined	One-to-one	Intensity change by factor, Negative image-inversion.
Area/Local	Spatial	Neighbouring pixels	Coalesced	Tree	Convolution functions: Sobel, Sharpen, Emboss.
Geometric	Spatial	Whole frame	Recursive non-coalesced	Large reduction tree	Rotate, Scale, Translate, Reflect, Perspective and Affine.

2.2. Soft Processor Architectures

Numerous FPGA multiprocessor architectures have been created to accelerate applications. Strik et al. used a heterogeneous multiprocessor system with a reconfigurable network-on-chip to process multiple video streams concurrently in real-time [16]. VectorBlox MXP [7] is the latest of a series of vector-based soft core processor architectures designed to exploit DLP by processing vectors. Optimizations employed include replacing a vector register file with a scratchpad memory to allow for arbitrary data packing and access, removing vector length limits, enabling sub-word single-instruction, multiple-data (SIMD) within each lane and a DMA-based memory interface.

Zhang et al. has created composable vector units [17] and allows a vector program of a dataflow graph (DFG) to be statically compiled and clusters of operations to be composed together to create a new streaming instruction that uses multiple operators and operands. This is similar to traditional vector chaining but is not easily extended to support wide SIMD-style parallelism. The reported speed-ups were less than a factor of two. Further optimizations have been employed in a custom SVP Bluespec [18] where they compared a custom pipeline to the SVP implementation and found that performance was within a factor of two given similar resource usage. Kapre et al. has proposed a GraphSoC custom soft processor for accelerating graph algorithms [19]. It is a three-stage pipelined processor that supports graph semantics (node, edge operations). The processor was designed with Vivado HLS. Each core uses nine BRAMs and runs at 200 MHz.

Octavo [20] is a multi-threaded, ten-cycle processor that runs at 550 MHz on a Stratix IV, equivalent to the maximum frequency supported by memory blocks. A deep pipeline is necessary to support this high operating frequency, but suffers from the need to pad dependent instructions to overcome data hazards. The authors sidestep this issue by designing Octavo as a multi-processor, thus dependent instructions are always sufficiently far apart and NOP padding is not needed. Andryc et al. presented a GPGPU architecture called FlexGrip [8] which like vector processors, supports wide data parallel, SIMD-style computation using multiple parallel compute lanes, provides support for conditional operations, and requires optimized interfaces to on- and off-chip memory. FlexGrip maps pre-compiled CUDA kernels on soft core processors which are programmable and operate at 100 MHz.

3. System Implementation

Whilst earlier versions of FPGAs just comprised multiple Lookup Tables (LUT) connected to registers and accelerated by fast adders, FPGAs now comprise more coarse-grained functions such as dedicated, full-custom, low-power DSP slices. For example, the Xilinx DSP48E1 block comprises a 25-bit pre-adder, a 25 × 18-bit multiplier and a 48-bit adder/subtracter/logic unit, multiple distributed RAM blocks which offer high bandwidth capability (Figure 1), and a plethora of registers which supports high levels of pipelining.

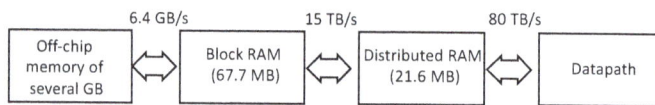

Figure 1. Bandwidth/memory distribution in Xilinx Virtex-7 FPGA which highlight how bandwidth and computation improves as we near the datapath parts of the FPGA.

Whilst FPGAs have been successfully applied in embedded systems and communications, they have struggled as a mainstream computational platform. Addressing the following considerations would make FPGAs a major platform rival for "data-intensive" applications:

- *Programmability*: there is a need for a design methodology which includes a flexible data communication interface to exchange data. Intellectual Property (IP) cores and HLS tools [15]/ OpenCL design routes increase programming abstraction but do not provide the flexible system infrastructure for image processing systems.
- *Dataflow support*: the dataflow model of computation is a recognized model for data-intensive applications. Algorithms are represented as a directed graph composed of nodes (actors) as computational units and edges as communication channels [21]. While the actors run explicitly in parallel decided by the user, actor functionality can either be sequential or concurrent. Current FPGA realizations use the concurrency of the whole design at a higher level but eliminate reprogrammability. A better approach is to keep reprogrammability while still maximizing parallelism by running actors on simple "pipelined" processors; the actors still run their code explicitly in parallel (user-specified).
- *Heterogeneity*: the processing features of FPGAs should be integrated with CPUs. Since dataflow supports both sequential and concurrent platforms, the challenge is then to allow effective mapping onto CPUs with parallelizable code onto FPGA.
- *Toolset availability*: design tools created to specifically compile user-defined dataflow programs at higher levels to fully reprogrammable heterogeneous platform should be available.

High-Level Programming Environment

The proposed methodology employs a reprogrammable model comprising multi-core processors supporting SIMD operation and an associated inter-processor communication methodology. A dataflow design methodology has chosen as the high-level programming approach as it offers concurrency, scalability, modularity and provides data driven properties, all of which match the design requirements associated with image processing systems. A dataflow model allows algorithms to be realized as actors with specific firing rules that are mapped into directed graphs where the nodes represent computations and arcs represent the movement of data. The term data-driven is used to express the execution control of dataflow with the availability of the data itself. In this context, an actor is a standalone entity, which defines an execution procedure and can be implemented in the IPPro processor. Actors communicate with other actors by passing data tokens, and the execution is done through the token passing through *First-In-First-Out* (FIFO) units. The combination of a set of actors with a set of connections between actors constructs a network, which maps well to the system level architecture of the IPPro processors. An earlier version of the programming environment has been is detailed in [11] allowing the user to explore parallel implementation and providing the necessary back-end compilation support.

In our flow, every processor can be thought of as an actor and data is fired through the FIFO structures but the approach needs to be sensitive to FPGA-based limitations such as restricted memory. *Cal Actor Language* (CAL) [22] is a dataflow programming language that has been focussed at image processing and FPGAs and it offers the necessary constructs for expressing parallel or sequential coding, bitwise types, a consistent memory model, and a communication between parallel tasks through queues. RVC-CAL is supported by an open source dataflow development environment and compiler framework, Orcc, that allows the trans-compilation of actors and generates equivalent code depending on the chosen back-ends [23]. An RVC-CAL based design is composed of a dataflow network file (.xdf file) that supports task and data-level parallelism.

Figure 2 illustrates the possible pipelined decomposition of dataflow actors. These dataflow actors need to be balanced as the worst-case execution time of the actor determines the overall achievable performance. Data-level parallelism is achieved by making multiple instances of an actor and requires SIMD operations that shall be supported by the underlying processor architecture. In addition, it requires software configurable system-level infrastructure that manages control and data distribution/collection tasks. It involves the initialisation of the soft core processors (programming the decomposed dataflow actor description), receiving data from the host processor, distributing them to first-level actors, gathering processed data from the final-level actors and send it back to host processor.

Data-level parallelism directly impacts the system performance; the major limiting factor is the number of resources available on FPGA. An example pipeline structure with an algorithm composed of four actors each having different execution times, and multiple instances of the algorithm realised in SIMD fashion is shown in Figure 2. The performance metric, frames-per-second (fps) can be approximated using $N_{(total\_pixels)}$ the number of pixels in a frame, $N_{(pixel\_consumption)}$ the number of pixels consumed by an actor in each iteration and $f_{(processor)}$ is operating frequency of processor.

$$fps \approx \frac{f_{(processor)} * N_{(pixel\_consumption)}}{N_{(total\_pixels)}} \tag{1}$$

To improve the fps, the following options are possible:

- *Efficient FPGA-based processor design* that operates at higher operating frequency $f_{(processor)}$.
- *Reducing the actor's execution time* by decomposing it into multiple pipelined stages, thus reducing $t_{(actor)}$ to improve the fps. Shorter actors can be merged sequentially to minimise the data transfer overhead by localising data into FIFOs between processing stages.
- *Vertical scaling to exploit data parallelism* by mapping an actor on multiple processor cores, thus reducing ($n * \frac{N_{(total\_pixels)}}{N_{(pixel\_consumption)}}$) at the cost of additional system-level data distribution, control, and collection mechanisms.

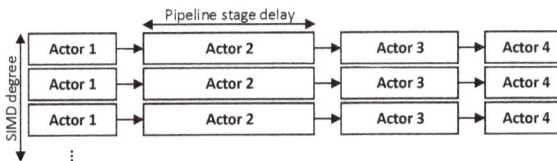

Figure 2. Illustration of possible data and task parallel decomposition of a dataflow algorithm found in image processing designs where the numerous of rows indicate the level of parallelism.

The developed tool flow (Figure 3) starts with a user-defined RVC-CAL description composed of actors selected to execute in FPGA-based soft cores with the rest to be run in the host CPUs. By analyzing behaviour, software/hardware partitioning is decided by two main factors, the actors with the worse execution time (determined exactly by number of instructions and the average waiting time to receive the input tokens and send the produced tokens), and the overheads incurred in transferring the image data to/from the accelerator. The behavioural description of an algorithm could be coded in different formats:

- No explicit balanced actors or actions are provided by the user.
- The actors include actions which are balanced without depending on each other, e.g., no global variables in an actor is updated by one action and then used by the other ones; otherwise, these would need to be decomposed into separate actors.
- The actors are explicitly balanced and only require hardware/software partitioning.

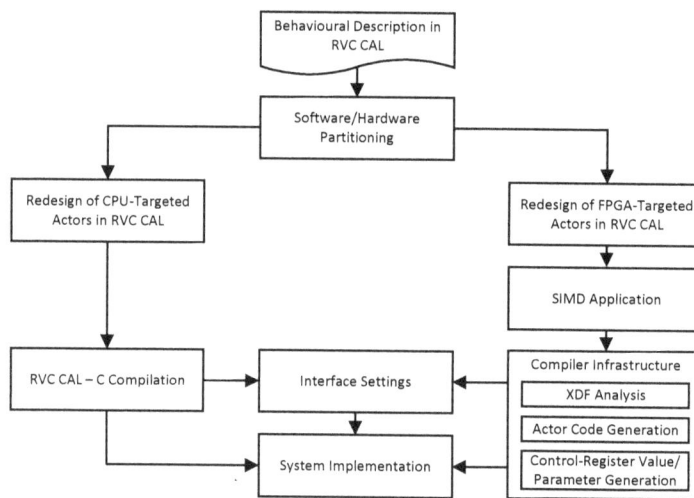

Figure 3. A brief description of the design flow of a hardware and software heterogeneous system highlighting key features. More detail of the flow is contained in reference [11].

There are two types of decomposition, "row-" and "column-wise". The newly generated data-independent actors can be placed row-wise at the same pipeline stage; otherwise they can be placed column-wise as consecutive pipeline stages. Row-wise is preferred as the overhead incurred in token transmission can be a limiting factor but typically a combination is employed.

If the actors or actions are not balanced, then they need to be decomposed. This is done by detecting a sequence of instructions without branches (unless this occurs at the end) and then breaking the program into basic blocks. The "balance points" whereby the actor needs to be divided into multiple sets of basic blocks such that if each set is placed in a new actor, then need to be found; this will ensure that the overhead of transferring tokens among the sets will not create a bottleneck and infer the selection and use of one with the lowest overhead (See Ref. [11]). Once the graph is partitioned, the original xdf file no longer represents the network topology, so each set of actors must be redesigned separately and their input/output ports fixed and a new set of xdf dataflow network description files, generated. The actors to run on the host CPU are compiled from RVC-CAL to C using the C backend of Orcc development environment, whereas the FPGA-based functionality is then created using the proposed compiler framework.

The degree of SIMD applied will affect the controller interface settings. For a target board, the design will have a fixed number of IPPro cores realized and interconnected with each other and controllers, determined by the FPGA resources and fan-out delay; for the Zedboard considered here, 32 cores are selected. The compilation infrastructure is composed of three distinctive steps:

- Examination of the xdf dataflow network file and assignment and recording of the actor mapping to the processors on the network.
- Compilation of each actor's RVC-CAL code to IPPro assembly code.
- Generation of control register values, mainly for AXI Lite Registers, and parameters required by the developed C-APIs. running on the host CPU

While FPGA-targeted actor interaction is handled by the compiler, the processes for receiving the image data and storing the output in the edge actors need to be developed. Multiple controllers (programmable by the host CPU) are designed to provide the interface to transfer the data to the accelerators, gather the results and transfer them back to the host. With the host CPU running part of the design and setting control registers, and the IPPro binary codes of the other actors loaded to the proper cores on the accelerator, and the interface between the software/hardware sections set accordingly, the system implementation is in place and ready to run.

4. Exploration of Efficient FPGA-Based Processor Design

Image processing applications extensively use multiply and accumulate operations for image segmentation and filtering which can be efficiently mapped to FPGA. On the FPGA, the dedicated memory blocks are located next to the DSP blocks to minimise any timing delays and it is this that determines the maximum operating frequency (f_{max}) of the processor. It is one of the reasons that many-core and multi-core architectures use simple, light-weight processing datapaths over complex and large out-of-order processors. However, to maintain the balance among soft processor functionality, scalability, performance and efficient utilisation of FPGA resources remain an open challenge.

Figure 4 presents the impact of different configurations of DSP48E1 and BRAM on f_{max} and the parameters required by the developed C-APIs running on the host CPU using different FPGAs. The DSP48E1 has five configurations that offer different functionalities (multiplier, accumulator, pre-adder and pattern detector) based on different internal pipeline configurations that directly impacts f_{max}. It varies 15–52% for the same speed grade and reduces by 12–20% when the same design is ported from −3 to −1 speed grade. Configuring the BRAM as a single and true-dual port RAM, Figure 4b has been created to show that a true-dual port RAM configuration gives a reduction of 25% in f_{max}. However an improvement of 16% is possible by migrating the design from Artix-7 to Kintex-7 FPGA technology.

Table 2 shows the distribution of compute (DSP48E1) and memory (BRAM) resources, and highlights the raw performance in GMAC/s (giga multiply-accumulates per second) across the largest FPGA devices covering both standalone and Zynq SoC chips. A BRAM/DSP ratio metric is reported to quantify the balance between compute and memory resources. In Zynq SoC devices, it is higher than standalone devices because more memory is required to implement substantial data buffers to exchange data between FPGA fabric and the host processor, while it is close to unity for standalone devices. This suggests that BRAM/DSP ratio can be used to quantify area efficiency of FPGA designs.

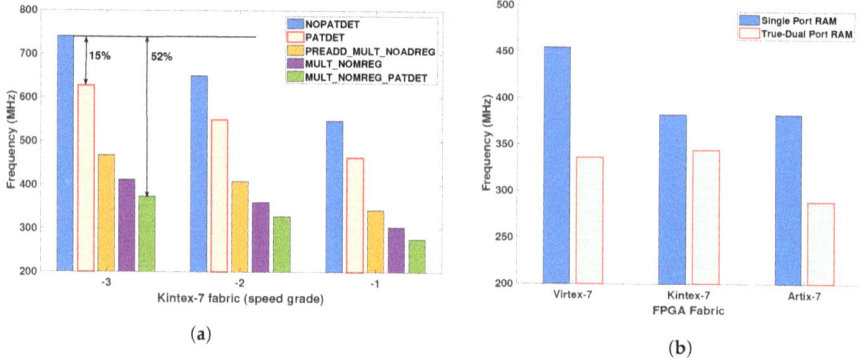

(a)

(b)

Figure 4. (**a**) Impact of DSP48E1 configurations on maximum achievable clock frequency using different speed grades using Kintex-7 FPGAs for fully pipelined with no (NOPATDET) and with (PATDET) PATtern DETector, then multiply with no MREG (MULT_NOMREG) and pattern detector (MULT_NOMREG_PATDET) and a Multiply, pre-adder, no ADREG (PREADD_MULT_NOADREG) (**b**) Impact of BRAM configurations on the maximum achievable clock frequency of Artix-7, Kintex-7 and Virtex-7 FPGAs for single and true-dual port RAM configurations.

Table 2. Computing resources (DSP48E1) and BRAM memory resources for a range of Xilinx Artix-7, Kintex-7, Virtex-7 FPGA families implemented using 28nm CMOS technology.

Product	Family	Part Number	BRAM (18 Kb Each)	DSP48E1	GMAC/s	BRAM/ DSP
Standalone	Artix-7	XC7A200T	730	740	929	0.99
Standalone	Kintex-7	XC7K480T	1910	1920	2845	0.99
Standalone	Virtex-7	XC7VX980T	3000	3600	5335	0.83
Zynq SoC	Artix-7	XC7Z020	280	220	276	1.27
Zynq SoC	Kintex-7	XC7Z045	1090	900	1334	1.21

4.1. Exploration of FPGA Fabric for Soft Core Processor Architecture

A system composed of light-weight and high-performance soft core processors that supports modular computation with fine and coarse-grained functional granularity is more attractive than fixed dedicated hardware accelerators. A lightweight, soft core processor allows more programmable hardware accelerators to be accommodated onto a single SoC chip which would lead to better acceleration possibilities by exploiting data and task-level parallelism.

Gupta et al. [24,25] have reported different dataflow graph models where the functionality corresponds to soft core datapath models ①, ② and ③ as shown in Figure 5. These dataflow models are used to find a trade-off between the functionality of soft core processor and f_{max} and laid the foundation to find the suitable soft core datapath to map and execute the dataflow specification. The input/output interfaces are marked in red while the grey box represents the mapped functionality onto the soft core datapath models as shown in Figure 6.

The first model ① exhibits the datapath of a programmable ALU as shown in Figure 6a. It has an *instruction register* (IR) that defines a DFG node (OP1) programmed at system initialisation. On each clock cycle, the datapath explicitly reads a token from the input FIFO, processes it based on the programmed operation and stores the result into the output FIFO that is then consumed by the following dataflow node (OP3). This model only allows the mapping of data independent, fine-grained dataflow nodes as shown in Figure 5a which limits its applicability due to lack of control and data dependent execution, commonly found in image processing applications where the output pixel depends on the input or neighbouring pixels. This model is only suitable for mapping a single dataflow node.

The second model ② increases the datapath functionality to a fine-grained processor by including BRAM-based *instruction memory* (IM), *program counter* PC and *kernel memory* (KM) to store constants as shown in Figure 6b. Conversely, ② can support mapping of multiple data independent dataflow nodes as shown in Figure 5b. The node (OP2) requires a memory storage to store a variable (t1) to compute the output token (C) which feeds back from the output of the ALU needed for the next instruction in the following clock cycle. This model supports improved dataflow mapping functionality over ① by introducing an IM which comes at the cost of variable execution time and throughput proportional to the number of instructions required to implement the dataflow actor. This model is suitable for accelerating combinational logic computations.

The third model ③ increases the datapath functionality to map and execute a data dependent dataflow actor as shown in Figure 5c. The datapath has memory in the form of a *register file* (RF) which represents a coarse-grained processor shown in Figure 6c. The RF stores intermediate results to execute data dependent operations, implements (feed-forward, split, merge and feedback) dataflow execution patterns and facilitates dataflow transformations (actor fusion/fission, pipelining etc.) constraints by the size of the RF. It can implement modular computations which are not possible in ① and ②. In contrast to ① and ②, the token production/consumption (P/C) rate of ③ can be controlled through program code that allows software-controlled scheduling and load balancing possibilities.

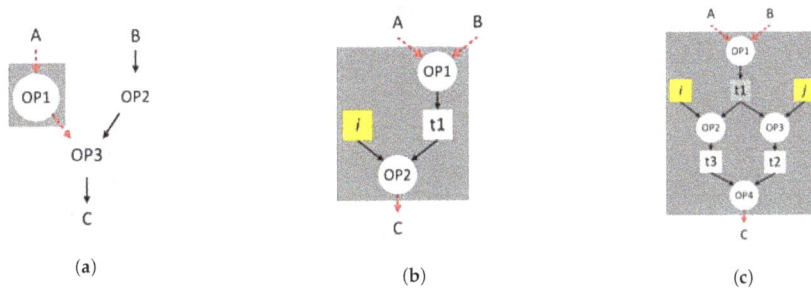

(a)   (b)   (c)

Figure 5. A range of dataflow models taken from [24,25]. (**a**) DFG node without internal storage called configuration ①; (**b**) DFG actor without internal storage t1 and constant i called configuration ②; (**c**) Programmable DFG actor with internal storage t1, t2 and t3 and constants i and j called configuration ③.

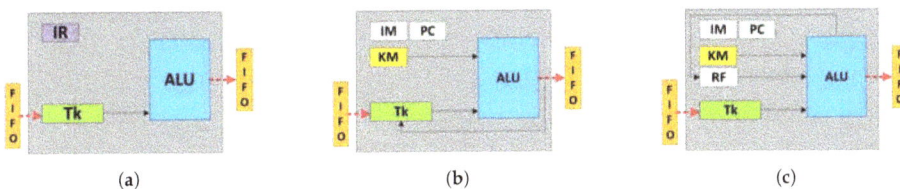

(a)   (b)   (c)

Figure 6. FPGA datapath models resulting from Figure 5. (**a**) Programmable ALU corresponding to configuration ①; (**b**) Fine-grained processor corresponding to configuration ②; (**c**) Coarse-grained processor corresponding to configuration ③.

4.2. Functionality vs. Performance Trade-Off Analysis

The presented models show that the processor datapath functionality significantly impacts the dataflow decomposition, mapping and optimisation possibilities, but also increases the processor critical path length and affects f_{max} by incorporating more memory elements and control logic.

Figure 6 shows the datapath models and their memory elements, where the memory resources (IM, KM, RF) have been incrementally allocated to each model. Each presented model has been coded in Verilog HDL, synthesised and placed and routed using the Xilinx Vivado Design Suite v2015.2 on Xilinx chips installed on widely available development kits which are Artix-7 (Zedboard), Kintex-7 (ZC706) and Virtex-7 (VC707). The obtained f_{max} results are reported in Figure 7.

In this analysis, f_{max} is considered as the performance metric for each processor datapath model and has a reduction of 8% and 23% for ② and ③ compared to ① using the same FPGA technology. For ②, the addition of memory elements specifically IM realised using dedicated BRAM affects f_{max} by ≈ 8% compared to ①. Nevertheless, the instruction decoder (ID) which is a combinational part of a datapath significantly increases the critical path length of the design. A further 15% f_{max} degradation from ② to ③ has resulted by adding memory elements KM and RF to support control and data dependent execution, which requires additional control logic and data multiplexers. Comparing different FPGA fabrics, a f_{max} reduction of 14% and 23% is observed for Kintex-7 and Artix-7. When ③ is ported from Virtex-7 to Kintex-7 and Artix-7, a maximum f_{max} reduction of 5% and 33% is observed.

This analysis has laid firm foundations by comparing different processor datapath and dataflow models and how they impact the f_{max} of the resultant soft-core processor. The trade-off analysis shows that an area-efficient, high-performance soft core processor architecture can be realised that supports requirements to accelerate image pre-processing applications. Among the presented models, ③ provides the best balance among functionality, flexibility, dataflow mapping and optimisation possibilities, and performance. This model is used to develop a novel FPGA-based soft core IPPro architecture in Section 4.3.

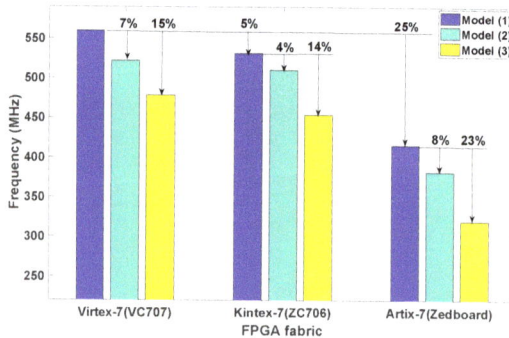

Figure 7. Impact of the various datapath models ①, ②, ③ on f_{max} across Xilinx Artix-7, Kintex-7 and Virtex-7 FPGA families.

4.3. Image Processing Processor (IPPro)

The IPPro is a 16-bit signed fixed-point, five-stage balanced pipelined RISC architecture that exploits the DSP48E1 features and provides balance among performance, latency and efficient resource utilization [10]. The architecture here is modified to support mapping of dataflow graphs by replacing the previously memory mapped, data memory by stream driven blocking input/output FIFOs as shown in Figure 8. The IPPro is designed as in-order pipeline because: (1) it consumes fewer area resources and can achieve better timing closure leading to the higher processor operating frequency f_{max}; (2) the in-order pipeline execution is predictable and simplifies scheduling and compiler development. The datapath supports the identified execution and memory access patterns (Table 1), and can be used as a coarse-grained processing core. IPPro has an IM of size 512 × 32, a RF of size 32 × 16 to store pixels and intermediate results, a KM of size 32 × 16 to store kernel coefficients and constant values, blocking input/output FIFOs to buffer data tokens between a producer, and a consumer to realise pipelined processing stages.

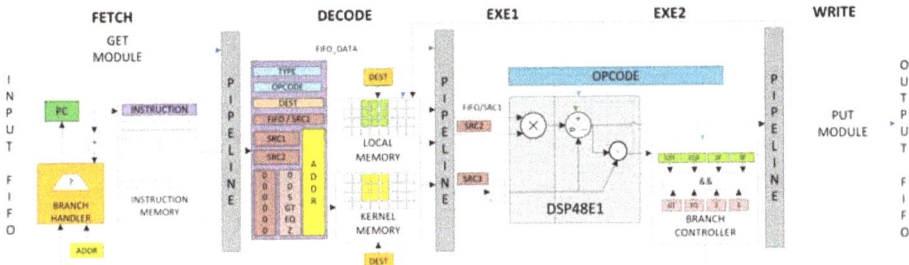

Figure 8. Block diagram of FPGA-based soft core Image Processing Processor (IPPro) datapath highlighting where relevant the fixed Xilinx FPGA resources utilised by the approach.

Table 3 outlines the relationship between data abstraction and the addressing modes, along with some supported instructions for the IPPro architecture, facilitating programmable implementation of point and area image processing algorithms. The *stream access* reads a stream of tokens/pixels from the input FIFO using GET instruction and allows processing either with constant values (Kernel Memory-FIFO) or neighbouring pixel values (Register File-FIFO or Register File-Register File). The processed stream is then written to the output FIFO using PUSH instruction. The IPPro supports arithmetic, logical, branch and data handling instructions. The presented instruction set is optimized after profiling use cases presented in [10,26].

Table 3. IPPro supported addressing modes highlighting the relation to the data processing requirements and the instruction set.

Addressing Mode	Data Abstraction	Supported Instructions
FIFO handling	Stream access	get, push
Register File–FIFO	Stream and randomly accessed data	addrf, subrf, mulrf, orrf, minrf, maxrf etc
Register File–Register File	Randomly accessed data	str, add, mul, mulacc, and, min, max etc.
Kernel Memory–FIFO	Stream and fixed values	addkm, mulkm, minkm, maxkm etc.

The IPPro supports branch instructions to handle control flow graphs to implement commonly known constructs such as if-else and case statements. The DSP48E1 block has a *pattern detector* that compares the input operands or the generated output results depending on the configuration and sets/resets the PATTERNDETECT (PD) bit. The IPPro datapath uses the PD bit along with some additional control logic to generate four flags zero (ZF), equal (EQF), greater than (GTF) and sign (SF) bits. When the IPPro encounters a branch instruction, the branch controller (BC) compares the flag status and branch handler (BH) updates the PC as shown in Figure 8.

The IPPro architecture has been coded in Verilog HDL and synthesized using Xilinx Vivado v2015.4 design suite on Kintex-7 FPGA fabric giving a f_{max} of 337 MHz. Table 4 shows that the IPPro architecture has achieved 1.6–3.3× times higher operating frequency (f_{max}) than the relevant processors highlighted in Section 2.2 by adopting the approach presented in Section 4. Comparing the FPGA resource usage of Table 4, the flip-flop utilisation (FF) is relatively similar except for the FlexGrip which uses 30× more flip-flops. Considering LUTs, the IPPro uses 50% less LUT resources compared to MicroBlaze and GraphSoC. To analyse design efficiency, a significant difference (0.76–9.00) in BRAM/DSP ratio can be observed among processors. Analysing design area efficiency, a significant difference 0.76–9.00 in BRAM/DSP ratio is observed which makes IPPro an area-efficient design based on the proposed metric.

Table 4. Comparison of IPPro against other FPGA-based processor architectures in terms of FPGA resources used and timing results achieved.

Resource	IPPro	Graph-SoC [19]	FlexGrip 8 SP * [8]		MicroBlaze
FFs	422	551	(103,776/8 =)	12,972	518
LUTs	478	974	(71,323/8 =)	8916	897
BRAMs	1	9	(120/8 =)	15	4
DSP48E1	1	1	(156/8 =)	19.5	3
Stages	5	3	5		5
Freq. (MHz)	337	200	100		211

* Scaled to a single streaming processor.

4.4. Processor Micro-Benchmarks

A commonly used performance metric for a processor is the time required to accomplish a defined task. Therefore, a set of commonly used micro-benchmarks [9,27] has been chosen and implemented on the IPPro and compared against a well-established MicroBlaze soft core processor as shown in Table 5a. Each of the chosen micro-benchmarks are fundamental kernels of larger algorithms and often the core computation of more extensive practical applications. The micro-benchmarks were written in standard C and implemented using Xilinx Vivado SDK v2015.1 Xilinx, San Jose, CA, USA. MicroBlaze has been configured for performance with no debug module, instruction/data cache and single AXI-Stream link enabled to stream data into the MicroBlaze using *getfsl* and *putfsl* instructions in C, equivalent to (GET and PUT) in assembly.

Table 5a reports the performance results of the micro-benchmarks and Table 5b shows the area utilisation comparison of the IPPro and the MicroBlaze both implemented on the same Xilinx Kintex-7 FPGA. It shows that the IPPro consumes 1.7 and 2.3 times fewer FFs and LUTs respectively than the MicroBlaze. It can be observed that for streaming functions (3 × 3 filter, 5-tap FIR and Degree-2 Polynomial), the IPPro achieved 1.80, 4.41 and 8.94 times better performance compared to MicroBlaze due to support of single cycle multiply-accumulate with data forwarding and get/push instructions in the IPPro processor. However, as the IPPro datapath does not support branch prediction that impacts its performance implementing data dependent or conditional functions (Fibonacci and Sum of absolute differences); thus, the SAD implementation using the IPPro resulted in a 5% performance degradation compared to Microblaze. On the other hand, for memory-bounded functions such as Matrix Multiplication, IPPro performed 6.7 times better than MicroBlaze due to higher frequency.

Table 5. Performance comparison of IPPro and MicroBlaze implementations (**a**) Comparison of micro-benchmarks. (**b**) Area comparison.

a			
Processor	**MicroBlaze**	**IPPro**	
FPGA Fabric	Kintex-7		
Freq (MHz)	287	337	
Micro-benchmarks	Exec. Time (us)		Speed-up
Convolution	0.60	0.14	4.41
Degree-2 Polynomial	5.92	3.29	1.80
5-tap FIR	47.73	5.34	8.94
Matrix Multiplication	0.67	0.10	6.7
Sum of Abs. Diff.	0.73	0.77	0.95
Fibonacci	4.70	3.56	1.32

b			
Processor	**MicroBlaze**	**IPPro**	**Ratio**
FFs	746	422	1.77
LUTs	1114	478	2.33
BRAMs	4	2	2.67
DSP48E1	0	1	0.00

5. System Architecture

The *k*-means clustering and Traffic Sign Recognition algorithms has been used to explore and analyse the impact of both data and task parallelism using a multi-core IPPro implemented on a ZedBoard. The platform has a Xilinx Zynq XC7Z020 SoC device interfaced to a 256 MB flash memory and 512 MB DDR3 memory. The SoC is composed of a host processor known as programmable system (PS) which configures and controls the system architecture, and the FPGA programmable logic (PL) on which the IPPro hardware accelerator is implemented, as illustrated in Figure 9. The SoC data communication bus (ARM AMBA-AXI) transfers the data between PS and PL using the AXI-DMA protocol and the Xillybus IP core is deployed as a bridge between PS and PL to feed data into the image processing pipeline. The IPPro hardware accelerator is interfaced with the Xillybus IP core via FIFOs. The Linux application running on PS streams data between the FIFO and the file handler opened by the host application. The Xillybus-Lite interface allows control registers from the user space program running on Linux to manage the underlying hardware architecture.

Figure 9 shows the implemented system architecture which consists of the necessary control and data infrastructure. The data interfaces involve stream (Xillybus-Send and Xillybus-Read); uni-directional memory mapped (Xillybus-Write) to program the IPPro cores; and Xillybus-Lite to manage Line buffer, scatter, gather, IPPro cores and the FSM. Xillybus Linux device drivers are used to access each of these data and control interfaces. An additional layer of C functions is developed using Xillybus device drivers to configure and manage the system architecture, program IPPro cores and exchange pixels between PS and PL.

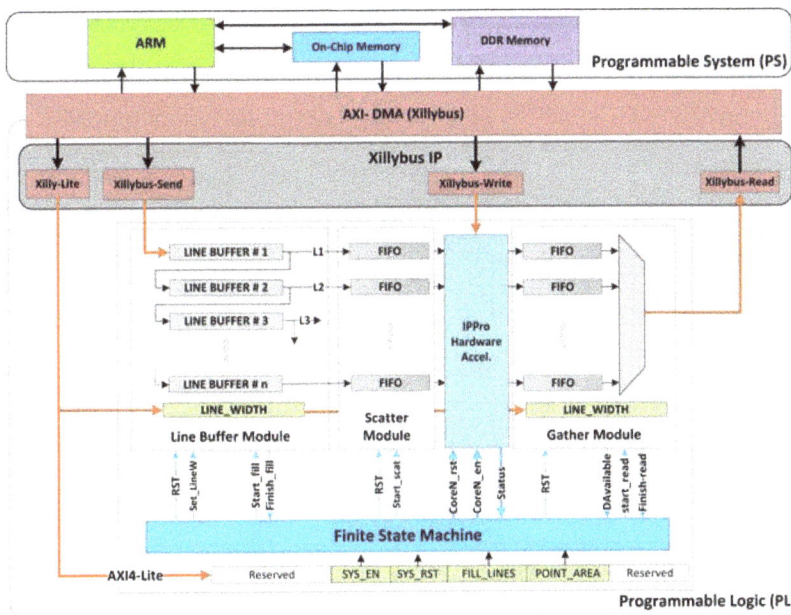

Figure 9. System architecture of IPPro-based hardware acceleration highlighting data distribution and control infrastructure, FIFO configuration and Finite-State-Machine control.

Control Infrastructure

To exploit parallelism, a configurable control infrastructure has been implemented using the PL resources of the Zynq SoC. It decomposes statically the data into many equal-sized parts, where each part can be processed by a separate processing core. A row-cyclic data distribution [28] has been used because it allows buffering of data/pixels in a pattern suitable for point and area image processing operations after storing them into the line buffers. The system-level architecture (Figure 9) is composed of line buffers, a scatter module to distribute the buffered pixels, a gather module to collect the processed pixels and a finite-state-machine (FSM) to manage and synchronise these modules.

6. Case Study 1: *k*-Means Clustering Algorithm

k-means clustering classifies a data set into *k* centroids based on the measure e.g., a distance between each data item and the *k* centroid values. It involves: *Distance Calculation* from each data point to the centroids which gives *k* distances and the associated pixels, and a minimum distance is computed from the *k* distance values; *Averaging* where data pixels in the dimension are added up and divided by the number in their dimensions for each cluster, giving an updated centroid value for the following frame. Here we accelerate a functional core of the *k*-means clustering algorithm with 4 centroids to be applied to a 512×512 image.

6.1. High-Level System Description

The behavioural description is captured in RVC-CAL using Orcc and includes mainly the actor CAL files and the xdf network, derived from .xml format. A dataflow network is constructed with FIFO channels between actors to allow high-throughput passage of tokens from one actor's output port to another's input port. The size of FIFO channels can be set. Whilst the length of execution times are the key factor for FPGA acceleration, overheads incurred in transferring the data to/from the PL and accelerators are also important. The SIMD degree was explored by redesigning the FPGA-targeted actors in RVC-CAL and using the compiler to generate the IPPro assembly code. This is done by analysing the xdf file to decide the allocation of actors to the processors and then compiling the function and interconnections.

Every IPPro core sets the hardware units around input/output port connections for the proper flow of tokens, and the compiler is designed to provide the proper signals required by each core. The compiler also generates the setup registers settings and C-APIs parameters, in order to help the controllers distribute the tokens among the cores and gather the produced results. Figure 10 shows the two stages of *k*-means clustering algorithm to be accelerated, and also cores port connections, sample distance calculation code in RVC-CAL and its compiled IPPro assembly code. As Xillybus IP has been used in the system architecture (Section 5), it restricts the clock rate to 100 MHz on Zedboard. To evaluate the IPPro architecture and different dataflow mapping possibilities by exploiting data and task-level parallelism, the *k*-means clustering is accelerated using four acceleration designs listed in Table 6 and illustrated in Figure 11.

Table 6. Dataflow actor mapping and supported parallelism of IPPro hardware accelerator design presented in Figure 11.

Design	Acceleration Paradigm	Mapping	Parallelism	
			Data	Task
①	Single core IPPro	Single actor	No	No
②	8-way SIMD IPPro	Single actor	Yes	No
③	Dual core IPPro	Dual actor	No	Yes
④	Dual core 8-way SIMD IPPro	Dual actor	Yes	Yes

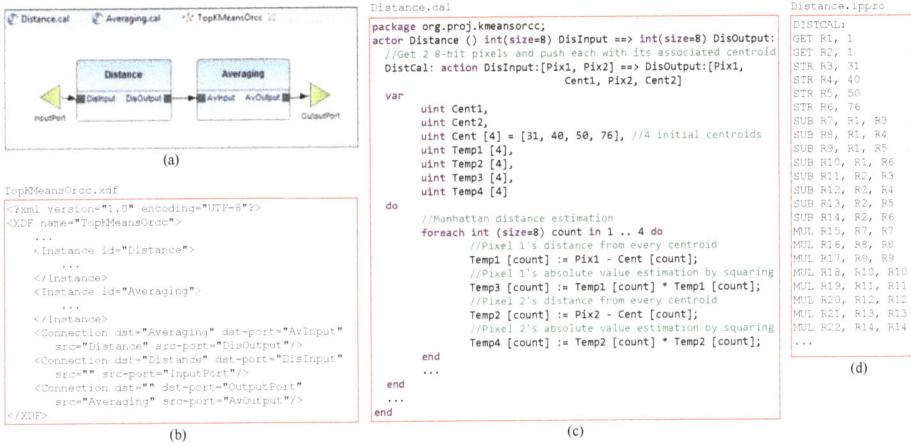

Figure 10. High-level implementation of *k*-means clustering algorithm: (**a**) Graphical view of Orcc dataflow network; (**b**) Part of dataflow network including the connections; (**c**) Part of `Distance.cal` file showing distance calculation in RVC-CAL where two pixels are received through an input FIFO channel, processed and sent to an output FIFO channel; (**d**) Compiled IPPro assembly code of `Distance.cal`.

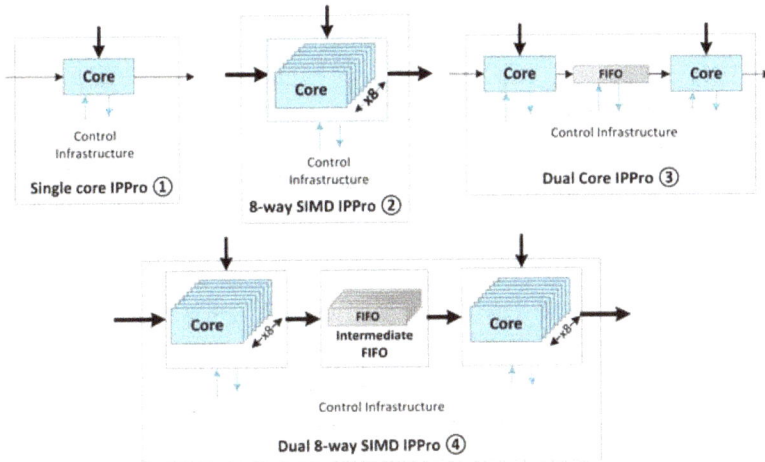

Figure 11. IPPro-based hardware accelerator designs to explore and analyse the impact of parallelism on area and performance based on Single core IPPro ①, eight-way parallel SIMD IPPro ②, parallel Dual core IPPro ③ and combined Dual core 8-way SIMD IPPro called ④.

6.2. IPPro-Based Hardware Acceleration Designs

Table 6 shows the dataflow actor mapping and the exploited parallelism for each design. The block diagram of each IPPro hardware acceleration design is illustrated in Figure 11. Design ① and ② are used to accelerate *Distance Calculation* and *Averaging* stages, where each stage is mapped separately onto individual IPPro cores. To investigate the impact of data and task parallelism, design ③ and ④ are used to accelerate both *Distance Calculation* and *Averaging* stages as shown in Figure 11. The detailed area and performance results are reported in Tables 7 and 8. The execution time depends on the number of IPPro instructions required to compute the operation and the time require to execute a instruction which corresponds to the operating frequency (f_{max}) of IPPro.

Table 7 reports the results obtained by individually accelerating the stages of k-means clustering using ① and ②. In each iteration, the distance calculation takes two pixels and classifies them into one of the four clusters which take an average of 45 cycles/pixel. To classify the whole image, it takes 118.2 ms which corresponds to 8.45 fps. On the other hand, the averaging takes four tokens and produces four new cluster values, which takes an average of 55 clock cycles/pixel results in 145 ms or 6.88 fps. Both the stages involve point-based pixel processing. Therefore design ② was developed and used to exploit data-level parallelism. As a result, the execution time is reduced to 23.32 ms and 27.02 ms for distance calculation and averaging respectively. This is an improvement of 5.1 and 5.4 times over ① (and not the expected 8 times) of the 8-way SIMD implementation (② over ①) as the overhead of data transfer time from/to the accelerator restricts the performance improvement. This came at the cost of 4.1, 2.3 and 8.0 times more BRAMs, LUTs and DSP blocks respectively as reported in Table 8. The major contributor to increased area utilisation is data distribution and control infrastructure.

Table 8 reports the execution time and performance (fps) numbers of both stages together to exploit task and data parallelism using designs ③ and ④. The reported results of ① and ② were obtained by combining the execution time of both stages previously reported in Table 7. Using design ③, the effect of task parallelism implemented via intermediate FIFO results in an average of 63 clock cycles/pixel which is 163 ms (6 fps). By pipelining both actors, ③ has achieved 1.6 times better performance compared to ① at the cost of 1.6 and 2.0 times more BRAM and DSP blocks using the same Xillybus IP infrastructure as ①. The reason for the improvement is the localisation of intermediate data within FPGA fabric using an intermediate FIFO, which hides the data transfer overhead to and from host processor as shown in Figure 11. Investigating the reported area utilisation numbers in Table 8 shows that the area utilisation for design ③ and ④ is not twice as big as ① and ② respectively due to the FPGA resources utilised by the input and output data ports of Xillybus IP. Design ① and ③ requires a single input and output data port, while ② and ④ requires eight input and output data ports. Therefore, a part of FPGA logic used by the Xillybus IP is constant/fixed for ①, ③ and ②, ④.

Analysing the impact of exploiting both task and data-level parallelism using ④ results on average 14 clock cycles/pixel and an execution time of 35.9 ms (2 fps). It is 1.4, 4.5 and 7.3 times better than ②, ③ and ① respectively. For comparison, both stages were coded in C language and executed on an embedded ARM Cortex-A7 processor that achieved execution time of 286 ms (354 fps) which is 8 times slower than the performance achieved by ④.

Table 7. Performance measurements for designs ① and ② highlighted in Figure 11.

Single Actor	① Single Core IPPro		② 8-Way SIMD IPPro	
	Exec. (ms)	fps	Exec. (ms)	fps
Distance Calculation	118.21	8.45	23.37	42.78
Averaging	145.17	6.88	27.02	37.00

Table 8. Area utilisation and performance results of IPPro-based hardware accelerator designs in Figure 11 exploiting data and task parallelism namely ①, ②, ③ and ④.

k-Means Acceleration	Area				Performance	
	LUT	FF	BRAM	DSP	Exec. (ms)	fps
① Combined stages using Single-core IPPro	4736	5197	4.5	1	263.38	3.8
② Combined stages using 8-way SIMD IPPro	10,941	12,279	18.5	8	50.39	19.8
③ Dual-core IPPro	4987	5519	4.5	2	163.2	6
④ Dual 8-way SIMD IPPro	13,864	16,106	18.5	16	35.9	28
Software implementation on ARM Cortex-A7	-	-	-	-	286	3.5

6.3. Power Measurement

This section presents the details of adopted power measurement methods and compares the IPPro-based implementation to the equivalent *k*-means implementation on GPU and CPU. The IPPro power measurements obtained by running post-implementation timing simulation. A *Switch activity interchange format* (SAIF) file is used to record the switching activity of designs data and control signals of each presented IPPro designs. The Xilinx Power Estimator (XPE) takes the SAIF file and reports the power consumption. An equivalent version of *k*-means in CUDA and OpenCL was implemented and profiled on nVIDIA GeForce GTX980 (desktop GPU), ODRIOD-XU3 (Embedded GPU) and ARM Cortex-A7 (CPU) due to in-house availability of both GPU platforms. The nVIDIA desktop GPU card supports 2048 CUDA cores running at a base frequency of 1126 MHz. OpenCL and CUDA were used for programming the GPU, and both stages merged into the single kernel. For performance measurement, OpenCL's profiling function *clGetEventProfilingInfo* is used which returns the execution time of kernel in nanoseconds. The power consumption during kernel execution was logged using nVIDIA *System Management Interface* (nvidia-smi) which allows to measure the power consumed by the GPU and the host processor separately. It is a command line utility, based on top of the nVIDIA Management Library (NVML), intended to aid the management and monitoring of nVIDIA GPUs.

To set the base line figures and for fair comparison of the FPGA against the GPU technology, an embedded CPU (ARM Cortex-A7) and an embedded GPU (ARM Mali-T628) implementation were carried out on a ODROID-XU3 platform. This is a heterogeneous multi-processing platform that hosts 28 nm Samsung Exynos 5422 application processor which has on-chip ARM Cortex-A7 CPUs and an ARM Mali-T628 embedded GPU. The platform is suitable for power constraint application use cases where the ARM Cortex-A7 CPU and mid-range ARM Mali-T628 GPU runs at 1.2 GHz and 600 MHz respectively. The platform have separate current sensors to measure the power consumption of ARM Cortex-A7 and ARM Mali-T628, thus allowing component-level power measurement capability.

Table 9 shows the results of IPPro-based accelerator designs running on Zedboard where both data and task parallel implementation achieved 4.6 times better performance over task only implementation at the cost of 1.57 times higher power consumption. Table 10 shows the performance results of the *k*-means implementation on Kintex-7 FPGA and compares them against equivalent embedded CPU (ARM Cortex-A7), embedded GPU (ARM Mali-T628) and desktop GPU (nVIDIA GeForce GTX680) implementations in terms of speed (MHz), Power (W) and transistors utilised (TU). The presented embedded CPU results has been considered as a baseline for the comparison.

Table 9. Power, resource and combined efficiency comparisons of IPPro-based *k*-means clustering implementations on Zedboard (Xilinx Zynq XC7Z020 Artix-7).

| | Power (mW) | | | Freq. | Exec. | | Power | TU | Efficiency | |
Impl.	Static	Dyn.	Tot.	(MHz)	(ms)	fps	Efficiency (fps/W)	($\times 10^6$)	(fps/TU) ($\times 10^{-8}$)	(fps/W/TU) ($\times 10^{-9}$)
③	118	18	136	100	163.2	6	44.1	591 (9%)	1.0	74.6
④	122	92	214	100	35.9	28	130.8	1564 (23%)	1.8	83.6

Table 10. Power, resource and combined efficiency comparisons for *k*-means clustering for Xilinx Zynq XC7Z045 Kintex-7 FPGA, nVIDIA GPU GTX980, embedded ARM Mali-T628 GPU and embedded ARM Cortex-A7 CPU.

| | | Power (W) | | | Freq. | Exec. | | Power | TU | Efficiency | |
Plat.	Impl.	Static	Dyn.	Tot.	(MHz)	(ms)	fps	Effic. (fps/W)	($\times 10^9$)	(fps/TU) ($\times 10^{-8}$)	(fps/W/TU) ($\times 10^{-9}$)
FPGA	③	0.15	0.03	0.19	337	48.43	21	114.1	0.6 (9%)	3.6	193.1
	④	0.16	0.15	0.31	337	10.65	94	300.3	1.0 (6%)	6.0	192.0
GPU	OpenCL	37	27	64	1127	1.19	840	13.1	1.3 (26%)	63.1	9.8
	CUDA	37	22	59	1127	1.58	632	10.7	1.2 (24%)	51.5	8.7
eGPU	Mali	0.12	-	1.56	600	3.69	271	173	-	-	-
eCPU	Cortex	0.25	-	0.67	1200	286	3.49	5.2	-	-	-

Both FPGA implementations achieved 6 and 27 times better fps performance than the embedded CPU, whilst the embedded GPU delivered 6.7 times better performance over the FPGA by exploiting parallelism and higher operating frequency. Focusing on the power consumption results, the FPGA consumed 2.1 and 4.9 times less power than both the embedded CPU and embedded GPU respectively. It shows that the FPGA technology delivers a power-optimised solution while the GPU approach provides a performance-optimised solution. Considering the performance and power together, the power efficiency (fps/W) numbers shows that FPGA and embedded GPU implementations are 57 and 33 times more power efficient than embedded CPU and that the FPGA implementation is 24 times more power efficient than embedded GPU. Nevertheless, this power efficiency edge can be further improved by applying dataflow transformations and increasing the number of IPPro cores.

Table 10 compares the FPGA results against desktop GPU and reports resource efficiency as a metric due to significant difference in the power consumption numbers. The resource efficiency has been presented in terms of frames-per-second-per-Transistor-Utilisation (fps/TU) which is 6 and 63 for the 28 nm FPGA and GPU technologies. For embedded CPU and GPU, these results are not reported due to unavailability of transistor count numbers for the ARM. The reported resource efficiency results shows that GPU utilises area resources more efficiently than the FPGA when power is kept out of the equation. Combining all three metrics (fps/W/TU) shows that the advantage gained from FPGA designs is significant i.e., 22 times more efficient than GPU. This advantage becomes more valuable when it is acknowledged that the FPGA-based SoC design is adaptable and allows exploration, profiling and implementation of different dataflow transformation possibilities over dedicated FPGA approaches to accelerate image processing applications for low energy applications.

7. Case Study 2: Traffic Sign Recognition

Traffic sign recognition is applied in driver assistance systems [29]. In the detection stage, sign candidate areas are extracted from the original image and matched against a list of known templates in the recognition stage. The processing stages along with their execution time and percentage contribution to the overall execution time for 600 × 400 image sign recognition implemented on ARM Cortex-A9 are shown in Figure 12. It involves a colour filter to convert RGB to HSV, morphology filters (erosion and dilation) using 3 × 3 and 5 × 5 circular kernels, edge detection, circles detection to guide the matching process and reduce the number of shapes, bounding box detection to transform the remaining objects into their convex hulls, classification by shape and then template matching. The colour and morphology filters have been chosen for hardware acceleration as they are dominant processing components as shown in Figure 12.

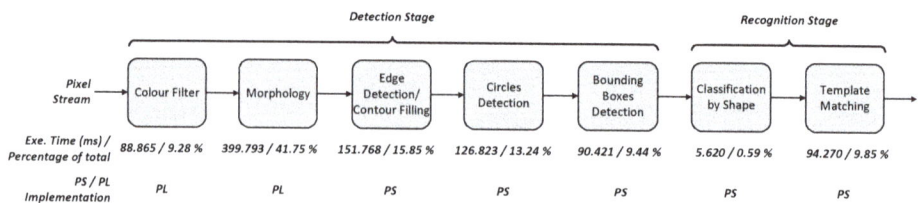

Figure 12. Section execution times and ratios for each stage of the traffic sign recognition algorithm.

7.1. Acceleration of Colour and Morphology Filter

The IPPro-based hardware accelerators for colour and morphology filter were implemented on Zedboard using the system architecture presented in Section 5 that allows to distribute pixels for *point* and *window* image processing operations. The high-level system description of colour filter actor from RVC-CAL produced program code consists of 160 IPPro assembly instructions. A 3 × 3 circular mask has been used for morphology filter as shown in Figure 13a, to find the maximum (dilation) or minimum (erosion) value in a set of pixels contained within a masked region around the input pixel.

The simplified generated code of RVC CAL-IPPro compilation is shown in Figure 13a. GET and PUSH instructions set the input or output port numbers through which the tokens are received or sent. GET instructions read 9 pixels values and stores them into the register file from R1 to R9. Then, the corner pixels are ignored to impose 3 × 3 circular mask, a maximum value among the remaining pixels max(R1, R4, R5, R6, R8) is computed and stored in R7 to apply dilation operation. This value is then pushed to the output using PUSH instruction. The output result of the implemented design are shown in Figure 13b.

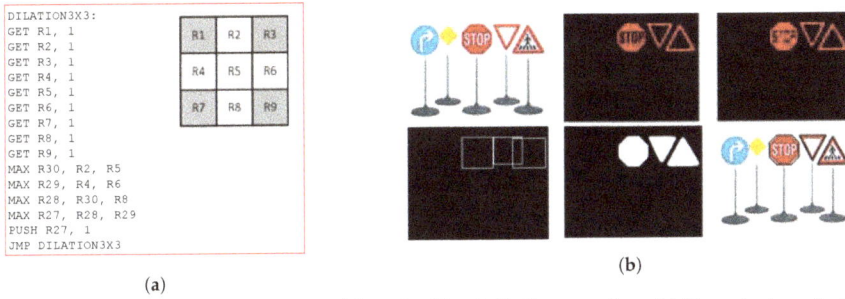

(a)

(b)

Figure 13. (a) The simplified IPPro assembly code of 3 × 3 dilation operation. (b) The output result of implemented design.

Table 11 presents the results from the Zedboard implementation that has been tested with a set of real images. The hardware accelerated implementation of colour filter stage using 32 IPPro cores reduces the execution time from 88.87 ms down to 19.71 ms compared to software implementation on-chip ARM Cortex-A9. Similarly, the morphology filter stage using 16 IPPro cores has reduced the execution time from 399 ms down to 41.3 ms. The presented IPPro-based hardware acceleration design has achieved a speed-up of 4.5 and 9.6 times over ARM for colour and morphology filters respectively. The achieved speed up for colour filter stage using 32 cores is lower than that of morphology stage using 16 cores, because of the higher number of clock cycles spent on every pixel for colour filter stage; this is due to larger execution time of division coprocessor used for colour filtering.

Table 11. IPPro-based acceleration of colour and morphology operations implemented on Zedboard.

Description	Colour	Morphology
No. of cores	32	16
FF	41,624 (39%)	43,588 (41%)
LUT	29,945 (56%)	33,545 (63%)
DSP48E1	32 (15%)	48 (22%)
BRAM	60 (42%)	112 (80%)
Cycles/Pixel	160	26
Exec. (ms)	19.7 (8.7 *)	41.3 (18.3 *)
Speed-up	4.5× (10.3× *)	9.6× (21.75× *)

* The achievable performance using Zynq XC7Z045 Kintex-7.

Figure 14 shows the stage-wise acceleration of traffic sign recognition by accelerating colour and morphology filters. Edge/contours detection and bounding boxes stages were improved partially by accelerating the morphology operations. The edge detection is based on the morphology operations by taking the difference between erosion and dilation. Therefore the morphology results obtained by acceleration are further exploited in the host to factor out some operations when doing edge detection.

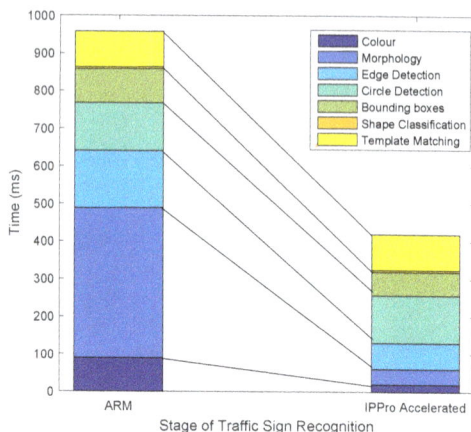

Figure 14. Stage-wise comparison of traffic sign recognition acceleration using ARM and IPPro based approach.

8. Conclusions and Future Work

The paper has presented an FPGA-based hardware acceleration approach for image processing applications using soft core processors which maps efficiently to FPGA resources thereby maintaining performance. By using the DFG model of computations, a design flow has been created which allows the user to partition the design based on processing needs and allows programming of each function. The work has been demonstrated for a k-means clustering function and a traffic sign recognition example where maximum speed up of 8 and 9.6 times, respectively, were achieved when compared to software implementation on ARM CPU. For k-means clustering, the 16 IPPro cores implementation is 57, 28 and 1.7 times more power efficient (fps/W) than ARM Cortex-A7 CPU, nVIDIA GeForce GTX980 GPU and ARM Mali-T628 embedded GPU. The future work to improve this work is to investigate further dataflow decomposition/mapping optimisations and software-controlled power optimisation techniques such as on-demand enable/disable the IPPro cores.

Author Contributions: The project was conceptualized by R.W., F.S. and S.A. and R.W. and K.R. provided both project supervision and project administration. The implementation was carried out primarily by F.S. and S.A. and validation was undertaken by F.S., U.I.M. and T.D. The writing of the original draft was carried out by F.S., R.W., S.A. and D.C. and edits done by R.W. and F.S.

Funding: This work has been undertaken in collaboration with Heriot-Watt University in a project funded by the Engineering and Physical Science Research Council (EPSRC) through the EP/K009583/1 grant.

Conflicts of Interest: The authors declare no conflict of interest.

References

1. Conti, F.; Rossi, D.; Pullini, A.; Loi, I.; Benini, L. PULP: A Ultra-Low Power Parallel Accelerator for Energy-Efficient and Flexible Embedded Vision. *J. Signal Process. Syst.* **2016**, *84*, 339–354. [CrossRef]
2. Lamport, L. The Parallel Execution of DO Loops. *Commun. ACM* **1974**, *17*, 83–93. [CrossRef]
3. Markov, I.L. Limits on Fundamental Limits to Computation. *Nature* **2014**, *512*, 147–154. [CrossRef] [PubMed]
4. Bacon, D.F.; Rabbah, R.; Shukla, S. FPGA Programming for the Masses. *ACM Queue Mag.* **2013**, *11*, 40–52. [CrossRef]
5. Gort, M.; Anderson, J. Design re-use for compile time reduction in FPGA high-level synthesis flows. In Proceedings of the IEEE International Conference on Field-Programmable Technology (FPT), Shanghai, China, 10–12 December 2014; pp. 4–11.

6.   Yiannacouras, P.; Steffan, J.G.; Rose, J. VESPA: Portable, scalable, and flexible FPGA-based vector processors. In Proceedings of the 2008 International Conference on Compilers, Architectures and Synthesis for Embedded Systems, Atlanta, GA, USA, 19–24 October 2008; pp. 61–70.

7.   Severance, A.; Lemieux, G.G. Embedded supercomputing in FPGAs with the VectorBlox MXP matrix processor. In Proceedings of the Ninth IEEE/ACM/IFIP International Conference on Hardware/Software Codesign and System Synthesis, Montreal, QC, Canada, 29 September–4 October 2013; pp. 1–10.

8.   Andryc, K.; Merchant, M.; Tessier, R. FlexGrip: A soft GPGPU for FPGAs. In Proceedings of the 23rd International Conference on Field Programmable Logic and Applications (FPL 2013), Porto, Portugal, 2–4 September 2013; pp. 230–237.

9.   Cheah, H.Y.; Brosser, F.; Fahmy, S.A.; Maskell, D.L. The iDEA DSP block-based soft processor for FPGAs. *ACM Trans. Reconfig. Technol. Syst.* **2014**, *7*, 19. [CrossRef]

10. Siddiqui, F.M.; Russell, M.; Bardak, B.; Woods, R.; Rafferty, K. IPPro: FPGA based image processing processor. In Proceedings of the IEEE Workshop on Signal Processing Systems, Belfast, UK, 20–22 October 2014; pp. 1–6.

11. Amiri, M.; Siddiqui, F.M.; Kelly, C.; Woods, R.; Rafferty, K.; Bardak, B. FPGA-Based Soft-Core Processors for Image Processing Applications. *J. Signal Process. Syst.* **2017**, *87*, 139–156. [CrossRef]

12. Bourrasset, C.; Maggiani, L.; Sérot, J.; Berry, F. Dataflow object detection system for FPGA-based smart camera. *IET Circuits Devices Syst.* **2016**, *10*, 280–291. [CrossRef]

13. Nugteren, C.; Corporaal, H.; Mesman, B. Skeleton-based automatic parallelization of image processing algorithms for GPUs. In Proceedings of the 2011 International Conference on Embedded Computer Systems: Architectures, Modeling and Simulation, Samos, Greece, 18–21 July 2011; pp. 25–32. [CrossRef]

14. Brodtkorb, A.R.; Dyken, C.; Hagen, T.R.; Hjelmervik, J.M.; Storaasli, O.O. State-of-the-art in Heterogeneous Computing. *Sci. Program.* **2010**, *18*, 1–33. [CrossRef]

15. Neuendorffer, S.; Li, T.; Wang, D. *Accelerating OpenCV Applications with Zynq-7000 All Programmable SoC Using Vivado HLS Video Libraries*; Technical Report; Xilinx Inc.: San Jose, CA, USA, 2015.

16. Strik, M.T.; Timmer, A.H.; Van Meerbergen, J.L.; van Rootselaar, G.J. Heterogeneous multiprocessor for the management of real-time video and graphics streams. *IEEE J. Solid-State Circuits* **2000**, *35*, 1722–1731. [CrossRef]

17. Zhang, J.; Zhang, Z.; Zhou, S.; Tan, M.; Liu, X.; Cheng, X.; Cong, J. Bit-level Optimization for High-level Synthesis and FPGA-based Acceleration. In Proceedings of the 18th Annual ACM/SIGDA International Symposium on Field Programmable Gate Arrays, Monterey, CA, USA, 21–23 February 2010; pp. 59–68.

18. Nikhil, R. Bluespec System Verilog: Efficient, correct RTL from high level specifications. In Proceedings of the Second ACM and IEEE International Conference on Formal Methods and Models for Co-Design (MEMOCODE '04), San Diego, CA, USA, 23–25 June 2004; pp. 69–70.

19. Kapre, N. Custom FPGA-based soft-processors for sparse graph acceleration. In Proceedings of the 2015 IEEE 26th International Conference on Application-specific Systems, Architectures and Processors (ASAP), Toronto, ON, Canada, 27–29 July 2015; pp. 9–16.

20. LaForest, C.E.; Steffan, J.G. Octavo: An FPGA-centric processor family. In Proceedings of the ACM/SIGDA International Symposium on Field Programmable Gate Arrays, Monterey, CA, USA, 22–24 February 2012; pp. 219–228.

21. Sutherland, W.R. On-Line Graphical Specification of Computer Procedures. Technical Report, DTIC Document. Ph.D. Thesis, Massachusetts Institute of Technology, Cambridge, MA, USA, 1966.

22. Eker, J.; Janneck, J. *CAL Language Report*; Tech. Rep. UCB/ERL M; University of California: Berkeley, CA, USA, 2003; Volume 3.

23. Yviquel, H.; Lorence, A.; Jerbi, K.; Cocherel, G.; Sanchez, A.; Raulet, M. Orcc: Multimedia Development Made Easy. In Proceedings of the 21st ACM International Conference on Multimedia (MM '13), Barcelona, Spain, 21–25 October 2013; pp. 863–866.

24. So, H.K.H.; Liu, C. FPGA Overlays. In *FPGAs for Software Programmers*; Springer: Berlin, Germany, 2016; pp. 285–305.

25. Gupta, S. *Comparison of Different Data Flow Graph Models*; Technical Report; University of Stuttgart: Stuttgart, Germany, 2010.

26. Kelly, C.; Siddiqui, F.M.; Bardak, B.; Woods, R. Histogram of oriented gradients front end processing: An FPGA based processor approach. In Proceedings of the 2014 IEEE Workshop on Signal Processing Systems (SiPS), Belfast, UK, 20–22 October 2014; pp. 1–6.

27. Schleuniger, P.; McKee, S.A.; Karlsson, S. Design Principles for Synthesizable Processor Cores. In *Proceedings of the 25th International Conference on Architecture of Computing Systems (ARCS)*; Springer: Berlin/Heidelberg, Germany, 2012; pp. 111–122.
28. García, G.J.; Jara, C.A.; Pomares, J.; Alabdo, A.; Poggi, L.M.; Torres, F. A survey on FPGA-based sensor systems: Towards intelligent and reconfigurable low-power sensors for computer vision, control and signal processing. *Sensors* **2014**, *14*, 6247–6278. [CrossRef] [PubMed]
29. Mogelmose, A.; Trivedi, M.M.; Moeslund, T.B. Vision-Based Traffic Sign Detection and Analysis for Intelligent Driver Assistance Systems: Perspectives and Survey. *IEEE Trans. Intell. Transp. Syst.* **2012**, *13*, 1484–1497. [CrossRef]

Journal of
Imaging

MDPI

Article

Optimized Memory Allocation and Power Minimization for FPGA-Based Image Processing

Paulo Garcia [1,*], Deepayan Bhowmik [2], Robert Stewart [3], Greg Michaelson [3] and Andrew Wallace [4]

1. Department of Systems and Computer Engineering, Carleton University, Ottawa, ON K1S 5B6, Canada
2. Div. of Computing Science and Mathematics, University of Stirling, Stirling FK9 4LA, UK; deepayan.bhowmik@stir.ac.uk
3. School of Mathematical and Computer Sciences, Heriot Watt University, Edinburgh EH14 4AS, UK; rstewart@hw.ac.uk (R.S.); gmichaelson@hw.ac.uk (G.M.)
4. School of Engineering and Physical Sciences, Heriot Watt University, Edinburgh EH14 4AS, UK; a.m.wallace@hw.ac.uk
* Correspondence: paulogarcia@cunet.carleton.ca

Received: 19 November 2018; Accepted: 27 December 2018; Published: 1 January 2019

Abstract: Memory is the biggest limiting factor to the widespread use of FPGAs for high-level image processing, which require complete frame(s) to be stored in situ. Since FPGAs have limited on-chip memory capabilities, efficient use of such resources is essential to meet performance, size and power constraints. In this paper, we investigate allocation of on-chip memory resources in order to minimize resource usage and power consumption, contributing to the realization of power-efficient high-level image processing fully contained on FPGAs. We propose methods for generating memory architectures, from both Hardware Description Languages and High Level Synthesis designs, which minimize memory usage and power consumption. Based on a formalization of on-chip memory configuration options and a power model, we demonstrate how our partitioning algorithms can outperform traditional strategies. Compared to commercial FPGA synthesis and High Level Synthesis tools, our results show that the proposed algorithms can result in up to 60% higher utilization efficiency, increasing the sizes and/or number of frames that can be accommodated, and reduce frame buffers' dynamic power consumption by up to approximately 70%. In our experiments using Optical Flow and MeanShift Tracking, representative high-level algorithms, data show that partitioning algorithms can reduce total power by up to 25% and 30%, respectively, without impacting performance.

Keywords: field programmable gate array (FPGA); memory; power; image processing; design

1. Introduction

Advances in Field Programmable Gate Array (FPGA) technology [1] have made them the de facto implementation platform for a variety of computer vision applications [2]. Several algorithms, e.g., stereo-matching [3], are not feasibly processed in real-time on conventional general purpose processors and are best suited to hardware implementation [4,5]. The absence of a sufficiently comprehensive, *one size fits all* hardware pipeline for the computer vision domain [6] motivates the use of FPGAs in a myriad of computer vision scenarios, especially in applications where processing should be performed in situ, such as in smart cameras [7], where FPGAs embed data acquisition, processing and communication subsystems. Adoption of FPGA technology by the computer vision community has accelerated during recent years thanks to the availability of High Level Synthesis (HLS) tools which enable FPGA design within established software design contexts.

However, since FPGAs have limited on-chip memory capabilities (e.g., approx. 6MB of on-chip memory on high end Virtex 7 FPGAs), external memory (i.e., DDR-RAM chips connected to the FPGA) is often used to accommodate frames [8,9]. This causes penalties on *performance* (latency is much higher for off-chip memory access) and perhaps more importantly, on *size* (two chips, FPGA and DDR, rather than just FPGA), *power* (DDR memories are power hungry [10]) and have associated monetary costs, hindering the adoption of FPGAs.

In this paper, we research allocation of on-chip memory resources in order to minimize resource usage and power consumption, contributing to the realization of power-efficient high-level image processing systems fully contained on FPGAs. We propose methods for generating on-chip memory architectures, applicable from both HLS and Hardware Description Languages (HDL) designs, which minimize FPGA memory resource usage and power consumption for image processing applications. Our approach does not exclude external memory access: rather, it is orthogonal to any memory hierarchy, and applicable to any instances of on-chip memory. Specifically, this paper offers the following contributions:

- A formal analysis of on-chip memory allocation schemes and associated memory usage for given frame sizes and possible on-chip memory configurations.
- Methods for selecting a memory configuration for optimized on-chip memory resource usage and balanced usage/power for a given frame size.
- A theoretical analysis of the effects on resource usage and power consumption of our partitioning methods.
- Empirical validation of resource usage, power and performance of the proposed methods, compared to a commercial HLS tool.

Our experiments show that on-chip memory dynamic power consumption can be reduced by up to approximately 70%; using representative high-level algorithms, this corresponds to a reduction of total power by up to 25% and 30%, respectively, without impacting performance. The remainder of this paper is organized as follows: Section 2 describes related work within FPGA memory systems architecture and design for image processing. In Section 3, we formally describe the research problem of power-size optimization, present a motivational example that highlights the limitations of standard HLS approaches, and present alternative partitioning methods. Section 4 describes our experimental methodology and experimental results, and Section 5 presents a thorough discussion of said results. Finally, Section 6 presents our concluding remarks.

Throughout this paper, we use the term BRAM (Block Random Access Memory), a Xilinx nomenclature for on-chip memories, to refer to on-chip FPGA memories in general.

2. Background and Related Work

Within FPGA processing sub-systems, algorithms evolve from typical software-suitable representations into more hardware-friendly ones [6,11] which can fully exploit data parallelism [11] through application-specific hardware architectures [3], often substantially different from the traditional Von Neumann model, such as dataflow [12,13] or biologically inspired processing [14]. These heterogeneous architectures are customized for FPGA implementation not just for performance (e.g., by exploiting binary logarithmic arithmetic for efficient multiplication/division [15]), but also for power efficiency (e.g., by static/dynamic frequency scaling across parallel datapaths for reduced power consumption [16]).

More often than not, computer vision applications deployed on FPGAs are constrained by performance, power and real-time requirements [3]. Real time streaming applications (i.e., performing image processing on real-time video feeds [6]) require bounded acquisition, processing and communication times [16] which can only be achieved, while maintaining the required computational power, through exploitation of data parallelism [11] by dedicated functional blocks [7].

However, the greatest limiting factor to the widespread use of FPGAs for complex image processing applications is memory [9]. Algorithms that perform only point or local region operators (e.g., sliding window filters) [15] are relatively simple to implement using hardware structures such as line buffers [3]. However, complex algorithms based on global operations require complete frame(s) to be stored in situ [11]; examples of contemporary applications that require global operations are object detection, identification and tracking, critical to security. Notice we use the term "global operations" to simultaneously refer to two characteristics: the use of *global operators* (atomic operations which require the whole image, such as transposition or rotation) and *undetermined* (unpredictable) access patterns (e.g., a person identification system might only need a subset of a frame, but which subset cannot be decided at design time, as it depends on person location at runtime).

A possible approach is to refine image processing algorithms so they can perform on smaller frame sizes that can be contained on an FPGA [2]. Several algorithms maintain robustness for downscaled images [17], e.g., the Face Certainty Map [18]) or employ intelligent on-chip memory allocation schemes [8] to accommodate complete frames that take into account power profiles. The latter requires methods to optimize on-chip memory configurations in order to maximize valuable usage; often at odds with performance-oriented allocation schemes standard in HLS code generators. Other possible approaches include stream-processing algorithm refactoring to minimize memory requirements [19] or programming-language abstractions for efficient hardware pipeline generation [20]; these are orthogonal to our approach, and outside the scope of this work.

In our context, the most significant related work on the use of FPGA on-chip memory for image processing applications has focused on four aspects: processing-specific memory architectures, caching systems for off-chip memory access, partitioning algorithms for performance and on chip memory power reduction.

2.1. Processing-Specific Memory Architectures

Memory architectures specialized for specific processing pipelines typically exhibit poor BRAM utilization. Torres-Huitzil and Nuno-Maganda [9] presented a mirrored memory system: in order to cope with dual access required by computational datapaths; data is replicated in two parallel memories and a third one is used for intermediate computations. The need for data replication to support paralellism inhibits scaling for higher frame sizes. Mori et al. [21] described the use of neighbourhood loader: input pixels are fed to shift registers which de-serialize the input stream into a neighbourhood region. Their approach supports only one output port, and sequential region read (no random access). This approach does not exploit datapath parallelism, nor does it support classes of algorithms which require disparate region access. Chen et al. [22] use distributed data buffers for expediting Fast Fourier computations; they partially exploit spatial parallelism, focusing on time-multiplexing as a means for reducing resource-usage and power consumption. Although time-multiplexing is a convenient technique for certain classes of applications, it cannot be used in real-time streaming where input pixels arrive at steady rates (without discarding frames). Klaiber et al. [23] have developed a distributed memory that divides input frames into vertical regions stored in separate memories. Their approach allows fine grained parallelism, but is only capable of handling single-pass algorithms, i.e., which do not require storage of intermediate values. While this suffices for simple computations, it does not satisfy the requirements of sophisticated computer vision algorithms which process data iteratively (e.g., MeanShift Tracking [24]).

2.2. Caching Systems

Delegating frame storage to off-chip memory solves the capacity problem, at the cost of performance and monetary expense. Caching techniques are used to minimize the performance implications: e.g., Sahlbach et al. [25] use parallel matching arrays for accelerating computation; however, each array is only capable of holding one row of interest (the complete frame is stored in off-chip memory) and their results do not discriminate resource usage across modules, making it hard to estimate the precise array costs. This approach can only support a limited class of algorithms: column-wise operations, for instance, require off-chip memory re-ordering for data to be loaded on-chip as rows, consuming precious processing time. Similarly, Chou et al. [26] have shown the use of vector scratchpad memories for accelerating vector processing on FPGAs, but still rely on random-access external memories; a similar approach is followed by Naylor et al. [27] in the context of FPGAs as accelerators. The use of external memories solves the storage limitation: however, it greatly limits parallelism (only one access per external memory chip can be performed at once) or greatly exacerbates financial and power costs, if several external memories are used.

2.3. Partitioning Algorithms

For HLS-based designs, computer vision algorithms are naturally expressed by assuming frames are stored in unbounded address spaces [28]. This software approach to FPGA design not only easily exceeds FPGA memory capabilities but is also not easily integrated in streaming designs without significant refactoring. This has led to the development of custom hardware blocks and APIs for software integration [29]: "naive" C-based HLS results in several on-chip memory structures, whose sizes and interfaces are dependent on variables' types, often sub-utilizing available on-chip memory. Most HLS tools offer compiler directives—*pragmas*—which guide the synthesis tool according to the designer's intention: optimizing for performance through loop unrolling, or selecting different implementations (on-chip memories or LUTs). We advocate that more directives, invoking different synthesis strategies, are required in order to tackle design constraints such as space and power.

The majority of research into partitioning algorithms has mainly focused on performance: namely, throughput. Gallo et al. [30] have shown how to construct efficient parallel memory architectures through High-Level Synthesis: however, their approach is predicated on re-organizing memory placement at algorithm level, by examining computational behavior and placing data accordingly through lattice-based partitioning, which is not feasible on streaming applications where pixels are inputted sequentially. Although possible, it would require a complex memory addressing mechanism between pixel input and memory structure. The authors then expanded their work to incorporate information about loop unrolling [31], providing new partitioning algorithms for maximizing parallelism; however, they did not tackle the utilization problem. Similarly, Wang et al. [32] have demonstrated an extremely efficient algorithm for improving throughput, by creating memory structures that facilitate loop pipelining in high level synthesis. Their approach saves up to 21% of BRAMs compared to previous work [33]; still, since their objective is maximizing throughput, supporting loop pipelining, their approach does not achieve optimized memory allocation in terms of utilization efficiency.

2.4. Memory Power Reduction

The impact of memory partitioning on power consumption has been researched by Kadric et al. [34]. Their approach investigates the impact of parallelism, i.e., how data placement can be leveraged for parallel access, minimizing communication power. A similar approach is taken in [35]. Tessier et al. [36] show on chip memory power reduction through partitioning, similar to our approach and previous work by the same authors [37], and more recently in [38]. However, none of these investigations assume constraints on memory availability. In contrast, we investigate tradeoffs between power and scarce availability, inherent to the image processing domain, future work need clearly identified by Tessier et al: "an investigation to determine the optimal size and availability of different-sized embedded memory blocks is needed".

3. Memory Partitioning on FPGA

In this paper we describe how to partition image frames into BRAMs in order to maximize utilization (i.e., minimize the number of required on-chip memories), subject to minimization of power consumption. We begin by by formulating the utilization efficiency problem, without paying any consideration to power aspects; the following section integrates power consumption in our problem formulation. We assume that only one possible BRAM configuration is used for each image frame buffer.

3.1. Problem Formulation: Utilization Efficiency

Definition 1. *Given a BRAM storage capacity C, and a number of possible configurations i, the configurations set **Cfg** is a vector of i elements:*

$$\mathbf{Cfg} = \begin{pmatrix} (M_1, N_1) \\ (M_2, N_2) \\ \cdot \\ \cdot \\ \cdot \\ (M_i, N_i) \end{pmatrix} = \begin{pmatrix} \mathrm{Cfg}_1 \\ \mathrm{Cfg}_2 \\ \cdot \\ \cdot \\ \cdot \\ \mathrm{Cfg}_i \end{pmatrix} \tag{1}$$

where the first component of each element depicts BRAM width M and the second component depicts BRAM height N, such that:

$$M_x \times N_x \leq C, \forall x \in [0, i-1] \tag{2}$$

For any given frame size, several possible BRAM topologies are possible (Different BRAM configurations do not always equal the same logical bit capacity. Whilst the total physical capacity is the same, in some configurations parity bits can be used as additional data bits. E.g., configuration (1,16384) can store 16384 bits, whilst configuration (9,2048) can store 18432 bits). A frame is a 3-dimensional array, of dimensions width W, height H, and pixel bit width B_w (typically defined as a 2-dimensional array where the type defines the bit width dimension). BRAM topologies are defined based on a *mapping* of 3-D to 2-D arrays and a *partitioning* of a 2-D array to a particular memory structure (Figure 1).

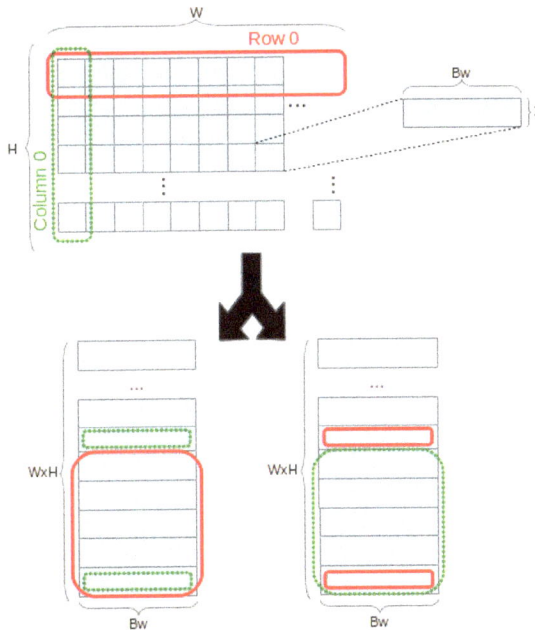

Figure 1. Mapping a 3-D array into row-major and colum-major order 2-D arrays.

Throughout the remainder of this paper, we assume the use of a mapping scheme which assigns B_w to the x dimension and H and W to the y dimension, in both row-major and column-major order (where x and y are 2-D array width and height, respectively). This is the default approach in software implementations, where the type/bit width dimension is considered implicit, and a sensible approach for hardware implementations. Mapping bit width B_w across the y dimension would result in implementations where different bits of the same array element (pixel) would be scattered among different memory positions of the same BRAM. This would require sequential logic to read/write a pixel, accessing several memory positions, creating performance, power and size overheads. It should be noted that this approach might offer performance advantages for certain classes of algorithms which might want to compare individual bits of different elements; however, we delegate this aspect to future work. Hence, we define only the default mapping scheme:

Definition 2. *A mapping scheme m transforms a 3-D array A3 into a 2-D array A2 of dimensions x and y by assigning B_w to the x dimension and ordered combinations of W and H to the y dimension, for a total of two possible configurations, as depicted in Figure 1. Mapping schemes are defined as:*

$$(x, y) = m(W, H, B_w) \tag{3}$$

$$A2_{x,y} = A3_{y \setminus W, y\%W, x}, \; x = B_w, y = W \times H \tag{4}$$

$$A2_{x,y} = A3_{y\%H, y \setminus H, x}, \; x = B_w, y = W \times H \tag{5}$$

where $\setminus$ *and* $\%$ *represent integer division and modulo, respectively.*

Definition 3. *Given a 2-D mapped image frame of dimensions x and y, a partitioning scheme p which assigns pixels across a $\times$ b BRAMs, depicted in Figure 2, is defined as the linear combination:*

$$p(x, y) = \mathbf{Cfg} * \Big((a_1, b_1), (a_2, b_2), ..., (a_i, b_i) \Big) \tag{6}$$

where $*$ *stands for linear combination, such that only one $(a_x, b_x), \forall x \in [0, i-1]$ pair has non-zero components (such a pair is generated as a function of x and y), selecting M_p and N_p subject to:*

$$((a \times M_p) \geq x) \cap ((b \times N_p) \geq y) \tag{7}$$

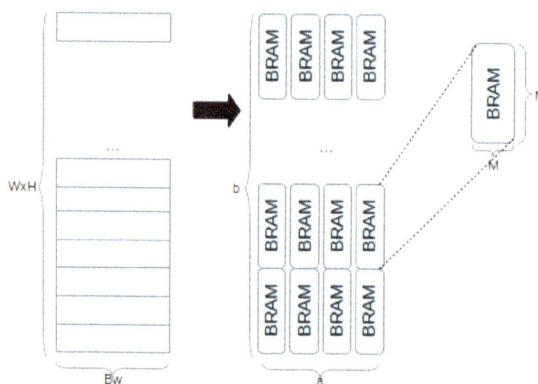

Figure 2. Mapping 2-D array of dimensions $x = B_w$ and $y = W \times H$ to $a \times b$ BRAMs configured for width M and height N.

Different partitioning schemes p, implementing different functions of x and y, result in different addressing, input and output logic requirements, each with a particular impact on performance and resource usage. As this is the greatest bottleneck in implementing high-level image processing pipelines on an FPGA, it is paramount to define BRAM usage efficiency, i.e., the ratio between the total data capacity of the assigned BRAMs and the amount of data which is actually used.

Definition 4. *Given a partitioning scheme p and maximum BRAM capacity C, the utilization efficiency E is defined as the ratio:*

$$E = \frac{x \times y}{a_p \times b_p \times C} \tag{8}$$

The default mapping and partitioning schemes in state of the art HLS tools are geared towards minimizing addressing logic (abundant in contemporary FPGAs), resulting in sub-par efficiency in BRAMs usage (still scarce for the requirements of high-level image processing systems). Alternative schemes must be used in order to ensure memory availability within HLS design flows. We define the problem as:

Problem 1 (Utilization Efficiency). *Given an image frame of width W, height H and pixel width B_w, select a partitioning scheme, in order to:*

Maximize $E = \frac{x \times y}{a_p \times b_p \times C}$

Subject to $((a \times M_p) \geq x) \cap ((b \times N_p) \geq y)$

3.2. Utilization Example

Consider an image frame of width $W = 320$ and height $H = 240$, where each pixel is 8 bits (monochrome), and BRAMs which can be configured according to:

$$\mathbf{Cfg} = \begin{pmatrix} (1, 16384) \\ (2, 8192) \\ (4, 4096) \\ (9, 2048) \\ (18, 1024) \\ (36, 512) \end{pmatrix} \tag{9}$$

which is representative of state of the art FPGAs (Xilinx Virtex 7 family 18Kbits BRAM.), where total BRAM capacity C is given by $C = 36 \times 512$. Using a partitioning scheme

$$p(m(320, 240, 8)) = \mathbf{Cfg} * \begin{pmatrix} (8, 8) \\ (0, 0) \\ (0, 0) \\ (0, 0) \\ (0, 0) \\ (0, 0) \end{pmatrix}^T \tag{10}$$

where $m(320, 240, 8) = (8, 76800)$ (Equation (3)), yields a BRAM usage count of 64 (8×8 BRAMs configured for width 1 and height 16384), with storage efficiency:

$$E = \frac{8 \times (320 \times 240)}{8 \times 8 \times (36 \times 512)} = 0.520833333 \tag{11}$$

We have observed that this is the default behaviour for Xilinx Vivado HLS synthesis tools: empirical results show that configuration $(M_1, N_1) = (1, 16384)$ is selected through a partitioning scheme where $a_1 = B_w$ and

$$b_1 = \frac{W \times H}{N_1} \tag{12}$$

rounded up to the nearest power of 2. Our experiments show that for any frame size, the synthesis tools' default partitioning scheme can be given by:

$$p(m(W, H, B_w)) = \mathbf{Cfg} * \begin{pmatrix} (B_w, 2^{\lceil log_2(\frac{W \times H}{N_1}) \rceil}) \\ (0, 0) \\ (0, 0) \\ (0, 0) \\ (0, 0) \\ (0, 0) \end{pmatrix}^T \tag{13}$$

where $2^{\lceil log_2(\frac{W \times H}{N_1}) \rceil}$ should be read as 2 to the *rounded up* (ceiled) result of the logarithm operation (i.e., 2 to an integer power).

Now consider the same mapping ($x = B_w$, $y = W \times H$), but with a partitioning scheme:

$$p(m(320, 240, 8)) = \mathbf{Cfg} * \begin{pmatrix} (8, 5) \\ (0, 0) \\ (0, 0) \\ (0, 0) \\ (0, 0) \\ (0, 0) \end{pmatrix}^T \tag{14}$$

which partitions data unevenly across BRAMs, rather than evenly. This scheme yields a BRAM usage count of 40, with storage efficiency:

$$E = \frac{320 \times 240 \times 8}{8 \times 5 \times (36 \times 512)} = 0.833333333 \tag{15}$$

Yet a better partitioning scheme for the same mapping would be:

$$p(m(320, 240, 8)) = \mathbf{Cfg} * \begin{pmatrix} (0, 0) \\ (0, 0) \\ (2, 19) \\ (0, 0) \\ (0, 0) \\ (0, 0) \end{pmatrix}^T \tag{16}$$

yielding a BRAM count of 38 and efficiency:

$$E = \frac{320 \times 240 \times 8}{2 \times 19 \times (36 \times 512)} = 0.877192982 \tag{17}$$

Clearly, partitioning schemes depend on the frame dimensions, width, height, and bit width, to enable efficient use of on-chip memory blocks.

3.3. Power Considerations

Having formalized the utilization problem, we may proceed to analyse the power implications of each configuration. We model BRAM dynamic power consumption using the model described by Tessier et al. [37]: a power quantum is consumed per read and/or write. BRAM static power is directly proportional to utilization, hence addressed in the utilization problem.

For any given BRAM cell, the *read* power is consumed by a sequence of operations: the clock signal is strobed; the read address is decoded; the read data is strobed into a column multiplexer; the read data passes to BRAM external port. *Write* power is consumed by the following sequence: the clock signal is strobed; the write enable signal transfers write data to the write buffers; a line is selected by address decoding; data is stored in the RAM cell.

Now consider the partitioning presented in Equation (10) where each datum is distributed across eight BRAMs, and the partitioning presented in Equation (16), where each datum is distributed across two BRAMs. Each read/write operation in the former must consume power across four times the number of BRAMs in the latter. Figures 3 and 4 depict examples of power consumption for two partitioning schemes.

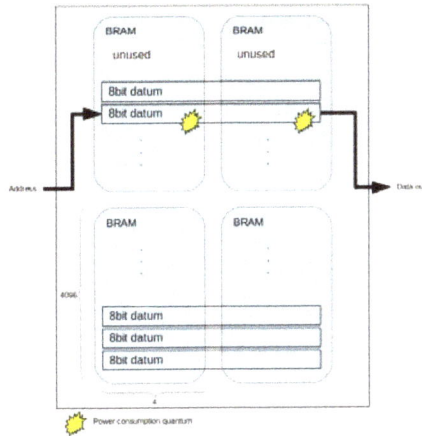

Figure 3. Partitioning across two BRAMs horizontally. Each access consumes two power consumption quantums.

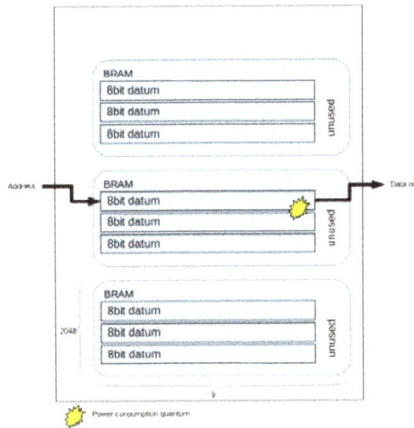

Figure 4. Partitioning across one BRAM horizontally. Each access consumes 1 power consumption quantum.

A partitioning scheme which minimizes horizontal usage of BRAMs (i.e., across x) is more suitable for clock gating. Since fewer BRAMs must be accessed per operation, the proportian of unused ones, which can be effectively gated, increases. It is straightforward to implement clock gating through chip enable selection [39] which is enabled/disabled based on address decoding. colorred In other words, BRAM power consumption is proportional to the number of BRAMs required to access each pixel: and this number depends on which configuration is selected.

An intuitive approach to balance power consumption and utilization is to always use the widest BRAM configuration that suffices for B_w, or multiples of the widest available.

This, however, is not an optimized strategy. While it is true that dynamic power is reduced, static power might increase when moving from one configuration to a wider one since the total number of

BRAMs might increase: utilization efficiency is modified. Additionally, the logic required for address (and chip enable) signals increases when moving to a wider configuration. This aspect makes the utilization and power problems indivisible. In the following section, we describe our approach to balance these two aspects.

3.4. Partitioning for Power and Utilization

We begin by presenting a brute force optimized partitioning procedure for maximizing utilization efficiency, described in Algorithm 1 in pseudo code notation.

Algorithm 1 Optimized Utilization Efficiency can be achieved by:

1: **procedure** OPTIMIZED PARTITION
2:      *efficiency* ← 0
3:      *best* ← 0
4:      **for** x=0 : *i*-1 **do**
5:          $(Mx,Nx) \leftarrow Cfg_x$
6:          $a \leftarrow Bw/Mx$
7:          $b \leftarrow W \times H/Nx$
8:          $efficiency \leftarrow (W \times H \times Bw)/(a \times b \times C)$
9:          **if** efficiency **greater than** best **then**
10:             $best \leftarrow efficiency$
11:             $configuration \leftarrow (Mx, Nx)$
12:         **end if**
13:     **end for**

For each element in the configurations set **Cfg** (possessing a total of *i* elements), the procedure calculates the required number of BRAMs to store a frame of width *W*, height *H* and bit width *Bw*, the efficiency of such a configuration and compares it with the highest efficiency found so far. The focus here is solely on utilization. Effectively, this is an exhaustive search as the number of possible memory configurations is finite and this is an off-line process.

Table 1 depicts the configurations selected by procedure 1 for a representative number of frame sizes and pixel bit widths. Several of the configurations are not power-optimised: notice that for pixels of widths 10, 14 and 22, BRAM configuration 2 × 8192 is chosen most often (consuming power on 5, 7 and 11 BRAMs per access, respectively). This is intuitive from a utilization efficiency perspective: it is the only configuration that divides the width, and is in accordance with the selection of configuration 4 × 4096 for pixels of width 8, 12, 20 and 24 and configuration 18 × 1024 for pixels of width 18.

Table 1. BRAM configurations based on optimized utilization procedure.

Frame	Pixel Width								
	8	10	12	14	16	18	20	22	24
160 × 120	4 × 4096	4 × 4096	4 × 4096	18 × 1024	18 × 1024	18 × 1024	4 × 4096	9 × 2048	4 × 4096
320 × 240	4 × 4096	2 × 8192	4 × 4096	2 × 8192	18 × 1024	18 × 1024	4 × 4096	2 × 8192	4 × 4096
512 × 512	4 × 4096	2 × 8192	4 × 4096	2 × 8192	4 × 4096	18 × 1024	4 × 4096	2 × 8192	1 × 16384
640 × 480	4 × 4096	2 × 8192	4 × 4096	2 × 8192	18 × 1024	18 × 1024	4 × 4096	2 × 8192	4 × 4096
1280 × 720	4 × 4096	2 × 8192	4 × 4096	2 × 8192	18 × 1024	18 × 1024	4 × 4096	2 × 8192	4 × 4096

This non-linearity complicates the derivation of an optimized procedure for partitioning for both utilization and power efficiencies. Hence, we take a more relaxed approach and define a procedure through user defined *tradeoffs* (i.e., an estimation of how much BRAM utilization can be traded for power reduction) and power and space *heuristics*, based on empirical properties. Our brute force balanced method is described in Algorithm 2. It is assumed that the *tradeoff* is expressed in percentage points.

Algorithm 2 Balanced Power-Utilization can be achieved by:

1: **procedure** BALANCED PARTITION
2:     *efficiency* ← 0
3:     *configuration* ← **get_MxNx**(*OptimizedPartition*())
4:     *best* ← **get_efficiency**(*OptimizedPartition*())
5:     *j* ← **get_index**(*OptimizedPartition*())
6:     **for** x=j+1 : *i*-1 **do** efficiency
7:         (*Mx*,*Nx*) ← Cfg$_x$
8:         *a* ← *Bw*/*Mx*
9:         *b* ← *W* × *H*/*Nx*
10:        *efficiency* ← (*W* × *H* × *Bw*)/(*a* × *b* × *C*)
11:       **if** efficiency **less than** best - tradeoff **then**
12:           **break**
13:       **end if**
14:       *configuration* ← (*Mx*, *Nx*)
15:     **end for**

Procedure 2 begins by selecting the optimized utilization solution and iterating over wider BRAM configurations (in the *x* dimension), calculating utilization efficiency. As long as the utilization is above the threshold limit, given by the difference between best utilization and tradeoff, in percentage points, the procedure continues. When it finds the first solution below the threshold, it exits, returning the last solution above the threshold limit. This approach follows the power model heuristics [37] described in the previous section: power consumption decreases as BRAM horizontal width increases (Figures 3 and 4).

Table 2 depicts the BRAM configurations selected by the balanced procedure, with the tradeoff set to 12 percentage points. Compared to the optimized configurations, the majority of widths are increased, resulting in a more power efficient solution based on the aforementioned heuristics.

Table 2. BRAM configurations based on balanced procedure with tradeoff equal to twelve percentage points.

Frame	Pixel Width								
	8	10	12	14	16	18	20	22	24
160 × 120	9 × 2048	4 × 4096	4 × 4096	18 × 1024	18 × 1024	18 × 1024	4 × 4096	9 × 2048	9 × 2048
320 × 240	9 × 2048	4 × 4096	4 × 4096	18 × 1024	18 × 1024	18 × 1024	4 × 4096	9 × 2048	9 × 2048
512 × 512	9 × 2048	2 × 8192	4 × 4096	18 × 1024	18 × 1024	18 × 1024	4 × 4096	9 × 2048	9 × 2048
640 × 480	9 × 2048	2 × 8192	4 × 4096	18 × 1024	18 × 1024	18 × 1024	4 × 4096	9 × 2048	9 × 2048
1280 × 720	9 × 2048	2 × 8192	4 × 4096	18 × 1024	18 × 1024	18 × 1024	4 × 4096	9 × 2048	9 × 2048

3.5. Applying Memory Partitioning: Methodology

Our procedures can be utilized in both HDL and HLS design flows: in an HDL design flow, by guiding the designer's implementation and/or refactoring; in an HLS design flow, through integration in the synthesis tools code generation subsystem. Figure 5 depicts the proposed design flows. The additional steps can be performed manually, either starting from HDL designs or by modifying HLS outputs pre-synthesis; through automated refactoring tools which compute the proposed procedures; or by the HLS tool prior to code generation. We describe the manual process used in our experiments.

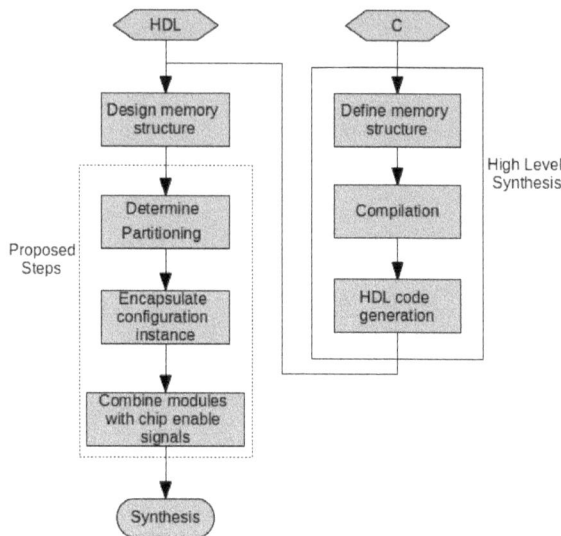

Figure 5. Proposed design flow from HDL and HLS, highlighting the additional steps required for minimizing utilization and power.

After a memory structure has been derived from the procedure specification, according to Equations (3)–(5), procedures 1 and/or 2 are computed to determine BRAM partitioning. BRAMs of the computed configuration are instantiated and contained in modules (i.e., hardware entities). A top module instantiates all sub-modules, providing interfaces identical to the base HDL design or to the specification of the HLS tool. Addressing logic within the top module controls chip enable signals to each sub-module, ensuring that non-addressed BRAMs are not enabled. This careful partitioning of HDL logic in hierarchical modules, where addressing logic is determined by the top-level interconnect and BRAM configuration is determined by module configuration parameters ensures that the desired configurations are used (this is based on our experiments using Vivado: different synthesis tools might require additional compiler pragmas).

4. Experimental Results

Our experiments target state of the art FPGA devices (Xilinx Virtex 7 device xc7vx690tffg1761-1C and Zynq xc7z020clg484-1). We use Vivado v2016.1 for HDL design, Vivado HLS v2016.1 for High Level Synthesis, and Xilinx Power Estimator for power characterization of implemented designs. We begin by generating frame buffers in several configurations, in order to characterise utilization efficiency and power consumption. We then compare utilization and power against equivalent frame buffers generated by a HLS tool. We conclude by implementing two high level image processing algorithms through HLS, and modifying frame buffers according to the proposed strategies, in order to quantify our algorithms' impact on resource usage and power consumption within complete image processing systems.

4.1. Frame Buffers: BRAM Configuration Impact

Our first set of experiments characterises utilization and power consumption for two frame sizes as a function of several possible configurations. The goal of this set of experiments was to validate the utilization efficiency of the partitioning algorithms and the power heuristics used in the previous section.

We implemented frame buffers in Verilog HDL in Vivado v2016.1, explicitly instantiating BRAMs according to the desired configurations. Logic in our design hierarchy routes data, addresses and control signals accordingly. Analysis of post-implementation reports was performed in order to ensure that BRAMs were instantiated according to the desired configuration (depending on the design hierarchy, synthesis tool optimizations could feasibly re-organize BRAM allocation). We performed a *sequential read/write* experiment, where a complete frame is written to memory (sequential pixel input, in row-major order) and then read in the same order. This allows us to validate the power model heuristics assumed in the previous section. Table 3 depicts power and utilization results for monochrome frames of sizes 320 × 240 and 512 × 512.

Table 3. FPGA power usage and utilization efficiency (Eff.) for monochromatic (8 bits) frames of sizes 320 × 240 and 512 × 512 for different BRAM configurations.

	320 × 240				512 × 512				
Configuration	Static	Power (W) Dynamic	BRAM	Eff. (%)	Configuration	Static	Power (W) Dynamic	BRAM	Eff. (%)
8 × 5–1 × 16384	0.328	0.054	0.036	83.33	8 × 16–1 × 16384	0.332	0.07	0.036	88.88
4 × 10–2 × 8192	0.327	0.036	0.018	83.33	4 × 32–2 × 8192	0.331	0.053	0.018	88.88
2 × 19–4 × 4096	0.327	0.026	0.009	87.72	2 × 64–4 × 4096	0.331	0.043	0.009	88.88
1 × 38–9 × 2048	0.327	0.027	0.005	87.72	1 × 128–9 × 2048	0.331	0.046	0.005	88.88

4.2. Frame Buffers: HLS Comparison

Our second set of experiments compares the proposed partitioning algorithms with default strategies employed by commercial HLS tools. The goal of this set of experiments was to confirm that the proposed methodology outperforms commercial HLS tools in both utilization and power consumption.

We performed C-based high level synthesis using Xilinx Vivado HLS, describing frames in the standard format (array type determines bit width, indices determine frame width and height). For each frame size, we report BRAM usage and additional resources (slice registers and LUTs). We utilized standard pixel widths (8 bits for monochrome images, 24 bits for RGB). We estimated optimized BRAM usage using the optimized utilization algorithm and according to the balanced partitioning algorithm in order to compare the power and utilization impact—algorithms were run offline; we have not integrated them in any HLS tool at this point. We implemented the frame buffers in Verilog HDL according to each algorithm, ensuring external interfaces (i.e., read/write data, address and control singals ports) are identical to the ones generated by Vivado HLS from C. We then replaced the frame buffers generated from HLS with our hand-coded Verilog HDL versions. For each frame size, we report BRAM usage and additional resources (slice registers and LUTs) required to implement addressing logic.

Table 4 depicts results obtained from the three configurations, for monochromatic and RGB frames respectively, and Figure 6 compares BRAM utilization efficiency. We characterised the power consumption implications of each generated system using Xilinx Power Estimator for access patterns representative of image processing applications. In our *sequential read/write* experiment, a complete frame is written to memory (sequential pixel input, in row-major order) and then read in the same order. In our *sliding window* experiment, a complete frame is read through 3 × 3 sliding window. Figure 7 depicts static power consumption; Figures 8 and 9 depict total dynamic power consumption by the three architectures, for sequential read/write and sliding window test cases, respectively; and Figures 10 and 11 depict BRAM power consumption for sequential read/write and sliding window test cases, respectively.

Table 4. FPGA resource usage for monochromatic frames: generated from Vivado HLS versus hand-coded modifications according to the proposed algorithms.

8 bits	HLS		Optimized Utilization				Balanced			
			BRAMs					BRAMs		
Frame	BRAMs	LUTs	Usage	Mode	Reduction	LUTs	Usage	Mode	Reduction	LUTs
160 × 120	16	0	10	4 × 4096	−37.5%	22	10	9 × 2048	−37.5%	48
320 × 240	64	9	38	4 × 4096	−40.6%	79	38	9 × 2048	−40.6%	186
512 × 512	128	17	128	4 × 4096	0%	285	128	9 × 2048	0%	596
640 × 480	256	34	150	4 × 4096	−41.4%	337	150	9 × 2048	−41.4%	742
1280 × 720	512	64	450	4 × 4096	−12.1%	1039	450	9 × 2048	−12.1%	2284

24 bits	HLS		Optimized Utilization				Balanced			
			BRAMs					BRAMs		
Frame	BRAMs	LUTs	Usage	Mode	Reduction	LUTs	Usage	Mode	Reduction	LUTs
160 × 120	48	0	30	4 × 4096	−37.5%	41	30	9 × 2048	−37.5%	91
320 × 240	192	25	114	4 × 4096	−40.6%	140	114	9 × 2048	−40.6%	308
512 × 512	384	49	384	1 × 16384	0%	504	384	9 × 2048	0%	1109
640 × 480	768	98	450	4 × 4096	−41.4%	584	450	9 × 2048	−41.4%	1285
1280 × 720	1536	192	1350	4 × 4096	−12.1%	1760	1350	9 × 2048	−12.1%	3877

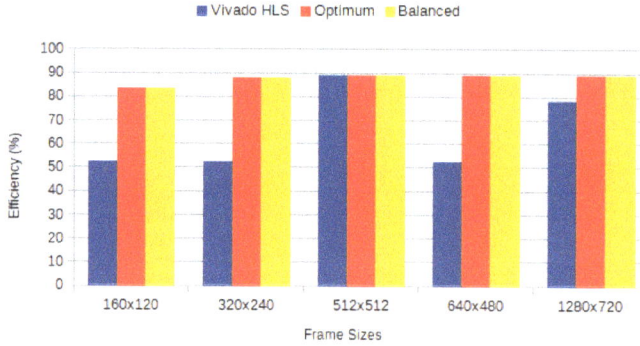

Figure 6. BRAM utilization efficiency for RGB frames: Vivado HLS versus proposed methods.

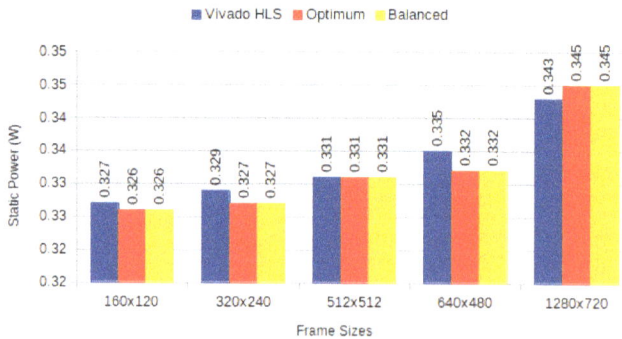

Figure 7. Static power consumption: Vivado HLS versus proposed methods.

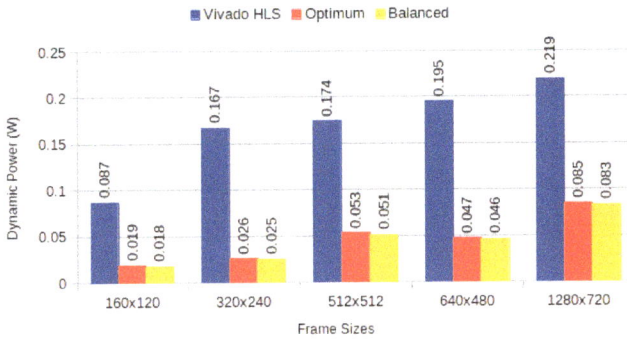

Figure 8. Total dynamic power consumption for sequential read/write: Vivado HLS versus proposed methods.

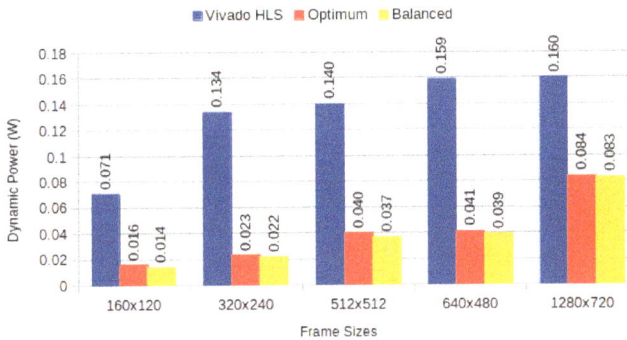

Figure 9. Total dynamic power consumption for 3 × 3 sliding window read: Vivado HLS versus proposed methods.

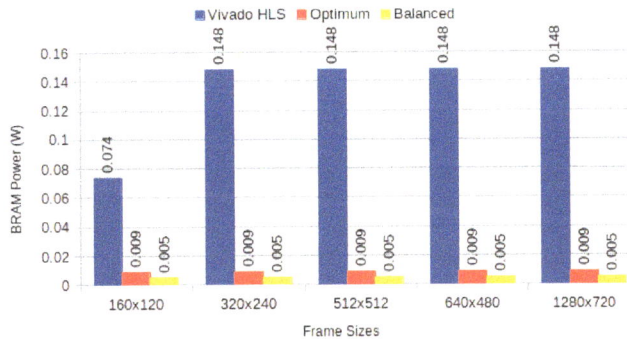

Figure 10. BRAM power consumption for sequential read/write: Vivado HLS versus proposed methods.

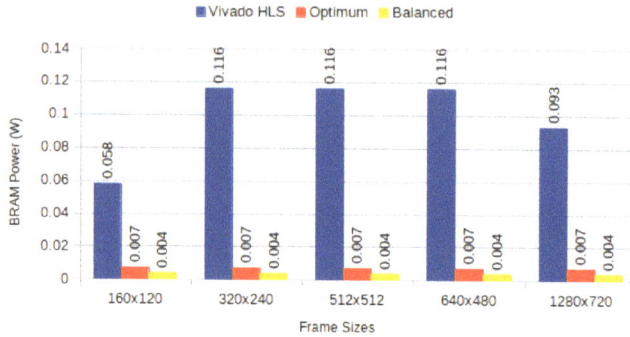

Figure 11. BRAM power consumption for 3 × 3 sliding window read: Vivado HLS versus proposed methods.

4.3. High-Level Image Processing

Out third set of experiments contextualises the impact of memory allocation on high-level image processing systems. The goal of this set of experiments was to quantify how much frame buffers impact resource usage and power consumption within complete image processing systems, based on default and proposed partitioning strategies.

We use Optical Flow and MeanShift Tracking as case studies. Optical Flow estimates the apparent motion of objects caused by the relative motion of an observer; i.e., for two sequential frames, Optical Flow estimates the movement of each pixel (or larger regions) from one frame to the other. It belongs to the *temporal* class of image processing algorithms, i.e., it performs computations across time (different frames). Our Optical Flow implementation is based on the code available from [40] using the TV-L1 method, refactored so it complies with Vivado HLS C synthesis requirements (e.g., dynamic memory allocation was replaced by static memory allocation); we performed no other optimizations. We compute a single scale, rather than multiple scales, for images of size 160 × 120: an example is depicted in Figure 12. We used the publicly available dataset from [41]. We developed three versions: with default memory allocation and following the optimized utilization and balanced algorithms. FPGA utilization results for Xilinx Virtex 7 are depicted in Table 5 (optimized and balanced strategies yield the same BRAM utilization, although different configurations, for our implementation). For the default strategy, BRAMs were insufficient to accommodate all memory requirements, causing the synthesis tool to infer Memory LUTs for parts of the design. Using our approach, BRAMs suffice to implement the complete system. Power consumption per version is depicted in Figure 13.

Table 5. Optical Flow FPGA resource usage and performance on Virtex 7 xc7vx690tffg1761-1: generated from Vivado HLS versus hand-coded modifications according to the proposed algorithm.

	Vivado HLS Default	Optimized
FF	24101 (3%)	24101 (3%)
LUTs	200205 (47%)	208724 (49%)
Memory LUT	126114 (73%)	-
IOs	568 (67%)	568 (67%)
BRAM	1008 (35%)	2157 (74%)
DSPs	232 (7%)	232 (7%)
fps	24	24

(a) First frame

(b) Second frame

(c) 1 scale optical flow

(d) 5 scales optical flow

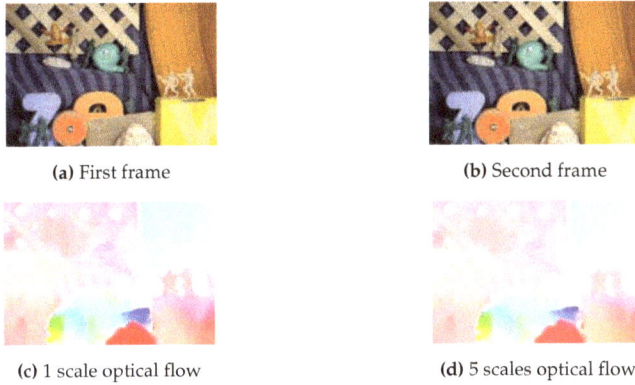

Figure 12. Optical Flow results using the implementation from [40]. (**a,b**): source frames. (**c**): output from 1 scale optical flow (used in our FPGA implementation). (**d**): output from 5 scales optical flow.

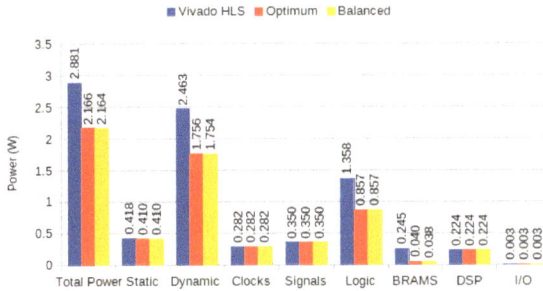

Figure 13. TV-L1 Optical Flow power consumption on Virtex 7.

MeanShift Tracking [24] calculates a confidence map for object position on an image, based on a colour histogram of such object on a previous image: i.e., for an object whose position is known and colour histogram is calculated in frame k, MeanShift Tracking determines the most likely object position in frame $k + 1$, based on colour histogram comparison. It is a *temporal* and *dynamic* algorithm: it performs computations across more than one frame, requiring an unpredictable number of iterations (up to a predefined maximum) on unpredictable frame positions (depending on runtime object position). It was described in C and implemented through Vivado HLS; our implementation was highly optimized for hardware implementation. MeanShift Tracking stores the first input frame (writing the full frame to memory in sequential, row-major order) and calculates a color histogram of a region of width M and height N, centered on an initial object position (reading $M \times N$ pixels). Every subsequent frame is stored, and color histograms for possible new positions are calculated in a region around the previous known position. The new position is decided when the difference between previous and current position is below a pre-defined error bound or a maximum number of iterations is reached. The MeanShift tracking access patterns are not regular or predictable as they depend on the input images; it is representative of memory-intensive image processing algorithms as the output depends on complete (or unpredictable subsets of) scenes, rather than well-defined pixels or regions.

Our tracking system was implemented on a Zynq 7020 chip on a Zedboard, connected to an external camera OV7670 (Figure 14). The processed data (image plus tracked object position) are sent to the on-board ARM processor which re-transmits to a remote desktop computer over Ethernet. However, it is important to stress that this for communication and display only, the complete algorithm is implemented on the FPGA. Figure 15 shows real-time operation of our setup.

Figure 14. Zedboard connected to PC through Ethernet.

Figure 15. MeanShift Tracking: real-time face tracking displayed on PC. Image sent from Zedboard over Ethernet connection.

We developed three system versions: with default memory allocation, optimized utilization memory allocation and balanced allocation for image sizes of 320×240 where each pixel is 24 bits (RGB), with a region of interest of size $M = 16$ and $N = 21$. Identical to the previous experiment, our baseline is the MeanShift Tracking implementation generated by Vivado HLS. The versions used for comparison replace the HLS frame buffer with hand-coded implementations: all other MeanShift Tracking modules are unmodified (generated from C through Vivado HLS). Resource usage for each version is depicted in Table 6. Power consumption per version is depicted in Figure 16.

Table 6. MeanShift Tracking FPGA resource usage and performance on Zynq 7020: generated from Vivado HLS versus hand-coded modifications according to the proposed algorithms.

	Vivado HLS Default	Optimized	Balanced
FF	6264 (5%)	6264 (5%)	6264 (5%)
LUTs	9197 (17%)	9310 (17.5%)	9475 (17.8%)
IOs	64 (32%)	64 (32%)	64 (32%)
BRAM	228 (81%)	150 (54%)	150 (54%)
DSPs	8 (3%)	8 (3%)	8 (3%)
fps	134	134	134

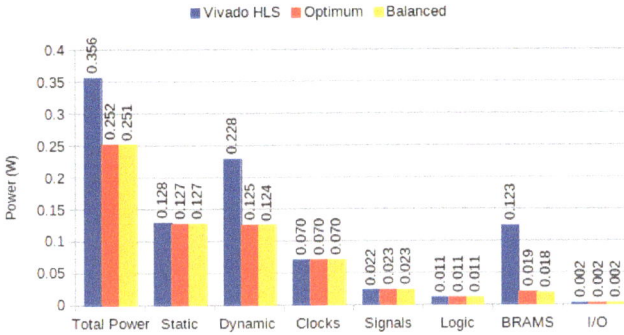

Figure 16. MeanShift Tracking power consumption on Zedboard.

5. Discussion of Results

Regarding the experiments in Section 4.1, we purposely chose these configurations in order to highlight the non-linear relationship between efficiency and power; while for frames of size 320 × 240, different configurations yield different efficiency and different power consumption, efficiency is identical across configurations for frames of size 512 × 512, while power consumption still varies. It is worthwhile noticing that for both sizes, BRAM configuration 9 × 2048 is less power efficient than configuration 4 × 4096, despite achieving the same efficiency; although BRAM power is decreased (from 0.009 W to 0.005 W in both cases), total dynamic power (comprised of BRAM, clocks, signals, logic and I/O) increases due to more complex logic, as previously described.

Experiments show that our partitioning algorithms achieve higher efficiency than default synthesis strategies, except for frames of size 512 × 512 where the efficiency is unchanged. This is the case where default strategies perform equally well in terms of utilization since the image height and width are powers of 2 (refer back to Equation (13)). This confirms that modified partitioning strategies are required, according to requirements, in order to improve memory usage.

Static power consumption depicted in Figure 7 decreases across frame sizes, except for frames of sizes 512 × 512 and 1280 × 720, where the utilization efficiency difference between default and proposed strategies is smallest (Figure 6) and additional addressing logic becomes too (static) power hungry. This confirms the utilization and power problems are indivisible, and must be treated in synergy.

Total dynamic power, on experiments performed on frame buffers, is reduced on average by 74.708% ($\sigma = 7.819\%$) for read/write experiments (Figure 8), and on average by 72.206% ($\sigma = 12.546\%$) for read-only experiments (Figure 9). This confirms our hypothesis that memory partitioning offers opportunities for power reduction, despite the need for logic overhead. Considering BRAM dynamic power only, our partitioning methods result in 95.945% average power reduction ($\sigma = 1.351\%$) for read/write experiments (Figure 10) and 95.691% average power reduction ($\sigma = 1.331\%$) for read-only experiments (Figure 11).

On our experiments using Optical Flow, where BRAM and Memory LUT power accounts for 25.9% of total power consumption, and 30% of dynamic power, we show that the proposed partitioning algorithms can reduce total power by approximately 25% (Figure 13). For MeanShift Tracking, where BRAM power accounts for 34.55% of total power consumption, and 53.94% of dynamic power, we show that the proposed partitioning algorithms can reduce total power by approximately 30% (Figure 16). Algorithm performance (i.e., frames per second) was unaffected by our partitioning methodologies, both in Optical Flow and MeanShift Tracking, since our strategies do not affect memory access latencies and maximum clock frequencies remained unchanged (frame buffers were not responsible for clock critical path). Our results compare favorably to the results presented in [36], which achieved up to

26% BRAM power reduction, at the expense of 1.6% clock frequency reduction; our methodology achieves up to 74% BRAM power reduction, without sacrificing clock frequency. This is due to the fact that their approach does not consider the power consumption differences caused by different BRAM configurations, a key aspect of our methodology.

5.1. Power Consumption

In Section 3.3, we illustrated how different BRAM configurations affect power consumption: depending on how many BRAMs must be strobed in order to access a pixel (in other words, depending on which configuration is used for memory allocation), different power consumption quanta are expended (assuming the remaining ones are clock gated, as per our methodology). The interested reader may refer to [37] for a detailed explanation of this power model. Figures 3 and 4 visually display this phenomenon. Table 4 showed how, for the same frame size, different configurations can reduce power consumption expended on BRAMs by up to 82%; this corresponded to total dynamic power reduction of up to 50%. These results showed how severely BRAM configuration affects power consumption. Note that it is possible that a very small reduction in BRAM utilization (i.e., the number of BRAMs required to implement frame storage) can yield substantial power reductions.

In our experiments using complex high level algorithms, we showed that BRAM power constitutes a substantial portion of total power consumption: namely, using the default Vivado HLS strategy, BRAMs account for 8% of Optical Flow power consumption and 34% of Meanshift Tracking power consumption (Figures 13 and 16). Additionally, significant power is spent on logic due to BRAM output change (prevented in our approach due to clock gating strategies).

5.2. Hardware Overhead

The default memory allocation strategy employed by HLS tools appears to be focused on minimizing addressing logic (implemented through LUTs), at the expense of memory usage. In contrast, our approach minimizes memory usage (a scarcer resource than LUTs) at the expense of more complex addressing. i.e., due to the use of different BRAM configurations, memory control logic (write-enable signals, address decoding, etc.) becomes slightly more complex, consuming more LUTs to implement. In our experiments using high level algorithms (Meanshift tracking and Optical Flow), this LUT overhead was of 0.8 and 2.0 percentage points, respectively (see Tables 5 and 6).

6. Conclusions

Efficient mapping of high-level descriptions of image frames to low-level memory systems is an essential enabler for the widespread adoption of FPGAs as deployment platforms for high-level image processing applications. Partitioning algorithms are one of the design techniques which provide routes towards power-and-space efficient designs which can tackle contemporary application requirements.

Based on a formalization of BRAM configuration options and a memory power model, we have demonstrated how partitioning algorithms can outperform traditional strategies in the context of High Level Synthesis. Our data show that the proposed algorithms can result in up to 60% higher utilization efficiency, increasing the sizes and/or number of frames that can be accommodated on-chip, and reduce frame buffers dynamic power consumption by up to approximately 70%. In our experiments using Optical Flow and MeanShift Tracking, representative high-level image processing algorithms, data show that partitioning algorithms can reduce total power by up to 25% and 30%, respectively, without any performance degradation. Our strategies can be applied to any FPGA family and can easily scale as required for future FPGA platforms with novel on-chip memory capabilities and configurations.

The majority of HLS design techniques have focused on programmability and performance. However, our results show that further research is required in order to improve design strategies towards accommodating other constraints; namely, size and power. Models which describe low-level non-functional properties such as power consumption can support high-level constructs in order to display early cost estimation, guiding the design flow. This requires not only fine-grained

J. Imaging **2019**, *5*, 7

characterization of technologies' properties, but also sufficiently powerful modeling abstractions which can lift these properties to high-level descriptions. It will also be interesting to profile and refactor image processing algorithms to determine if alternative mappings (refer back to Equations (4) and (5)) could provide higher performance and utilization; this could be pursued in future work involving multi-objective optimizations.

Research in FPGA dynamic reconfiguration has focused on overcoming space limitations; whether this capability can be exploited for image processing power reduction, based on heuristics and runtime decisions, essentially transforming approximate computing design from a static to a dynamic paradigm, remains an open question.

Author Contributions: Conceptualization and methodology, P.G. and D.B.; methodology and software, P.G. and R.S.; validation, P.G., R.S. and A.W.; writing—original draft preparation, P.G., D.B.and A.W.; writing—review and editing, A.W. and G.M.; project administration and funding acquisition, A.W. and G.M.

Funding: We acknowledge the support of the Engineering and Physical Research Council, grant references EP/K009931/1 (Programmable embedded platforms for remote and compute intensive image processing applications) and EP/K014277/1 (MOD University Defence Research Collaboration in Signal Processing).

Conflicts of Interest: The authors declare no conflict of interest. The funders had no role in the design of the study; in the collection, analyses, or interpretation of data; in the writing of the manuscript, or in the decision to publish the results.

References

1. Wang, J.; Zhong, S.; Yan, L.; Cao, Z. An Embedded System-on-Chip Architecture for Real-time Visual Detection and Matching. *IEEE Trans. Circuits Syst. Video Technol.* **2014**, *24*, 525–538. [CrossRef]
2. Mondal, P.; Biswal, P.K.; Banerjee, S. FPGA based accelerated 3D affine transform for real-time image processing applications. *Comput. Electr. Eng.* **2016**, *49*, 69–83. [CrossRef]
3. Wang, W.; Yan, J.; Xu, N.; Wang, Y.; Hsu, F.H. Real-Time High-Quality Stereo Vision System in FPGA. *IEEE Trans. Circuits Syst. Video Technol.* **2015**, *25*, 1696–1708. [CrossRef]
4. Jin, S.; Cho, J.; Pham, X.D.; Lee, K.M.; Park, S.K.; Kim, M.; Jeon, J.W. FPGA Design and Implementation of a Real-Time Stereo Vision System. *IEEE Trans. Circuits Syst. Video Technol.* **2010**, *20*, 15–26.
5. Perri, S.; Frustaci, F.; Spagnolo, F.; Corsonello, P. Design of Real-Time FPGA-based Embedded System for Stereo Vision. In Proceedings of the 2018 IEEE International Symposium on Circuits and Systems (ISCAS), Florence, Italy, 27–30 May 2018; pp. 1–5.
6. Schlessman, J.; Wolf, M. Tailoring design for embedded computer vision applications. *Computer* **2015**, *48*, 58–62. [CrossRef]
7. Stevanovic, U.; Caselle, M.; Cecilia, A.; Chilingaryan, S.; Farago, T.; Gasilov, S.; Herth, A.; Kopmann, A.; Vogelgesang, M.; Balzer, M.; Baumbach, T.; Weber, M. A Control System and Streaming DAQ Platform with Image-Based Trigger for X-ray Imaging. *IEEE Trans. Nucl. Sci.* **2015**, *62*, 911–918. [CrossRef]
8. Dessouky, G.; Klaiber, M.J.; Bailey, D.G.; Simon, S. Adaptive Dynamic On-chip Memory Management for FPGA-based reconfigurable architectures. In Proceedings of the 2014 24th International Conference on Field Programmable Logic and Applications (FPL), Munich, Germany, 2–4 September 2014; pp. 1–8.
9. Torres-Huitzil, C.; Nuño-Maganda, M.A. Areatime Efficient Implementation of Local Adaptive Image Thresholding in Reconfigurable Hardware. *ACM SIGARCH Comput. Arch. News* **2014**, *42*, 33–38. [CrossRef]
10. Appuswamy, R.; Olma, M.; Ailamaki, A. Scaling the Memory Power Wall With DRAM-Aware Data Management. In Proceedings of the 11th International Workshop on Data Management on New Hardware, Melbourne, Australia, 31 May–4 June 2015; p. 3.
11. Memik, S.O.; Katsaggelos, A.K.; Sarrafzadeh, M. Analysis and FPGA implementation of image restoration under resource constraints. *IEEE Trans. Comput.* **2003**, *52*, 390–399. [CrossRef]
12. Jiang, H.; Ardo, H.; Owall, V. A Hardware Architecture for Real-Time Video Segmentation Utilizing Memory Reduction Techniques. *IEEE Trans. Circuits Syst. Video Technol.* **2009**, *19*, 226–236. [CrossRef]
13. Baskin, C.; Liss, N.; Zheltonozhskii, E.; Bronstein, A.M.; Mendelson, A. Streaming architecture for large-scale quantized neural networks on an FPGA-based dataflow platform. In Proceedings of the 2018 IEEE International Parallel and Distributed Processing Symposium Workshops (IPDPSW), Vancouver, BC, Canada, 21–25 May 2018; pp. 162–169.

14. Fowers, S.G.; Lee, D.J.; Ventura, D.A.; Archibald, J.K. The Nature-Inspired BASIS Feature Descriptor for UAV Imagery and Its Hardware Implementation. *IEEE Trans. Circuits Syst. Video Technol.* **2013**, *23*, 756–768. [CrossRef]
15. Pandey, J.; Karmakar, A.; Shekhar, C.; Gurunarayanan, S. An FPGA-Based Architecture for Local Similarity Measure for Image/Video Processing Applications. In Proceedings of the 2015 28th International Conference on VLSI Design, Bangalore, India, 3–7 January 2015; pp. 339–344.
16. Ali, K.; Ben Atitallah, R.; Fakhfakh, N.; Dekeyser, J.L. Using hardware parallelism for reducing power consumption in video streaming applications. In Proceedings of the 2015 10th International Symposium on Reconfigurable Communication-centric Systems-on-Chip (ReCoSoC), Bremen, Germany, 29 June–1 July 2015; pp. 1–7.
17. Atkinson, P.M. Downscaling in remote sensing. *Int. J. Appl. Earth Obser. Geoinf.* **2013**, *22*, 106–114. [CrossRef]
18. Jin, S.; Kim, D.; Nguyen, T.T.; Kim, D.; Kim, M.; Jeon, J.W. Design and Implementation of a Pipelined Datapath for High-Speed Face Detection Using FPGA. *IEEE Trans. Ind. Inf.* **2012**, *8*, 158–167. [CrossRef]
19. Stewart, R.; Michaelson, G.; Bhowmik, D.; Garcia, P.; Wallace, A. A Dataflow IR for Memory Efficient RIPL Compilation to FPGAs. In Proceedings of the International Workshop on Data Locality in Modern Computing Systems, Granada, Spain, 14–16 December 2016.
20. Hegarty, J.; Brunhaver, J.; DeVito, Z.; Ragan-Kelley, J.; Cohen, N.; Bell, S.; Vasilyev, A.; Horowitz, M.; Hanrahan, P. Darkroom: Compiling High-level Image Processing Code into Hardware Pipelines. *ACM Trans. Graph.* **2014**, *33*, 144:1–144:11. [CrossRef]
21. Mori, J.Y.; Kautz, F.; Hübner, M. Applied Reconfigurable Computing. In Proceedings of the 12th International Symposium, Mangaratiba, RJ, Brazil, 22–24 March 2016; pp. 328–333.
22. Chen, R.; Park, N.; Prasanna, V.K. High throughput energy efficient parallel FFT architecture on FPGAs. In Proceedings of the High Performance Extreme Computing Conference (HPEC), Waltham, MA, USA, 10–12 September 2013; pp. 1–6.
23. Klaiber, M.J.; Bailey, D.G.; Ahmed, S.; Baroud, Y.; Simon, S. A high-throughput FPGA architecture for parallel connected components analysis based on label reuse. In Proceedings of the 2013 International Conference on Field-Programmable Technology (FPT), Kyoto, Japan, 9–11 December 2013; pp. 302–305.
24. Ning, J.; Zhang, L.; Zhang, D.; Wu, C. Robust mean-shift tracking with corrected background-weighted histogram. *IET Comput. Vis.* **2012**, *6*, 62–69. [CrossRef]
25. Sahlbach, H.; Ernst, R.; Wonneberger, S.; Graf, T. Exploration of FPGA-based dense block matching for motion estimation and stereo vision on a single chip. In Proceedings of the Intelligent Vehicles Symposium (IV), Gold Coast, Australia, 23–26 June 2013; pp. 823–828.
26. Chou, C.H.; Severance, A.; Brant, A.D.; Liu, Z.; Sant, S.; Lemieux, G.G. VEGAS: Soft Vector Processor with Scratchpad Memory. In Proceedings of the 19th ACM/SIGDA International Symposium on Field Programmable Gate Arrays, Monterey, CA, USA, 27 February–1 March 2011; pp. 15–24.
27. Naylor, M.; Fox, P.J.; Markettos, A.T.; Moore, S.W. Managing the FPGA memory wall: Custom computing or vector processing? In Proceedings of the 2013 23rd International Conference on Field Programmable Logic and Applications (FPL), Porto, Portugal, 2–4 September 2013; pp. 1–6.
28. Schmid, M.; Apelt, N.; Hannig, F.; Teich, J. An image processing library for C-based high-level synthesis. In Proceedings of the 2014 24th International Conference on Field Programmable Logic and Applications (FPL), Munich, Germany, 2–4 September 2014; pp. 1–4.
29. Chen, Y.T.; Cong, J.; Ghodrat, M.A.; Huang, M.; Liu, C.; Xiao, B.; Zou, Y. Accelerator-rich CMPs: From concept to real hardware. In Proceedings of the 2013 IEEE 31st International Conference on Computer Design (ICCD), Asheville, NC, USA, 6–9 October 2013; pp. 169–176.
30. Gallo, L.; Cilardo, A.; Thomas, D.; Bayliss, S.; Constantinides, G.A. Area implications of memory partitioning for high-level synthesis on FPGAs. In Proceedings of the 2014 24th International Conference on Field Programmable Logic and Applications (FPL), Munich, Germany, 2–4 September 2014; pp. 1–4.
31. Cilardo, A.; Gallo, L. Interplay of Loop Unrolling and Multidimensional Memory Partitioning in HLS. In Proceedings of the 2015 Design, Automation & Test in Europe Conference & Exhibition (DATE '15), Grenoble, France, 9–13 March 2015; EDA Consortium: San Jose, CA, USA; pp. 163–168.
32. Wang, Y.; Li, P.; Zhang, P.; Zhang, C.; Cong, J. Memory Partitioning for Multidimensional Arrays in High-level Synthesis. In Proceedings of the 50th Annual Design Automation Conference, Austin, TX, USA, 29 May–7 June 2013; pp. 12:1–12:8.

33. Cong, J.; Jiang, W.; Liu, B.; Zou, Y. Automatic Memory Partitioning and Scheduling for Throughput and Power Optimization. *ACM Trans. Des. Autom. Electron. Syst.* **2011**, *16*, 15:1–15:25. [CrossRef]
34. Kadric, E.; Lakata, D.; Dehon, A. Impact of Parallelism and Memory Architecture on FPGA Communication Energy. *ACM Trans. Reconfigurable Technol. Syst.* **2016**, *9*, 30:1–30:23. [CrossRef]
35. Kadric, E.; Lakata, D.; DeHon, A. Impact of Memory Architecture on FPGA Energy Consumption. In Proceedings of the 2015 ACM/SIGDA International Symposium on Field-Programmable Gate Arrays, Monterey, CA, USA, 22–24 February 2015; pp. 146–155.
36. Tessier, R.; Betz, V.; Neto, D.; Egier, A.; Gopalsamy, T. Power-Efficient RAM Mapping Algorithms for FPGA Embedded Memory Blocks. *IEEE Trans. Comput.-Aided Des. Integr. Circuits Syst.* **2007**, *26*, 278–290. [CrossRef]
37. Tessier, R.; Betz, V.; Neto, D.; Gopalsamy, T. Power-aware RAM Mapping for FPGA Embedded Memory Blocks. In Proceedings of the 2006 ACM/SIGDA 14th International Symposium on Field Programmable Gate Arrays, Monterey, CA, USA, 22–24 February 2006; pp. 189–198.
38. Kaur, I.; Rohilla, L.; Nagpal, A.; Pandey, B.; Sharma, S. Different Configuration of Low-Power Memory Design Using Capacitance Scaling on 28-nm Field-Programmable Gate Array. In *System and Architecture*; Springer: New York, NY, USA, 2018; pp. 151–161.
39. Rivoallon, F. Reducing Switching Power with Intelligent Clock Gating. *Xilinx White Paper*. Available online: https://www.xilinx.com/support/documentation/white_papers/wp370_Intelligent_Clock_Gating.pdf (accessed on 1 January 2019).
40. Sánchez Pérez, J.; Meinhardt-Llopis, E.; Facciolo, G. TV-L1 Optical Flow Estimation. *Image Process. Line* **2013**, *3*, 137–150. [CrossRef]
41. Baker, S.; Scharstein, D.; Lewis, J.; Roth, S.; Black, M.J.; Szeliski, R. A database and evaluation methodology for optical flow. *Int. J. Comput. Vis.* **2011**, *92*, 1–31. [CrossRef]

Journal of
Imaging

MDPI

Article

High-Throughput Line Buffer Microarchitecture for Arbitrary Sized Streaming Image Processing

Runbin Shi[ID], Justin S.J. Wong[ID] and Hayden K.-H. So *[ID]

Department of Electrical and Electronic Engineering, The University of Hong Kong, Pok Fu Lam, Hong Kong;
rbshi@eee.hku.hk (R.S.); jsjwong@hku.hk (J.S.J.W.)
*   Correspondence: hso@eee.hku.hk

Received: 21 January 2019; Accepted: 25 February 2019; Published: 6 March 2019

Abstract: Parallel hardware designed for image processing promotes vision-guided intelligent applications. With the advantages of high-throughput and low-latency, streaming architecture on FPGA is especially attractive to real-time image processing. Notably, many real-world applications, such as region of interest (ROI) detection, demand the ability to process images continuously at different sizes and resolutions in hardware without interruptions. FPGA is especially suitable for implementation of such flexible streaming architecture, but most existing solutions require run-time reconfiguration, and hence cannot achieve seamless image size-switching. In this paper, we propose a dynamically-programmable buffer architecture (D-SWIM) based on the Stream-Windowing Interleaved Memory (SWIM) architecture to realize image processing on FPGA for image streams at arbitrary sizes defined at run time. D-SWIM redefines the way that on-chip memory is organized and controlled, and the hardware adapts to arbitrary image size with sub-100 ns delay that ensures minimum interruptions to the image processing at a high frame rate. Compared to the prior SWIM buffer for high-throughput scenarios, D-SWIM achieved dynamic programmability with only a slight overhead on logic resource usage, but saved up to 56% of the BRAM resource. The D-SWIM buffer achieves a max operating frequency of 329.5 MHz and reduction in power consumption by 45.7% comparing with the SWIM scheme. Real-world image processing applications, such as 2D-Convolution and the Harris Corner Detector, have also been used to evaluate D-SWIM's performance, where a pixel throughput of 4.5 Giga Pixel/s and 4.2 Giga Pixel/s were achieved respectively in each case. Compared to the implementation with prior streaming frameworks, the D-SWIM-based design not only realizes seamless image size-switching, but also improves hardware efficiency up to 30×.

Keywords: streaming architecture; low-latency; high-throughput; FPGA; D-SWIM; line buffer

---

1. Introduction

Real-time image processing applications, such as for high-speed image-guided vehicle control [1], requires the underlying image-processing hardware to be both high-throughput and low-latency. Furthermore, for many real-world scenarios, such as in detecting and processing the region of interest (ROI) of arbitrary sizes, the underlying hardware must also be flexible to adapt to the varying input-sized images as needed [2]. With ample high-bandwidth I/O and on-chip programmable logic resources, researchers have demonstrated the benefits of using Field Programmable Gate Arrays (FPGAs) to address the throughput and latency challenges in a wide range of image processing applications. For instance, Wang et al. [3] demonstrated that by using an FPGA to directly process output from a high-speed time-stretch imaging camera, they can successfully classify cell images in real-time with data throughput exceeding 4 Giga Pixels Per Second (GPPS). Similarly, Ma et al. [4] demonstrated an automatic tool for porting general Deep Neural Networks (DNN) to FPGA, which achieves a maximum processing throughput of 710 Giga Operations Per Second (GOPS) and a latency of 31.85 ms for each image frame.

As illustrated by the above examples, one key to achieving high-throughput low-latency image processing on FPGAs is by leveraging carefully pipelined hardware that can operate on the input image as pixel streams without excessive buffering. These hardware architectures are able to commence processing of the image as soon as the necessary pixels are received and continue processing the rest of the arriving image as a pipeline, giving rise to both low-latency and high-throughput operations. Indeed, to facilitate the design of complex streaming image-processing hardware, some FPGA-hardware generators have already been proposed, often relying on the use of domain-specific languages (DSLs) as a bridge between the algorithm designer and the lower-level hardware [5–8]. In our previous work, SWIM [9], a streaming line buffer generator, was also proposed to address the complexities of rearranging misaligned multi-pixel blocks for ultra high-input throughput applications. It demonstrated that by carefully arranging on-chip memory resources to align with the input image size, a fully pipelined image processing system on FPGA could be realized that operates close to the FPGA maximum clock frequency.

However, while these hardware generation frameworks can efficiently produce designs for a particular target application, they must be pre-configured to a fixed input image size before the FPGA synthesis. The FPGA has to be reconfigured when the input image size changes, limiting their use in real-time applications that operate on input images with varying sizes.

Building on top of the work of SWIM, we present in this paper an improved high-throughput hardware architecture that can adapt to the size of the input image dynamically during runtime without hardware reconfiguration. The improved scheme, called Dynamic-SWIM (D-SWIM), utilizes an improved on-chip memory organization that can adapt to changing the image size dynamically. Different to SWIM, the D-SWIM framework generates light-weighted control instructions for different image sizes. The hardware architecture can be rapidly programmed in sub-100 nanoseconds instead of seconds to half a minute of FPGA reconfiguration, making it suitable to process images of different sizes seamlessly. Such dynamic programmability with D-SWIM is achieved with only a slight overhead on logic resource usage. Furthermore, D-SWIM lowers overall power consumption by 45.7% due to reduced BRAM usage. This paper also provides a D-SWIM based hardware design method with two real-world applications as a case study.

The rest of the paper is organized as follows: Section 2 presents the basis of streaming architecture and the motivative scenarios of high-throughput and arbitrary sized image processing. Section 3 describes the D-SWIM framework, including the hardware structure and instruction compilation for any image size. Section 4.2 gives the logic implementation of the fully pipelined hardware. We deeply evaluated the D-SWIM with practical image applications. Section 5 shows the experiments and the results compared to SWIM and other streaming architectures. Section 6 is the conclusion.

2. Background

2.1. Streaming Architecture for Image Processing on FPGA

Similarly to the traditional computer system, memory hierarchy exists in FPGA-centric systems. On-chip memory inside the FPGA has low access latency, but relatively small capacity. In contrast, off-chip memory (DRAM) has a larger capacity, but longer latency and lower bandwidth. Furthermore, DRAM access consumes significantly more energy than on-chip memory. Therefore, in the field of FPGA architecture for image processing, it is a hot topic to trade off the on-chip buffer cost and system performance. For streaming architecture, it is widely adopted that the FPGA receives the pixels line-by-line as they are captured by the image sensor. The on-chip buffer is employed to store multiple lines for the 2D pixel access in the computation. Note that the buffer is optimized to the minimum size, and only the stores the pixels if they will be reused in subsequent computations.

Previous works presented general methods for designing a streaming architecture for image processing with a 2D access pattern [5,7,10]. Figure 1 shows an example. There are three components within this streaming architecture: *Buffer* (BUF), *operator*, and *interconnections*. The BUF stores multiple image lines that arrive sequentially in a line-by-line manner from the input stream, and the *operators* can simultaneously access pixels across multiple lines within a local area defined by a 2D window or stencil pattern. For instance, in Figure 1, the operator 1 (OP1) performs 2D filtering with a 3 × 3 sliding window, and the step size of sliding window is one pixel in both vertical and horizontal directions. Assuming the FPGA receives one new pixel from the input stream per cycle to sequentially fill the input Buffer 1 (BUF1). Concurrently, BUF1 outputs 3 × 3 pixels in a window that is needed by OP1 to produce one resultant pixel. In each clock cycle, the window advances to the right by one step, and the output pixel is stored in BUF2. Note that while the window is moving to the boundary of each line, the output window of BUF1 concatenates the pixel columns from both the end and start in the buffer, as Figure 1a shows. The windows across the boundary are invalid, and the corresponding resultant pixels are dropped, such that the line width of BUF2 is less than the width of BUF1.

As illustrated, BUF1 dynamically maintains three image lines that will be reused. Note that the on-chip BUF can be optimized to a minimum size where the new pixels are consumed as soon as they become available in the BUF and the old pixels are discarded. The BUF design for the other 2-D stencil patterns follows a similar principle. *Operator* is composed of arithmetic units (adder, multiplier, etc.) tailored for the image application. The results from the operators can be either output as the final result, or stored in another BUF which provides the input of the subsequent operator. The *interconnections* are the dedicated data paths that follows the data flow graph (DFG) of the application. For instance, in Figure 1d, Operator 2 (OP2) uses both the pixels in the initial BUF1 and the output of OP1 stored in BUF2 for further processing. In addition to the direct wires, *first-in, first-out (FIFO)* was inserted on the data flow path to guarantee all pixels of the required pattern arrived at the operator in the correct clock cycle.

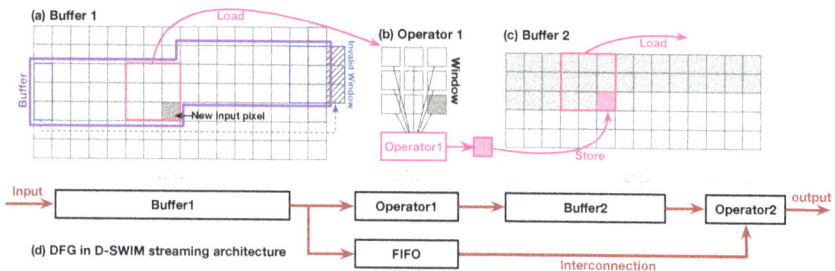

Figure 1. A streaming architecture example for image processing with a 2D pattern. The architecture has three components: buffer, operator, and interconnections.

2.2. Demand on Arbitrary Sized Image Processing

In many real-world image processing scenarios, the size of the image is unpredictable before the system run-time. To demonstrate, Figure 2 presents two example cases.

The first case is the Region of Interest (ROI) processing. As Figure 2a shows, the ROI is selected from the entire view of the image for analysis. This mechanism exists in most image applications that effectively reduce the computation workload. However, the ROI is defined by the end-user—hence, the size of ROI is unpredictable during the hardware design time. Furthermore, multiple ROIs may exist on the same view, such that the hardware is required to accommodate images of different sizes in processing one frame.

The second case presents how the arbitrary size image processing is also demanded in cloud computing. As Figure 2b shows, the users at the edge side upload images to the cloud for the computation-intensive applications (such as inference of deep learning, etc.). The cloud server sends the workload to the FPGA accelerator to reduce CPU processing time.

In both cases, the streaming architecture on FPGA is required to process arbitrary sized images. Furthermore, the working mode of hardware should be quickly switched for seamlessly processing the images. The conventional FPGA reconfiguration costs seconds to half a minute, which greatly reduces the system efficiency. Thus, we investigate a streaming architecture that can be rapidly programmed to process images in an arbitrary size.

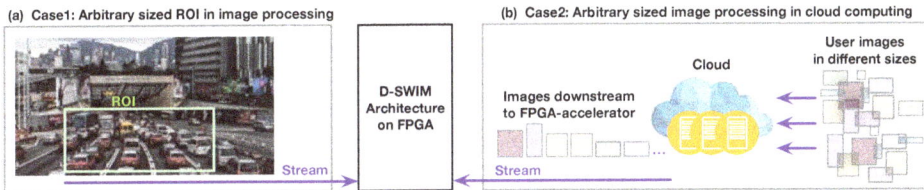

Figure 2. Motivation for arbitrary sized image processing: (**a**) user-defined Region of Interest (ROI) processing; (**b**) arbitrary sized image processing in cloud computing.

2.3. Demand on Ultra-Fast Stream Processing

In previous works, the FPGA streaming architectures accept pixel streams with a throughput of one or two pixels per clock cycle (pix/cycle) [5,7]. Due to the fast-growing bandwidth of peripherals, demand comes that FPGA should process multi-pixel blocks instead of independent pixels in each cycle. For instance,

- **Near-storage processing:** High-bandwidth memory (HBM) stacks multiple DRAM dies to achieve a bandwidth of 250 GByte/s [11]. Assuming the operating frequency of FPGA is 250 MHz, the max data rate of a FPGA input stream is 1000 Byte/cycle. For images with 1 byte per pixel, this translates into a pixel throughput of 1000 pix/cycle.
- **Near-sensor processing:** The high-resolution image sensor represents a high pixel throughput. For instance, the up-to-date CMOS sensor Sony IMX253 is capable of capturing 68 frames per second, with a resolution of 4096×3000 [12]. Thus, the minimum processing throughput on FPGA is 4 pix/cycle ($\lceil 4096 \times 3000 \times 68/250 \text{ MHz} \rceil$).

2.4. BRAM-Misalignment Challenge and SWIM Framework

An increase in processing throughput demands a more complex buffer that relies on the parallel pixel access using multi-pixel blocks. This, however, introduces potential memory alignment issues when utilizing BRAMs in the buffer design. An example in Figure 3a illustrates this problem, where the original image lines are sequenced into a high-throughput 1D pixel stream, and then clipped to pixel blocks by the serial-to-parallel hardware (deserializer) inside the FPGA. The image-processing logic accepts one pixel block in each cycle. Complication due to memory block misalignment arises when the pixel number of one image line (denoted as N_{line}) is not an integer multiple of the pixel number in an input block (N_{blk}). In this case, some of the blocks ended up encapsulating pixels from two image lines. As an example, in Figure 3a, we have $N_{line} = 36$ and $N_{blk} = 16$. Thus, blk2, blk4, blk6, at the end of line0, line1, line2, contains 12, 8, and 4 pixels, respectively, that belong to the start of the next line. These pixels are labeled as *remainder pixels* in the example. As Figure 3b shows, the general pixel buffer is composed of multiple line buffers (LBs) and each LB stores an entire image line. The LB is implemented with one BRAM with a size of N_{blk} to fulfill the parallel pixel access. We annotated the BRAM index (n) and the address ($addr$) in the diagram as $Bn(addr)$ to present the storage pattern. Note that the remainder of the pixels within the last block of each line will be stored in the following LB. Therefore, the storage of subsequent blocks may inherit an alignment offset relative to the BRAM boundary. For example, in Figure 3b, the last block of line0(blk2) contains 12 remainder pixels that are written to LB1. To store the `blk3` continuously in LB, two addresses of LB1 ($B1(0)$, $B1(1)$) are accessed. However, this behavior overwrites the pixels of `blk2` stored in $B1(0)$.

To address the misalignment issue, Wong et al. [9] proposed SWIM, a BRAM partition method for the pixel buffer design. With the same case, Figure 3c shows the SWIM buffer architecture and the pixel storage pattern. Each LB is composed of two BRAMs, and the width of the first BRAM is equal to the number of remainder pixels. For example, LB0 is composed of only one BRAM because there is no remainder pixel at the end of the previous line; LB1 is partitioned into BRAM1 and BRAM2 with widths of 12 and 4, respectively. Thus, the 12 remainder pixels in `blk2` are stored at $B1(0)$, and `blk3` are stored separately at $B2(0)$ and $B1(1)$. With this method, SWIM guarantees that the block storage is aligned to the BRAM boundary. Although the SWIM framework generates BRAM partition configurations that avoid the BRAM-misaligned access, the hardware configuration needs to be re-generated through FPGA synthesis flow for a different image width (N_{line}). Even if the FPGA configuration files for different N_{line} can be pre-generated before the run-time, the long disruption caused by FPGA reconfiguration for differently sized images significantly decreases the throughput.

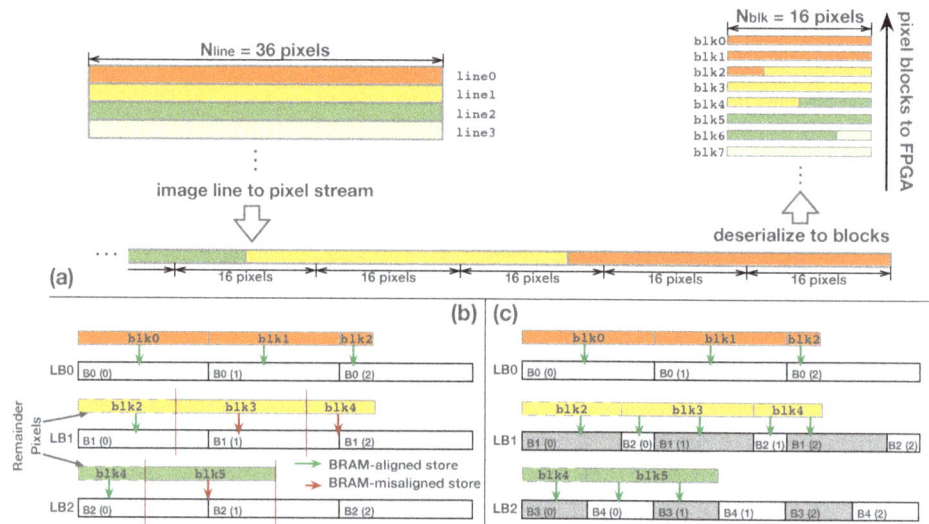

Figure 3. (**a**) Shows that the image lines are sequenced into a stream and then clipped to multi-pixel blocks; FPGA accepts one block in each cycle. (**b**) Shows the general pixel buffer in which the BRAM-misalignment issue occurs. (**c**) Shows the SWIM buffer avoids the BRAM-misalignment using specific BRAM partition.

3. Method

This section describes the Dynamic-SWIM (D-SWIM), a flexible buffer architecture that can be rapidly reconfigured to accommodate arbitrary sized images via instruction updates. First, an overview of the D-SWIM framework (hardware-, software-tools, and design parameters) is given; then, the hardware of D-SWIM is described. Subsequently, the control method of D-SWIM and the custom instruction-set are described, followed by the system working-flow illustration.

3.1. Framework Overview

As shown in Figure 4, the D-SWIM framework is composed of two parts: the *software compilation tool*, (SW tool), and *hardware generation tool* (HW tool). The HW tool generates hardware components following the D-SWIM method. Note that D-SWIM mainly optimizes the buffer hardware which is a general component of the streaming architecture, where specific arithmetic units (operators) are generated by FPGA synthesis tools without further optimization. According to the principle of stream processing in Figure 1, the `Buffer` of D-SWIM is composed of multiple line buffers (LBs), and the number of LB (N_{LB}) is equal to the height of a 2D stencil (denoted as H). Details on the construction of LBs will be elaborated in Section 3.2. Inside the buffer hardware, the `Controller` module provides the control signals to the underlying BRAMs to realize certain buffer behavior. Note that we employed an `Instruction Memory` to provide the control words which can be pre-generated and loaded into the memory during run-time. By doing so, the D-SWIM hardware can accommodate the arbitrary image size by quickly switching the control words in the `Instruction Memory` in a few cycles instead of performing FPGA reconfiguration. The SW tool generates the specific instruction words for the `Controller` based on the pixel block size and image size, that will be described in Section 3.3.

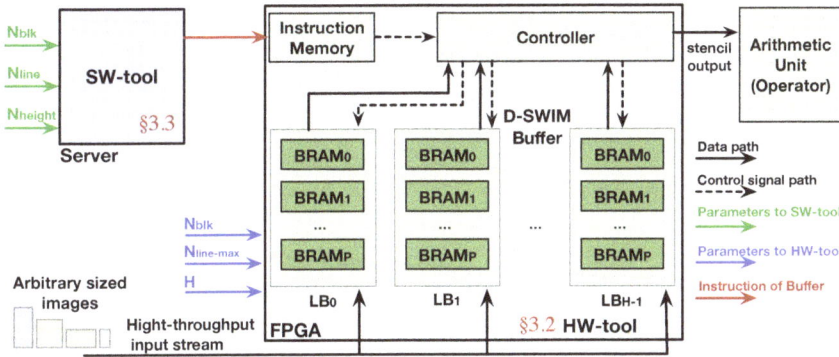

Figure 4. Overview of D-SWIM framework.

The design parameters used in D-SWIM are listed in Table 1. N_{blk} is the number of pixels in one block; N_{line} is the number of pixels in one image line (image width), and N_{height} is the image height; $N_{line-max}$ is the largest possible value of N_{line} that decides the volume of the `Buffer`; and H is the height of the 2D stencil pattern that determines the number of image lines stored in the buffer (number of LB). Table 1 also highlighted the use scope of each parameter. Note that the HW tool only invokes N_{blk}, $N_{line-max}$, and H, which are independent to the image size.

Table 1. Design parameters in D-SWIM framework.

Design Parameters	Description	Use Scope
N_{blk}	Number of pixels in one stream block	HW & SW
N_{line}	Number of pixels in the image line (image width)	SW
N_{height}	Image height	SW
$N_{line-max}$	Largest possible value of N_{line}	HW
H	Height in the vertical axis of the 2D stencil pattern	HW

3.2. Buffer Architecture in D-SWIM

3.2.1. BRAM Organization of Line Buffer

Similarly to SWIM, the D-SWIM buffer is composed of BRAM that saves the FPGA hardware resource and avoids the complex routing requirement. This section describes the BRAM-centric technique for the D-SWIM buffer construction.

BRAM Configuration: D-SWIM directly employs the BRAM primitive for the buffer. The port width of BRAM can be configured. To accommodate the parallel pixels access of the input block and fully utilize the BRAM bandwidth, we configured all the BRAMs to a port width of 64 bits in the simple dual-port (SDP) mode. Note that the real maximum port width is 72 bits, whereas only 64 bits are under the control of the byte-wise write-enabling signal. The conventional usage of BRAM considers all bits in one address as an element in memory access. As Figure 5a shows, the store of the input block should align to the BRAM boundary—otherwise, the misaligned store will overwrite the other bits in the same address. To avoid interference between two consecutive blocks which is misaligned with the BRAM, we used the BRAM primitive instantiation within Xilinx Vivado that provides a *byte-wise write-enable signal* [13]. For instance, in Figure 5b, the input block (8 pixels, 8 bits/pixel) is misaligned to the BRAM boundary because the 4 pixels in the head of BRAM0 are stored along with the previous block. With the byte-wise write enable, the specific control bits in BRAM0 and BRAM1 are set to indicate the store positions of the incoming 8 pixels and the 4 remainder pixels ahead will not be overwritten. In summary, with the BRAM primitive instantiation, the controlling of the pixel-block store becomes more fine-grained. Furthermore, the write enable signal can be changed in the FPGA run-time such that the LB accommodates arbitrary writing offset introduced by the remainder pixels.

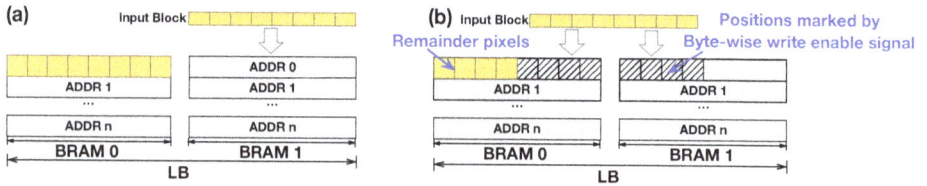

Figure 5. (**a**) shows LB write behavior with conventional BRAM usage. (**b**) shows LB write behavior with the byte-wise write enable signal using BRAM primitive instantiation.

Number of BRAM in LB: The number of BRAM invoked by one LB (denoted as N_{bram}) is determined by the system parameters in Table 1. D-SWIM targets minimizing the BRAM consumption under the constraints in Equation (1). Firstly, the capacity of the LB should be larger than $N_{line\text{-}max}$. Secondly, the overall port width of the LB should be large enough to tackle the pixel block and ensure that only one address in each BRAM will be accessed in one cycle, such as the minimum N_{bram} is 2 in the Figure 5b case. Otherwise, two addresses of BRAM0 will be accessed in the same cycle that violates the port limitation of BRAM in the SDP mode.

$$\text{minimize} \quad N_{bram}$$
$$\text{subject to} \quad N_{bram} \times D_{bram} \times W_{bram} \geq N_{line\text{-}max} \times 8(bits/pix)$$
$$N_{bram} \times W_{bram} \geq (N_{remain\text{-}max}\%(W_{bram}/8) + N_{blk}) \times 8$$
$$N_{bram} \in \mathbb{Z}_{>0}. \tag{1}$$

In Equation (1), D_{bram} and W_{bram} is the depth and width of a BRAM that is equal to 512 and 64, respectively, in Xilinx FPGA. $N_{remain\text{-}max}$ is the largest possible number of the remainder pixel which is equal to $N_{blk} - 1$. % is the modulo operation. Therefore, we obtained the value of N_{bram} as Equation (2).

$$N_{bram} = \max(N_{line\text{-}max}/4096, \lceil ((N_{blk} - 1)\%8 + N_{blk})/8\rceil) \tag{2}$$

3.2.2. Line-Rolling Behavior of Line Buffers

The buffer in D-SWIM stores and loads the successive image lines with the line-rolling mechanism. To demonstrate the line-rolling clearly, we show an example with $H = 3$, $N_{blk} = 4$ in Figure 6. At the beginning, the LB0-LB2 are stored in the Line0-Line2, respectively. When the buffer receives the incoming Line3, the input block is stored in LB0 and replaces the old pixels of Line0 which is no longer needed. With this *line-rolling* mechanism, the successive image lines are stored in all LBs in a cyclic manner.

Meanwhile, the buffer outputs a 2D window including pixels from H image lines, and the blocks in the window are spatially aligned to the input block. As Figure 6 shows, the first two blocks of the output window are loaded from the LBs, while the last one is directly sourced from the input block. Because the output blocks are aligned in the vertical direction, the 2D windows are continuous in the horizontal direction. Thus, the output 2D windows cover all the pixels required by an arbitrary 2D pattern with a height of H.

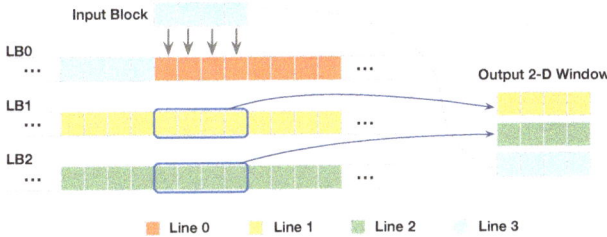

Figure 6. Example of buffer load and store with the line-rolling behavior.

3.3. Line Buffer Access Pattern and Control Instruction

3.3.1. Access Pattern of Line Buffer

Since the image lines are vertically aligned in the LBs, the load addresses are synchronized to the store address of the LB which accepts the input block. We use an example in Figure 7 to demonstrate the pixel access pattern in the underlying BRAMs. The parameters, N_{line}, N_{blk} and H are set to $44, 16, and 3$, respectively in the example. With the D-SWIM method, we set 3 LBs ($H = 3$) in the streaming architecture, and each LB is composed of 3 BRAMs ($N_{bram} = 3$). The store position of input blocks (blk0-blk15) are highlighted in the LBs. In each cycle, one BRAM address is accessed at most to ensure that the previous constraint of BRAM port is not violated. For the blocks that are not aligned to the BRAM boundary, such as blk3-blk5, a byte-wise write enable signal was used to make sure only the positions marked by the enable signal were updated and the other pixels in the same address are not overwritten. Note that the remainder pixels in the last block of each line are duplicated and stored at the beginning of the successive LB. For example, blk2 contains 4 pixels of Line1 ($N_{remain} = 4$). Thus, these pixels are written to both BRAM2 of LB0 and BRAM0 of LB1, concurrently.

Note that from the Blk11, the storage pattern in LBs will be the same as that from Blk0. This is because the values of N_{remain} in continuous lines show a periodic pattern, and the period is determined by N_{line} and N_{blk}. The period measured in clock cycle (P_{clk}) or in image line (P_{line}) is given by Equation (3).

$$P_{clk} = LCM(N_{line}, N_{blk}) / N_{blk}$$
$$P_{line} = LCM(N_{line}, N_{blk}) / N_{line}$$

(3)

where LCM is the least common multiple. In addition, N_{remain} of line l (denoted as $N_{remain,l}$) is calculated as Equation (4).

$$N_{remain,l} = \begin{cases} N_{blk} - N_{line} \% N_{blk}, & l = 0 \\ N_{blk} - (N_{line} - N_{remain,l-1}) \% N_{blk}, & l \in [1, P_{line}) \end{cases}$$

(4)

where l is the index of the line. With the equations above, the buffer access pattern is deterministic. Thus, in the Figure 7 example, every 4 lines have the same LB storage pattern, and the value of $N_{remain,l}$ shows a periodic pattern of $\{4, 8, 12, 0\}$.

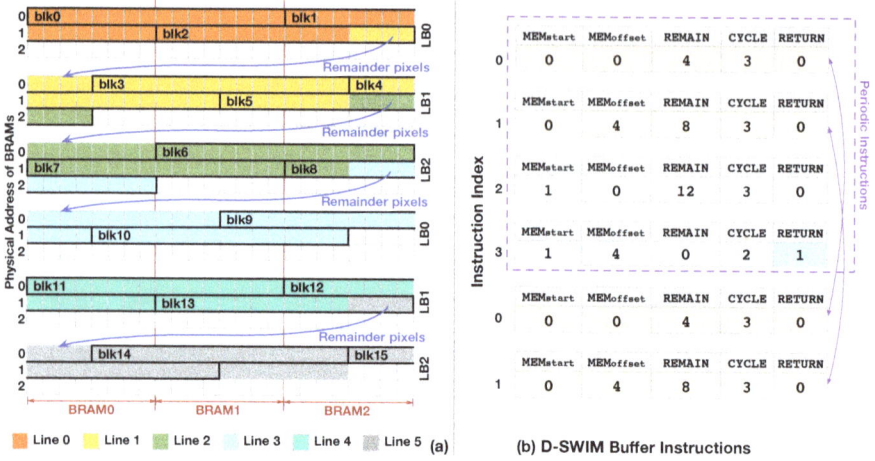

Figure 7. (**a**) shows an example of the block storage pattern with parameters $N_{line} = 44$, $N_{blk} = 16$, and $H = 3$. (**b**) shows the buffer instruction list for achieving the access pattern in (**a**).

3.3.2. Control Code Generation

To perform the buffer store and load with the proposed access pattern, D-SWIM adopts customized instructions along with hardware logic to control the LBs. The BRAM control signals inside each LB are given by the instruction codes and decode logic, and the line-rolling behavior (store block/load block) is controlled by the hardware logic. The instruction codes for a specific image size were generated and loaded into the Instruction Memory before run-time. The instruction-based control method has two key benefits: firstly, it saves hardware logic for control signal generation; and secondly, the content in the Instruction Memory can be rapidly switched for processing differently sized images. Note that each instruction manages the buffer behavior over multiple cycles corresponding to one image line.

As Table 2 listed, the customized instruction is composed of five sections, and each of them is translated into specific BRAM control signals by the control logic. Because an arbitrary number of remainder pixels (N_{remain}) may exist ahead of the first block of a line (line-initial block), we set section MEM$_{start}$ to give the BRAM index from which to store the line-initial block. Furthermore, since the block access may not be aligned to the BRAM boundary, the offset position inside a BRAM is given by section MEM$_{offset}$. In the D-SWIM design, we constrained N_{blk} to be an integer multiple of the BRAM width ($N_{blk}/(W_{bram}/8) \in \mathbb{Z}$). Thus, all pixel blocks in one image line have the same offset inside a BRAM, which is given by MEM$_{offset}$. This constraint leads to a regular storage pattern and reduces the hardware logic usage for control signal generation. Section REMAIN gives the value of N_{remain}, which represents the number of pixels in the last block of a line that overflows into the successive line, and they are duplicated and stored in the next LB. Section CYCLE gives the number of blocks in the line, which indicates the cycle number of the control period for the current instruction code. In addition, CYCLE determines the interval period of fetching a new instruction.

The periodic access pattern of continuous image lines presented in Equation (3) enables instruction reuse. For instance, P_{line} is 4 in Figure 7a; thus, only four instructions are needed. To reuse the instruction periodically, section RETURN gives the flag to reset the instruction-fetch address and restart a new period of the access pattern. The periodic reuse of control code saves the instruction memory and reduces time delay caused by instruction reloading while switching the image size. Theoretically, the maximum possible number of instruction is N_{blk}.

Table 2. Sections of the customized instruction for D-SWIM architecture.

Section	Bit-Length	Description
MEM$_{\text{start}}$	$\lceil \log_2 N_{bram} \rceil$	Start BRAM index of line-initial block
MEM$_{\text{offset}}$	$\lceil \log_2 W_{bram} \rceil$	Start position (inside BRAM) of line-initial block
REMAIN	$\lceil \log_2 N_{blk} \rceil$	N_{remain} of the current image line
CYCLE	$\lceil \log_2 \lceil N_{line\text{-}max} / N_{blk} \rceil \rceil$	Number of blocks in the current image line
RETURN	1	Flag to reset the instruction-fetch address

Algorithm 1 gives the instruction generation flow in D-SWIM's SW-tool. Each iteration of the program calculates five sections and then assembles the instruction to binary codes. The iteration continues till N_{remain}(value of REMAIN section) gets to zero. In the last instruction of the list, RETURN is set to 1, that leads to re-execution of the entire instruction list. For instance, Figure 7b gives the instruction code for each image line in Figure 7a, which is generated by Algorithm 1. For Line0, the line-initial block starts from BRAM0 without pixel offset. Thus, MEM$_{\text{start}}$ and MEM$_{\text{offset}}$ are 0. It takes 3 blocks to fulfill the Line0, and the last block contains 4 pixels belonging to the following Line1. Thus REMAIN and CYCLE is equal to 4 and 3, respectively. Algorithm 1 starts with an initial state that all variables are set to 0, and input parameters N_{line}, N_{blk}, and W_{bram} are set to 44, 16, and 64, respectively. In the loop iteration, the variables are calculated sequentially, and they are corresponding to the value of each instruction section for Line0. Then, the values of five sections are assembled into the Instruction0 and appended to the instruction list. Following the Line0, the line-initial block of Line1 starts from BRAM0 of LB1 with a inner-BRAM offset of 4 pixels, which can be translated to MEM$_{\text{start}}$= 0 and MEM$_{\text{offset}}$= 4 in Instruction1, respectively. The other sections are conducted using the same manner as Instruction0. In particular, only 2 blocks are required to fulfill Line3 (CYCLE in Instruction3= 2), because there are 12 remainder pixels contained in the last block of Line2. The Line3 does not contain remainder pixels, that results in pixel blocks from Blk11 which perform the same storage pattern with that of blocks from Blk0. Therefore, in the algorithm loop iteration for Instruction3, variable RETURN is set to 1, and the loop stops. Then, the algorithm outputs the instruction list (Instruction0-3) that can be periodically executed in processing continuous image lines.

Algorithm 1: Instruction Generation Algorithm in D-SWIM Streaming Architecture

---

Input: Application parameters: N_{line}, N_{blk}, Hardware information: W_{bram}

Output: Instruction code: Inst

Inst$= \emptyset$;

MEM$_{\text{start}}$ = 0; MEM$_{\text{offset}}$ = 0; REMAIN = 0; RETURN = 0;

while RETURN== 0 **do**

    MEM$_{\text{start}}$= $\lfloor$REMAIN$/(W_{bram}/8)\rfloor$;

    MEM$_{\text{offset}}$=REMAIN%$(W_{bram}/8)$;

    CYCLE=$\lceil (N_{line} -$ REMAIN$)/N_{blk}\rceil$;

    REMAIN=$N_{blk} - (N_{line} -$ REMAIN$)$%N_{blk};

    if REMAIN=0 **then**

        | RETURN=1;

    end

    Inst.append(Assemble(MEM$_{\text{start}}$, MEM$_{\text{offset}}$, REMAIN, CYCLE, RETURN));

end

return Inst

3.4. Run-Time Dynamic Programming for Arbitrary-Sized Image

With the specific instruction set, the D-SWIM buffer can be rapidly re-programmed for processing arbitrary sized images. Figure 8 demonstrates the system workflow on both the FPGA and the server. The server obtains the images from users and prepares the D-SWIM instruction list for the image size. Due to the low complexity of the instruction generator in Algorithm 1, the server generates the instruction list online and then writes it to the Instruction Memory of D-SWIM at the FPGA side. Besides the instruction, the server also sends the value of image height (N_{height}) to the control register in D-SWIM that determines the life-cycle of the instruction list. Subsequently, the server sends the corresponding image to the FPGA and obtains the computational results in a continuous data stream. Note that the communication latency is hidden in the fully pipelined workflow. Thus, the image computation logic on FPGA only stalls for a brief period of time during instruction loading.

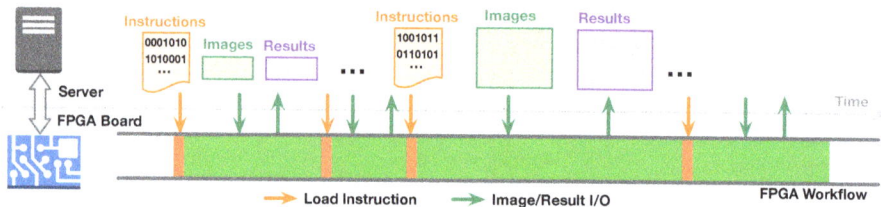

Figure 8. D-SWIM workflow with dynamic programming for arbitrary sized image processing.

4. Logic Implementation of D-SWIM

This section explains the detailed implementation of the underlying logic hardware of D-SWIM. Note that the main focus here is a universal buffer design for image-processing-based streaming architectures on modern FPGA architectures. Further optimizations may apply to specific applications on FPGA architectures, but it is outside the scope of this section.

4.1. Logic of Line Buffer

Figure 9 shows the hardware composition of the Line Buffer (LB) and the related control signals from the Controller module. Each LB is composed of N_{bram} BRAMs and the associated control logic. According to the LB access pattern described in Section 3.3, the BRAM addressing pattern is sequential. Thus, we employed an AddrCounter module to each BRAM to manage the write address. The AddrCounter accepts the AddrInc and AddrRst signals from the Controller that determines whether to increase the address register by one or reset it to zero, respectively. The other signals related to the block store process, including WrMask, WrData, and WrEn, were generated by the Controller and directly connected to the BRAM primitives. Note that we annotate the width of each signal bus in the brace following the signal name in Figure 9.

According to the line-rolling buffer access behavior, the read addresses of multiple LBs were synchronized to the write address of the LB which stores the input block. In the logic design, the WrAddr from AddrCounters were sent to a MUX, and the MUX selected the proper value as the RdAddr signal of all LBs under the control of the AddrSel signal.

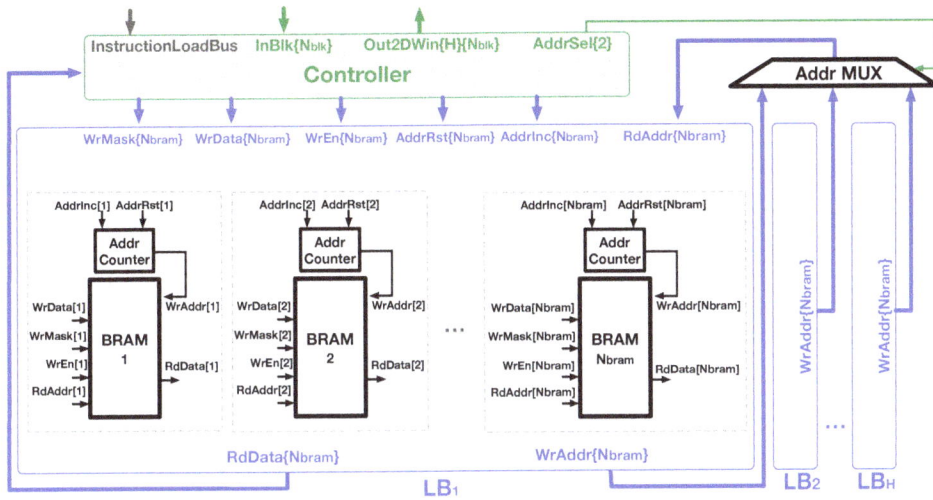

Figure 9. The D-SWIM buffer is composed of LBs and Controller. Each BRAM in the LB is equipped with an Address Counter to manage the write address. It performs address incrementation or reset according to the signal on the controller bus. The Addr MUX allows the write addresses to be broadcasted during a block write operation of a specific LB as the read addresses of the other LBs for block loading.

4.2. Logic of Controller

The Controller performs three functions in D-SWIM: (1) decode the instruction word to the control signals of each LB; (2) transform the input pixel block (InBlk) to the proper storage pattern as the WrData signal of the BRAMs; (3) transform the pixels loaded from LBs to the certain 2D window required by the operators (Out2DWin). Thus, the buffer-write and buffer-read logic are implemented independently as follows.

4.2.1. Buffer-Write Logic

In the D-SWIM design, the length of input block (InBlk) is larger than the width of LB. Thus, the buffer-write logic extends the InBlk signal to the same width of LB in a certain pattern, and the BRAM byte-wise write enable signal (WrMask) is generated concurrently. As Figure 10 shows, two stages exist in the signal generation. In the first stage, place-holding bytes (cross marked in Figure 10) are padded at the beginning and the end of the input block. By doing so, the padded block has the same width as the LB. The number of place-holders at the start of the block is equal to MEM_{offset} in the instruction word. Thus, the PHPad hardware in this stage is controlled by the corresponding register decoded from the instruction. In the second stage, the pixels from the first stage are rearranged by a circular right-shift (CRS) operator. The shift distance is an integer multiple of the BRAM width, and it is given by MEM_{start} in the instruction that ensures the pixel-block storage starts from the proper BRAM in the LB. Note that the pattern of place-holder padding is fixed for blocks in the entire image line, but the shift distance in the second stage changes for every block. Thus, the CRS hardware in the second stage is controlled by the MEM_{start} and a run-time Counter which provides the input block index of one image line. Along with the WrData signal, the WrMask signal is generated in a similar manner. After the two-stage processing, a set of binary flags are generated, where 0 corresponds to the positions of the place-holders in WrData and 1 indicates that the BRAM byte position will be overwritten by the value in WrData.

In particular, when the input block exceeds the end of the image line, the logic stores the *remainder pixels* belonging to the next image line to the beginning of the next LB concurrently, where specific logics are set to process these remainder pixels. Because the number of remainder pixels is provided by the REMAIN section in the instruction, the MUX in the logic separates remain pixels (red pixels in Figure 10) and pads place-holders in the tail as the WrData signal of the next LB, while the WrMask signal with N_{remain} ones at the beginning of the binary set is generated. Subsequently, the WrData and WrMask signals from the circuits for general pixels and remainder pixels are concatenated as the output bus of the Controller. Other buffer-write related signals, WrEn, AddrInc, and AddrRst, were generated concurrently by the Counter and specific logics.

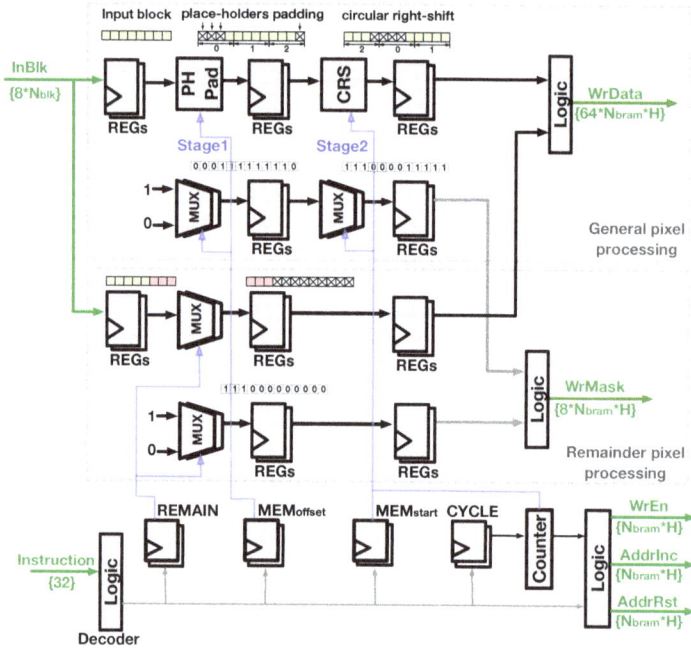

Figure 10. Buffer-write logic.

4.2.2. Buffer-Read Logic

As introduced previously, the BRAM read address was synchronized to the write address of the LB being written. Thus, the Controller generates the AddrSel signal to indicate the LB index that stores the input block. The RdData loaded from multiple LBs are processed by the buffer-read logic to form the output 2D pixel window (Out2DWin) from multiple image lines. The buffer-read logic reverses transformation performed during the buffer-write process, and the circuit is shown in Figure 11. The logic contains three stages to transform the RdData into Out2DWin. The first stage performs line-wise reordering that changes the line-order of the LBs' output blocks to the spatial order of the image. As per the line-rolling behavior in Figure 6, $(H-1)$ blocks of Out2DWin are read from the LBs, and the last block is directly sourced from InBlk with delay logic. The second stage performs a circular left-shift (CLS) which reorders the pixels from different BRAMs. The third stage removes several pixels at the beginning and the end of results from the previous stage, which ensures the output blocks are spatially aligned to the InBlk. Subsequently, the pixel blocks after the three-stage processing are concatenated with the delayed InBlk to construct the Out2DWin.

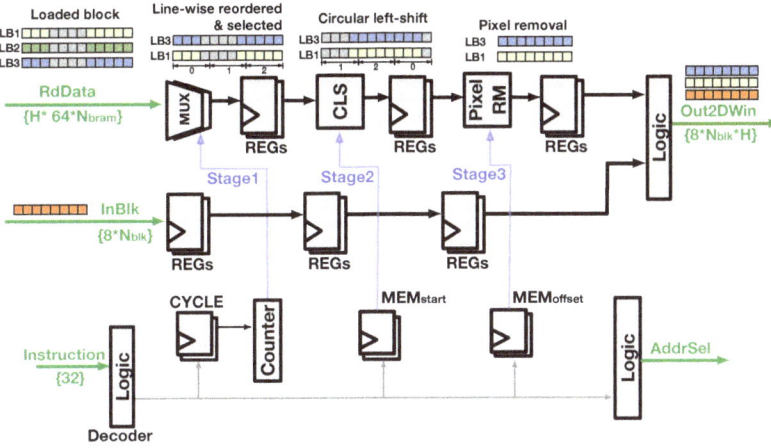

Figure 11. Buffer-read logic.

5. Evaluation

This section describes the experimental setup for evaluating the D-SWIM implementation. In the evaluation, we compare this work with SWIM in terms of hardware resource usage, timing, and power consumption on FPGA. Subsequently, we evaluate the D-SWIM workflow with dynamic programming for continuously processing images in different sizes. Furthermore, we present D-SWIM based hardware architectures for two real-world image applications (2D-Convolution and Harris Corner Detector). The implementations are compared to streaming architectures in prior works.

5.1. Experiment Setup and Evaluation Metric

The hardware generator of D-SWIM was realized using Verilog RTL and implemented with Xilinx Vivado. Our selected target FPGA device was Xilinx-XC7VX690, where the tool synthesizes the Verilog into logic circuits and generates FPGA-specific mapping. Meanwhile, it also gives the resource utilization and timing performance, which are generally employed as the evaluation metrics of FPGA implementation. The resource utilization can be broken down into four FPGA building-blocks: the look-up table (LUT), Flip-Flop Register (REG), BRAM, and DSP. On the timing performance, the worst negative slack (WNS) of the critical path is given by Vivado and can be translated to the maximum operating frequency (f_{max}). The vendor tool gives the power consumption of the D-SWIM module as well. Besides the hardware tools, we implemented the D-SWIM instruction generator on the server to provide the control codes for any given image width (N_{line}) and block size (N_{blk}).

5.2. Evaluation of Buffer Hardware

We evaluated the buffer design in D-SWIM and compared it with the previous work of SWIM, which tackles the similar BRAM-misalignment issue for the multi-pixel block but only supports static image sizes that are pre-defined before FPGA synthesis. In the experiment, we configure the SWIM and D-SWIM with different parameter sets for a complete evaluation. As Table 3 shows, the parameters (N_{line}, H, and N_{blk}) are set to different values, and the implementation results are listed. In Configurations 1–6, we set the image width (N_{line}) to arbitrary values. The window height (H) was set to 3 or 5, which are frequently used in image applications. The pixel number of one input block (N_{blk}) was set to 8, 16, 32. Note that in the SWIM method, the number of LB (N_{LB}) was deduced by N_{blk} and N_{line}; thus, it may exceed H, whereas N_{LB} is equal to H in D-SWIM. The optimization technique of multi-pass BRAM partitioning in SWIM was also invoked to reduced N_{LB}, and the corresponding results are shown in the SWIM-2pass column of Table 3.

Table 3. Buffer resource consumption in SWIM and D-SWIM.

Config.	Parameters				D-SWIM			SWIM				SWIM-2pass			
	N_{line}	H	N_{blk}	N_{LB}	LUT	REG	BRAM	N_{LB}	LUT	REG	BRAM	N_{LB}	LUT	REG	BRAM
1	630	3	8	3	1950 (1.45)	2140 (1.35)	6 (0.75)	4	1346	1589	8	4	1346	1589	8
2	630	3	16	3	3427 (1.33)	3553 (1.29)	9 (0.56)	8	3895	5127	32	4	2650	2653	16
3	1020	3	16	3	3427 (1.30)	3553 (1.16)	9 (0.56)	4	2643	3051	16	4	2643	3051	16
4	1020	3	32	3	7656 (1.18)	6338 (0.94)	15 (0.47)	8	8745	12662	60.5	4	6491	6743	32
5	1020	5	16	5	5608 (1.04)	4931 (0.80)	15 (0.47)	8	5367	6142	32	8	5367	6142	32
6	1375	5	16	5	5608 (0.87)	4931 (0.69)	15 (0.44)	16	10,833	13,305	64	8	6452	7182	34

5.2.1. Resource Evaluation

Table 3 lists the resource consumption of LUT, REG, and BRAM for different buffer schemes. Note that the results of D-SWIM and SWIM-2pass schemes are compared, and the ratio values of D-SWIM to SWIM-2pass are listed in the parenthesis of the D-SWIM column. In Configuration 1, D-SWIM consumes 44.9% and 34.7% more LUT and REG than that in SWIM. However, the BRAM consumption in D-SWIM is less—this is because N_{LB} is 4 in SWIM as 4 lines compose a BRAM-partition period, but this issue does not exist in D-SWIM. When N_{blk} is set to 16, as per Configuration 2, N_{LB} of SWIM increases to 8, which consumes more logic and BRAMs than D-SWIM. Although the 2-pass optimization halves the N_{LB}, the BRAM cost in SWIM is 16, which is 1.8 times that of 9 in D-SWIM. SWIM costs more BRAMs of specific widths to compose the LB, whereas D-SWIM sets all BRAM ports to the maximum width, which fully utilizes the bandwidth and reduces the resource. Note that the D-SWIM buffer accommodates arbitrary image width, and configurations use different N_{line} values but identical H and N_{blk} (e.g., Configuration 2 and Configuration 3) share the same hardware via dynamic programming. In Configurations 5–6 where H is 5, D-SWIM's consumptions of both logic and BRAM are less than SWIM. D-SWIM saves 13.1% LUT, 31.4% REG, and 55.9% BRAM compared with SWIM-2pass in Configuration 6. With Configuration 6, the N_{LB} of SWIM is 8, which costs more logic on the line-selection multiplexer.

We also investigate the impact of parameters on the resource consumption in the D-SWIM scheme. Comparing the results in Configurations 1–4, we note that N_{blk} greatly affects the logic and BRAM resources. This is because a larger N_{blk} requires more complex multiplexers for pixel-block manipulation. Note that H also affects the hardware (comparing Configuration 3 to Configuration 5) because a larger H costs more LUTs for the line-selecting multiplexer and more REGs on the temporary pixel-storage.

5.2.2. Timing and Power Evaluation

In addition to the hardware resource usage, timing performance and power consumption were also evaluated. The results of the post place-and-route design were obtained from the vendor tools (Xilinx Vivado) and presented in Figure 12, where (a) is the f_{max} with different configurations in Table 3 and (b) is the power consumption. Compared with SWIM, the D-SWIM design slightly decreases the f_{max}. This is because the multi-stage logics for dynamic controlling lengthen the critical path. We selected the proper pipeline stage as described in Section 4.2, while trading the f_{max} and resource overhead in further pipelining. We observed that N_{blk} is a significant factor to the f_{max}. In Configurations 1–6, the worst f_{max} is 329.5 MHz with Configuration 4 in which N_{blk} is 32.

Figure 12b presents the power consumption of buffer modules with SWIM and D-SWIM design methods. Each power bar is composed of two portions that represent static power (lighter part) and dynamic power (darker part). Apparently, SWIM and D-SWIM have identical static power with all configurations, but D-SWIM performs better in the dynamic power aspect. This is mainly due to fewer LBs (N_{LB}) used in the D-SWIM case, which leads to less BRAM usage. For example, with Configuration 5, SWIM consumes 2.1× BRAMs of that in D-SWIM; thus, the dynamic power is increased proportionally. Compared with SWIM, the D-SWIM buffer saves up to 45.7% power consumption in the case of Configuration 6.

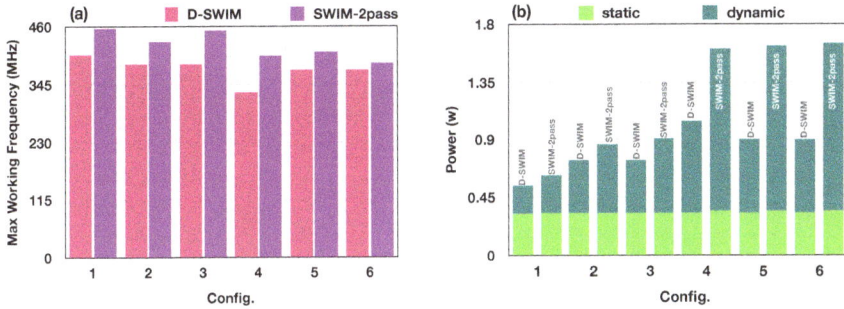

Figure 12. (**a**) shows the f_{max} of D-SWIM and SWIM designs with the configurations in Table 3. (**b**) shows the power consumption of D-SWIM and SWIM, with the breakdown of static and dynamic power.

5.3. Evaluation of Dynamic Programming in D-SWIM

The dynamic programming described in Section 3.4 contributes to the ability of rapid context-switching for arbitrary sized images. We evaluated the D-SWIM system with the workload containing images in different sizes. Table 4 lists the period of computation and dynamic programming for one image. The independent variables are *image size* and N_{blk} (input throughput), which affects the measured periods. The values were measured in clock cycles. However, for direct comparison, they were converted to the numbers in micro-seconds with an operating frequency of 350 MHz. The *proportion* column gives the ratio of the programming period to the entire working period (programming period + computation period). The overhead of dynamic programming in D-SWIM is significantly less than 1% in most cases, and the context-switching can be regarded as seamless.

In contrast, while employing the SWIM buffer for the same workload, a FPGA reconfiguration is required to switch the specific hardware corresponding to the size of the input image. The average period for reconfiguring the entire FPGA device (Xilinx-XC7VX690) is 20 s. For a fair comparison, we listed the time period for the partial reconfiguration technique [14], which reduces the reconfiguration time to the order of milliseconds via programming only a portion of the FPGA. Similarly, we obtained the proportion of FPGA reconfiguration time based on the image-processing period. Assuming the SWIM hardware is reconfigured for each image, the results show that the FPGA performs reconfiguration in over 80% of the entire working period. This means that the FPGA spends the most time on reconfiguration rather than actual image processing, causing a huge reduction in processing throughput.

Table 4. Time period of dynamic programming of D-SWIM and partial reconfiguration of SWIM.

Image Size	N_{blk}	Computation Time		D-SWIM Programming Time			SWIM Reconfiguration Time		
H×W (pixel)	(pixel)	(cycle)	(µs)	(cycle)	(µs)	Proportion	(cycle)	(µs)	Proportion
431 × 392	8	21,227	60.649	8	0.023	0.04%	465,500	1330	95.64%
431 × 392	16	10,614	30.326	16	0.046	0.15%	465,500	1330	97.77%
431 × 392	32	5307	15.163	32	0.091	0.60%	465,500	1330	98.87%
1342 × 638	8	107,360	306.743	4	0.011	0.00%	465,500	1330	81.26%
1342 × 638	16	53,680	153.371	8	0.023	0.01%	465,500	1330	89.66%
1342 × 638	32	26,840	76.686	16	0.046	0.06%	465,500	1330	94.55%

5.4. Case Study of Image Processing with D-SWIM

With the D-SWIM buffer, an architecture for a specific image application can be easily constructed. This section presents D-SWIM-based architectures for two real-world image applications and their performance study.

To evaluate the practicability of D-SWIM in real applications, we compare the D-SWIM designs with similar streaming architectures for image processing [7,10]. In prior studies, Reiche et al. [7] improved the HIPA^{CC} image-processing framework to generate effective High-level Synthesis (HLS) codes for FPGA with a specific memory architecture, and Özkan et al. [10] optimized the OpenCL framework of Intel (Altera) FPGA to a domain-specific language (DSL) for image processing. These works are widely accepted by the community, and were developed based on the latest tools from the industry and academia. Thus, we consider these two as the state-of-the-art works for comparison.

5.4.1. Conv2D

2D convolution (Conv2D) is a popular operation for image feature extraction. Figure 1 shows a typical Conv2D operation with 3×3 convolutional kernels. Pixels in a kernel-sized window were fetched and multiplied to the kernel weights and then accumulated to the Conv2D result. The subsequent operation moves the window 1 pixel to the right, and performs the same arithmetic. In the high-throughput scenario of D-SWIM, multiple overlapped windows are processed in the same clock cycle. Thus, the logic components are connected as Figure 13. In every clock cycle, the buffer output pixel block has a height of H, and width of N_{blk}. The pixels were directly delivered to the parallel operators (OP) which performed the MACC operation. The results of OPs were concatenated to the output block. Note that there are windows, such as Win0 and Win1, in Figure 13, containing pixels from two consecutive output blocks of the buffer. Thus, we set registers to store the last pixel-columns of the previous cycle to construct these windows.

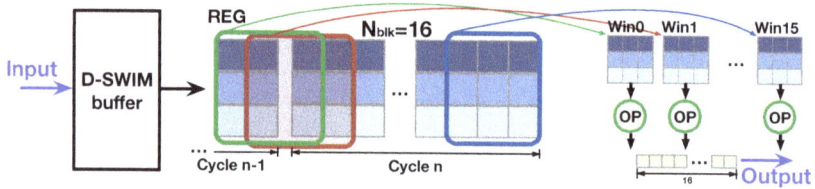

Figure 13. D-SWIM-based architecture for Conv2D (3×3 window).

Following the architecture above, we implemented the Conv2D with $N_{blk} = 16$ and $H = 3$. For a fair comparison, the hardware of OP was simply implemented with naïve RTL with a pre-defined pipeline stage. The implementation results are listed in Table 5. We name the works in [7,10] Design2 and Design1, respectively, in the following content. The devices adopted in each work have been listed as a reference. Note that the size of BRAM in Intel FPGA is 20 Kbits, whereas it is 36 Kbits in Xilinx FPGA. N_{blk} represents the hardware throughput (pixel/cycle). Meanwhile, the f_{max} of each design has been given, and we obtained the system pixel throughput (giga pixel per second (GPPS)) by $N_{blk} \times f_{max}$.

Because D-SWIM and Design1–2 have different throughputs, it was unfair to compare the resource number in Table 5 directly. Thus, we obtained the hardware efficiency of FPGA logic (LUT and REG) with Equation (5). Comparing with the highest-throughput design (Design1), the hardware efficiency of D-SWIM is 4.8× and 8.2× in LUT and REG, respectively. Comparing with the smallest design (Design2), D-SWIM also achieves competitive hardware efficiency. Note that Design2 achieves higher hardware efficiency on LUT, as it has traded off throughput severely for simpler logic. Moreover, it does not consider the issues in the multi-pixel input scenario (such as BRAM-misalignment), which allows further reduction in overall hardware usage.

$$Efficiency = Throughput/Hardware\ Consumption \times 10^5 \qquad (5)$$

Table 5. Hardware resource consumption and throughput in a Conv2D implementation.

Work	Device	N_{blk} (pixel)	Precision (bit/pixel)	Hardware Consumption LUT	REG	BRAM	DSP	f_{max} (MHz)	Throughput (GPPS)	Efficiency LUT	REG
Design1 [10]	Intel-5SGXEA7	32	8	47,045	73,584	363	0	303.6	9.71	20.7	1.3
Design2 [7]	Xilinx-XC7Z045	1	8	288	521	2	0	349.9	0.35	121.5	6.7
D-SWIM	Xilinx-XC7VX690	16	8	4514	4232	9	76	283	4.5	100.3	10.7

5.4.2. Harris Corner (HC) Detector

The Harris Corner (HC) detector [15] is commonly used in computer vision applications that detects the corner position for feature matching. The HC operator swaps the window (e.g., 3×3 pixels in the benchmark) on the image and determines if the window contains a corner pattern. The HC algorithm on each window is listed in Equation (6). Firstly, HC obtains the gradient matrix **M**, where $I(i,j)$ is the intensity value of the pixel inside the window; $\frac{\partial I(i,j)}{\partial x}$ and $\frac{\partial I(i,j)}{\partial y}$ are the intensity derivative in the horizontal and vertical axes, respectively. Secondly, R was calculated to estimate the eigenvalue of **M**, where k is a constant of 0.04–0.06, and det and trace calculates the determinant and trace of the matrix, respectively. If the value of R is larger than the threshold, the current window contains the corner pattern.

$$\mathbf{M} = \begin{bmatrix} \sum_{i,j}^{W}(\frac{\partial I(i,j)}{\partial x})^2 & \sum_{i,j}^{W}(\frac{\partial I(i,j)}{\partial x})(\frac{\partial I(i,j)}{\partial y}) \\ \sum_{i,j}^{W}(\frac{\partial I(i,j)}{\partial x})(\frac{\partial I(i,j)}{\partial y}) & \sum_{i,j}^{W}(\frac{\partial I(i,j)}{\partial y})^2 \end{bmatrix}$$
$$R = \det(\mathbf{M}) - k \times \text{trace}(\mathbf{M})^2 \qquad (6)$$

Figure 14 demonstrates the D-SWIM-based architecture for HC. This streaming architecture is composed of a buffer (rectangular shape), operator (circular shape), and interconnections. Note that the derivative calculation in different axes can be realized by a Conv2D operation with the Sobel kernels. We used a 3×3 Sobel kernel in the example, and the operators are denoted as dx and dy for the two axes. The derivative results ($\frac{\partial I(i,j)}{\partial x}$, $\frac{\partial I(i,j)}{\partial y}$) were stored in Buf2 and Buf3 because they were accessed with a 2D window pattern in the subsequent operations. The sx, sy, and sxy operators perform the element-wise multiplication and accumulate the values in the window. After **M** is obtained, operator rc calculates the R in Equation (6) and compares it with the threshold to determine whether the window contains a corner or not.

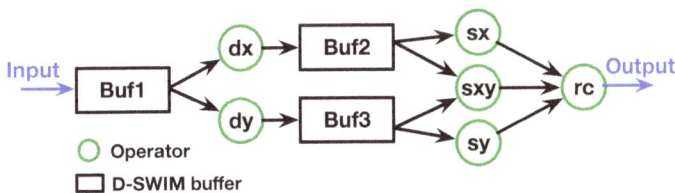

Figure 14. D-SWIM-based architecture for HC detector (3×3 window).

The evaluation method of HC is the same as the Conv2D case. Table 6 shows the implementation results of D-SWIM and Design1–2. In the HC case, the D-SWIM-based design achieves both the highest throughput and the best hardware efficiency. Comparing with the superior design (Design1), D-SWIM increases the throughput to 3.5×. Furthermore, with D-SWIM, the efficiency of LUT and REG is 25× and 30× that in prior studies.

Table 6. Hardware resource consumption and throughput in HC detector implementation.

Work	Device	N_{blk} (pixel)	Precision (bit/pixel)	Hardware Consumption				f_{max} (MHz)	Throughput (GPPS)	Efficiency	
				LUT	REG	BRAM	DSP			LUT	REG
Design1 [10]	Intel-5SGXEA7	4	8	135,808	192,397	493	36	303.4	1.2	0.9	0.1
Design2 [7]	Xilinx-XC7Z045	1	8	23,331	31,102	8	254	239.4	0.24	1.0	0.1
D-SWIM	Xilinx-XC7VX690	16	8	16769	14439	27	444	267	4.2	25.5	3.0

6. Conclusions

This work has presented D-SWIM, a dynamic programmable line buffer microarchitecture for arbitrary sized streaming image processing on FPGAs. The D-SWIM architecture facilitates high-throughput realignment of multi-pixel blocks into line buffers suitable for further streaming image processing. In addition, through a rapid instruction code update, D-SWIM allows for the size of line buffers to adjust dynamically to accommodate varying size requirements of the application during run time. Compared to prior studies where SWIM can only work on a predetermined image size, D-SWIM achieves dynamic programmability for varying image sizes with a slight logic resource overhead. In our experiment, the D-SWIM buffer reached a maximum operating frequency of 329.5 MHz and saved BRAM resources up to 56% that contributed to a power consumption reduction of 45.7%. When compared to other state-of-the-art FPGA-based streaming architectures using two real-world image applications as benchmarks, D-SWIM contributes to a significant hardware efficiency improvement of $25\times$ in LUT and $30\times$ in REG. For the benchmark cases, the D-SWIM based design reaches a pixel throughput of 4.2 GPPS when 16 pixels are input every cycle.

As more applications domain begin to take advantage of vision-based intelligence, the number of systems that demand high-performance image processing is going to increase. D-SWIM represents our first step in systematically generating flexible high-throughput low-latency streaming image processing hardware. In the future, we expect to further the capability of D-SWIM to facilitate generation of the complete intelligent image processing system automatically for FPGAs.

Author Contributions: Conceptualization, R.S. and H.K.-H.S.; Investigation and implementation, R.S. and J.S.J.W.; Validation, J.S.J.W.; Writing-original draft, R.S. and J.S.J.W.; Writing-review and editing J.S.J.W.; Funding acquisition, H.K.-H.S.

Funding: This research was funded in part by the Croucher Foundation (Croucher Innovation Award 2013) and the Research Grants Council of Hong Kong grant number CRF C7047-16G, GRF 17245716.

Conflicts of Interest: The authors declare no conflict of interest.

Abbreviations

The following abbreviations are used in this manuscript:

BRAM	Block Random Access Memory
CLS	Circular Left Shift
CRS	Circular Right Shift
DFG	Data Flow Graph
DNN	Deep Neural Networks
DRAM	Dynamic Random Access Memory
DSL	Domain Specific Languages
DSP	Digital Signal Processing
FIFO	First-In, First-Out
FPGA	Field Programmable Gate Array
GPPS	Giga Pixels Per Second
GOPS	Giga Operations Per Second
LB	Line Buffer
LUT	Look-up Table
REG	Register

ROI	Region of Interest
RTL	Register Transfer Level
SDP	Simple Dual Port
SWIM	Stream-Windowing Interleaved Memory
TDP	True Dual Port

References

1. Guo, C.; Meguro, J.; Kojima, Y.; Naito, T. A multimodal ADAS system for unmarked urban scenarios based on road context understanding. *IEEE Trans. Intell. Transp. Syst.* **2015**, *16*, 1690–1704. [CrossRef]

2. Rosenfeld, A. *Multiresolution Image Processing and Analysis*; Springer Science & Business Media: Berlin, Germany, 2013; Volume 12.

3. Wang, M.; Ng, H.C.; Chung, B.M.; Varma, B.S.C.; Jaiswal, M.K.; Tsia, K.K.; Shum, H.C.; So, H.K.H. Real-time object detection and classification for high-speed asymmetric-detection time-stretch optical microscopy on FPGA. In Proceedings of the 2016 International Conference on Field-Programmable Technology (FPT), Xi'an, China, 7–9 December 2016; pp. 261–264.

4. Ma, Y.; Cao, Y.; Vrudhula, S.; Seo, J.S. An automatic RTL compiler for high-throughput FPGA implementation of diverse deep convolutional neural networks. In Proceedings of the 2017 27th International Conference on Field Programmable Logic and Applications (FPL), Ghent, Belgium, 4–8 September 2017; pp. 1–8.

5. Pu, J.; Bell, S.; Yang, X.; Setter, J.; Richardson, S.; Ragan-Kelley, J.; Horowitz, M. Programming heterogeneous systems from an image processing DSL. *ACM Trans. Archit. Code Optim. (TACO)* **2017**, *14*, 26. [CrossRef]

6. Chugh, N.; Vasista, V.; Purini, S.; Bondhugula, U. A DSL compiler for accelerating image processing pipelines on FPGAs. In Proceedings of the 2016 International Conference on Parallel Architecture and Compilation Techniques (PACT), Haifa, Israel, 11–15 September 2016; pp. 327–338.

7. Reiche, O.; Schmid, M.; Hannig, F.; Membarth, R.; Teich, J. Code generation from a domain-specific language for C-based HLS of hardware accelerators. In Proceedings of the 2014 International Conference on Hardware/Software Codesign and System Synthesis, New Delhi, India, 12–17 October 2014; ACM: New York, NY, USA, 2014; p. 17.

8. Serot, J.; Berry, F.; Ahmed, S. Implementing stream-processing applications on fpgas: A dsl-based approach. In Proceedings of the 2011 International Conference on Field Programmable Logic and Applications (FPL), Chania, Greece, 5–7 September 2011; pp. 130–137.

9. Wong, J.S.; Shi, R.; Wang, M.; So, H.K.H. Ultra-low latency continuous block-parallel stream windowing using FPGA on-chip memory. In Proceedings of the 2017 International Conference on Field Programmable Technology (ICFPT), Melbourne, VIC, Australia, 11–13 December 2017; pp. 56–63.

10. Özkan, M.A.; Reiche, O.; Hannig, F.; Teich, J. FPGA-based accelerator design from a domain-specific language. In Proceedings of the 2016 26th International Conference on Field Programmable Logic and Applications (FPL), Lausanne, Switzerland, 29 August–2 September 2016; pp. 1–9.

11. Salehian, S.; Yan, Y. Evaluation of Knight Landing High Bandwidth Memory for HPC Workloads. In Proceedings of the Seventh Workshop on Irregular Applications: Architectures and Algorithms, Denver, CO, USA, 12–17 November 2017; ACM: New York, NY, USA, 2017; p. 10.

12. Mono Camera Sensor Performance Review 2018-Q1. Available online: https://www.ptgrey.com/support/downloads/10722 (accessed on 6 March 2019).

13. Xilinx. UG473-7 Series FPGAs Memory Resources. Available online: https://www.xilinx.com/support/documentation/user_guides/ug473_7Series_Memory_Resources.pdf (accessed on 6 March 2019).

14. Pezzarossa, L.; Kristensen, A.T.; Schoeberl, M.; Sparsø, J. Using dynamic partial reconfiguration of FPGAs in real-Time systems. *Microprocess. Microsyst.* **2018**, *61*, 198–206. [CrossRef]

15. Harris, C.; Stephens, M. A combined corner and edge detector. In Proceedings of the Alvey Vision Conference, Manchester, UK, 31 August–2 September 1988; Volume 15, pp. 10–5244.

Journal of
Imaging

MDPI

Article

Border Handling for 2D Transpose Filter Structures on an FPGA

Donald G. Bailey * and **Anoop S. Ambikumar**

School of Engineering and Advanced Technology, Massey University, Palmerston North 4442, New Zealand;
A.Ambikumar@massey.ac.nz
* Correspondence: D.G.Bailey@massey.ac.nz

Received: 31 October 2018; Accepted: 21 November 2018; Published: 26 November 2018

Abstract: It is sometimes desirable to implement filters using a transpose-form filter structure. However, managing image borders is generally considered more complex than it is with the more commonly used direct-form structure. This paper explores border handling for transpose-form filters, and proposes two novel mechanisms: transformation coalescing, and combination chain modification. For linear filters, coefficient coalescing can effectively exploit the digital signal processing blocks, resulting in the smallest resources requirements. Combination chain modification requires similar resources to direct-form border handling. It is demonstrated that the combination chain multiplexing can be split into two stages, consisting of a combination network followed by the transpose-form combination chain. The resulting transpose-form border handling networks are of similar complexity to the direct-form networks, enabling the transpose-form filter structure to be used where required. The transpose form is also significantly faster, being automatically pipelined by the filter structure. Of the border extension methods, zero-extension requires the least resources.

Keywords: stream processing; image borders; window filters; pipeline

1. Introduction

Image filtering is a common preprocessing operation in many image analysis applications. A local filter calculates the output for each pixel in an image as some function of the pixels within a local window in the input image. However, to produce an output for pixels on (or near) the image border, the input window extends past the edge of the input image. If such window pixels are not managed appropriately, the output pixels around the borders are invalid, and the effective image size shrinks. After a sequence of filters (especially if some of the filters are large), the effective image size can be substantially reduced, which is undesirable. Therefore, it is necessary to extend the input image through some form of extrapolation to provide suitable pixel values for the window pixels which extend past the borders of the input.

When processed using a field programmable gate array (FPGA), pipelined stream processing is the most common processing mode for implementing image filters [1]. Commonly, one pixel is processed per clock cycle (although this can be relatively easily generalized to two or more pixels per clock cycle [1]). To avoid memory bandwidth issues associated with reading all the input pixels for each window position, row buffers are typically used to cache pixels from previous image rows. Feeding the pixel stream through the window is equivalent to scanning the window through the image. Two commonly used window filter structures (ignoring image borders) are shown in Figure 1. The parallel structure shifts the window pixels in parallel with the row buffers, whereas the series structure uses the window pixels to extend the row buffers. When considering border handling, the parallel structure has the advantage that it decouples the vertical scanning (handled by the row buffers) from the horizontal scanning. These filter structures are direct form, where the window is formed directly, followed by the filter function.

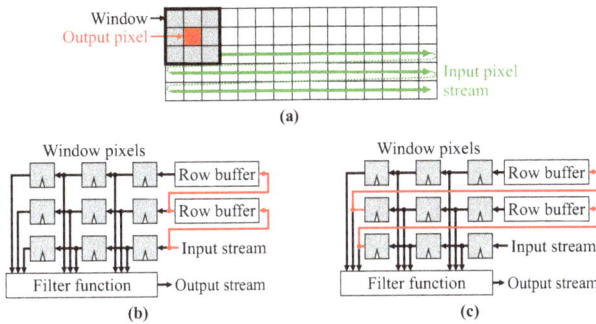

Figure 1. Window filters (without border handling). (**a**): window scanning; (**b**): parallel window structure; (**c**): series window structure; with the series and parallel connections highlighted in red.

The contribution of this paper is a systematic methodology for constructing border handling networks for 2D transpose-form filters. The remainder of this section reviews the transpose-form filter architecture, and commonly used border handling methods. Section 2 summarizes previously reported work on FPGA architectures for handling image borders. Two novel transpose-form border handling architectures are developed for 1D filters in Section 3, which are then extended to 2D filters in Section 4. Implementation of the architectures are discussed in Section 5 and compared experimentally in Section 6.

1.1. Transpose-Form Filter Structures

Although the filter function could be any function of the pixel values within the window, many useful filter functions can be represented as a transformation of each individual window pixel value, followed by a combination function which combines the transformed window pixels to produce a single output pixel value, as represented in Figure 2. Any filter which has an associative combination function can be restructured from direct form into a transpose form by [2]:

1. interchanging input and output nodes,
2. reversing all the paths through the filter,
3. replacing branch nodes (pick-off points) with combination functions, and
4. replacing combination functions with branch nodes.

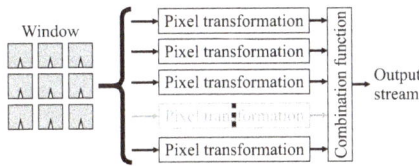

Figure 2. Filter function that can be arranged into transpose form.

Arguably, the most common filter function is the 2D finite impulse response (FIR) filter, where the output value is a weighted sum of the window pixels:

$$Q_{FIR}[x,y] = \sum_{i=-\frac{W-1}{2}}^{\frac{W-1}{2}} \sum_{j=-\frac{W-1}{2}}^{\frac{W-1}{2}} h_{i,j} I[x-i, y-j] \tag{1}$$

where $I[x,y]$ and $Q[x,y]$ are the input and output images respectively, with a $W \times W$ convolution kernel, $h_{i,j}$. The pixel transformation is multiplication of each window pixel by the corresponding filter coefficient, $h_{i,j}$, and the combination function is addition. Figure 3 shows the direct form 3×3 FIR filter restructured into its transpose form. Please note that reversing the computation order flips the filter coefficients relative to the direct form.

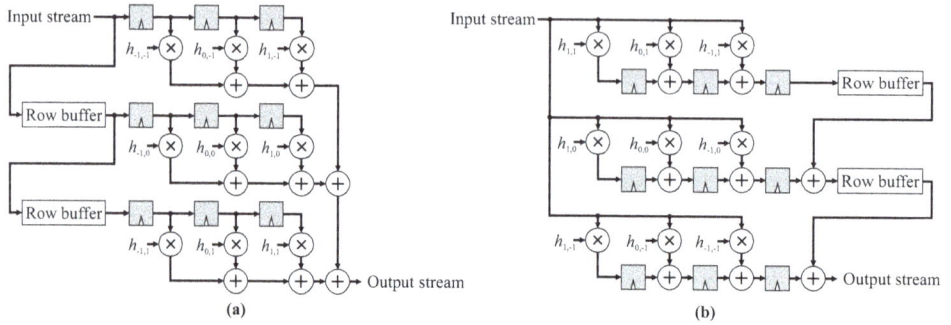

Figure 3. 3×3 FIR filter structure. (**a**): direct form; (**b**): transpose form.

Morphological erosion and dilation filters can also be arranged into transpose form. For example, greyscale dilation by a non-flat structuring element [3], $S[i,j]$, can be represented as:

$$Q_{dilation}[x,y] = \max_{i,j \in S} \{I[x-i, y-j] + S[i,j]\}. \tag{2}$$

The pixel transformation is an offset of each window pixel value by the corresponding value of the structuring element, and the combination function is maximum. Similarly, for greyscale erosion [3]:

$$Q_{erosion}[x,y] = \min_{i,j \in S} \{I[x-i, y-j] - S[-i,-j]\}. \tag{3}$$

The transpose form has the advantage that the combination function is automatically pipelined, by distributing the combination function over the window, as is clearly seen in Figure 3 for an FIR filter. Rather than calculating the output as the weighted sum of window pixels, the input pixels are weighted immediately, and are accumulated into the window position of the corresponding output pixel. Where there are common filter coefficients, for example with symmetric filters, the associated multiplications are in parallel, enabling the set of common multiplications to be replaced by a single multiplier [4]. In the direct form, this is equivalent to using the distributive property to factor out the common multiplications. When realized on an FPGA, the transpose form enables the multiplication, addition and register to be combined within a single digital signal processing (DSP) block, reducing the logic required for the implementation [5].

Similarly, with morphological filters (see Figure 4), the structuring element offsets (pixel transformations) are in parallel so any common offsets only need to be calculated once in transpose form. Again, the combination function is also pipelined automatically by the filter structure.

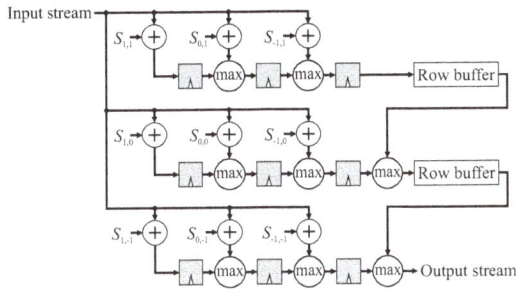

Figure 4. 3 × 3 greyscale dilation in transpose form.

When multiple filters are required in parallel (examples: Sobel filter, difference of Gaussians filter, sub-band filters, wavelet analysis), resources can be reduced by sharing the window structure (see left panel of Figure 5). However, when combining multiple filtered images together (examples: image fusion, high dynamic range imaging, wavelet synthesis), each filter must have its own window structure unless the transpose form is used (right panel of Figure 5). Of key importance is the ability to share the relatively expensive row buffers between all the parallel filters.

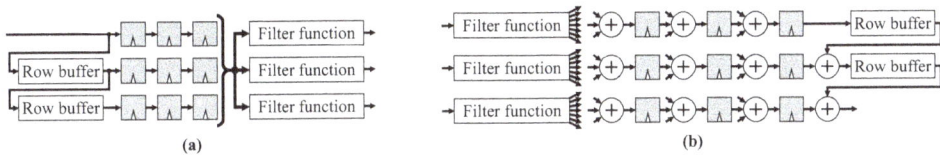

Figure 5. Shared windows for parallel filters (shown here for FIR filters). (**a**): direct form for distribution to multiple filters; (**b**): transpose form for collection from multiple filters.

One example where both direct form and transpose-form structures are used is in the parallel decomposition of morphological filters [6]. The flat structuring element is decomposed into parallel rectangular windows, which are each separable into row and column filters. Direct form is used to share resources (including row buffers) for the column filters, and transpose form is used to combine the results of the row filters, while sharing resources.

1.2. Border Handling

So far in this discussion, border handling issues have not been considered. The problem with simply processing the image is that pixels around the image border become corrupted because part of the window lies outside the image. In some machine vision applications, it may be possible to capture a larger image than required from the camera to allow for the reduction in image size as a result of subsequent filtering. Alternatively, it is important to ensure that the objects being imaged are kept sufficiently far from the image borders that important features of the objects are not corrupted by the processing. In such cases, no special processing is required around the image borders.

However, when filtering a video for enhancement, it is usually desirable for the output video to be the same size and format as the input. Some computer vision applications become less reliable when image borders are not processed appropriately. For example, Tan and Triggs [7] found that face detection (using difference of Gaussian filters) at the edges of the image was more reliable when the image was extended. Similarly, Jiang et al. [8] obtained improved saliency detection when the image was extended by reflecting edge super-pixels in the image border. For motion compensation with video coding, it is necessary to restrict the search for matching patches at the edges of the image. Sullivan and Baker [9] made the observation that appropriate image extrapolation gave major improvement in coding performance.

Please note that any form of extrapolation of the image beyond the borders is estimating data that is not actually available. Consequently, if care is not taken, artefacts can be introduced into the image depending on image contents and filter being applied. Generally, better results are obtained by extrapolating the image before filtering rather than replacing the lost pixels by extrapolation after filtering [10].

In software, image borders are commonly managed by additional code to provide appropriate processing of border pixels. However, in hardware this can result in considerable extra logic solely for processing border pixels [10]. There are several different commonly used border handling methods, with the particular method selected based on the type of filter, and the expected image contents. These are enumerated here, with key methods illustrated in Figure 6.

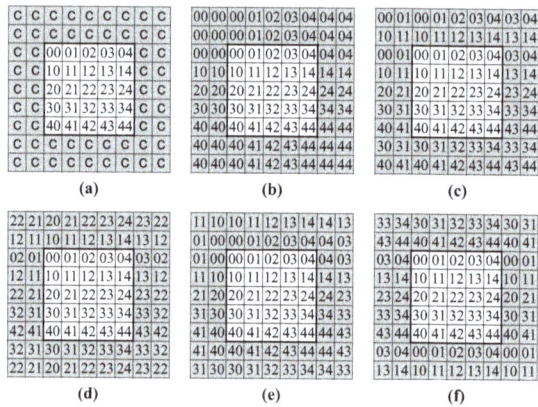

```
(a)                          (b)                          (c)
c  c  c  c  c  c  c  c  c     00 00 00 01 02 03 04 04 04    00 01 00 01 02 03 04 03 04
c  c  c  c  c  c  c  c  c     00 00 00 01 02 03 04 04 04    10 11 10 11 12 13 14 13 14
c  c 00 01 02 03 04 c  c      00 00 00 01 02 03 04 04 04    00 01 00 01 02 03 04 03 04
c  c 10 11 12 13 14 c  c      10 10 10 11 12 13 14 14 14    10 11 10 11 12 13 14 13 14
c  c 20 21 22 23 24 c  c      20 20 20 21 22 23 24 24 24    20 21 20 21 22 23 24 23 24
c  c 30 31 32 33 34 c  c      30 30 30 31 32 33 34 34 34    30 31 30 31 32 33 34 33 34
c  c 40 41 42 43 44 c  c      40 40 40 41 42 43 44 44 44    40 41 40 41 42 43 44 43 44
c  c  c  c  c  c  c  c  c     40 40 40 41 42 43 44 44 44    30 31 30 31 32 33 34 33 34
c  c  c  c  c  c  c  c  c     40 40 40 41 42 43 44 44 44    40 41 40 41 42 43 44 43 44
```

```
(d)                          (e)                          (f)
22 21 20 21 22 23 24 23 22    11 10 10 11 12 13 14 14 13    33 34 30 31 32 33 34 30 31
12 11 10 11 12 13 14 13 12    01 00 00 01 02 03 04 04 03    43 44 40 41 42 43 44 40 41
02 01 00 01 02 03 04 03 02    01 00 00 01 02 03 04 04 03    03 04 00 01 02 03 04 00 01
12 11 10 11 12 13 14 13 12    11 10 10 11 12 13 14 14 13    13 14 10 11 12 13 14 10 11
22 21 20 21 22 23 24 23 22    21 20 20 21 22 23 24 24 23    23 24 20 21 22 23 24 20 21
32 31 30 31 32 33 34 33 32    31 30 30 31 32 33 34 34 33    33 34 30 31 32 33 34 30 31
42 41 40 41 42 43 44 43 42    41 40 40 41 42 43 44 44 43    43 44 40 41 42 43 44 40 41
32 31 30 31 32 33 34 33 32    41 40 40 41 42 43 44 44 43    03 04 00 01 02 03 04 00 01
22 21 20 21 22 23 24 23 22    31 30 30 31 32 33 34 34 33    13 14 10 11 12 13 14 10 11
```

Figure 6. Image border extrapolation schemes (shaded pixels are extrapolated). (**a**): constant extension; (**b**): duplication; (**c**): two-phase duplication. (**d**): mirroring; (**e**): mirroring with duplication; (**f**): periodic extension.

1. Do nothing [5,10,11]: This does not handle borders, and the effective size of the output image shrinks.
2. Constant extension [5,10–12]: Pixels outside the image are assumed to be constant. Common constants are 0 (particularly with morphological processing) or the average value within the image.
3. Duplication or clamping [5,10–12]: The nearest valid pixel within the image is used (zero order extrapolation).
4. Two-phase duplication: Like duplication, but alternating the two outermost rows of the image. This is required, for example, when processing raw color images with a Bayer pattern or similar phased structure [13].
5. Mirroring [5,10,12,14]: Pixels are mirrored about the outside row and column of pixels.
6. Mirroring with duplication [5,10–12]: Pixels are mirrored about the image border such that the outside row and column are duplicated.
7. Periodic extension (tiling) [10,11]: Extends the image by periodically tiling the image horizontally and vertically. This scheme is impractical for stream processing [10] because the whole image must be buffered to obtain the bottom row before processing the top row of the image. Opposite borders of an image usually have little correlation, resulting in artefacts around the borders of the output image.
8. Modify the filter function [5,10–12]: An alternative to extending the input image is to explicitly modify the filter function to handle each scenario. When done naively, this can result in a large

amount of additional logic, making it less practical. It is generally more efficient to implicitly modify the filter function by modifying the formation of the window (using one of the other methods) and leaving the filter function unchanged [10].

With direct-form filters, window formation and the filter function are independent; managing borders simply involves selecting the required pixels to form the window that provides the pixel values to the filter function. The transpose form, however, is made more complicated because the window formation and filter function are more tightly integrated. The selection of pixels to form the windows generally requires multiplexing (depending on the position of the window relative to the border), and transforming structures containing multiplexers into transpose form is not trivial.

2. Prior Border Handling Architectures

The earliest work considering border handling architectures (other than zero-extension) was that of Chakrabarti [15], which proposed a routing network for mirroring (with duplication) the borders of 1D filters in the context of performing a discrete wavelet transform. The routing network was placed between the filter delay chain, and the filter function as shown in Figure 7. Although the original paper only considered a 4-pixel window and mirroring with duplication, it is easily generalized to wider windows and other border handling schemes.

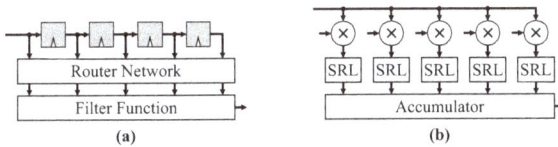

Figure 7. 1D border management techniques. (**a**): Chakrabarti [15]; (**b**): Benkrid et al. [14,16].

Benkrid et al. [16] used the FPGA logic elements as programmable shift register logic (SRL) to give variable delays for 1D FIR filters (see Figure 7). The accumulator was either an adder tree (direct form filter) or a pipelined adder chain (transpose form). Implementation details within [16] are sketchy; however more details are provided in a later paper [14]. The basic principle is that the shift register lengths are dynamically selected to route the required pixels to the accumulator to appropriately handle border conditions. Scheduling considerations increase the filter latency to the width of the window, a small but usually insignificant increase. However, this approach is only suitable for 1D filters, and cannot easily be generalized to 2D filter structures.

Bailey [10] considered direct-form 2D filters, using a parallel window structure to make the row and column processing independent. Two schemes were presented for row processing which exploited stream processing (where each pixel is only loaded once). Cached priming managed borders by routing pixels from where they were within the delay chain to where they were needed. The disadvantage of this method is that additional clock cycles are required between rows to flush the data from one row and load sufficient data to begin processing for the next row. The second method, overlapped priming and flushing, loaded the initial pixels from the next row into parallel registers while processing for the previous row was completed. At the end of the row, these were then transferred to appropriate locations within the window for the next row, avoiding the flushing and priming delays. These two methods are illustrated in Figure 8. For column processing, the row buffers were connected as a single chain, with multiplexing used to select the appropriate input for each window row. Column processing is therefore effectively the same as the routing network of [15].

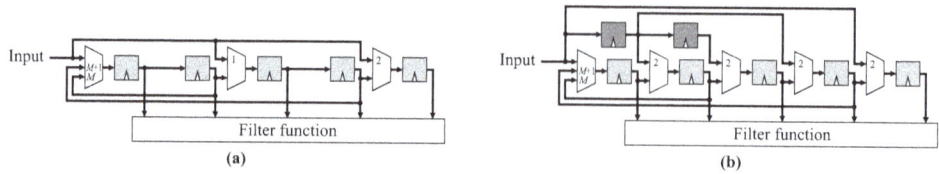

Figure 8. Row processing by Bailey [10] for mirroring without duplication. (**a**): cached priming; (**b**): overlapped priming and flushing.

Rafi and Din [11] also considered direct-form 2D filters, and replaced the parallel priming registers of [10] with multiplexers, effectively implementing the routing network of [15]. While this reduces the number of registers, the routing multiplexers are on the output of the window registers, potentially adding them to the critical path and reducing the clock frequency. Although this issue may be overcome by adding pipeline registers, this would negate the savings made.

Al-Dujaili and Fahmy's [5] focus was on optimizing speed by using DSP blocks for FIR filters. Although both direct and transpose filter forms were considered, for border management only the direct-form methods of [10] were implemented because of the complexities of border management with transpose filters.

3. Design for Transpose Filters

It is observed in Figure 6 that the border handling patterns are separable in the sense that extensions for the horizontal and vertical borders can be applied independently. This separability is independent of whether the underlying filter function is separable or not and enables the design of a 1-dimensional border handling mechanism and applying it to both the rows and columns within the window. This is made easier with the parallel window structure, where the row and column processing are separated. Referring to Figures 3 and 4, each row filter can be considered a pixel transformation for the vertical combination function performed via the row buffers. This section will therefore focus on structures for 1D transpose filtering, with the extension to 2D presented in Section 4.

For high speed processing, it is desirable to not introduce any additional clocking overheads between rows (and between frames). Therefore, when streaming one pixel per clock cycle, the last pixel in a row is immediately followed by the first pixel in the next row, and the last pixel in a frame is followed by the first pixel of the next frame. A complete $M \times N$ image is processed every $M \times N$ clock cycles, with the latency determined by the filter itself.

Consider the 1D linear FIR filter of width W with filter coefficients h_i given by

$$Q_{FIR}[x] = \sum_{i=-\frac{W-1}{2}}^{\frac{W-1}{2}} h_i I[x-i], \qquad 0 \le x < M \tag{4}$$

where I and Q are the input and output images, respectively. Input pixels outside the range $0 \le x < M$ are managed by the chosen border handling scheme. Figure 9 shows successive 5-pixel-wide row windows during the transition from one row to the next. Samples shaded grey represent invalid window pixels that must be replaced in the calculation through image border extension. The replacement is shown in bold, illustrating mirroring without duplication in Figure 9. These are linked to the corresponding source pixels with an arrow. The direction of the arrow is to the source pixel, because in the transpose form, the timing is governed by when a pixel is input. Additional processing is required therefore when the circled pixels are input.

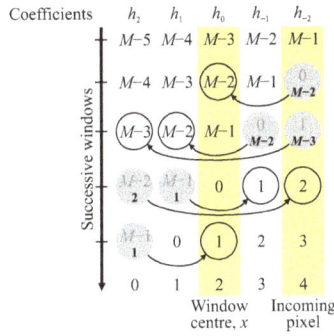

Figure 9. Border management for mirroring without duplication.

Two approaches to applying this additional processing are proposed. The first is to modify the filter function by coalescing the pixel transformations. The second applies the modification to the pipelined combination chain.

3.1. Transformation Coalescing

With border handling, some of the input pixel values appear at more than one position within the window and are therefore subjected to more than one-pixel transformation. For example, in an FIR filter, the input pixel is multiplied by more than one filter coefficient. Consider the window at $x = 0$ in Figure 9:

$$\begin{aligned} Q_{FIR}[0] &= h_{-2}I[2] + h_{-1}I[1] + h_0I[0] + h_1I[1] + h_2I[2] \\ &= h_0I[0] + (h_{-1} + h_1)I[1] + (h_{-2} + h_2)I[2] \\ &= h_0I[0] + h'_{-1}I[1] + h'_{-2}I[2]. \end{aligned} \tag{5}$$

The samples can be factored out, giving modified filter weights as combinations of the original filter weights, i.e.,

$$\begin{aligned} h'_{-1}[1] &= h_{-1} + h_1 \\ h'_{-2}[2] &= h_{-2} + h_2 \end{aligned} \tag{6}$$

These are labelled with positions 1 and 2 respectively, because these modified weights need to be applied to those corresponding input samples.

This pairing is applied for each arrow within Figure 9, with the label being given by the head of the arrow. The corresponding set of coalesced coefficients then become:

$$\begin{aligned} h'_2 \quad [M-3] &= h_2 + h_{-2} \\ h'_1 \quad [M-2] &= h_1 + h_{-1} \\ h'_0 \quad [M-2] &= h_0 + h_{-2} \\ h'_0 \quad [1] &= h_0 + h_2 \\ h'_{-1} \quad [1] &= h_{-1} + h_1 \\ h'_{-2} \quad [2] &= h_{-2} + h_2 \end{aligned} \tag{7}$$

It is also necessary to set the coefficients for the invalid samples (shaded grey in Figure 9) to 0 to prevent the invalid samples from being accumulated:

$$
\begin{aligned}
h'_2 \ [M-2] &= 0 \\
h'_2 \ [M-1] &= 0 \\
h'_1 \ [M-1] &= 0 \\
h'_{-1} \ [0] &= 0 \\
h'_{-2} \ [0] &= 0 \\
h'_{-2} \ [1] &= 0
\end{aligned}
\tag{8}
$$

The resulting coalesced coefficients can be formed using a multiplexer indexed by the sample number as demonstrated in Figure 10. Obviously, this can be simplified if the coefficients are constants because the sum of constants is also a constant.

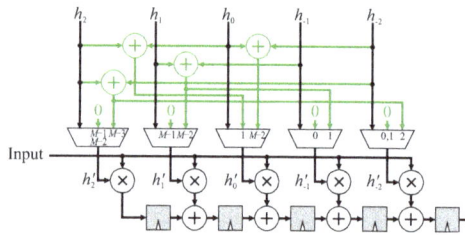

Figure 10. Coefficient coalescing for mirroring without duplication.

Please note that coefficient coalescing is only applicable to FIR filters. This technique may or may not be able to be adapted to other filter types depending on the filter function. For example, with a greyscale dilation filter, with structuring element offsets S_i

$$
Q_{dilation}[x] = \max_{i \in S} \{ I[x-i] + S_i \}, \qquad 0 \le x < M
\tag{9}
$$

From Figure 9, the window position at $x = 0$ gives:

$$
\begin{aligned}
Q_{dilation}[0] &= \max \{ I[2] + S_{-2},\ I[1] + S_{-1},\ I[0] + S_0,\ I[1] + S_1,\ I[2] + S_2 \} \\
&= \max \{ I[2] + \max(S_{-2}, S_2),\ I[1] + \max(S_{-1}, S_1),\ I[0] + S_0 \}
\end{aligned}
\tag{10}
$$

with the corresponding set of coalesced offsets, S', as:

$$
\begin{array}{llll}
S'_2 \ [M-3] &= \max(S_2, S_{-2}), & S'_{-2} \ [1] &= -\infty \\
S'_1 \ [M-2] &= \max(S_1, S_{-1}), & S'_{-1} \ [0] &= -\infty \\
S'_0 \ [M-2] &= \max(S_0, S_{-2}), & S'_{-2} \ [0] &= -\infty \\
S'_0 \ [1] &= \max(S_0, S_2), & S'_2 \ [M-1] &= -\infty \\
S'_{-1} \ [1] &= \max(S_{-1}, S_1), & S'_1 \ [M-1] &= -\infty \\
S'_{-2} \ [2] &= \max(S_{-2}, S_2), & S'_2 \ [M-2] &= -\infty
\end{array}
\tag{11}
$$

where the offsets of $-\infty$ correspond to the entries removed from the window (shaded grey in Figure 9). The resulting architecture, in Figure 11, has obvious parallels with coefficient coalescing for FIR filters in Figure 10.

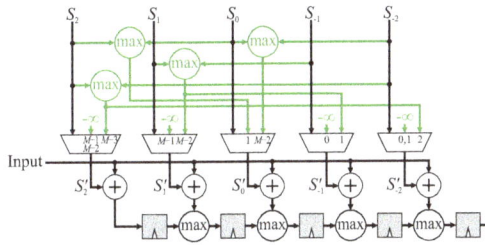

Figure 11. Transform coalescing for greyscale dilation using mirroring without duplication.

3.2. Combination Chain Modification

This next technique is applicable to all filters which are transposable. The pixel transformation is left unchanged, and the border handling is applied to the pipelined combination chain. This method works by combining the terms resulting from pixels outside the image into the appropriate place within the combination chain based on the source of the duplicated or mirrored pixel.

A 5×5 FIR filter using mirroring without duplication will be used to illustrate the method. Again, the parallel filter structure is used for separability, and the construction in Figure 9 is used to develop the modifications. Each arrow indicates where a transformed pixel needs to be combined into a different place within the output chain. Consider the window centered at $M - 2$. The window extension is $I[M - 2]$ (shown in grey) which is multiplied by h_{-2}. To arrive at the output at the correct time, the product $h_{-2}I[M - 2]$ must be added with the regular contribution from pixel $M - 2$ (shown by the circle), which is the center of the window. Since this combination is added only during clock cycle $M - 2$, a multiplexer is required. All 6 window extensions are shown in green in Figure 12.

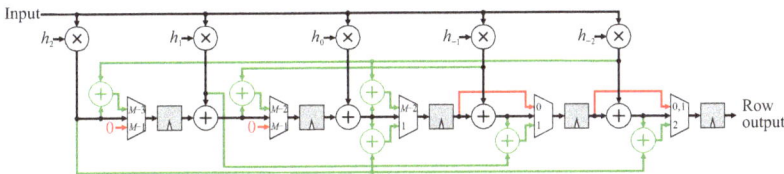

Figure 12. Row combination chain for mirroring without duplication.

It is also necessary to prevent the invalid pixels (grey circles in Figure 9) from being accumulated. On the right-hand part of the window, this may be achieved by bypassing the adder on those clock cycles. On the left-hand part of the window, it is easier to just clear the registers on the last pixel of a row. This may be accomplished either through multiplexing, or directly using a synchronous clear of the associated flip-flops. These modifications are shown in red in Figure 12.

Please note that the number of additional combination functions (additions in the case of FIR filters) and associated multiplexers is given by the number of shaded entries in Figure 9 and grows quadratically with the window size W (W is assumed odd here):

$$C_{1D} = \left(\frac{W-1}{2} \right) \left(\frac{W+1}{2} \right). \tag{12}$$

However, several of the combination terms are common, and this can be exploited by moving the multiplexers to the input of the combination chain. Where there are multiple combinations for a given stage, these will usually occur on different clock cycles. Moving the multiplexer to before the combination operation enables a single combination operation to be reused, as shown in Figure 13. This reduces the number of adders required to

$$C_{1D} \leq W, \tag{13}$$

which can result in a significant savings for larger windows. However, the complexity of the multiplexers increases with the size of the window as more terms must be multiplexed together before the combination for larger windows.

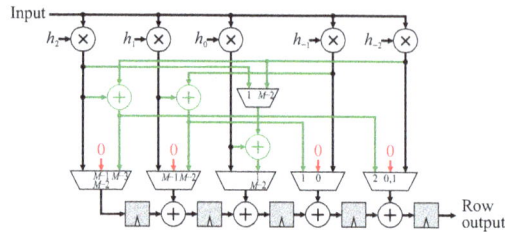

Figure 13. Optimization of row combination chain for mirroring without duplication.

3.3. Constant Extension

The above proposals manage the image border using a nearby window pixel. However, they do not work directly with constant extension.

The simplest is zero-extension. For FIR filters, when using coefficient coalescing, this can simply be achieved by setting the coefficients for invalid pixels to 0. For the modified combination chain, the extended combinations do not need to be added in (they are 0). It is only necessary to ensure that the invalid combinations are not added in, by bypassing the adders for the right-hand registers and clearing the left-hand registers. These approaches are shown in Figure 14. Note: they do not necessarily work directly with other filter types.

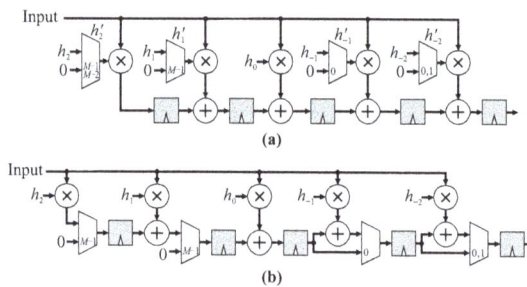

Figure 14. Zero-extension. (**a**): coefficient coalescing; (**b**): modified combination chain.

For constant extension, perhaps the simplest approach is to simply multiplex the input for those samples outside the image (shaded in grey in Figure 9). This is shown for row processing within an FIR filter in Figure 15.

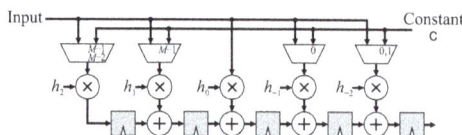

Figure 15. Constant extension.

4. 2D Filters

So far, all the examples that have been given apply to the 1D row filter components. Since border handling is separable (regardless of the separability of the underlying filter function) the same techniques can be applied for column handling. This is illustrated in Figure 16, where each row filter consists of a pixel transformation (multiplication by the FIR filter coefficient), combination network (for managing image borders, such as shown in Figure 13), followed by the combination chain. In 2D, pixel transformation consists of the set of row filters, the border managing combination network routes each row filter output into the appropriate tap of the combination chain, which now consists of row buffers rather than registers to combine data from different rows.

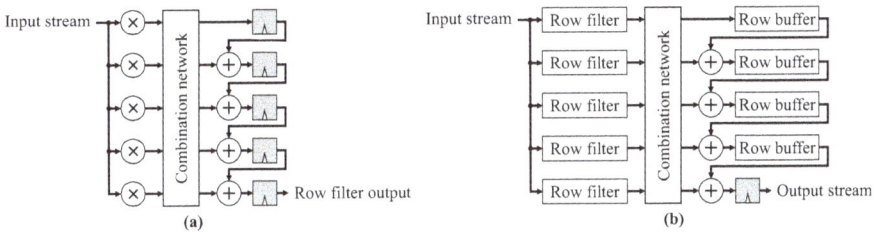

Figure 16. Extending 1D to 2D. (**a**): a 1D row FIR filter; (**b**): column combination processing for a 2D FIR filter.

If a 2D filter is not separable, then each row filter would be different. In transpose form, these row filters are in parallel, enabling reuse to be exploited (for example in the case of symmetry). The combination network manages the top and bottom image borders following the same principles as row border management. A specific example of the combination network for mirroring without duplication is illustrated in Figure 17. The combination network is identical to that shown in Figure 13 with the exception that the multiplexers are controlled by the row number rather than the column number.

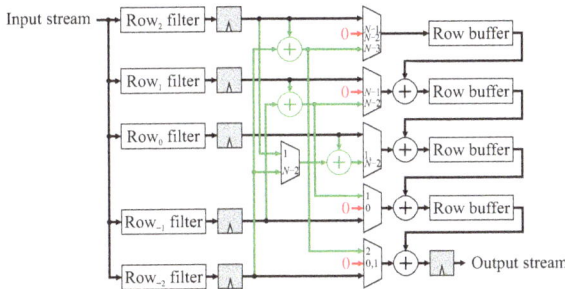

Figure 17. Column combination chain for mirroring without duplication.

Transform coalescing can also be extended to 2D. In the previous section, FIR filter coefficients were coalesced horizontally across the row. Since the border extension is separable, the same technique can be used to coalesce the resulting coefficients vertically. This is illustrated in Figure 18 where the coefficients $h'_{i,j}$ are formed from coalescing across row j. The same network is then applied vertically (down each column i), indexed by row number, with a second level of multiplexers selecting $h''_{i,j}$ from combinations of $h'_{i,j}$. Please note that 2D transform coalescing requires applying the coalescing to each column of the filter, rather than a single combination chain modification to the outputs of the row filters. The number of multiplexers is proportional to the number of pixels within the window, and the complexity of the multiplexers (number of terms that must be multiplexed) will also grow with the window width.

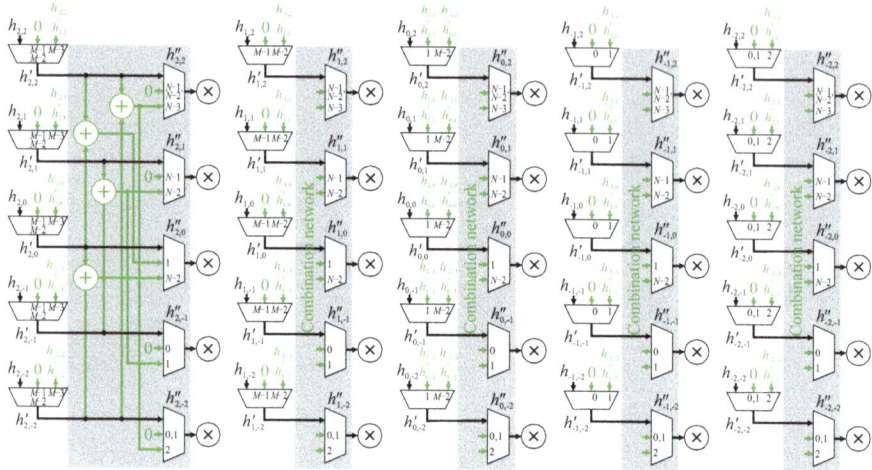

Figure 18. Coefficient coalescing by columns for 2D FIR filters (5 × 5 for mirroring without duplication).

The constant extension scheme shown in Figure 15 can similarly be adapted for 2D filtering by adding a second set of input multiplexers controlled by the row numbers.

Control Circuitry

In the proposed architectures, the multiplexers are controlled by the timing associated with the incoming pixel stream. This timing can easily be provided by a horizontal column (x) counter (modulo M) and a vertical row (y) counter (modulo N), which are reset by the corresponding stream synchronization signals. Rather than explicitly decode each of the required states, it is more efficient to decode the earliest state during a transition at an image border, and use a shift register to decode the subsequent states, as demonstrated in Figure 19. For the row counter and state shift register, providing a clock enable signal from the last column ($M - 1$) minimizes the additional circuitry required. (If the rows and columns are extended separately, then the clock enable can be shifted to a later tap to account for the latency of the row filters).

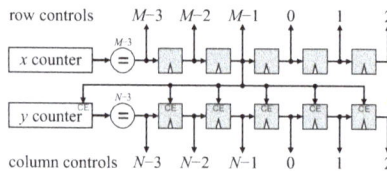

Figure 19. Control signal decoder.

5. Linear Filter Implementation Issues

One practical issue with implementing FIR filters is that the coefficients are usually scaled to enable integer arithmetic to be used. Where possible, the scale factor is a power of 2 (effectively representing the coefficients as binary fixed point), so the output of the filter can be obtained simply by bit-shifting (free in hardware). Rescaling is usually the last operation within the filter to minimize the precision loss through the adder chain. One implication of this is that the word length is larger on the output of the multipliers. In particular, this affects the word length (hence memory size) of the row buffers, which for transpose filters must be sized according to the adder chain rather than the filter input. The buffer word length may be reduced by distributing the rescaling (as illustrated in Figure 20), with a partial rescaling of the outputs of the row filters, and the balance applied at the final filter output. The output can be rounded by adding in the scaled equivalent of 0.5 at the start of the chain.

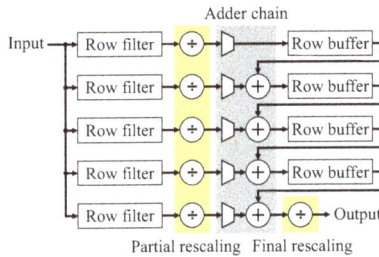

Figure 20. Distributed rescaling for transpose-form FIR filters.

If necessary for speed, coefficient coalescing can be pipelined, with a register placed between the multiplexer and multiplier. This would require adjusting the multiplexers to select the required coefficients 1 clock cycle earlier, which can easily be achieved. On an FPGA, this would generally use the flip-flop on the output of the multiplexer logic cell, which would otherwise be unused.

On modern FPGAs, the multiplication is realized within hard DSP blocks. Speed can be optimized, and additional resources minimized if the multiplication, addition, and following register can be implemented within a single DSP block [5]. Indeed, this is the case with the coefficient coalescing scheme, as seen in Figure 10. In fact, for Intel FPGAs, if the filter coefficients are constant and there are 8 or fewer combinations for each coalesced coefficient, then the coefficient multiplexing can also be implemented directly within the DSP block [17], although this requires direct instantiation of DSP primitives and cannot be inferred from the register transfer level (RTL) source code.

The disadvantage of coefficient coalescing is that it is no longer possible to reuse common multipliers within the filter. However, since the combination chain modification scheme moves the multiplexers to after the multipliers, such multiplier reuse is possible.

Modifying the combination chain prevents the implementation of both the multiplication and following addition within a single DSP block because the output of the multiplier is used in more than one place. However, for typical word sizes used for images, 2 or even 3 multipliers may be able to be realized by a single DSP block [17].

6. Experimental Comparison

To compare the different border management approaches, three experiments were performed. The first compares the cost of border management over doing nothing. For this, the transformation coalescing and combination chain modification techniques are compared for both FIR and morphological filters. For comparison, the transpose form is also compared against the more traditional direct-form filter structures. The second experiment compares the cost of different border extension methods for transpose-form filters. The third experiment investigates the scalability of border extension with window size.

All experiments were performed with symmetrical but non-separable square windows. Obviously, separable windows would significantly reduce resource requirements by implementing the 2D window as a cascade of two 1D windows. Non-separable filters require implementation of the full 2D window. Many filters are symmetrical, and resources can be reduced by exploiting symmetry where possible. However, border management will damage symmetry if care is not taken, for example with the transformation coalescing methods, and a symmetrical filter would enable this aspect to be explored.

The first two experiments used 5 × 5 filters, with the FIR filter coefficients and morphological filter structuring element offsets as shown in Figure 21. The FIR filter is a Gaussian filter, a frequently used filter, and although the Gaussian is technically separable, as a result of rounding, this filter is not separable, requiring implementation of a full two-dimensional window. The symmetry of both filters enables the number of computations to be reduced by a factor of approximately 2 when symmetry can be exploited. The test designs processed a 1024 × 768 × 8-bit image. For all FIR filter implementations, fixed-point arithmetic was used throughout, with the output pixel values obtained by rounding. Rounding was achieved by adding 0.5 at an appropriate point (usually at the start of the adder chains) and truncating the fraction bits of the final addition.

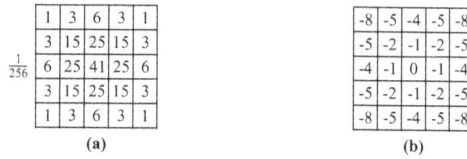

$\frac{1}{256}$

1	3	6	3	1
3	15	25	15	3
6	25	41	25	6
3	15	25	15	3
1	3	6	3	1

(a)

-8	-5	-4	-5	-8
-5	-2	-1	-2	-5
-4	-1	0	-1	-4
-5	-2	-1	-2	-5
-8	-5	-4	-5	-8

(b)

Figure 21. Coefficients for the sample filters used for testing in experiments 1 and 2. (**a**): FIR filter; (**b**): morphological filter structuring element offsets.

Designs were represented using VHDL, and synthesized using Quartus Prime Lite Edition 17.1.0 (Intel, Santa Clara, CA, USA), using "Balanced optimization (Normal flow)" targeting a Cyclone V FPGA (5CSEMA5F31C6) (Intel, Santa Clara, CA, USA) to give the resource requirements and the design speed. Modelsim-Intel FPGA Starter Edition 10.5b (Intel, Santa Clara, CA, USA) was used for design verification.

6.1. Experiment 1: Comparison of Approaches

The aim of this experiment was to compare the performance of the different architectural alternatives described in Sections 3 and 4 with both the FIR filter and the morphological filter. The synthesis results are summarized in Table 1.

Table 1. Resource requirements for the different approaches (adaptive lookup tables (ALUT), flip-flops (FF), 10 kbit memory blocks (M10K), DSP blocks (DSP), maximum clock frequency (Fmax) in MHz). Other than the cases with no border management (indicated by *), mirroring without duplication is used.

Method	5 × 5 FIR Filter					5 × 5 Morphological Filter			
	ALUT	FF	M10K	DSP	Fmax	ALUT	FF	M10K	Fmax
Transpose form, no borders									
– DSP-based (*)	164	100	7	9	175				
– Coefficient sharing (*)	312	237	7	2	176	285	167	4	179
Transformation coalescing	296	131	7	15	120	688	251	4	184
– Pipelined	296	135	7	15	173	710	300	4	186
Combination chain	410	251	7	2	180	439	171	4	172
– Partial rescaling 4/4	389	247	5	2	194				
– Partial rescaling 6/2	378	245	4	2	180				
Direct-form filter structures									
– No border handling (*)	331	265	4	5	55	731	265	4	56
– Multiplex network	503	267	4	5	57	745	266	4	56
– Adder/max tree	380	267	4	2	93	580	267	4	64
– Overlap prime and flush	404	346	4	5	56	807	346	4	56
– Adder/max tree	317	346	4	2	105	500	346	4	68
– Pipelined	343	398	4	2	152	473	395	4	117

As a baseline, the transpose form with no border management was implemented in two ways for the FIR filter. The first, exploited the use of DSP blocks on the FPGA, since these are specifically targeted for multiply and accumulate operations. The second exploited the fact that many of the filter coefficients were used multiple times, with only 6 multipliers (one for each unique coefficient) shared for the complete window.

As expected, the DSP-based design used the fewest resources. Only 3 rows of the filter were required, because of symmetry, and each row used 3 DSP blocks because two multiply-add and associated output registers able to be packed per DSP block. Coefficient sharing reduced the number of hardware multipliers to 2, since multiplication by 1, 3, 6, and 15 were optimized to additions. The adder chains were no longer implemented using DSP blocks, giving an increase in both logic and flip-flops. The four 16-bit wide row buffers (64 bits total) were packed into 7 M10K memory blocks.

For the morphological filter, coefficient sharing reduced the number of offsets required to 5. Any offset pixel values that went below 0 were clipped at 0. The four 8-bit wide row buffers (32 bits total) required 4 M10K memory blocks.

Transformation coalescing has two layers of multiplexers, one for coalescing the coefficients vertically, and a second for coalescing horizontally as illustrated in Figure 18. Coalescing destroys the symmetry, so all 5 rows of the filter are required, requiring more flip-flops. For the FIR filter, this also requires more DSP blocks. The clock speed for the FIR filter is lowered significantly by the coalescing multiplexers; this is recovered with minimal additional resources by inserting pipeline registers between the multiplexers and multipliers (these registers were absorbed into the inputs of the DSP blocks). The clock speed for the morphological filter is barely affected, although the critical path does change from the row buffer operation to the coefficient coalescing. However, the additional delay is negligible, so pipelining the coefficient coalescing only serves to increase resources and has negligible effect on the maximum clock frequency.

Modifying the combination chain can share the common multiplier terms for the FIR filter and requires additional logic for the adders and multiplexers. Since the filter function is naturally pipelined in transpose form, there is no loss of speed. Rather than perform the division by 256 at the output (rescaling by 0 bits for the rows then 8 bits at the output (0/8)), two partial rescaling options were considered: rescaling by 4 bits from the row filters (4/4) or 6 bits (6/2). The 4/4 option reduces the row buffer word width to 12 bits (48 bits for the 4 buffers) which can be packed into 5 M10Ks. Dropping a further 2 bits (the 6/2 option) reduces the row buffers to 10 bits wide (40 bits total), requiring only 4 M10Ks. The small reduction in logic results from partial rescaling requiring smaller adders within the column adder chain; however, the associated reduction in memory is significant. The effect of distributed partial rescaling on the output image is insignificant (at most 1-pixel value).

For the morphological filter, the combination chain modification allows the offsets to be reused, giving a significant drop in logic resources required. Again, since the maximum combinations are pipelined, there is no effect on the operating frequency.

It is instructive to compare these designs with the same filters realized using the traditional direct form. The row buffers are on the input, requiring only 8 bits per buffer (32 bits total). This is the same as the transpose-form morphological filter but is less than the transpose-form FIR filter.

The 5 DSPs for the FIR filter come from the multiplication by coefficients 25 and 41; the others are optimized to additions. The multiplex network [11,15] adds significantly to the logic requirements of the FIR filter, but not so much on the morphological filter. This latter effect may be the synthesis optimizing the logic by combining the multiplexer and the offset operation. The overlapped prime and flush approach [10] has significantly fewer multiplexers, but this comes at the cost of additional priming registers. For the morphological filter, the increase in resources is from the multiplexer and offset operations no longer being combined. The operating speed is the same for these designs, and results from the combination chains; row adder chains (in parallel) feed into a column adder chain for the FIR filter, and similarly maximum combination chains for the morphological filter. Replacing these chains by a tree structure reduces the propagation delay by a factor of approximately 2 for the

FIR filter, and to a lesser extent for the morphological filter. The tree structure also enables the common multipliers and offsets to be factored out, reducing the number of DSP blocks and logic. This provides a more realistic comparison with the coefficient sharing used by the combination chain modification scheme. The trade-off between using the multiplexer network or the overlapped prime and flush comes down to the number of logic cells and registers required, so would only depend on resource availability. The direct-form implementation though is still significantly slower than the transpose form (running at 60% speed for the FIR filter and at 36% speed for the morphological filter), with both direct and transpose forms having similar resource requirements. The difference in speed can be addressed by pipelining the combination tree, although this comes at the expense of increasing the number of registers required (results for a 2-stage pipeline are shown in Table 1, if necessary further pipelining could be used).

6.2. Experiment 2: Comparison of Border Management Schemes

The second experiment was to compare the resources required for the different border management schemes. The results are presented in Table 2.

Table 2. Transpose-form resource requirements for different border management schemes (adaptive lookup tables (ALUT), flip-flops (FF), 10 kbit memory blocks (M10K), DSP blocks (DSP), maximum clock frequency (Fmax) in MHz).

Method	5 × 5 FIR Filter					5 × 5 Morphological Filter			
	ALUT	FF	M10K	DSP	Fmax	ALUT	FF	M10K	Fmax
Zero-extension									
– Coalescing	215	130	7	15	174	660	250	4	185
– Combination chain	323	239	7	2	185	366	168	4	184
Constant extension	387	130	7	15	173	636	250	4	175
Duplication	448	247	7	2	159	576	170	4	138
Two-phase duplication	389	248	7	2	188	436	170	4	171
Mirroring	410	251	7	2	180	439	171	4	172
Mirroring with duplication	445	247	7	2	178	540	170	4	172

The two forms of zero-extension were transformation coalescing or to modify the combination chain. For the FIR filter, coalescing consisted of setting the filter coefficients to 0 for pixels outside the image and using DSP units for the multiply and accumulate. For the morphological filter, the offsets for pixels outside the image were set to $-\infty$ (in practice -255 for 8-bit images). Combination chain modification enabled the transformations to be shared (reuse of multipliers for FIR, or offsets for the morphological filter). The increase in resources for the FIR filter reflect the movement of adders and registers from the DSP blocks into logic. However, for the morphological filter, sharing the offsets significantly reduces resources.

Constant extension was managed by multiplexing between the input pixel and the constant. Consequently, the pixel transformations could not be shared. For the FIR filter the multiplexers are the source of the 80% increase in logic resources. For the morphological filter, the multiplexers were combined with the offset calculation so that resources were similar to those for zero-extension.

The remaining extension methods were achieved by modifying the combination chain. The small differences in the number of flip-flops result from differences in the control chain. The logic resources reflect the complexity in terms of the number of adder/maximum units that could be reused, and complexity of the multiplexing by the difference schemes. Two-phase duplication has the lowest resource requirements because there are several combination terms that can be reused. Extension by duplication is slightly slower than the other methods because it requires multiple combination operations in two of the window positions, and this increases the propagation delay. For the morphological filter, two-phase duplication and mirroring without duplication require fewer logic resources. It appears that for these two filters, the synthesis was able to combine the offsets with the combination chain giving better optimization. Otherwise there is little to distinguish between the different methods in terms of resources or speed.

In this experiment, for the FIR filters rescaling was performed at the end. With partial rescaling, it is expected that all these results would decrease by similar amounts to that shown in Table 1.

6.3. Experiment 3: Scalability with Window Size

For this experiment, a range of different morphological filters from 3 × 3 up to 15 × 15 using mirroring without duplication were synthesized to explore trends in resource requirements as a function of filter size. Combination chain modification was used because this is more efficient for implementing morphological filters. The results are listed in Table 3, with the resources normalized per pixel plotted in Figure 22.

Table 3. Resource requirements for the symmetrical morphological dilation filter as a function of filter size (adaptive lookup tables (ALUT), flip-flops (FF), 10 kbit memory blocks (M10K), maximum clock frequency (Fmax) in MHz). Normalized values are per window pixel. The last row shows the effect of pipelining.

Filter Size	Raw Resource Count				Normalized	
	ALUT	FF	M10K	Fmax	ALUT	FF
3 × 3	163	93	2	196	18.1	10.3
5 × 5	439	171	4	172	17.6	6.8
7 × 7	924	279	5	174	18.9	5.7
9 × 9	1621	419	7	155	20.0	5.2
11 × 11	2539	591	8	140	21.0	4.9
13 × 13	3695	795	10	135	21.9	4.7
15 × 15	5090	1031	12	123	22.6	4.6
15 × 15 (pipelined)	5054	2112	12	165	22.5	9.4

As expected, the resource requirements grow approximately in proportion to the number of pixels within the window. Part of this results from the filter function, which will be proportional to the window size, and part of this is for the combination network used to manage image borders. The number of ALUTs and FFs normalized by the number of window pixels makes this particularly clear. The number of ALUTs per window pixel increases because as the window grows larger, the width of the multiplexers in the combination network also grows. This growth is relatively slow, which shows that the combination network scales well with filter size. The higher numbers for the 3 × 3 window reflect the overhead of the control logic, which is a greater proportion for the small window. The number of FFs per window pixel decreases, reflecting the decreasing proportion used by the control logic and row buffer output (which are proportional to the window width rather than area). The asymptote here will be 4 FFs per window pixel reflecting the fact that only half of the row filters are required because of symmetry.

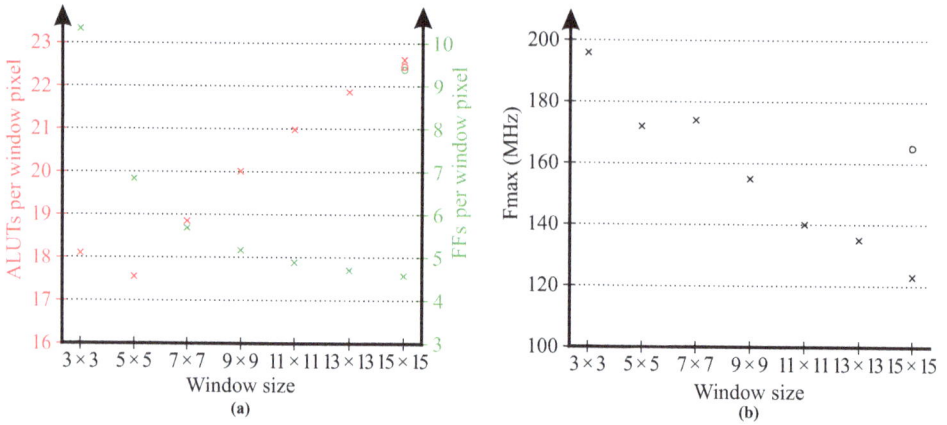

Figure 22. (**a**): resources required per window pixel; (**b**): maximum clock frequency. Pipelined results for the 15 × 15 window are shown with ∘.

The maximum clock frequency decreases with increasing window size. This results purely from the increase in the complexity of the multiplexers within the combination network, as these form the critical path for windows larger than about 7 × 7. If clock speed is critical, this can be mitigated by pipelining the output of the combination networks, as shown by the last row in Table 3. Although this more than doubles the number of flip-flops required, in an FPGA implementation, these flip-flops are associated with the logic cells used to realize the combination network and would be otherwise unused. The critical path in this case is still the combination network, so the speed would still be expected to decrease for larger filters unless additional pipelining was used.

Overall, these results indicate that the transpose-form filters scale well with increasing window size.

7. Conclusions

This paper has demonstrated that border management using transpose filter structures in not only feasible, but can have significant advantages over direct-form filter structures.

For FIR filters, coefficient coalescing enables DSP blocks to be used for realizing the multiply, add, and associated register resulting in the fewest required resources. However, this comes at the cost of not being able to exploit multiplier reuse and symmetry. Modifying the combination chain separates the multiplication and addition, approximately doubling the resources by forcing the additions and registers into the FPGA fabric. Reflecting this trade-off, coefficient coalescing would therefore be recommended for implementing FIR filters on FPGAs with plentiful DSP blocks.

For FIR filters, using the transpose filter structures requires wider memories for the row buffers because these come between the multiplications and the distributed additions. Since scaling of the output occurs at the end, more bits must be carried through the row buffers. It is demonstrated that this increase in RAM resources by the transpose structure for FIR filters can be effectively managed through distributing the rescaling between the row filters (before the row buffers) and the output.

For morphological filters, transform coalescing means that symmetry cannot effectively be exploited, making this a less viable option than modifying the combination chain.

Overall, the resources required by the transpose form with combination chain modification are similar for both linear and morphological filters to that for direct-form filters using the multiplexer network, especially if distributed partial rescaling is used with FIR filters to reduce the width of the row buffers. The transpose-form filter structures scale well with increasing filter size, with resources only growing slightly faster than the number of pixels within the window. The key advantage of the transpose form is that the filters are significantly faster than direct-form filters, primarily as a result of the pipelining inherent within their structure. Although direct-form filters can be pipelined to improve the speed, this comes at the cost of additional resources.

The disadvantage of using the transpose form for filter realization is that the filter function is no longer independent of the window formation. However, this paper has demonstrated that the complexities of border handling can be confined to an additional processing layer which implements the combination network. (For 2D filters, two such layers are required: one for the row filters, and one for the column combination.)

In conclusion, this paper has demonstrated that image border processing can effectively and efficiently be integrated within transpose-form filters, and that the complexity of the combination network is similar to that of the more conventional direct-form processing.

Author Contributions: Conceptualization, D.G.B.; Investigation, D.G.B. and A.S.A.; Methodology, D.G.B.; Project administration, D.G.B.; Supervision, D.G.B.; Validation, D.G.B. and A.S.A.; Writing—original draft, D.G.B.; Writing—review & editing, D.G.B. and A.S.A.

Funding: This research received no external funding.

Conflicts of Interest: The authors declare no conflict of interest.

Abbreviations

The following abbreviations are used in this manuscript:

ALUT   Adaptive Lookup Table
DSP   Digital Signal Processing
FF   Flip-Flop
FIR   Finite Impulse Response filter
FPGA   Field Programmable Gate Array
LUT   Lookup Table
M10K   10 kbit memory block
RTL   Register Transfer Level
SRL   Shift Register Logic

References

1. Bailey, D.G. *Design for Embedded Image Processing on FPGAs*; John Wiley and Sons (Asia) Pte. Ltd.: Singapore, 2011. [CrossRef]
2. Jackson, L.B. On the interaction of roundoff noise and dynamic range in digital filters. *Bell Syst. Tech. J.* **1970**, *49*, 159–184. [CrossRef]
3. Sternberg, S.R. Grayscale morphology filters. *Comput. Vis. Graph. Image Process.* **1986**, *35*, 333–355. [CrossRef]
4. Porikli, F. Reshuffling: A fast algorithm for filtering with arbitrary kernels. In Proceedings of the Real-Time Image Processing 2008, San Jose, CA, USA, 28–29 January 2008; Kehtarnavaz, N., Carlsohn, M.F., Eds.; SPIE: Washington, WA, USA, 2008; Volume 6811. [CrossRef]
5. Al-Dujaili, A.; Fahmy, S.A. High throughput 2D spatial image filters on FPGAs. *arXiv* **2017**, arXiv:1710.05154.
6. Bailey, D.G. Efficient implementation of greyscale morphological filters. In Proceedings of the International Conference on Field Programmable Technology (FPT 2010), Beijing, China, 8–10 December 2010; pp. 421–424. [CrossRef]
7. Tan, X.; Triggs, B. Enhanced local texture feature sets for face recognition under difficult lighting conditions. In Proceedings of the International Workshop on Analysis and Modeling of Faces and Gestures (AMFG 2007), Rio de Janeiro, Brazil, 20 October 2007; LNCS; Volume 4778, pp. 168–182. [CrossRef]
8. Jiang, B.; Zhang, L.; Lu, H.; Yang, C.; Yang, M. Saliency detection via absorbing Markov chain. In Proceedings of the 2013 IEEE International Conference on Computer Vision, Sydney, Australia, 1–8 December 2013; pp. 1665–1672. [CrossRef]

J. Imaging **2018**, *4*, 138

9. Sullivan, G.J.; Baker, R.L. Motion compensation for video compression using control grid interpolation. In Proceedings of the International Conference on Acoustics, Speech, and Signal Processing (ICASSP 91), Toronto, ON, Canada, 14–17 April 1991; Volume 4, pp. 2713–2716. [CrossRef]
10. Bailey, D.G. Image border management for FPGA based filters. In Proceedings of the 6th International Symposium on Electronic Design, Test and Applications, Queenstown, New Zealand, 17–19 January 2011; pp. 144–149. [CrossRef]
11. Rafi, M.; Din, N.U. A novel arrangement for efficiently handling image border in FPGA filter implementation. In Proceedings of the 2016 3rd International Conference on Signal Processing and Integrated Networks (SPIN), Noida, India, 11–12 February 2016; pp. 163–168. [CrossRef]
12. Ozkan, M.A.; Reiche, O.; Hannig, F.; Teich, J. Hardware design and analysis of efficient loop coarsening and border handling for image processing. In Proceedings of the 2017 IEEE 28th International Conference on Application-Specific Systems, Architectures and Processors (ASAP), Seattle, WA, USA, 10–12 July 2017; pp. 155–163. [CrossRef]
13. Bailey, D.; Li, J.S.J. FPGA based multi-shell filter for hot pixel removal within colour filter array demosaicing. In Proceedings of the 2016 International Conference on Image and Vision Computing New Zealand (IVCNZ), Palmerston North, New Zealand, 21–22 November 2016; pp. 196–201. [CrossRef]
14. Benkrid, A.; Benkrid, K. Novel area-efficient FPGA architectures for FIR filtering with symmetric signal extension. *IEEE Trans. Very Large Scale Integr. Syst.* **2009**, *17*, 709–722. [CrossRef]
15. Chakrabarti, C. A DWT-based encoder architecture for symmetrically extended images. In Proceedings of the 1999 IEEE International Symposium on Circuits and Systems (ISCAS'99), Orlando, FL, USA, 30 May–2 June 1999; Volume 4, pp. 123–126. [CrossRef]
16. Benkrid, A.; Benkrid, K.; Crookes, D. A novel FIR filter architecture for efficient signal boundary handling on Xilinx VIRTEX FPGAs. In Proceedings of the 11th Annual IEEE Symposium on Field-Programmable Custom Computing Machines (FCCM 2003), Napa, CA, USA, 9–11 April 2003; pp. 273–275. [CrossRef]
17. Altera. *Cyclone V Device Handbook*; Altera Corporation: San Jose, CA, USA, 2015; Volume CV-5V2.

Journal of
Imaging

MDPI

Article

Accelerating SuperBE with Hardware/Software Co-Design

Andrew Tzer-Yeu Chen *, Rohaan Gupta, Anton Borzenko, Kevin I-Kai Wang and Morteza Biglari-Abhari

Embedded Systems Research Group, Department of Electrical and Computer Engineering,
The University of Auckland, Auckland 1023, New Zealand; rgup275@aucklanduni.ac.nz (R.G.);
abor539@aucklanduni.ac.nz (A.B.); kevin.wang@auckland.ac.nz (K.I.-K.W.); m.abhari@auckland.ac.nz (M.B.-A.)
* Correspondence: andrew.chen@auckland.ac.nz

Received: 11 September 2018; Accepted: 16 October 2018; Published: 18 October 2018

Abstract: Background Estimation is a common computer vision task, used for segmenting moving objects in video streams. This can be useful as a pre-processing step, isolating regions of interest for more complicated algorithms performing detection, recognition, and identification tasks, in order to reduce overall computation time. This is especially important in the context of embedded systems like smart cameras, which may need to process images with constrained computational resources. This work focuses on accelerating SuperBE, a superpixel-based background estimation algorithm that was designed for simplicity and reducing computational complexity while maintaining state-of-the-art levels of accuracy. We explore both software and hardware acceleration opportunities, converting the original algorithm into a greyscale, integer-only version, and using Hardware/Software Co-design to develop hardware acceleration components on FPGA fabric that assist a software processor. We achieved a $4.4\times$ speed improvement with the software optimisations alone, and a $2\times$ speed improvement with the hardware optimisations alone. When combined, these led to a $9\times$ speed improvement on a Cyclone V System-on-Chip, delivering almost 38 fps on 320×240 resolution images.

Keywords: background estimation; image segmentation; System-on-Chip; embedded systems; real-time systems; hardware accelerators

1. Introduction

Many computer vision applications rely on scanning an image by applying a sliding window across the image, whether it is a simple filter operation or a more complex object detection and recognition task. The use of multi-scale image pyramids may mean that the entire image is effectively scanned multiple times. In many scenarios, this is wasteful because the regions or objects of interest only occupy some of the image space, while the majority of the camera view yields negative results. Background estimation (also known as background subtraction, background modelling, or foreground detection) is a popular method of segmenting images in order to isolate foreground regions of interest. This allows for further analysis with subsequent algorithms, saving computation time by processing a smaller image and therefore iterating over fewer window positions.

However, using background estimation has two limitations. Firstly, sequential frames in a video are usually required in order to compare frames to each other and classify similar parts of the images as background, and there is a general assumption that objects of interest are moving between frames. This eliminates the applicability of background estimation in some offline image processing applications where the images contain no notion of time or may be entirely independent, but for most real-world applications there is some continuous monitoring where multiple frames of the same view are captured. Secondly, background estimation is not free; it still requires some computation time, and that computation time must be sufficiently low to justify introducing background estimation before running more complex algorithms.

While computation time is a critical factor for justifying background estimation, most of the literature focuses on incrementally improving accuracy with new algorithms at any cost. Popular pixel-level models such as the Gaussian Mixture Model (GMM) [1] have been around for decades, but recent approaches have included applying adaptive weights and parameters [2,3], deep convolutional neural networks [4–6], and ensemble models with stochastic model optimisation [7], all of which significantly increase computation time while only marginally improving accuracy, failing to address the challenges of real-world implementation.

Instead of blindly pursuing gains in accuracy, once a sufficient level of accuracy has been reached we should focus on accelerating those approaches, in order to minimise the impact of background estimation in more complex image processing pipelines with multiple stages. In our previous work, we applied superpixels to ViBE [8], a popular background estimation algorithm, and incorporated further optimisations of computation time to develop an algorithm called SuperBE [9]. We were able to achieve real-time processing with speeds of approximately 135 fps on 320×240 resolution images on a standard desktop PC while maintaining comparable accuracy to other state-of-the-art algorithms. In this work, we make two contributions by exploring further acceleration in two directions. Firstly, since the original SuperBE algorithm used RGB images with floating-point mathematics, we target software acceleration by investigating the effect of reducing the amount of information being processed by using greyscale and integer-only versions of SuperBE. Secondly, we developed an embedded system implementation of the algorithm with constrained computational resources for a real-world use case, targeting hardware acceleration by using Hardware/Software Co-design techniques [10] to partition the algorithm on a System-on-Chip (SoC) with an ARM processor and connected Field Programmable Gate Array (FPGA) fabric. In both cases, we present quantitative results justifying our acceleration strategies, while also detailing the effects on accuracy. The primary intention of the paper is to show how an algorithm like SuperBE can be accelerated in a variety of ways, in detail, without requiring software developers to spend excessive amounts of time on learning how to develop hardware.

In Section 2, we present some related works in the area of real-time background estimation and acceleration of background estimation algorithms, including a summary of the SuperBE algorithm to provide full context for this paper. In Sections 3 and 4, we provide a detailed description of the software and hardware acceleration procedures explored in this work, as well as full experimental results demonstrating the effectiveness of these acceleration strategies in Sections 3.1 and 4.1. We present our conclusions and ideas for future work in Section 5.

2. Literature Review and Background

2.1. Fast Background Estimation

While basic background estimation algorithms such as frame differences, running averages, and median filters are very fast, they tend to suffer from an inability to deal with high-frequency salt and pepper noise as well as low-frequency environmental changes such as lighting variations over time [11]. First popularised by Stauffer and Grimson [1] in 1999 and improved upon by others including [12–14], the Gaussian Mixture Model (GMM) remains one of the most popular background estimation algorithms today, primarily because of its simplicity and wide availability as one of the default algorithms available in most image processing libraries. In many applications, a GMM approach is "good enough" for background estimation, even though it still produces a substantial amount of noise from false positives and negatives. For applications where false positives or negatives are costly, such as safety-critical systems, acceptable error rates will depend on the requirements of the specific application and may need to be further reduced. This can somewhat be alleviated through the use of post-processing filters, but this adds further computation time. On the challenging CDW2014 [15] dataset, the Zivkovic GMM [12] misclassifies just under 4% of all pixels across the 11 categories and

53 video sequences. The error rate is also known as the Percentage of Wrong Classifications (PWC). However, it is important to note that this is an average. Figure 1 shows the difference in segmentation quality between different levels of PWC on different video sequences. The figure shows that even a 4% PWC can appear to be poorly segmented, while a 1.3% PWC is perhaps sufficiently accurate, but this will strongly depend on the end application.

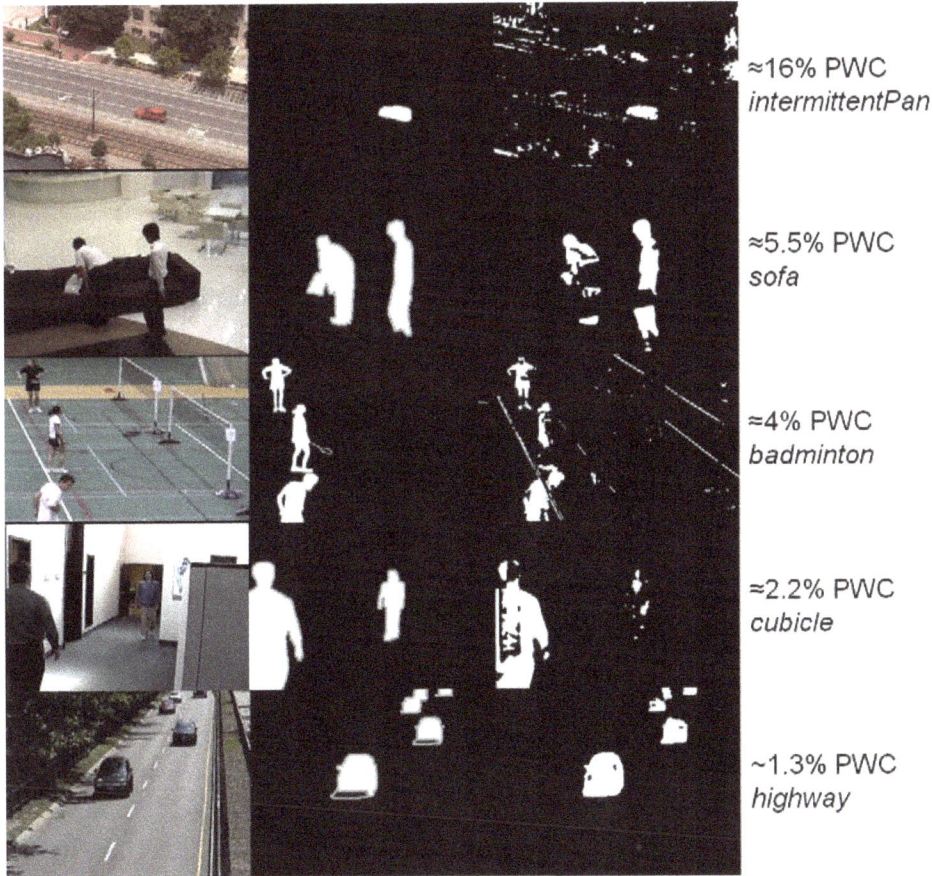

Figure 1. Examples of background estimation with different levels of PWC. In each row, the leftmost image is the raw image, the middle image is the ground truth, and the right image is the output of the Zivkovic GMM algorithm [12], with the approximate PWC and name of the sequence from the CDW2014 [15] dataset on the right.

Current state-of-the-art methods are able to reduce that error rate to less than 2%, but this has come with a heavy computation cost. Whereas the Zivkovic GMM can achieve around 49 fps on this dataset on a standard desktop computer, Ref. [6] requires a high-end Graphics Processing Unit (GPU) to achieve 18 fps, Ref. [16] achieves 8–9 fps on a desktop computer, and Ref. [3] only achieves 2 fps for 320 × 240 video on a high-end i5 CPU. While improving accuracy is important, the trade-off between accuracy and speed needs to be more carefully considered, as more accurate algorithms are unlikely to be adopted in the real world if they cannot justify slow computation times. Comprehensive background estimation survey papers are available in [17–19].

In most background estimation methods, the algorithm works at the pixel level. This means that for every pixel in the image, a background model is maintained and compared against pixels from newer frames to determine whether that pixel should be classified as background or foreground for the current frame. Colour is generally the feature that is used to describe the pixels and ascertain differences, although depth/range can also sometimes be used [20]. We also generally include a model update step to allow the model to adapt over time to changes in environmental conditions. The computation time is therefore strongly dependent on the number of pixels in the image, which presents an issue in terms of scalability as imaging technology continues to improve and image resolutions increase. SuperBE [9] addressed this by incorporating the use of superpixels (groups of pixels clustered together for colour and spatial coherency) into the popular background estimation algorithm ViBe [8]. Superpixels have been used in background estimation in the literature before [21–24], but most works in the literature still have very high computation times, particularly because superpixel segmentation is relatively expensive.

2.2. SuperBE

Using the SLICO [25] algorithm to generate superpixels, SuperBE essentially reduces the number of elements that need to be classified in background estimation, based on the assumption that all of the pixels within a superpixel cluster are very likely to have the same foreground or background classification. Reducing the number of elements means that fewer background models need to be maintained, compared against, and updated, decreasing both memory requirements and computation time. SuperBE is shown in Figure 2, and it can be seen how the superpixels form the main shape of the output background mask that can then be post-processed to form a contiguous region of interest.

Figure 2. SuperBE on the CDW2014 *backdoor* sequence, showing the superpixel segmentation **(top-left)**, the output mask without **(top-right)** and with **(bottom-left)** post-processing, and then with the mask applied to the original image **(bottom-right)**.

As shown in Figure 3, SuperBE is comprised of two main processes. The first process is model initialisation, where a single frame is provided to the algorithm so that the background model can be created for the first time. After pre-processing, we apply superpixel clustering to group the pixels in the image, identifying the bounds of background objects and grouping similarly coloured areas together. It is important to note that superpixel clustering is only performed once in the entire algorithm, during initialisation, and not performed again for each subsequent frame, leading to significant speed increases in comparison to other superpixel-based algorithms as clustering can be computationally expensive. This is generally suitable in static surveillance cases, although in scenarios with panning cameras or dynamically changing backgrounds it may be necessary to re-initialise the algorithm more regularly. Then, we use the clusters to initialise the background model based on the colour means and colour covariance matrices of each superpixel. For each superpixel, we store multiple background samples to maintain robustness over time, although initially they are set to be identical. This helps compensate for only performing superpixel clustering once at initialisation by allowing for some variation in the background model when matching.

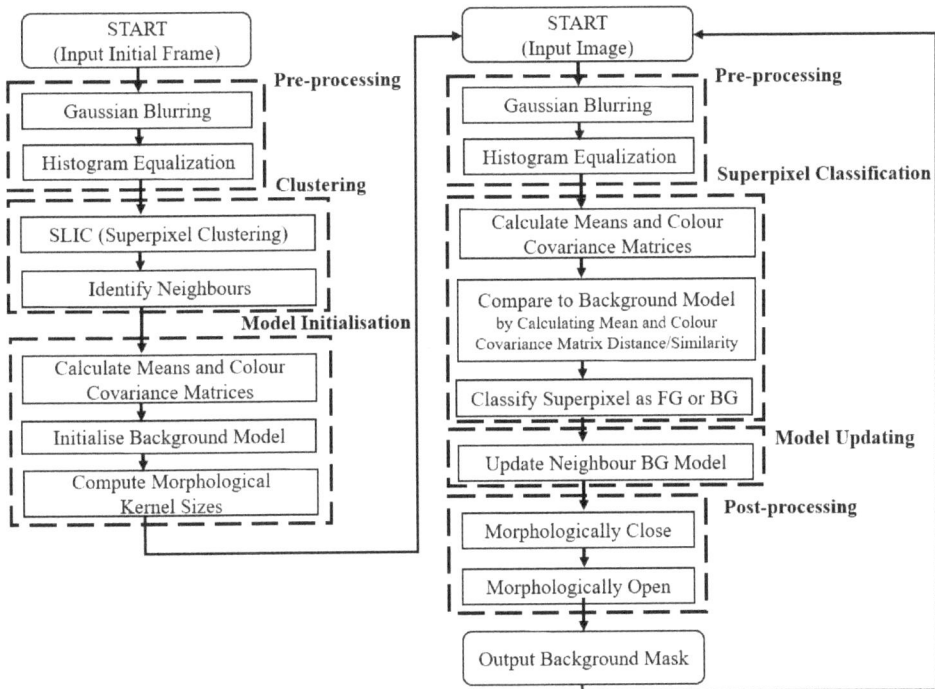

Figure 3. Flowcharts showing the background model initialisation (**left**) and frame masking (**right**) processes of SuperBE [9].

The second process is frame masking, where subsequent frames in the video sequence are presented to the algorithm and an output background mask is produced. For each frame, SuperBE applies the same superpixel segmentation obtained in the initialisation process, and then classifies each superpixel as background or foreground based on its similarity to the background model samples in terms of colour means and covariance. For each superpixel, the algorithm iterates through the background model samples, and checks if the similarity is below a parameterised threshold. Once enough background model samples have been found to be similar enough to the current superpixel (based on another parameter), then the algorithm exits that superpixel and classifies it as background. This is done to reduce time spent unnecessarily checking excess background model samples when only a few are required to accurately classify the superpixel as background.

While computing the mean and colour covariance matrix is relatively fast, computing the similarity of two colour covariance matrices is challenging. In SuperBE, the Jensen-Bregman LogDet Divergence was used for its computational efficiency, but that computational efficiency only holds true for complex processors that can compute logarithm operations quickly, making it less suitable for simpler processors or pure hardware implementation.

If the current superpixel values are sufficiently similar to those in the background model, then the content of the superpixel has not changed substantially and is probably also background. In this case, we also conduct a model update step by randomly replacing one of the background model samples with the values from the current superpixel, so that over time the background model incorporates minor variation in the background pixels in order to remain robust against low-frequency environmental changes. The algorithm also updates the background model for a random neighbouring superpixel with the values from the current superpixel. This helps improve robustness against small spatial shifts and allows neighbouring superpixels to "invade" each others models in order to erode false positives over time. These update procedures are relatively computationally light, as they are mostly comprised of control flow operations and memory reads/writes. The random selection of samples to be replaced is challenging to emulate in hardware, but it appears that the algorithm does not need true randomness, and some pseudorandom approach with a relatively uniform distribution should be sufficient. An optional post-processing step using morphological closing and opening can help reduce the amount of false positive noise patches and false negative holes in the resultant output mask. However, these morphological operations are very computationally expensive, as they tend to require multiple passes across the entire image and need to store multiple copies of the image in order to perform accurately.

The resulting algorithm is both fast and sufficiently accurate for most applications, reaching 135 fps on 320×240 images on an i7 CPU using only one core, while achieving an error rate of between 0.4–3% depending on the type of video. However, it is important to investigate how to make the algorithm even less computationally expensive so that it can still achieve good speeds on resource constrained systems with less powerful processing capabilities. This is especially important for enabling the development of useful smart cameras: imaging devices with embedded processing hardware, that either partially or fully process video streams at the point of image capture. In the subsequent acceleration, we mostly focus on the frame masking process (on the right of Figure 3), since the model initialisation process is only executed once and is therefore not an important factor in the long-run execution time. The key reason to focus on SuperBE is that it is more accurate that algorithms like GMM without introducing the significant computation costs of more modern background estimation approaches.

2.3. Hardware Implementations

Some literature does exist for describing systems that implement various background estimation algorithms on hardware platforms with the goal of achieving real-time speeds. Ref. [26] implements a GMM algorithm on a high-end GPU device, achieving speeds of over 50 fps for high-definition video. A separate work, Ref. [27], reports that a GPU implementation of GMM has a 5× speed-up over CPU implementations, reaching 58.1 fps for 352×288 resolution images. A competing FPGA implementation of GMM reported 20 fps at a 1920×1080 resolution [28], while a FPGA implemenation of ViBe achieved 60fps on 640×480 resolution images [29]. Alternatively, instead of taking an existing background estimation algorithm and merely porting it to a hardware device, algorithm designers could take the hardware architecture into account to leverage memory structures and parallelism. A method that is highly optimised for hardware using a codebook implementation on an FPGA achieved 50 fps on 768×576 resolution images [30]. Using a simple convolutional filter as the main processing step in their algorithm, Ref. [31] reports 60 fps on 800×480 images, although the simplicity of their approach is likely to lead to low accuracy on large images.

Unfortunately, the largest challenge with hardware design has generally been the high level of skill needed, and the associated high development time and cost required for well-optimised designs. While pure hardware designs can be very fast, this continuing challenge impedes adoption of faster hardware systems. This can partly be addressed through the use of Hardware/Software Co-Design. In these systems, the algorithm is still predominantly software-based and controlled on a standard CPU, but parts of the processing are offloaded to specialised hardware accelerator components that can decrease the computation time significantly. Ref. [32] leverages shared memory resources to compute multi-modal background masks based on a GMM approach on a FPGA, achieving 38 fps on 1024 × 1024 resolution images. In [33], a kernel based tracking system is implemented on an FPGA with a soft processor, reporting hundreds of frames per second based on a window size of 64 × 64 pixels with pipelining to process multiple frames at the same time. Ref. [34] implemented the Mixture of Gaussians (MoG) algorithm using many pipeline stages in hardware with an ARM processor to achieve real-time background estimation on Full-HD images. Nevertheless, there are relatively few HW/SW Co-design systems for background estimation published in the literature, and even fewer using modern background estimation techniques. In a bid to balance higher levels of accuracy with acceptably fast computation times, we propose to implement SuperBE on an embedded platform. While SuperBE as an algorithm is more complex and therefore slower than GMM or similar methods previously accelerated, it has an average PWC of 1.75%, much better than the 4% error rate expected from GMM (both scores measured on the CDW2014 dataset). In our work, we target a hard CPU with attached FPGA fabric, using a similar strategy from [10] to partition SuperBE into software and hardware components with the intention of accelerating computation on an embedded system. This improves upon the existing literature by accelerating a new algorithm that achieves better accuracy than most of the existing hardware implementations of background estimation algorithms, with real-time speeds on an embedded system.

3. Software Acceleration

Our main strategy for reducing computation time is to reduce the amount of information that needs to be processed while maintaining a sufficiently high accuracy. We produced three new versions of the algorithm: greyscale-only, integer-only, and a combined greyscale + integer version. In [8], it is reported that a greyscale variant of their background estimation algorithm is approximately 15% faster than the RGB version, with a less than one percentage point increase in the error rate. In the context of SuperBE, each superpixel is described by its colour means and colour covariance matrices. Since there are three colour channels, this results in three mean values and a 3 × 3 matrix for each superpixel. In a greyscale version, we still need to describe the superpixel in terms of its mean and variance, but this becomes much simpler as there is only one channel. While reducing the colour means from three to one would not have a large impact, replacing the colour covariance matrix calculation and the covariance matrix similarity calculation with a simple single-variable variance leads to a much lower computational complexity. By removing the covariance matrix similarity calculation, we also remove a number of logarithm operators that produce odd results at extreme values, which could lead to a positive effect on the accuracy. In addition to this, histogram equalisation tends to have less of an impact on greyscale images than colour images, so we removed this step from greyscale versions of SuperBE to further reduce computation time.

Since we will eventually target a hardware device, it is also worth considering the effect of casting/rounding all numbers in an integer-only version of the algorithm. For a standard desktop CPU, floating-point mathematics is well optimised, so there may not be a large speed improvement. On many smaller processors used in embedded devices, simpler processor architectures may not include specialised hardware for floating-point operations, causing these operations to be extremely costly. Implementing floating-point mathematics on hardware is also much more resource-intensive than fixed-point mathematics, restricting most designs to fixed-point or integer-based arithmetic [35]. We should expect there to be some increase in error as a result of losing precision, but it is likely to be small since background estimation is generally looking for relatively large changes in features. However, casting or rounding of the numbers is not the only effect of moving towards an integer-only version of the algorithm; operators such as log and square root also need to be approximated with integers, which could potentially lead to larger errors in output.

3.1. Software Evaluation

To test the effect of these optimisations, we used the Change Detection Workshop CDW2014 dataset [15], excluding the three categories PTZ, intermittent object motion, and thermal, which were also omitted in the original SuperBE paper as it is unsuitable for these video types. The tested video sequences included low framerates, shaky cameras, poor image quality, and a variety of image resolutions ranging from 320 × 240 to 720 × 576. As shown in Table 1, experiments were conducted both with and without post-processing, where the reference algorithm was the one provided in the original SuperBE paper [9]. The main metric that we used for accuracy was the Percentage of Wrong Classifications (PWC), which is equivalent to the error rate, calculated by dividing the number of incorrectly classified pixels by the total number of pixels and converting to a percentage. The speeds given in FPS are normalised for a 320 × 240 resolution image, meaning that we take all of the speeds from the different image resolutions, and then scale them based on the number of pixels to a 320 × 240 resolution image in order to make a fair comparison between methods. The relative speed for each version is given relative to the reference version. All experiments were conducted on the same laptop computer, with a 2.4 GHz i7-4700HQ CPU, 16GB of RAM, running Linux Kubuntu 17.04. The algorithms are implemented in C++, compiled with -O3.

Table 1. Software Acceleration Results.

Version	PWC (%)	Speed (FPS)	Relative Speed
Without Post-processing			
Reference	1.75	53.00	1.00
Integer-only	1.23	81.25	1.53
Grayscale	1.88	184.65	3.48
Grayscale + Integer	2.33	232.39	4.38
With Post-processing			
Reference	1.66	28.99	1.00
Integer-only	1.08	37.35	1.08
Grayscale	2.42	53.12	1.83
Grayscale + Integer	2.51	52.12	1.80

As expected, the software optimisations significantly increased the speed of the algorithm. In the integer-only case, there is an unexpected improvement to the accuracy as well—this was identified to be due to the approximated log function in the integer version, which was clamped to not return negative values, whereas the reference version included a log function that would sometimes give very negative values that could cause misclassification of superpixels. The grayscale version does increase the error rate, but this is still low enough to be suitable for many applications. It appears that the grayscale optimisation has a much larger impact on speed than the integer optimisation, which makes sense since there is substantially less data being processed in the grayscale version, while the integer version relies on the differences between integer processing units and floating-point processing units being significant.

It should be noted that with post-processing, the grayscale and grayscale + integer cases have very similar error rates and speeds, performing far worse than without post-processing. This would suggest that the current post-processing scheme of morphologically closing and then opening the background mask may not be as suitable when applied to an output derived from grayscale data. This is further supported by the fact that the grayscale and grayscale + integer versions have worse accuracy with post-processing than without. It appears that this post-processing method also does not justify itself in terms of computation time, as in the reference and integer-only cases it only reduces the error rate by about 0.1–0.2% but slows down the algorithm by 45–55%.

For a standard case where SuperBE is being used on a desktop PC or in the cloud, the grayscale version without post-processing is likely to be sufficient in terms of accuracy while delivering very fast speeds. If it is desirable to add the integer optimisation on top for hardware implementation, then the effect on accuracy is relatively limited and likely to be acceptable in exchange for the further improvement in speed. Based on these results, we targeted the grayscale + integer version without post-processing for embedded implementation and hardware acceleration. A flowchart of the resultant simplified algorithm is shown in Figure 4.

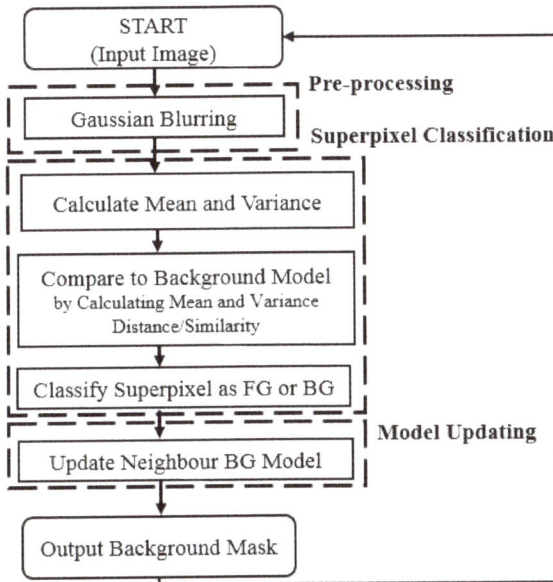

Figure 4. Flowchart of the simplified Greyscale + Integer algorithm for embedded implementation.

4. Hardware Acceleration

It is theoretically possible that SuperBE could be entirely implemented in hardware, for example by describing the algorithm through components in a Hardware Description Language (HDL) and then synthesising onto a FPGA. However, this is a very time consuming and high-skill task, and some of the components might not deliver any better performance than if the same functionality was implemented in software on a CPU. In our approach, we use HW/SW Co-design to achieve the maximum improvement in speed for the least amount of development time, while maintaining sufficient accuracy. This involves combining a Hard Processor System (HPS) which executes the software, with hardware circuits on FPGA fabric. The most important step in partitioning an algorithm between hardware and software is therefore determining which parts of the algorithm are the most computationally expensive, so that if accelerated, would have the largest effect on the computation time. In our case, we used Valgrind with Callgrind to perform execution profiling on the algorithm across a few thousand frames. The results are shown in Table 2. Note that the values in this table do not sum to 100% because we have not included steps that cannot be easily accelerated in our system, such as reading the image in from memory or initialising matrices and vectors.

Table 2. Runtime Analysis of SuperBE.

Task	Percentage Runtime (%)
Gaussian Blurring	4.17
Superpixel Classification	
- Mean/Variance Calculation	50.58
- Similarity Calculation	8.35
- Superpixel Classification	0.12
Model Updating	0.17

In addition to a timing analysis, the communication requirements need to be taken into consideration. In a HW/SW Co-design system, some data communication has to occur between the Hardware (HW) component and the Software (SW) component, which requires a non-zero amount of time. In [10], we identified that the communication channels can become the bottleneck that prevents faster speeds from being achieved. If multiple non-sequential tasks are partitioned onto the hardware, then data needs to be passed between the HW and SW units multiple times. Therefore, it is desirable, where possible, to complete a contiguous block of the algorithm together on the HW accelerator, and then pass the data to the SW processor for completion. Taking the computation and communication times into account, we decided to accelerate the two earliest stages of the algorithm, Gaussian blurring and the mean/variance calculation. It makes sense that these are the stages that may require the most computation time because they process the largest amount of data—after the mean/variance calculation, the algorithm represents each superpixels with two numbers, rather than all of the pixel values within the superpixel, essentially reducing the amount of data that needs to be processed in subsequent steps. We did not accelerate the similarity calculation step because there would be significant communication and memory overheads, as the background model values would need to be either transferred between the HPS and FPGA regularly or duplicated and updated on the FPGA side as well as the HPS side. A high-level block diagram of the hardware partition is shown in Figure 5, showing the data flow between the HPS and FPGA as well as the different hardware components. The buffers shown are modular Scatter Gather DMA (mSGDMA) IP blocks from Intel (Altera) that provide interfacing between the HPS and FPGA, allowing the memory-mapped interface of the HPS to feed into a streaming First-In-First-Out (FIFO) buffer on the FPGA. Control signals are omitted, since the only control signal comes from the HPS to the FPGA to tell the components to reset and start again when a new image is being transferred across.

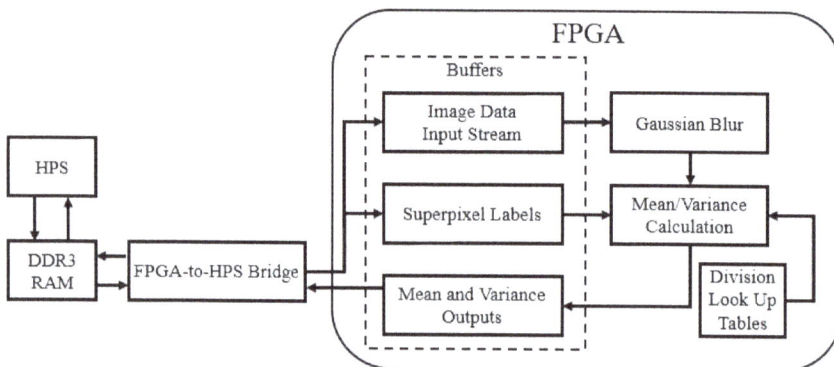

Figure 5. Top-level architectural diagram of the hardware partition, with arrows representing data flow.

Our target execution platform is the DE1-SoC development board, which has an Altera Cyclone V 5CSEMA5F31C6 System-on-Chip (SOC) device. This device includes a dual-core ARM Cortex A9 (which we refer to as the hard processor system or HPS) and FPGA logic cells, Digital Signal Processing

(DSP) blocks, and memory resources. A conceptual diagram of the HPS-FPGA system is shown in Figure 6, where the AMBA AXI bridges between the HPS and FPGA are shown in bold arrows. These bridges allow two-way communication, so that the master side can send an instruction to request data and have the result returned on the same bridge. Therefore, communication between the HPS and FPGA is not single-cycle, creating an overhead for each transaction. We do save some transfer time by interfacing the FPGA with the external memory (RAM) module so that image data can be read directly, rather than transferring the data from the RAM to the HPS and then through the HPS-to-FPGA bridge. We described our hardware components in VHDL, and then synthesised onto the FPGA fabric.

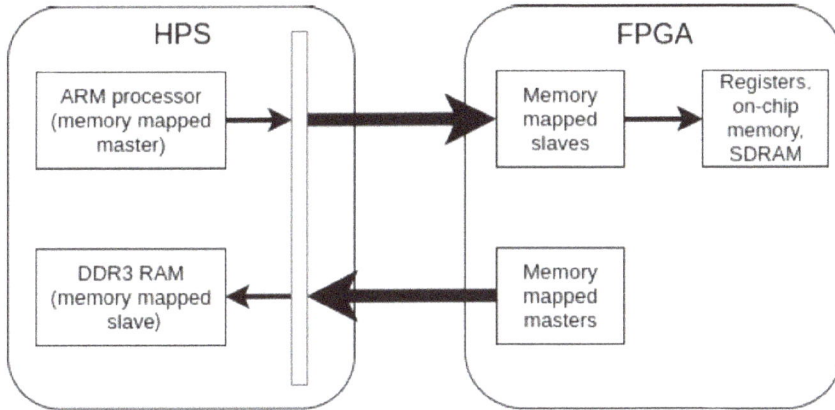

Figure 6. Block diagram showing the software (HPS) and hardware (FPGA) partitions of the Cyclone V SOC device.

The Gaussian blur was implemented using a sliding window approach based on [10,36], shown in Figure 7. Essentially, the filter operation is parallelised so that the convolution operator can be applied to $N \times N$ pixels simultaneously, with a Gaussian kernel to create a blurring effect. To further reduce hardware resource consumption, instead of implementing floating-point multipliers (since a standard Gaussian kernel has floating-point values), the kernel was approximated with powers of two so that the appropriate right shifts could be applied to the binary values instead using combinational logic. While this is not a perfect Gaussian blur, it should sufficiently filter out high frequency noise, while remaining a single-cycle operation with a small hardware footprint.

The mean and variance calculation was more challenging to implement in hardware, as it needs to iterate through all of the pixel values within each superpixel. Traditionally, a two-pass method is used, where the first pass calculates the mean, and then the second pass uses the previously computed mean to determine the variance. This has a critical drawback in that either we have to transfer the pixels between the SW and HW subsystems twice (once for each pass) to stream the data through, or we need a substantial amount of memory on the HW side to store an entire image's worth of pixels. Instead, we used the modified Welford algorithm [37,38], shown in Algorithm 1, which can compute mean and variance in a single pass but may introduce some small error.

This method does require the use of division, which normally requires multiple cycles and is relatively computationally expensive in comparison to addition or multiplication operations. To simplify the division operator, we used a multiply-shift approach and a Look Up Table (LUT) for all possible division values, since we know that the operation is limited to integer values between 1 and 255. Empirically we found that for the image resolutions we were working with, the largest superpixel contained 165 pixels, so we set a safe upper bound of 255 for the denominator, allowing us to store a finite number of multiply-shift parameters. Using the LUT, we can approximate any division operation by multiplying the numbers together and then shifting right, which is the same as dividing by a power of two. While this method does introduce some error since it is an integer approximation, it can be completed in a single pass of all the pixels and is much faster than a standard division operation.

Algorithm 1 Modified Welford algorithm for calculating mean and variance in a single pass

---

1: n = 0, mean = 0, var = 0, delta1 = 0, delta2 = 0
2: **for** pixel in superpixel **do**

3:     n += 1
4:     delta1 += pixel - mean
5:     mean += delta1 / n
6:     delta2 = pixel - mean
7:     var += delta1 * delta2
8: **end for**
9: var /= n-1

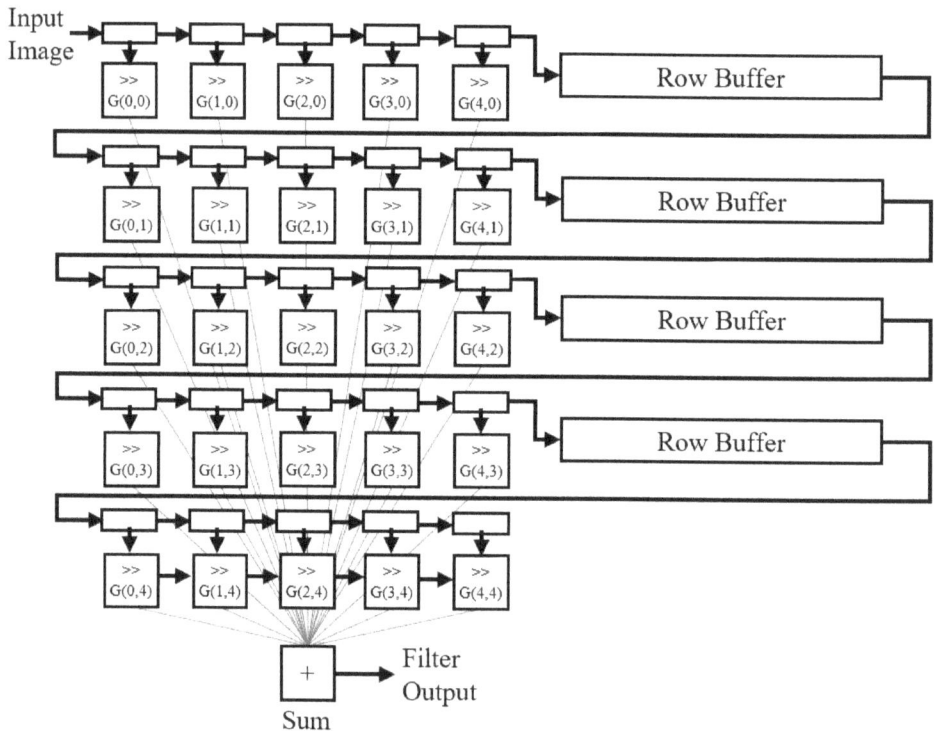

Figure 7. A block diagram showing a 5×5 Gaussian blur operator in hardware, where $>>$ indicates a right shift and G is a matrix representing the Gaussian kernel.

To summarise the communication requirements between the FPGA and HPS shown in Figure 5, for each image being processed, the image data input stream receives one value per pixel (the greyscale intensity of that pixel), the superpixel labels register receives one value per pixel (representing the superpixel number for that pixel), and the mean and variance outputs register returns two numbers per superpixel (a mean and a variance). In order to make full use of the communication buses between the FPGA fabric and HPS, we use the full-size 128-bit bridge, with data packing to concatenate as much data together before transmission in order to minimise the number of transactions and therefore the communication overheads. The FPGA was clocked at 50 MHz during testing, with interconnect logic clocked at 150 MHz, although it could potentially be run at a higher clock frequency depending on the device.

4.1. Hardware Evaluation

As shown in Table 3, running SuperBE in software alone (using the HPS only) is much slower than on a Desktop PC. This is predominantly caused by the fact that the embedded processor is much slower, running at 800 MHz with a Reduced Instruction Set Computer (RISC) architecture in comparison to the 2.4 GHz+ CPU on a laptop or desktop. We use the HPS-only version as the reference embedded benchmark against which hardware accelerated versions should be compared. Firstly, parallelising the Gaussian blur operator has a negligible effect on speed, as the speed gain through parallelisation in hardware barely covers the added communication overheads. It is theoretically possible to increase the throughput of the Gaussian blur component further by instantiating multiple copies of the component and dividing the image into blocks for processing in parallel [39], but this further increases the hardware cost and is likely to still be constrained by the communication bandwidth between the HPS and FPGA.

Table 3. Hardware Acceleration Results.

Version	PWC (%)	Speed (FPS)
Original Reference, HPS only	1.49	4.18
Grayscale + Integer, HPS only	1.74	18.31
Gaussian Blurring on FPGA	1.55	18.56
Mean/Variance on FPGA	3.22	29.16
Gaussian Blurring + Mean/Variance on FPGA	2.88	37.91

The hardware versions of the mean and variance operations add speed to the system, although this is at the cost of also introducing significant error, which should be expected since we are using multiple approximations in that calculation. This is an approximate computing trade-off, where we could have a higher level of accuracy, but this would require more hardware resources and likely reduce the speed. The final HW/SW Co-design version with both Gaussian blurring and the mean/variance calculation accelerated on FPGA in one contiguous block yields a speed of 37.91 fps (normalised for 320 × 240 resolution images), a 2× increase from the HPS-only Grayscale + Integer version. This comes at the cost of approximately 1% extra error introduced into the system, which is likely to be acceptable for most purposes. More importantly, we can compare the final version to the original colour SuperBE algorithm being run on the HPS to find the overall improvement from both the software and hardware optimisations on the same test platform. The overall 9x speed improvement more than justifies the 1.4% higher error.

In all previous results in this paper, the computation times have been normalised for a 320 × 240 image size. In the first part of Table 4, we show how that time varies as the image resolution becomes larger, reaching 720p. As the image becomes larger, the computation time will increase, which is due to the fact that there are more pixels to process when calculating the mean and variance of each superpixel. As the modified Welford algorithm allows this to be done in one pass, the increase in computation time is linear, or in other words, this part of the algorithm is O(n) complex. Since this algorithm is superpixel-based, the classification and model update steps do not increase based on the image resolution, since the number of superpixels remains relatively similar. However, the resolution is not the only factor that influences the computation time; the more dominating factor is how much of the image is foreground, since SuperBE has to spend more time comparing superpixel values to past model values to confirm that the superpixel is foreground. This is reflected in the second part of Table 4, where the sequences with a grey background are from the *lowFramerate* and *nightVideos* categories, where the processing time per frame is considerably slower for the same image resolutions as the first part of the table. This is the primary reason that the normalised 320 × 240 speed is so much lower than the computation time for the *backdoor* sequence even though it is also 320 × 240—the more computationally expensive sequences pull the average computation time up (and therefore push the fps down).

Table 4. Average Computation Times on Selected Sequences from CDW2014.

Image Resolution and Sequence	ms	fps
320 × 240 on *backdoor*	15.3	65.2
352 × 240 on *peopleInShade*	16.9	59.3
360 × 240 on *bungalows*	17.3	58.0
380 × 244 on *copyMachine*	18.5	54.0
432 × 288 on *fountain02*	30.8	32.5
540 × 360 on *skating*	74.6	13.4
645 × 315 on *turbulence2*	75.7	13.2
720 × 480 on *cubicle*	69.0	14.5
720 × 576 on *PETS2006*	89.9	11.1
720 × 480 on *blizzard*	132.5	7.5
720 × 540 on *wetsnow*	149.1	6.7
320 × 240 on *turnpike*	57.0	17.6
480 × 295 on *tramStation*	97.7	10.2
595 × 245 on *streetCornerAtNight*	100.6	9.9
640 × 350 on *tramCrossroad*	166.2	6.0
700 × 450 on *fluidHighway*	217.4	4.6

5. Conclusions and Future Work

This work presents the acceleration of a background estimation algorithm, SuperBE, in both the software and hardware worlds, through a systematic approach towards improving speed while maintaining acceptable levels of accuracy. In software, the main optimisations focused on reducing the amount of data to be processed by converting the algorithm into greyscale and integer-only versions, yielding a 4.38× speed improvement over the original algorithm (without post-processing) at the cost of a 0.6% higher error rate. In hardware, the main optimisations focused on accelerating the Gaussian blur and mean/variance calculation steps, parallelising these steps and adding more specialised computation units. This resulted in a further 2× speed improvement within the embedded implementation. When combined, there is a 9× speed improvement over the original SuperBE algorithm when executed on an embedded processor. This work shows that Hardware/Software Co-design is a valid approach for improving the performance of algorithms, without needing to invest significant resources to develop a pure hardware design. This work also provides evidence that SuperBE can be accelerated sufficiently to be used in embedded real-time processing contexts, especially where background estimation is used as a first step in an image processing pipeline to reduce the workload of subsequent algorithms.

In future work, there is opportunity for improvements to be made to both speed and accuracy if needed. One of the major challenges with Hardware/Software Co-design is always the introduction of increase communication time between the hardware and software platforms, which is often assumed by developed to be free but is actually non-zero and can contribute to a significant portion of the overall computation time. Further reducing the usage of the HPS-FPGA bridges would decrease the communication time, which could be done by directly loading images onto the FPGA and completing preliminary processing there, and then only sending the mean and variance values for each superpixel back across to the CPU for model comparison and updating. This may be challenging, as the first frame still needs to be provided to the CPU for model initialisation, as it would be very difficult to implement superpixel segmentation in hardware. Additionally, the value of doing so would be limited since it is only executed once, during initialisation. Alternatively, a device with wider or faster communication buses between the HPS and FPGA systems would reduce the communication and co-ordination costs. There is also potential for further parallelisation—the SOC CPU has more than one core, and multiple copies of the hardware components could be made to allow independent superpixels to be processed simultaneously if more hardware resourcing was available on a larger device. It is important to consider that most modern cameras provide HD 1080p image resolutions, so some further acceleration may be necessary to achieve real-time processing of high resolution imagery and video.

J. Imaging **2018**, *4*, 122

Lastly, accuracy could be improved by further investigating the effect of different data widths in the hardware components; increasing the bit widths of the mean/variance component would likely make the results more accurate, but would also consume more hardware resources. Investigating more suitable post-processing schemes that clean up the output background masks, particularly in hardware, would also improve accuracy but introduce additional computational complexity.

Author Contributions: Conceptualization, A.T.-Y.C. and K.I.-K.W.; Methodology, A.T.-Y.C., R.G. and A.B.; Project administration, K.I.-K.W. and M.B.-A.; Development/Software, R.G. and A.B.; Supervision, A.T.-Y.C. and K.I.-K.W.; Validation, R.G. and A.B.; Writing—original draft, A.T.-Y.C.; Writing—review & editing, A.T.-Y.C., K.I.-K.W. and M.B.-A.

Funding: This research received no external funding.

Conflicts of Interest: The authors declare no conflict of interest.

References

1. Stauffer, C.; Grimson, E. Adaptive Background Mixture Models for Real-time Tracking. In Proceedings of the 1999 IEEE Computer Society Conference on Computer Vision and Pattern Recognition, Collins, CO, USA, 23–25 June 1999; pp. 246–252.
2. Hofmann, M.; Tiefenbacher, P.; Rigoll, G. Background segmentation with feedback: The Pixel-Based Adaptive Segmenter. In Proceedings of the 2012 IEEE Computer Society Conference on Computer Vision and Pattern Recognition Workshops, Providence, RI, USA, 16–21 June 2012; pp. 38–43.
3. Jiang, S.; Lu, X. WeSamBE: A Weight-Sample-Based Method for Background Subtraction. *IEEE Trans. Circuits Syst. Video Technol.* **2017**, *28*, 2105–2115. [CrossRef]
4. Babaee, M.; Dinh, D.T.; Rigoll, G. A deep convolutional neural network for video sequence background subtraction. *Pattern Recognit.* **2018**, *76*, 635–649. [CrossRef]
5. Wang, Y.; Luo, Z.; Jodoin, P.M. Interactive deep learning method for segmenting moving objects. *Pattern Recognit. Lett.* **2017**, *96*, 66–75. [CrossRef]
6. Lim, L.A.; Keles, H.Y. Foreground Segmentation Using a Triplet Convolutional Neural Network for Multiscale Feature Encoding. *arXiv* **2018**, arXiv:1801.02225.
7. Bianco, S.; Ciocca, G.; Schettini, R. Combination of Video Change Detection Algorithms by Genetic Programming. *IEEE Trans. Evol. Comput.* **2017**, *21*, 914–928. [CrossRef]
8. Barnich, O.; van Droogenbroeck, M. ViBe: A Universal Background Subtraction Algorithm for Video Sequences. *IEEE Trans. Image Process.* **2011**, *20*, 1709–1724. [CrossRef] [PubMed]
9. Chen, A.T.Y.; Biglari-Abhari, M.; Wang, K.I.K. SuperBE: Computationally-Light Background Estimation with Superpixels. *J. Real-Time Image Process.* **2018**, *11*, 1–17. [CrossRef]
10. Chen, A.T.Y.; Biglari-Abhari, M.; Wang, K.I.K.; Bouzerdoum, A.; Tivive, F.H.C. Convolutional Neural Network Acceleration with Hardware/Software Co-design. *Appl. Intell.* **2017**, 1–14. [CrossRef]
11. Horprasert, T.; Harwood, D.; Davis, L.S. A statistical approach for real-time robust background subtraction and shadow detection. In Proceedings of the International Conference on Computer Vision, Kerkyra, Greece, 20–27 September 1999; pp. 1–19.
12. Zivkovic, Z. Improved Adaptive Gaussian Mixture Model for Background Subtraction. In Proceedings of the 17th International Conference on Pattern Recognition, Cambridge, UK, 26 August 2004; Volume 2, pp. 28–31.
13. KaewTraKulPong, P.; Bowden, R. An improved adaptive background mixture model for real-time tracking with shadow detection. *Video-Based Surveill. Syst.* **2002**, *1*, 135–144.
14. Tian, Y.L.; Lu, M.; Hampapur, A. Robust and efficient foreground analysis for real-time video surveillance. In Proceedings of the 2005 IEEE Computer Society Conference on Computer Vision and Pattern Recognition (CVPR'05), San Diego, CA, USA, 20–25 June 2005; Volume 1, pp. 1182–1187.
15. Wang, Y.; Jodoin, P.; Porikli, F.M.; Konrad, J.; Benezeth, Y.; Ishwar, P. CDnet 2014: An Expanded Change Detection Benchmark Dataset. In Proceedings of the Conference on Computer Vision and Pattern Recognition, Columbus, OH, USA, 24–27 June 2014; pp. 393–400.
16. Sajid, H.; Cheung, S.C.S. Universal Multimode Background Subtraction. *IEEE Trans. Image Process.* **2017**, *26*, 3249–3260. [CrossRef] [PubMed]

17. Brutzer, S.; Höferlin, B.; Heidemann, G. Evaluation of background subtraction techniques for video surveillance. In Proceedings of the Conference on Computer Vision and Pattern Recognition, Colorado Springs, CO, USA, 20–25 June 2011; pp. 1937–1944.

18. Bouwmans, T. Traditional and recent approaches in background modeling for foreground detection: An overview. *Comput. Sci. Rev.* **2014**, *11*, 31–66. [CrossRef]

19. Sobral, A.; Vacavant, A. A comprehensive review of background subtraction algorithms evaluated with synthetic and real videos. *Comput. Vis. Image Underst.* **2014**, *122*, 4–21. [CrossRef]

20. Gordon, G.; Darrell, T.; Harville, M.; Woodfill, J. Background estimation and removal based on range and color. In Proceedings of the 1999 IEEE Computer Society Conference on Computer Vision and Pattern Recognition, Fort Collins, CO, USA, 23–25 June 1999; Volume 2, pp. 459–464.

21. Giordano, D.; Murabito, F.; Palazzo, S.; Spampinato, C. Superpixel-based video object segmentation using perceptual organization and location prior. In Proceedings of the IEEE Conference on Computer Vision and Pattern Recognition (CVPR), Boston, MA, USA, 7–12 June 2015; pp. 4814–4822.

22. Lim, J.; Han, B. Generalized Background Subtraction Using Superpixels with Label Integrated Motion Estimation. In Proceedings of the European Conference on Computer Vision, Zurich, Switzerland, 6–12 September 2014; pp. 173–187.

23. Schick, A.; Bäuml, M.; Stiefelhagen, R. Improving foreground segmentations with probabilistic superpixel Markov random fields. In Proceedings of the 2012 IEEE Computer Society Conference on Computer Vision and Pattern Recognition Workshops, Providence, RI, USA, 16–21 June 2012; pp. 27–31.

24. Shu, G.; Dehghan, A.; Shah, M. Improving an Object Detector and Extracting Regions Using Superpixels. In Proceedings of the IEEE Conference on Computer Vision and Pattern Recognition, Portland, OR, USA, 23–28 June 2013; pp. 3721–3727.

25. Achanta, R.; Shaji, A.; Smith, K.; Lucchi, A.; Fua, P.; Süsstrunk, S. SLIC Superpixels Compared to State-of-the-Art Superpixel Methods. *IEEE Trans. Pattern Anal. Mach. Intell.* **2012**, *34*, 2274–2282. [CrossRef] [PubMed]

26. Pham, V.; Vo, P.; Hung, V.T. GPU Implementation of Extended Gaussian Mixture Model for Background Subtraction. In Proceedings of the 2010 IEEE RIVF International Conference on Computing & Communication Technologies, Research, Innovation, and Vision for the Future, Hanoi, Vietnam, 1–4 November 2010; pp. 1–4.

27. Carr, P. GPU Accelerated Multimodal Background Subtraction. In Proceedings of the International Conference on Digital Image Computing: Techniques and Applications, Canberra, Australia, 1–3 December 2008; pp. 279–286.

28. Genovese, M.; Napoli, E. FPGA-based architecture for real time segmentation and denoising of HD video. *J. Real-Time Image Process.* **2013**, *8*, 389–401. [CrossRef]

29. Kryjak, T.; Gorgon, M. Real-time implementation of the ViBe foreground object segmentation algorithm. In Proceedings of the 2013 Federated Conference on Computer Science and Information Systems, Krakow, Poland, 8–11 September 2013; pp. 591–596.

30. Rodriguez-Gomez, R.; Fernandez-Sanchez, E.J.; Diaz, J.; Ros, E. Codebook hardware implementation on FPGA for background subtraction. *J. Real-Time Image Process.* **2015**, *10*, 43–57. [CrossRef]

31. Sánchez-Ferreira, C.; Mori, J.Y.; Llanos, C.H. Background subtraction algorithm for moving object detection in FPGA. In Proceedings of the 2012 Southern Conference on Programmable Logic, Bento Goncalves, Spain, 20–23 March 2012; pp. 1–6.

32. Jiang, H.; Ardo, H.; Owall, V. Hardware accelerator design for video segmentation with multi-modal background modelling. In Proceedings of the 2005 IEEE International Symposium on Circuits and Systems, Kobe, Japan, 23–26 May 2005; Volume 2, pp. 1142–1145.

33. Ali, U.; Malik, M.B. Hardware/software co-design of a real-time kernel based tracking system. *J. Syst. Archit.* **2010**, *56*, 317–326. [CrossRef]

34. Tabkhi, H.; Sabbagh, M.; Schirner, G. An Efficient Architecture Solution for Low-Power Real-Time Background Subtraction. In Proceedings of the 2015 IEEE 26th International Conference on Application-specific Systems, Architectures and Processors, Toronto, ON, Canada, 27–29 July 2015; pp. 218–225.

35. MacLean, W.J. An Evaluation of the Suitability of FPGAs for Embedded Vision Systems. In Proceedings of the Conference on Computer Vision and Pattern Recognition Workshops, San Diego, CA, USA, 20–26 June 2005; pp. 131–137.
36. Bailey, D.G. *Design for Embedded Image Processing on FPGAs*; Wiley: Singapore, 2011.
37. Ling, R.F. Comparison of Several Algorithms for Computing Sample Means and Variances. *J. Am. Stat. Assoc.* **1974**, *69*, 859–866. [CrossRef]
38. Welford, B.P. Note on a Method for Calculating Corrected Sums of Squares and Products. *Technometrics* **1962**, *4*, 419–420. [CrossRef]
39. Draper, B.A.; Beveridge, J.R.; Bohm, A.P.W.; Ross, C.; Chawathe, M. Accelerated image processing on FPGAs. *IEEE Trans. Image Process.* **2003**, *12*, 1543–1551. [CrossRef] [PubMed]

Journal of
Imaging

MDPI

Article

High-Level Synthesis of Online K-Means Clustering Hardware for a Real-Time Image Processing Pipeline

Aiman Badawi and Muhammad Bilal *

Electrical and Computer Engineering Department, King Abdulaziz University, Jeddah 21589, Saudi Arabia;
abadawi0018@stu.kau.edu.sa
* Correspondence: meftekar@kau.edu.sa

Received: 29 November 2018; Accepted: 7 March 2019; Published: 14 March 2019

Abstract: The growing need for smart surveillance solutions requires that modern video capturing devices to be equipped with advance features, such as object detection, scene characterization, and event detection, etc. Image segmentation into various connected regions is a vital pre-processing step in these and other advanced computer vision algorithms. Thus, the inclusion of a hardware accelerator for this task in the conventional image processing pipeline inevitably reduces the workload for more advanced operations downstream. Moreover, design entry by using high-level synthesis tools is gaining popularity for the facilitation of system development under a rapid prototyping paradigm. To address these design requirements, we have developed a hardware accelerator for image segmentation, based on an online K-Means algorithm using a Simulink high-level synthesis tool. The developed hardware uses a standard pixel streaming protocol, and it can be readily inserted into any image processing pipeline as an Intellectual Property (IP) core on a Field Programmable Gate Array (FPGA). Furthermore, the proposed design reduces the hardware complexity of the conventional architectures by employing a weighted instead of a moving average to update the clusters. Experimental evidence has also been provided to demonstrate that the proposed weighted average-based approach yields better results than the conventional moving average on test video sequences. The synthesized hardware has been tested in real-time environment to process Full HD video at 26.5 fps, while the estimated dynamic power consumption is less than 90 mW on the Xilinx Zynq-7000 SOC.

Keywords: image segmentation; K-Means; image processing pipeline; FPGA; high-level synthesis

1. Introduction

The inclusion of advanced frame analysis techniques in live video streams has now become mandatory in modern smart surveillance systems. Thus, the conventional image processing pipeline of video cameras has transformed in the recent years to include some form of object, scene, and/or event analysis mechanism as well [1]. Strict real-time and minimal power consumption constraints, however, limit the number and the complexity of operations that can be included within the camera modules [2]. Thus, some pre-processing tasks, such as motion estimation, image segmentation, and trivial object detection tasks have attracted the attention of contemporary researchers [3]. Furthermore, the increasing complexity of computer vision systems has led designers to resort to higher-level programming and synthesis tools, to shorten the design time. In this regard, Xilinx High-Level Synthesis (HLS) [4] and Simulink Hardware Description Language (HDL) Coder [5] are two widely cited tools. The latter is particularly suitable for the design of large computer vision systems, since it incorporates extensive functional verification and the ability to compare with built-in standard algorithms. Thus, the HDL coder supports quick synthesis and the functional verification of a large number of image processing algorithms, such as custom filtering, colorspace conversion and image statistics collection, etc. However, the current toolbox version lacks the explicit support for image segmentation tasks. To this end, we have developed a Simulink model to extend the capability of this toolbox to support this vital function. Although, various advance algorithms for scene segmentation have been put forward by researchers in recent years [6,7], we have chosen "Online K-Means" [8,9] to be incorporated in our proposed hardware, to keep logic resource utilization at minimum. Furthermore, it has been demonstrated that the use of weighted averaging in the place of moving averaging leads to a reduction in logic resource requirements, without compromising the result precision. Thus, the contributions of the conducted work can be summarized as follows:

- Development of a synthesizable Simulink model for the K-Means clustering operation, which is currently not available as an intrinsic block in the Simulink HDL Coder/Vision HDL Coder toolbox (Matlab R2018b)
- Logic resource conservation through the use of the weighted average in the place of the moving average, which requires costly division operation
- Provision of experimental evidence to demonstrate the utility of the weighted average in preserving the result fidelity of the on-line K-Means algorithm for image segmentation

The proposed design can be downloaded (https://sites.google.com/view/4mbilal/home/rnd/image-segmentation, see Supplementary Materials) as an open-source HDL IP core for its direct incorporation into the image processing pipeline hardware on Xilinx FPGAs. The associated Simulink model and the testing environment are also available for practitioners and researchers, to facilitate further development.

The rest of the paper is organized as follows. Section 2 contains the necessary background, and it discusses the relevant works reported in the literature. Section 3 describes the details of the hardware implementation of the online K-Means algorithm for scene segmentation, using the Simulink HDL Coder toolbox. Section 4 presents the FPGA synthesis and implementation results, as well as a comparison with contemporary works. The discussion is concluded with the identification of possible future directions.

2. Background and Literature Review

Image or scene segmentation refers to the classification/grouping of pixels, such that each class/group represents a differently perceived object. For this purpose, different features are employed to discriminate one object from another. Texture, boundary, edges, and color are some of the most widely employed features to distinguish distinct objects [6,7,10]. The corresponding numeric representation of these features themselves are obtained through various arithmetic operations, such as gradient filtering, colorspace conversion, and local histogram population [7,11–13] etc. The extracted features are then "clustered" to form groups of pixels that are perceived to belong to the same objects. Various clustering algorithms, such as Gaussian Mixture Modelling (GMM) [12,14], Expectation-Maximization (EM) [11,13], K-Means [15,16], and their derivative algorithms [17] have been used by different studies reported in the literature. Some form of post-processing operations, such as 'region growing', are also required to assign unclassified pixels or outliers to form a neat and closed boundary around the finally perceived objects. Figure 1 depicts an example of color-based segmentation using a K-Means clustering algorithm without any post-processing.

Figure 1. Image segmentation examples: (a) Input image [18]; (b) Segmented image with each pixel classified as one of the four best matching dominant color clusters (prominent objects) in the input image.

As mentioned earlier, the inclusion of the image segmentation option as a hardware module inside the image processing pipeline of a camera is constrained by its low-power and complexity requirements. Benetti et al. [19] have recently described the design of an ultra-low-power vision chip for video surveillance, which can detect motion as well as segment the significant portions of the input frames in real-time. This design is limited to specific scenarios with rigid hardware requirements. Moreover, the camera sensor is severely limited in spatial resolution, and is hence, unsuitable for general-purpose applications. Lie et al. [20] have described another neural network-based design for medical imaging applications. Another hardware architecture proposed by Genovese and Napoli [21] uses GMM-based segmentation to extract the foreground (moving objects) from the background. Liu et al. [22] have proposed support vector machine-based image segmentation hardware. These designs target specific applications (e.g., medical imaging and surveillance, etc.), and they are not tailored for inclusion in general-purpose cameras. For general-purpose applications, simpler pixel-based operations are generally preferred over a window-based operation, to reduce the memory and associated power consumption requirements. Color-based segmentation satisfies this requirement, and thus, it naturally stands out favorably over other options, which inevitably require line memory buffers for their operation. Despite being algorithmically simple, color-based segmentation yields promising results, and it has been the subject of various research efforts reported in the literature. Furthermore, since pixel data are presented to the processing hardware in the raster scan order (stream), 'online' cluster update algorithms are required. Liang and Klein [23] have demonstrated that 'online EM'-based clustering in fact performs better than batch processing. Liberty et al. [24] have demonstrated similar results for 'online K-Means' algorithm. The latter is more suitable for hardware implementation, since it involves fewer computations, involving fixed-point arithmetic.

Hussain et al. [25] have described an FPGA architecture of a K-Means clustering algorithm for a bioinformatics application to process large genome datasets. Similarly, Kutty et al. [26] have described a fully pipelined hardware for the K-Means algorithm that is capable of running at 400 MHz on a Xilinx target FPGA. These designs, however, lack the ability to classify the incoming data (pixels) online. Thus, these designs necessarily require full-frame storage in the external memory for classification at a later stage. Moreover, the latter work fails to describe how the problem of the inherent feedback loop in the K-Means algorithm has been handled while aggressively pipelining the hardware. Thus, although the attainment of higher speed has been mentioned as a result of the simple insertion of pipeline registers in the distance calculation module, the cluster update feedback loop has been ignored in the overall speed calculation. Recently, Raghavan and Perera [27] have proposed another FPGA-based design for big-data applications. This design also involves frequent memory accesses, and is hence, not suitable for insertion into image processing pipeline. Cahnilho et al. [28] have described a hardware-software co-design approach to implement the clustering algorithm. The involvement of the processor in the operation necessarily complicates the data flow while processing the pixel stream, and is hence, not desirable in real-time systems. Li et al. [29] have used the Xilinx HLS tool to implement AXI4 bus compliant K-Means hardware accelerator. However, this design also uses main memory for the cluster update feedback loop, and it is not suitable for its incorporation in a camera module as a low-complexity add-on. Khawaja et al. [30] have described a multiprocessor architecture to accelerate the K-Means algorithm. This design is meant for parallel processing at several nodes, and it is hence, not suitable for insertion in a real-time image processing pipeline.

It can be noticed from the description of these hardware designs reported earlier in the literature that the color-based online K-Means clustering is a popular choice among researchers, due to its simpler architecture and performance. However, all of these designs allocate a large amount of logic resources for the centroid update mechanism, due to the presence of a divider inside this module. In this work, we propose to circumvent this huge cost by employing a weighted average instead of a moving average for the cluster update. Weighted averaging replaces an explicit division operation with multiplication by constants, and hence, it reduces circuit complexity. This mechanism relies on the temporal redundancy in pixel values of adjacent video frames, and has been shown to work without noticeable loss in accuracy. Moreover, the proposed design is implemented by using high-level synthesis tools (Simulink) for quick insertion into larger systems, and it has been made publicly available as a downloadable FPGA IP core.

3. Online K-Means Clustering Hardware Design Using Simulink

The proposed image segmentation hardware accelerator uses an online K-Means clustering algorithm, and it has been designed with a standard Xilinx AXI4 streaming interface, so that it can be inserted as an FPGA IP core within any image processing pipeline flexibly. This section gives a brief overview of the underlying algorithm with some desired modifications, to minimize the hardware resource requirements. This is followed by a detailed description of the proposed hardware architecture.

3.1. The Online K-Means Algorithm for Color-Based Image Segmentation

The Online K-Means clustering algorithm is listed as follows.

Algorithm 1: Online K-Means clustering algorithm for color-based image segmentation

---

1:    Initialize the 'k' number of centroids, $C_1, C_2, C_3 \ldots C_k$ with random values.
2:    Initialize the counts $n_1, n_2, n_3 \ldots n_k$ to zero.
3:    **while** 'pixel stream continues' **do**
4:        $p \leftarrow \text{RGB2YCbCr}(p)$
5:        Match the input pixel, 'p', to a single centroid C_i by minimizing the distance $\|p - C_i\|^2$
6:        Increment n_i
7:        Update the matching centroid, C_i, using moving average
8:        $\hat{C}_i \leftarrow C_i + (1/n_i)(p - C_i)$
9:        Classify the input pixel, 'p', as 'i'.
10:   **end**

In our work, we have fixed the number of clusters, 'k', to be eight. The RGB format for pixel representation is quite commonly used by frame capture and display devices. This representation has been, however, found to be less favorable for color matching in various studies [31–33]. The reason for this is that RGB does not yield a perceptually uniform result when different colors are characterized, based on a numeric distance. For this purpose, various researchers have suggested that RGB be converted to LUV or LAB colorspaces [34,35], which yield a much better response (perceptually uniform) to Euclidean distance when differentiating colors. These colorspaces achieve this by decoupling the luminance (illumination) from the color (hue) information, using complex floating-point operations. In our experiments, we have used the YCbCr format, which works similar to LUV and LAB in decoupling the illumination from color information, but it is not as perceptually uniform. The advantage of this, however, is that it is commonly employed by many commercial cameras and almost all compression schemes. Moreover, it can be computed from the intrinsic RGB space by using simpler arithmetic operations as follows:

$$\begin{bmatrix} Y \\ C_b \\ C_r \end{bmatrix} = \begin{bmatrix} 0.299 & 0.587 & 0.114 \\ -0.169 & -0.331 & 0.500 \\ 0.500 & -0.419 & -0.081 \end{bmatrix} \begin{bmatrix} R \\ G \\ B \end{bmatrix} \tag{1}$$

Thus, complex colorspace conversion operations can be entirely skipped if the incoming video stream is already in this format. Figure 2 compares the results of using LAB, YCbCr, and RGB colorspaces for segmentation with the Matlab intrinsic k-means function (L2-norm) on test images. Eight clusters are considered in each case, and they have been depicted by using eight corresponding pseudo-colors. It can be noticed that both LAB and YCbCr colorspaces give visually comparable results. The difference is perceptively discernable only in 'Akiyo' and 'Container'. In fact, in these two cases, YCbCr gives better clustering of the blue screen (Akiyo) and the ocean (Container) than LAB. Prasetyo et al. [36] and Shaik et al. [37] have also noted the utility of the YCbCr colorspace in segmentation operation. Sajid et al. [38] have similarly employed YCbCr for background–foreground clustering. Figure 2 shows that the RGB colorspace works well in the case of pixel groups with markedly different shades of hue and illumination values. However, it fails to account for subtle changes in the illumination values of the pixels belonging to the same object (i.e., similar hue information) and clusters these separately. Thus, the thin outline of the screen in the background of 'Akiyo' is wrongly identified as a different object. Similarly, the field is not clustered properly in 'Soccer'. Both YCbCr and LAB yield a better clustering solution in these cases.

After colorspace conversion, the luminance (intensity) is depicted by the "Y" channel, while chrominance (color information) is described by the other two components, i.e., "Cb" and "Cr". All three channels can be used to compute the vector distance of the current pixels from the centroids of the respective clusters. However, omitting the luminance channel (Y/L) while computing the distance has favorable results in some cases, as shown in Figure 3. It can be observed that including the luminance information leads to an incorrect segmentation of the sky into two segments, due to the brightness variation (Y/L channel). Removing this channel from the distance calculation rectifies the situation for both the YCbCr and LAB colorspaces. Moreover, using L1-norm in place of L2-norm for distance calculation gives almost identical results. This finding is in line with the extensive experimental results reported by Estlick et al. [39]. They found L1-norm to not only reduce the computational complexity, but also to improve the segmentation results in some cases. In our hardware, the use of L1 or L2-norm and the inclusion/exclusion of the "Y" channel can be selected via independent switches under software control, to facilitate catering to different environments.

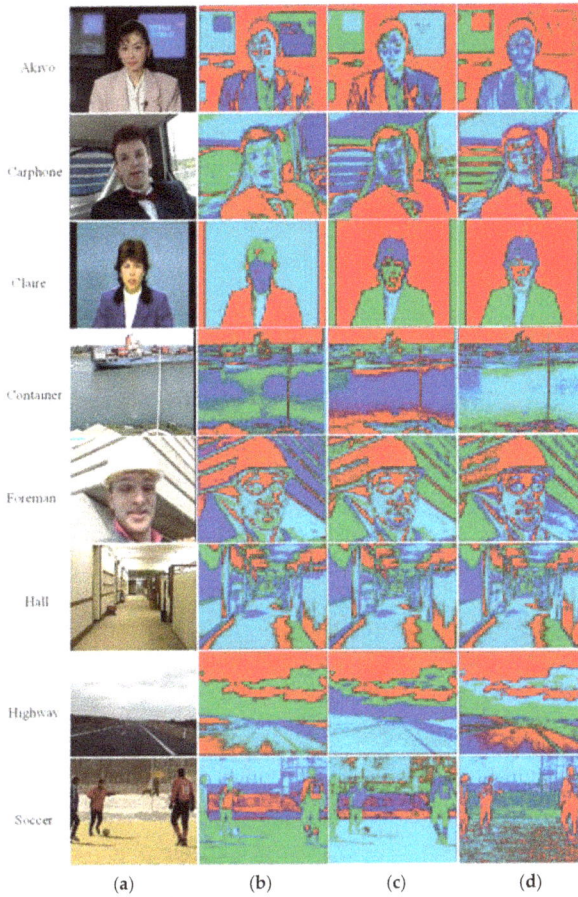

Figure 2. Color-based segmentation using the Matlab intrinsic k-means function: (**a**) Input image; (**b**) Output using the "LAB" colorspace; (**c**) Output using the "YCbCr" colorspace; (**d**) Output using the "RGB" colorspace.

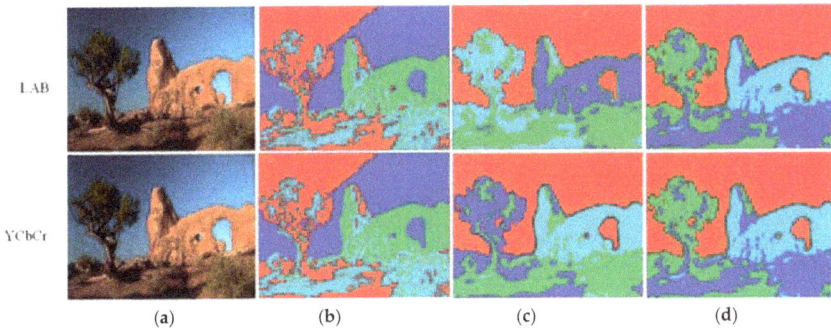

Figure 3. The Effect of using the luminance channel and the distance measure on clustering performance: (**a**) Original image; (**b**) Including the Y/L channel with L2 norm; (**c**) Excluding the Y/L channel with L2 norm; (**d**) Excluding the Y/L channel with L1 norm.

In offline applications, the centroids are determined after processing all of the pixels in the given image/frame. The output classification is calculated during the second pass, once all of the centroids are available. In real-time applications, on the other hand, the centroids of the matched cluster (minimum distance) are updated by using the moving average formula. This involves a division operation, and it is the source of major complexity in hardware implementations, as discussed in the previous section. The pixel classification, the matching cluster's index, 'I', is simultaneously output.

In order to remove the division operation from the algorithm, we have incorporated the "weighted average" instead of the moving average in step 8 of Algorithm 1. This can be rewritten as:

$$\hat{C}_i = C_i\left(\frac{n_i - 1}{n_i}\right) + p\left(\frac{1}{n_i}\right) \tag{2}$$

The weighted average formula, on the other hand, yields the following formulation:

$$\hat{C}_i = C_i(\propto) + p(1 - \propto) \tag{3}$$

where '$\propto$' is a predetermined constant that is close to 1, e.g., ≈ 0.999. It can be noticed that although the weighted averaging does not involve division, it approximates the moving average in the limit:

$$\lim_{n \to \infty}\left(\frac{n_i - 1}{n_i}\right) \approx 1 \tag{4}$$

Practically, this limit is reached before processing even 10 lines of pixels in a moderate-resolution video frame, such as VGA (640 × 480). Thus, the revised formulation of the averaging operation in Equation (3) removes the need for expensive division operation. This alteration, however, does not affect the clustering performance of the overall algorithm noticeably, since the cluster centroids invariably depict similar variations during the processing of the whole frame, for both the moving and weighted average operations in the online clustering methodology. This behavior has been depicted for a representative centroid during the first 15 frames of the test video sequence "Hall" in Figure 4. It can be observed that both the moving and the weighted averages fluctuate during the processing of the frame, as new pixels are processed in the raster scan order. For reference, centroid values from an offline implementation of K-Means (Matlab intrinsic function) have also been plotted alongside. These have been labelled "True Average", since offline methods access whole frames at a time to determine the centroid values. These a-priori values remain constant during the second pass of the offline algorithm when pixels are classified. We have plotted these values as references to judge the performance of the moving and weighted average-based on-line methods, respectively. Both the moving and weighted average-based methods initialize the cluster centroids with identical values (seeds) at the start of the first frame. It was noticed that for $\propto = 0.999$, the moving average tracks the static true value very well. However, at the start, it takes roughly six frames for all three values (YCbCr) to settle. This "settling" time will be needed whenever rapid scene changes occur in the video frames, and the centroids shift positions. At 15 frames per seconds (fps), this translates to less than half a second. A higher value will further increase this delay. Decreasing $\propto$ to 0.99, decreases the settling time to just one frame but also leads to more fluctuation. It is worth noting that even at this rate, it causes lower fluctuations than the moving average. Thus, the weighted average is a better choice in either case.

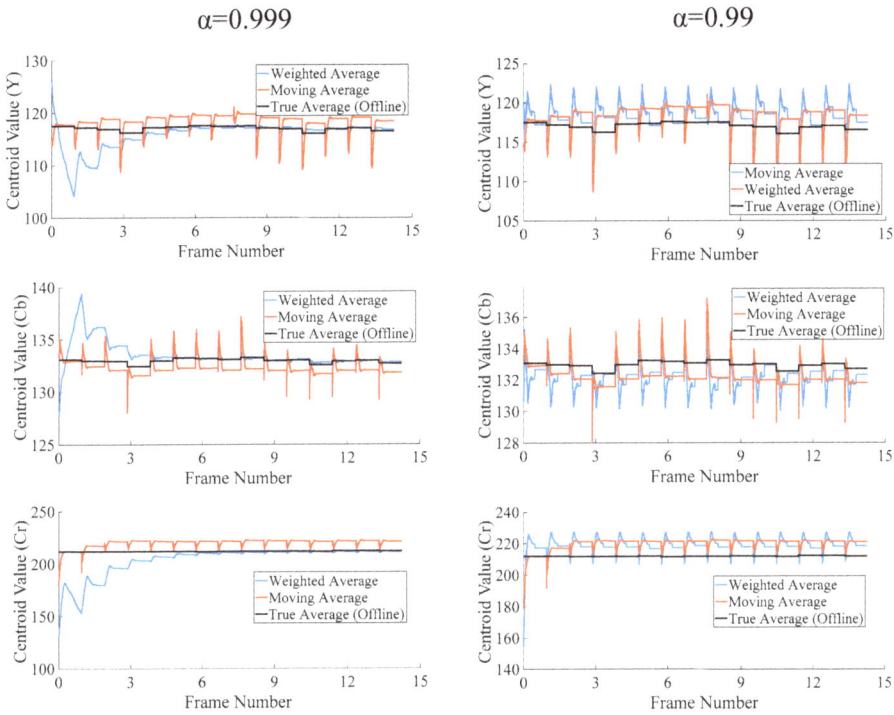

Figure 4. Effect of choice of 'α' on a representative centroid's values for the first 15 frames of 'Hall' test video sequence.

To further investigate the performance of weightage average-based on-line algorithm, the combined error in the calculation of all of the centroid centers with reference to standard offline implementation has been gathered on test video sequences. The root means squared error (RMSE) has been used as the metric to evaluate different settings, and it has been reported on per-frame basis. Eight clusters have been considered in all of the experiments. "Y" information is included and L2-norm is used for distance calculation. The centroids are randomly initialized around the middle value, 127, of the dynamic range [0 255] of the pixels. Figure 5 plots the RMSE per frame for three video sequences, with high motion content. These plots further confirm the observations made in Figure 4. Weighted average with ∝ = 0.999, yields the lowest RMSE for most of the frames. At the start and during rapid scene changes, however, it rises to higher values, as discussed previously. The moving average performs poorly in all if the cases considered, except during a few frames in 'Foreman' and 'Ice' sequences. Thus, even for high-motion video sequences, the error in the centroid's values, calculated through the weighted average (∝ = 0.999) is upper-bounded by the error for the moving average, with reference to the corresponding offline implementation.

Figure 5. Error deviation in the centroid of the online K-Means algorithms with respect to reference offline algorithm on test video sequences with high motion content.

RMSE values for the full test video sequences have been reproduced in Table 1. It can be observed from these values that the weighted average performs better than moving average on all the sequences on average. The former only occasionally performs poorly in sudden scene changes, and at the very start of the algorithm as observed in Figures 4 and 5.

Table 1. A comparison of online K-Means algorithms in terms of the average error in centroid values from the offline approach.

Video Sequence	Resolution	Number of Frames	RMSE	
			Moving Average	Weighted Average $\alpha = 0.999$
Akiyo	352 × 288	300	11.82	7.14
Container	352 × 288	300	7.51	7.13
Foreman	352 × 288	300	9.04	6.44
Carphone	352 × 288	382	6.62	5.77
Claire	176 × 144	494	9.56	6.75
Hall	352 × 288	300	5.96	4.21
Highway	352 × 288	2000	7.26	4.61
Soccer	352 × 288	150	8.06	4.71
Ice	352 × 288	240	3.75	3.01
Tennis	352 × 288	150	8.63	6.83

In conclusion, weighted average is a better choice than the moving average, not only due to its lower computational complexity, but also its better performance. Experimental evidence dictates that $\alpha = 0.999$ yields better results than the other choices. Decreasing this value leads to poorer overall performance. On the other hand, further increasing this value leads to poorer response on startup and high-motion-content frames. Moreover, increasing this value requires further precision in its representation which leads to subsequently more complex hardware.

3.2. Simulink Design Entry and High-Level Synthesis

The online K-Means algorithm has been implemented as a Simulink model to generate the corresponding Xilinx AXI4 streaming protocol-compatible IP core. The top-level module has been depicted in Figure 6.

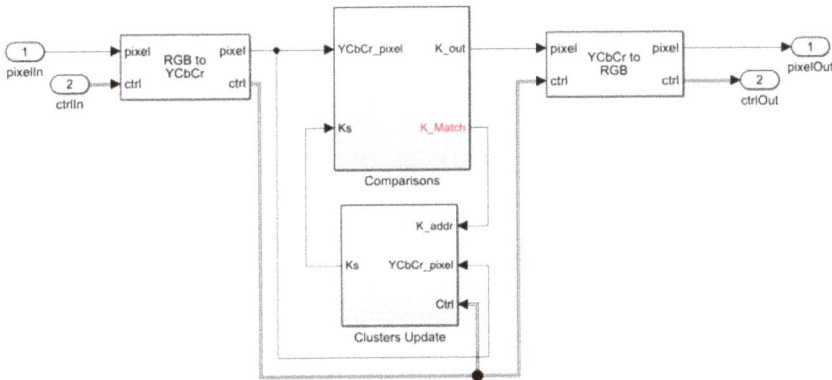

Figure 6. The Simulink model developed for the online K-Means clustering algorithm with Xilinx AXI-4 compliant standard pixel streaming interfaces.

As discussed earlier, the first operation performed on the pixel stream is the conversion from RGB to the YCbCr colorspace, in order to use only color components for segmentation. On the output side, the reverse transformation is necessary if the pixel values are replaced with their associated cluster values. The other option is to simply output the fixed colors that correspond to each identified cluster (pseudo-coloring), as shown in Figure 7. The former option gives a more pleasing output, but the latter may be more suitable for certain downstream tasks. For demonstration purposes, our hardware uses the former option, and this leads to slightly more resources being utilized by the YCbCr2RGB conversion. Both of these conversion modules are available in the Simulink Vision HDL toolbox.

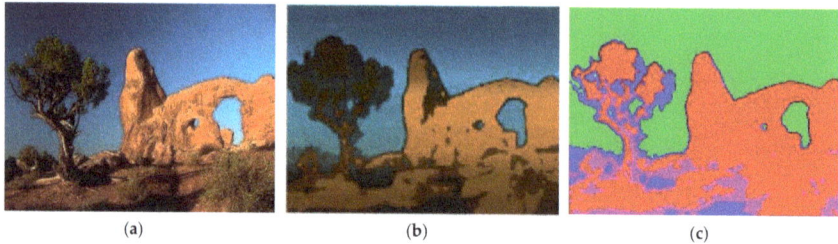

Figure 7. Image segmentation output options: (**a**) Input image [18]; (**b**) Output image with each pixel replaced by its corresponding cluster's centroid value; (**c**) Output image with pseudo-colors to denote clustering.

After the colorspace conversion, the color components, i.e., the *Cb* and *Cr* values of each pixel, are compared against the current centroids of each cluster (eight in our model) in the 'Comparisons' module. These centroids are initialized at random to ensure the proper operation of the K-Means clustering, as discussed in the literature. The "Comparisons" module outputs the classification value of the current pixel (Figure 8), as well as the address of the matched cluster for updating its centroid in the "Clusters Update" module. The updated module uses Equation (3) to output the new centroids for the next cycle. These two modules are elaborated below.

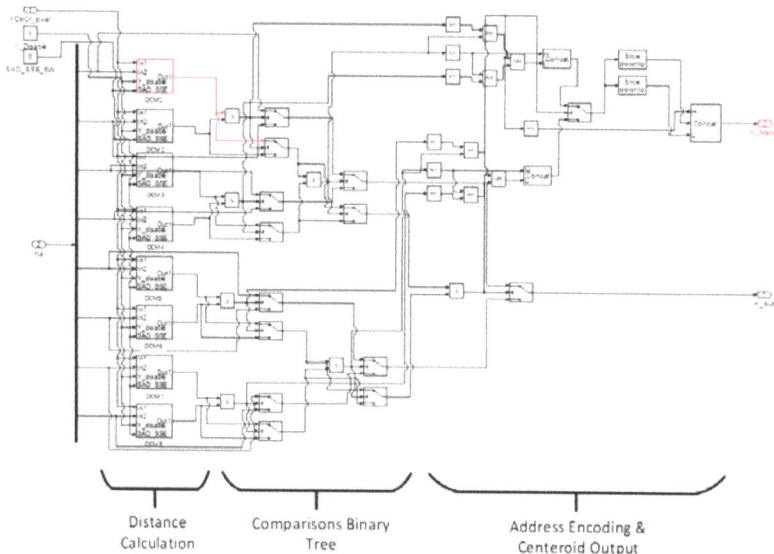

Figure 8. Comparison module to find the matching cluster's centroid.

3.2.1. Comparisons Module

The comparisons module takes in pixel data in the YCbCr format, and compares it with the corresponding centroids of eight clusters in the first stage. For this purpose, eight "Distance Calculation Modules" (DCM) are employed. These DCMs have the option to use either the L1 or L2-norm as the heuristic for a match, using "SAD_SSE_SW" switch. They can also include or exclude the 'Y' (luminance) component, while finding the best match between current pixel and the corresponding centroid through "Y_Disable" switch. The second stage is a binary tree of the comparators and multiplexers which successively propagates the centroid with minimum distance forward. Finally, the centroid of the best matching cluster and its 3-bit encoded address is output based on the logical outcome of each comparator.

3.2.2. Clusters Update Module

The centroids of eight clusters are updated using the output from 'Comparisons Module' and the current pixel. The centroid values are stored in registers as fixed-point values using a word size of 18 bits with eight fractional bits. The precision for fractional bits has been decided, based on the accuracy loss behavior that is depicted in Figure 9. RMSE for test video sequences were gathered for different bit precisions. It was observed that the RMSE error metric shows a sharp rise when the fractional bits are reduced below 6. On the other hand, the allocation of up to 14 bits yields a performance that is at par with the double-precision floating point software implementation. Thus, eight fractional bits seems to be a reasonable choice. Ten further bits were allocated for the sign and magnitude, with a 1-bit margin for overflows. The centroids are initialized to random values around 127 at the start, as used in the experimental setup described in Section 3.1.

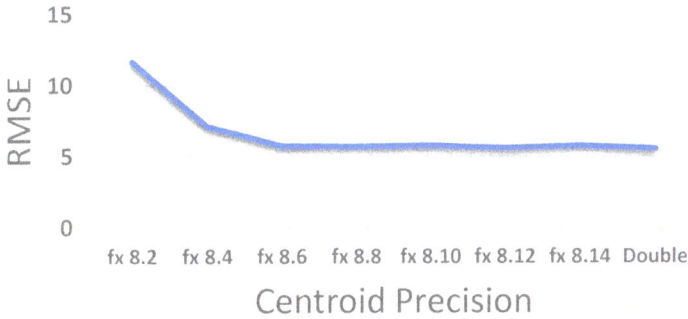

Figure 9. Effect of the fixed-point arithmetic on result accuracy.

The update method (Equation (3)) has been implemented as a user-defined function module with the option to initialize the centroids at startup, using the 'vStart' signal that is available from AXI4 streaming bus. All other components have been implemented by using Simulink intrinsic modules that support direct synthesis. Hence, the entire design framework is highly flexible, with support for functionality testing by using Simulink media interfaces. Moreover, fixed-point hardware implementation can be compared against the corresponding full-precision software model.

Finally, the Simulink HDL Coder is invoked to convert the hardware model into AXI4 streaming bus compliant IP core in the form of HDL sources. To test the functionality of this IP core in a practical environment, a Hardware–Software co-design (HW-SW) has been setup on a Xilinx Zedboard, which houses Xilinx Zynq-7000 AP SoC XC7Z020-CLG484 FPGA running at 100 MHz. The hardware portion has been implemented in the Xilinx Vivado tool, with all the peripherals, as well as the segmentation IP core connected across a single bus, as shown in Figure 10. The software environment is based on Xillinux, an operating system based on Ubuntu for ARM. The application to test the IP core functionality makes use of OpenCV computer vision library as well. This setup ensures that three different sources of video streams can be used to feed the developed IP core, i.e., the High Definition Multimedia Interface (HDMI) on the Zedboard, USB webcam or the stored files on the flash memory card decoded through software library. For the former two sources, the AXI Video DMA core accesses a dedicated section of Random Access Memory (RAM) to read/write input/output frames.

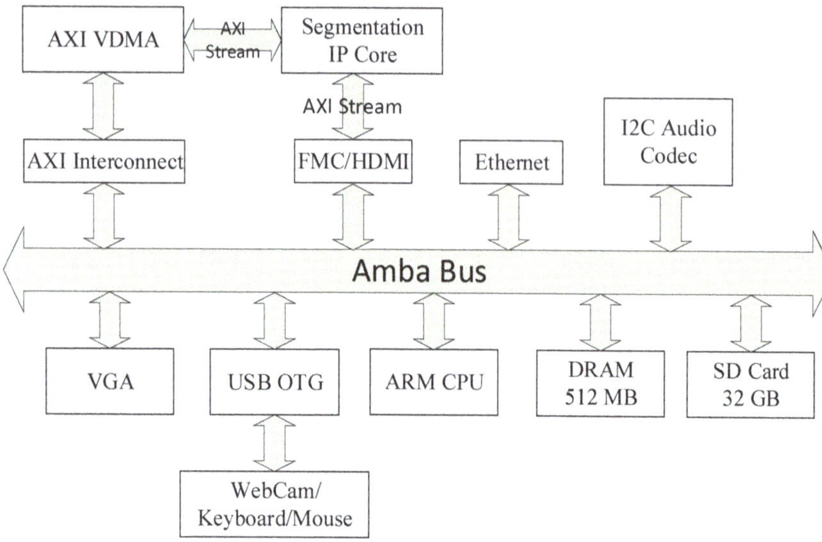

Figure 10. Hardware-software co-design architecture.

Figure 11 shows an operating scenario where an image that is stored on the flash memory card is written to RAM in software. The segmentation IP core reads (via DMA) this image, processes it and then writes the output image (via DMA) to a different RAM segment. The software subsequently displays the output via OpenCV library functions. The continuous video stream from a USB webcam can be used as input in the similar fashion. For HDMI/FMC input/output, however, video capture and display devices need to be connected to the respective peripheral channel. For experimentation, the input/output frame size has been fixed at VGA resolution (640 × 480). The entire framework, including the Simulink models, the Vivado project files for the HW-SW co-design, and software routines are available for download as open-source code, to facilitate researchers and practitioners.

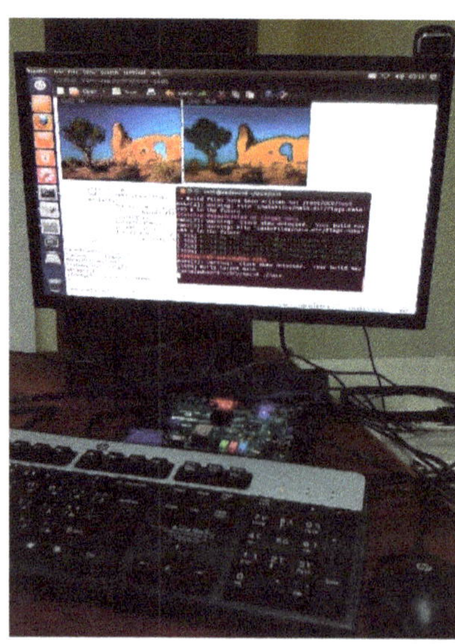

Figure 11. Hardware–software co-design implemented on the Zedboard FPGA platform.

4. Results

The proposed IP core for image segmentation, using the online K-Means algorithm, has been synthesized, along with the entire HW-SW co-design, using Vivado 2016. The synthesis results have been reproduced in Table 2, and compared with those for similar structures reported in the literature.

Table 2. FPGA synthesis results.

Design		FPGA	Slice LUT	Slice Registers	BRAM	DSP	Dynamic Power
Hussain [25]		Xilinx Virtex-IV	2208	3022	90 Kb	-	-
Kutty [26]		Xilinx Virtex-VI	2110	8011	288 Kb	112	-
Raghavan [27]		Xilinx Virtex-6	6916	14,132	-	88	-
Cahnilho [28]		Xilinx Zynq-7000	1583	1016	36 Kb	7	-
Li [29]		Xilinx Zynq-7000	178,185	208,152	5742 Kb	412	-
Proposed	Full IP	Xilinx Zynq-7000	3402	2443	0	62	86 mW
	AXI		458	538	0	0	4 mW
	CSC		719	1014	0	14	7 mW
	Clusters Update		1643	876	0	48	72 mW
	Comparisons		582	15	0	0	3 mW

Hussain's hardware [25] for bioinformatics applications also uses fixed eight clusters, but it does not include the logic resources that are utilized by the interfaces in their final report. This design also does not include the colorspace conversion modules. Thus, in comparison, our design delivers more functionality for similar Look Up Table (LUT) resource consumption without utilizing any Block Random Access Memory (BRAM) parts. Their design is heavily parallelized, and it runs at 126 MHz. As a result, many more slice registers are consumed by the circuit. Furthermore, it requires on-chip BRAM, as well as the external main memory, for complete operation. Similarly, Kutty's architecture [26] consumes a comparable number of logic resources, but even more registers and BRAM resources. This design also achieves a high operating frequency of 400 MHz by heavily pipelining the circuit. However, both of these designs require the external RAM for the cluster update feedback loop, as discussed in Section 2. Thus, achieving higher clock rates for the hardware through pipelining without the loop is meaningless, since the overall operation is much slower, due to the required accesses to the main memory. This fact has been recognized by Raghavan et al. [27] as well, who have described another hardware architecture for big-data applications. Cahnilho et al. [28] have only reported the hardware resource utilization for the comparisons module, and not for the full operation. Moreover, their design requires software intervention which prohibits its inclusion in an image processing pipeline. Li's design [29] is based on a map-reduce technique, which may be suitable for big-data applications, but not for real-time image segmentation, since it requires an exorbitant amount of logic and Digital Signal Processing (DSP) resources for its implementation.

Table 2 also gives the breakup of the logic resource utilization and the estimated dynamic power consumption for the different constituent components in the proposed design. These values have been noted from the Vivado power estimation tool after a place-and-route task for the FPGA bit-stream generation. As expected, the clusters update module consumes the most resources, due to the presence of the fixed-point arithmetic implementation using Equation (3), and the associated registers. It also consumes the most dynamic power, i.e., 72 mW, due to these clocked registers. It should be noted, however, that these estimated power numbers have limited accuracy, and their absolute values are likely to be very different in practical scenarios. It should be noted that the colorspace conversion modules take up to 21% of the share of the slice LUTs, and almost 40% of the registers. These modules are synthesized via the built-in Simulink Vision HDL toolbox blocks.

In conclusion, the proposed hardware design is very well suited for real-time image segmentation, since it requires minimal logic resources, and it does not depend on the external memory for complete operation. As described earlier, and as is evident from Figure 10, the proposed design can be readily

J. Imaging **2019**, *5*, 38

inserted into any generic image processing pipeline as a stand-alone IP core. Despite using high-level synthesis tool for its development, the developed core is efficient both in terms of resource utilization, speed and power consumption. The final synthesized core is able to run at 55 MHz, which translates to 59.7 fps and 26.5 fps for HD (1280 × 720) and Full HD (1920 × 1080) video resolutions respectively while consuming only little power (≈86 mW). To accommodate this lower clock, the AXI interface runs off a slower clock instead of the default 100 MHz system-wide clock. It may be reiterated that the designs reported earlier in the literature do not use the immediate feedback loop in their calculation, and hence, their mentioned speeds are not representative of the full-operation conditions. The low values of estimated power consumption further affirm the suitability of the developed IP core for low-power image processing pipelines.

In this paper, a fixed number of clusters, i.e., eight, was used to illustrate the design principle with weighted average in place of moving average. The extension to a larger number of clusters in powers of two is straightforward, given the modular nature of the design shown in Figure 8 (the comparisons module). The developed Simulink framework for the online K-Means clustering algorithm can be extended to include the EM and GMM algorithms, with minimal effort in the future. For this purpose, the online calculation of variance needs to be added, along with modifications to the distance calculation modules.

Supplementary Materials: The described hardware accelerator IP core and the relevant Simulink models, as well as the Vivado project for HW-SW co-design, are available for download at (https://sites.google.com/view/4mbilal/home/rnd/image-segmentation).

Author Contributions: Conceptualization, M.B.; Methodology, M.B.; Software/Hardware, A.B.; Validation, A.B. and M.B.; Formal Analysis, A.B.; Investigation, A.B. and M.B.; Resources, M.B.; Writing—Original Draft Preparation, A.B.; Writing—Review & Editing, A.B. and M.B.; Supervision, M.B.; Project Administration, M.B.

Funding: This research received no external funding.

Acknowledgments: The authors would like to acknowledge the logistical support provided by Ubaid Muhsen Al-Saggaf, the director of Center of Excellence in Intelligent Engineering System at King Abdulaziz University, Jeddah, KSA.

Conflicts of Interest: The authors declare no conflict of interest.

References

1. New Eyes for the IoT—[Opinion]. *IEEE Spectr.* **2018**, *55*, 24. [CrossRef]
2. Lubana, E.S.; Dick, R.P. Digital Foveation: An Energy-Aware Machine Vision Framework. *IEEE Trans. Comput. Aided Des. Integr. Circuits Syst.* **2018**, *37*, 2371–2380. [CrossRef]
3. Seib, V.; Christ-Friedmann, S.; Thierfelder, S.; Paulus, D. Object class and instance recognition on RGB-D data. In Proceedings of the Sixth International Conference on Machine Vision (ICMV 13), London, UK, 16–17 November 2013; p. 7.
4. Muslim, F.B.; Ma, L.; Roozmeh, M.; Lavagno, L. Efficient FPGA Implementation of OpenCL High-Performance Computing Applications via High-Level Synthesis. *IEEE Access* **2017**, *5*, 2747–2762. [CrossRef]
5. Hai, J.C.T.; Pun, O.C.; Haw, T.W. Accelerating video and image processing design for FPGA using HDL coder and simulink. In Proceedings of the 2015 IEEE Conference on Sustainable Utilization and Development in Engineering and Technology (CSUDET), Selangor, Malaysia, 15–17 October 2015; pp. 1–5.
6. Yuheng, S.; Hao, Y. Image Segmentation Algorithms Overview. *arXiv*, 2017; arXiv:1707.02051.
7. Cardoso, J.S.; Corte-Real, L. Toward a generic evaluation of image segmentation. *IEEE Trans. Image Process.* **2005**, *14*, 1773–1782. [CrossRef]
8. Pereyra, M.; McLaughlin, S. Fast Unsupervised Bayesian Image Segmentation with Adaptive Spatial Regularisation. *IEEE Trans. Image Process.* **2017**, *26*, 2577–2587. [CrossRef]
9. Isa, N.A.M.; Salamah, S.A.; Ngah, U.K. Adaptive fuzzy moving K-means clustering algorithm for image segmentation. *IEEE Trans. Consum. Electron.* **2009**, *55*, 2145–2153. [CrossRef]

10. Ghosh, N.; Agrawal, S.; Motwani, M. A Survey of Feature Extraction for Content-Based Image Retrieval System. In Proceedings of the International Conference on Recent Advancement on Computer and Communication, Bhopal, India, 26–27 May 2017; pp. 305–313.

11. Belongie, S.; Carson, C.; Greenspan, H.; Malik, J. Color- and texture-based image segmentation using EM and its application to content-based image retrieval. In Proceedings of the Sixth International Conference on Computer Vision (IEEE Cat. No. 98CH36271), Bombay, India, 7 January 1998; pp. 675–682.

12. Farid, M.S.; Lucenteforte, M.; Grangetto, M. DOST: A distributed object segmentation tool. *Multimed. Tools Appl.* **2018**, *77*, 20839–20862. [CrossRef]

13. Carson, C.; Belongie, S.; Greenspan, H.; Malik, J. Blobworld: Image segmentation using expectation-maximization and its application to image querying. *IEEE Trans. Pattern Anal. Mach. Intell.* **2002**, *24*, 1026–1038. [CrossRef]

14. Liang, J.; Guo, J.; Liu, X.; Lao, S. Fine-Grained Image Classification with Gaussian Mixture Layer. *IEEE Access* **2018**, *6*, 53356–53367. [CrossRef]

15. Dhanachandra, N.; Manglem, K.; Chanu, Y.J. Image Segmentation Using K-means Clustering Algorithm and Subtractive Clustering Algorithm. *Procedia Comput. Sci.* **2015**, *54*, 764–771. [CrossRef]

16. Qureshi, M.N.; Ahamad, M.V. An Improved Method for Image Segmentation Using K-Means Clustering with Neutrosophic Logic. *Procedia Comput. Sci.* **2018**, *132*, 534–540. [CrossRef]

17. Bahadure, N.B.; Ray, A.K.; Thethi, H.P. Performance analysis of image segmentation using watershed algorithm, fuzzy C-means of clustering algorithm and Simulink design. In Proceedings of the 2016 3rd International Conference on Computing for Sustainable Global Development (INDIACom), New Delhi, India, 16–18 March 2016; pp. 1160–1164.

18. Martin, D.; Fowlkes, C.; Tal, D.; Malik, J. A database of human segmented natural images and its application to evaluating segmentation algorithms and measuring ecological statistics. In Proceedings of the Eighth IEEE International Conference on Computer Vision (ICCV 2001), Vancouver, BC, Canada, 7–14 July 2001; Volume 412, pp. 416–423.

19. Benetti, M.; Gottardi, M.; Mayr, T.; Passerone, R. A Low-Power Vision System With Adaptive Background Subtraction and Image Segmentation for Unusual Event Detection. *IEEE Trans. Circuits Syst. I Regul. Pap.* **2018**, *65*, 3842–3853. [CrossRef]

20. Liu, Z.; Zhuo, C.; Xu, X. Efficient segmentation method using quantised and non-linear CeNN for breast tumour classification. *Electron. Lett.* **2018**, *54*, 737–738. [CrossRef]

21. Genovese, M.; Napoli, E. ASIC and FPGA Implementation of the Gaussian Mixture Model Algorithm for Real-Time Segmentation of High Definition Video. *IEEE Trans. Very Large Scale Integr. (VLSI) Syst.* **2014**, *22*, 537–547. [CrossRef]

22. Liu, H.; Zhao, Y.; Xie, G. Image segmentation implementation based on FPGA and SVM. In Proceedings of the 2017 3rd International Conference on Control, Automation and Robotics (ICCAR), Nagoya, Japan, 24–26 April 2017; pp. 405–409.

23. Liang, P.; Klein, D. Online EM for unsupervised models. In Proceedings of the Human Language Technologies: The 2009 Annual Conference of the North American Chapter of the Association for Computational Linguistics, Boulder, CO, USA, 1–3 June 2009; pp. 611–619.

24. Liberty, E.; Sriharsha, R.; Sviridenko, M. An Algorithm for Online K-Means Clustering. *arXiv*, 2014; arXiv:1412.5721.

25. Hussain, H.M.; Benkrid, K.; Seker, H.; Erdogan, A.T. FPGA implementation of K-means algorithm for bioinformatics application: An accelerated approach to clustering Microarray data. In Proceedings of the 2011 NASA/ESA Conference on Adaptive Hardware and Systems (AHS), San Diego, CA, USA, 6–9 June 2011; pp. 248–255.

26. Kutty, J.S.S.; Boussaid, F.; Amira, A. A high speed configurable FPGA architecture for K-mean clustering. In Proceedings of the 2013 IEEE International Symposium on Circuits and Systems (ISCAS2013), Beijing, China, 19–23 May 2013; pp. 1801–1804.

27. Raghavan, R.; Perera, D.G. A fast and scalable FPGA-based parallel processing architecture for K-means clustering for big data analysis. In Proceedings of the 2017 IEEE Pacific Rim Conference on Communications, Computers and Signal Processing (PACRIM), Victoria, BC, Canada, 21–23 August 2017; pp. 1–8.

28. Canilho, J.; Véstias, M.; Neto, H. Multi-core for K-means clustering on FPGA. In Proceedings of the 2016 26th International Conference on Field Programmable Logic and Applications (FPL), Lausanne, Switzerland, 29 August–2 September 2016; pp. 1–4.
29. Li, Z.; Jin, J.; Wang, L. High-performance K-means Implementation based on a Coarse-grained Map-Reduce Architecture. *CoRR* **2016**.
30. Khawaja, S.G.; Akram, M.U.; Khan, S.A.; Ajmal, A. A novel multiprocessor architecture for K-means clustering algorithm based on network-on-chip. In Proceedings of the 2016 19th International Multi-Topic Conference (INMIC), Islamabad, Pakistan, 5–6 December 2016; pp. 1–5.
31. Kumar, P.; Miklavcic, J.S. Analytical Study of Colour Spaces for Plant Pixel Detection. *J. Imaging* **2018**, *4*, 42. [CrossRef]
32. Guo, D.; Ming, X. Color clustering and learning for image segmentation based on neural networks. *IEEE Trans. Neural Netw.* **2005**, *16*, 925–936. [CrossRef]
33. Sawicki, D.J.; Miziolek, W. Human colour skin detection in CMYK colour space. *IET Image Process.* **2015**, *9*, 751–757. [CrossRef]
34. Wang, X.; Tang, Y.; Masnou, S.; Chen, L. A Global/Local Affinity Graph for Image Segmentation. *IEEE Trans. Image Process.* **2015**, *24*, 1399–1411. [CrossRef]
35. Scharr, H.; Minervini, M.; French, A.P.; Klukas, C.; Kramer, D.M.; Liu, X.; Luengo, I.; Pape, J.-M.; Polder, G.; Vukadinovic, D.; et al. Leaf segmentation in plant phenotyping: A collation study. *Mach. Vis. Appl.* **2016**, *27*, 585–606. [CrossRef]
36. Prasetyo, E.; Adityo, R.D.; Suciati, N.; Fatichah, C. Mango leaf image segmentation on HSV and YCbCr color spaces using Otsu thresholding. In Proceedings of the 2017 3rd International Conference on Science and Technology—Computer (ICST), Yogyakarta, Indonesia, 11–12 July 2017; pp. 99–103.
37. Shaik, K.B.; Ganesan, P.; Kalist, V.; Sathish, B.S.; Jenitha, J.M.M. Comparative Study of Skin Color Detection and Segmentation in HSV and YCbCr Color Space. *Procedia Comput. Sci.* **2015**, *57*, 41–48. [CrossRef]
38. Sajid, H.; Cheung, S.S. Universal Multimode Background Subtraction. *IEEE Trans. Image Process.* **2017**, *26*, 3249–3260. [CrossRef]
39. Estlick, M.; Leeser, M.; Theiler, J.; Szymanski, J.J. Algorithmic transformations in the implementation of K-means clustering on reconfigurable hardware. In Proceedings of the 2001 ACM/SIGDA Ninth International Symposium on Field Programmable Gate Arrays, Monterey, CA, USA, 11–13 February 2001; pp. 103–110.

Journal of
Imaging

MDPI

Article

Efficient FPGA Implementation of Automatic Nuclei Detection in Histopathology Images

Haonan Zhou, Raju Machupalli and Mrinal Mandal *

Department of Electrical and Computer Engineering, University of Alberta, Edmonton, AB T6G 2R3, Canada; haonan8@ualberta.ca (H.Z.); machupal@ualberta.ca (R.M.)
* Correspondence: mmandal@ualberta.ca

Received: 30 November 2018; Accepted: 11 January 2019; Published: 17 January 2019

Abstract: Accurate and efficient detection of cell nuclei is an important step towards the development of a pathology-based Computer Aided Diagnosis. Generally, high-resolution histopathology images are very large, in the order of billion pixels, therefore nuclei detection is a highly compute intensive task, and software implementation requires a significant amount of processing time. To assist the doctors in real time, special hardware accelerators, which can reduce the processing time, are required. In this paper, we propose a Field Programmable Gate Array (FPGA) implementation of automated nuclei detection algorithm using generalized Laplacian of Gaussian filters. The experimental results show that the implemented architecture has the potential to provide a significant improvement in processing time without losing detection accuracy.

Keywords: FPGA implementation; hardware architecture; image processing; histopathology; generalized Laplacian of Gaussian filter; nuclei detection; mean Shift clustering

1. Introduction

Many diseases are diagnosed based on the cellular structures in their respective tissue specimens as the cellular structures can provide quantitative information about the diseases and help in the study of disease progression. For example, the density of cell nuclei in histological images is an important feature for automatic breast or skin tumor grading [1]. The difference between normal skin cells and abnormal skin cells can be seen in Figure 1. In human intervened diagnosis procedure, histopathologists typically examine the tissue under a microscope, and the diagnostic accuracy depends on the pathologists' personal experience, which sometimes leads to intra and inter observer variability [2]. To overcome these limitations, several computer-aided diagnosis (CAD) techniques have been proposed in the literature for the diagnosis. Due to a wide variety of nuclei appearances in different organs, and staining procedures, accurate and efficient segmentation of cell nuclei is an important step in most histopathology-based CAD techniques. The detection of cells in a histology image may also be the first step towards cell segmentation.

Since cell nuclei typically have circular shapes, they can be considered as blob-like structures which can be detected efficiently using scale-space theory. Xu et al. [1] proposed an efficient technique for nuclei detection using directional gLOG (generalized Laplacian of Gaussian) kernels on red channel image of H&E (Hematoxylin and Eosin) strained color histopathology images. The technique generates intermediate response maps using directional gLOG kernels. It is possible to obtain more than one point from different response maps, corresponding to the same nuclei in the input image. Therefore, seeds from these response maps are merged using mean-shift clustering. It gives a promising performance in nuclei seeds detection.

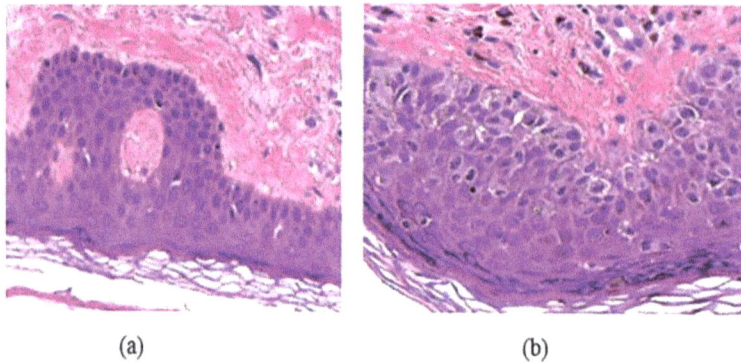

Figure 1. Example of a skin Whole Slide image (WSI), (**a**) normal skin image, (**b**) melanoma affected skin image.

The histological images typically have a large size. For example, a 20 mm^2 glass slide tissue scanned with a resolution of 0.11625 µm/pixel (at 40× magnification) will consist of about 2.96×10^{10} pixels, and will approximately require 80 GB of storage space in an uncompressed color format (24bits/pixel) [2]. In addition, gLoG kernels generally require significant computation. As a result, the nuclei detection techniques typically have high computational complexity, and software implementation on general purpose processors (GPP) requires a significant amount of processing time. For real-time diagnosis, it would be helpful to develop a hardware accelerator for faster nuclei detection. With advances in CMOS and fabrication technology, Field Programmable Gate Array (FPGA) and Graphical Processing Unit (GPU) are being widely used as a High-Performance Computing (HPC) solution to overcome the GPP limitations. GPUs are efficient for data parallel applications with high memory bandwidth requirement and are typically programmed using high-level languages, such as CUDA. On the other hand, FPGAs have more flexibility than GPUs and are efficient for both *data* and *task* parallel applications.

In this paper, we propose an FPGA-based hardware architecture for cell nuclei detection in a histology image obtained using H&E stain. The proposed architecture uses data parallelism. To reduce the computation burden and power consumption, floating point arithmetic is implemented in a fixed-point form without losing much accuracy. The architecture has low latency. The organization of the rest of the paper is as follows. Section 2 gives details on nuclei detection algorithm and its implementation. Section 3 presents experimental results and performance evaluation. Discussion on results is presented in Section 4, followed by conclusion in Section 5.

2. Materials and Methods

The schematic of the proposed accelerator architecture for nuclei detection is shown in Figure 2. It has been found that [1] the nuclei can be detected efficiently using the red channel of the H&E stained RGB image. Therefore, the red channel of the histology image is used as the input gray scale image. The architecture mainly contains six modules: Gaussian filter, gLoG filter, Regional Maxima, Thresholding, Masking and Mean-shift clustering. The Gaussian filter smooths an input image. The gLoG filter is then applied to generate response maps corresponding to different scales and orientation of the gLoG kernels. The Regional Maxima module generates nuclei seed candidates from the response maps. In order to reduce the number of false positive seeds, a mask is generated by applying the Thresholding module on the Gaussian filter output and Masking is done on the nuclei seed candidates generated from Regional Maxima module. Finally, the Mean-shift clustering module clusters the remaining seed candidates to obtain coordinates of different nuclei centers. The anticipated results of different modules are also shown in Figure 2. Implementation details of each module is given in the following sections.

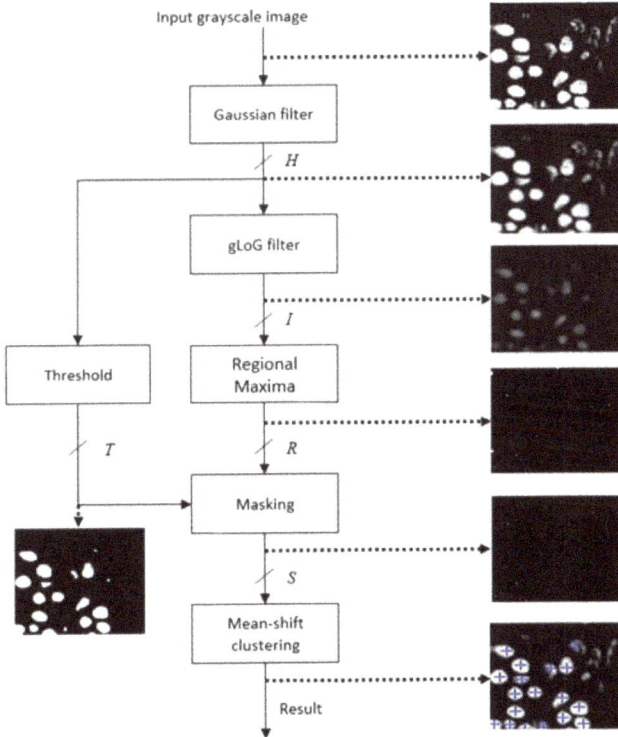

Figure 2. Schematic of the proposed nuclei detection technique.

2.1. Gaussian Filter

The architecture for the Gaussian filter is shown in Figure 3, which mainly consists of a coefficient table, an image register unit, an image window and a convolution module [3]. The coefficients of the $M \times M$ Gaussian filter are generated offline. The normalized filter coefficients (in floating-point data type) are converted into fixed-point data type. In this implementation, 16-bit fixed-point representation (with fraction length of 14) has been used (without any significant loss of accuracy). The filter coefficients are stored in ROM IP core on the FPGA board.

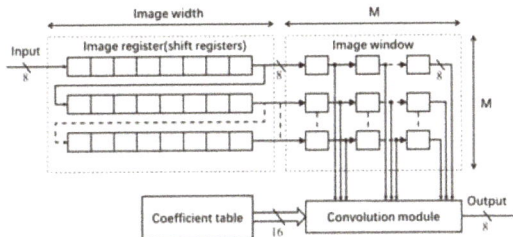

Figure 3. Architecture of 2-D Gaussian Filter.

To enable the process of shifting the window of 2-D filter coefficients for a raster scan of the entire image, M shift register IP cores of length equal to the image width (see Figure 3) are used for generating a Serial-In-Parallel-Output (SIPO) image register unit [3]. Each shift register stores one row of image data. Input to this register unit is an 8-bit image pixel data comes at a rate of one pixel per clock. The M pixels from each shift register are transferred to the image window to access randomly in convolution.

The architecture of the convolution module is shown in Figure 4. The module uses the image data r (stored in the image window) and filter coefficients f (stored in the coefficient table) to calculate the output h. The entire convolution process with $M \times M$ size filter is divided into M cycles. In each cycle, one column (e.g., ith column) of the image window data r and coefficient table data f pass through the multiplier array and first stage adder tree, and is then stored in the register queue. In each subsequent cycle, the register data shifts right by one unit, and the next columns of image data and filter coefficients go through the module and the output is stored in the register queue. This process continues for M times. After M cycles, the outputs of every column (stored in register queue) are added by the second stage adder to calculate the convolution output h (pixel value in the Gaussian filter output image H). In this work, h is truncated into 8-bit precision and the output image H is stored in the FPGA block RAM.

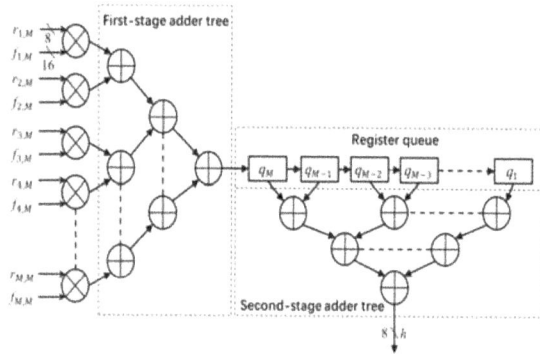

Figure 4. Convolution module. Multiplication of data and coefficients are shown for Mth column.

2.2. 2-D gLoG Filter

Because the cell nuclei in digital histopathological images typically have circular or elliptical shapes, the 2-D gLoG filters are used for nuclei detection [1]. The nuclei are detected by convolving the image H with a 2-D gLoG filter. The gLoG filters are generated from a bank of gLoG kernels $\nabla^2 G(x,y)$ as defined below [1]:

$$\nabla^2 G(x,y) = \frac{\partial^2 G(x,y)}{\partial x^2} + \frac{\partial^2 G(x,y)}{\partial y^2},$$

where $G(x,y)$ is a 2-D Gaussian function defined as follows.

$$G(x,y) = \lambda \cdot e^{-(ax^2+2bxy+cy^2)}$$

Note that a, b and c are functions of scale (σ_x, σ_y) and orientation θ of the Gaussian kernels [1,4]. By changing the scales and the orientation, a set of gLoG kernels can be obtained. In this paper, we generate gLoG kernels (σ_x, σ_y) with $\sigma_x > \sigma_y$ ranging from 6 to 12 insteps of 0.5 and nine orientations θ, $\{\theta = n\pi/9, n = 0, 1, ..., 8\}$. The nine gLoG filters corresponding to nine orientations are generated by adding up gLoG kernels of the same orientation, but with different scales. Special kernels, whose $\sigma_x = \sigma_y$ are rotational symmetric and their structures are independent of the orientation, are summed separately to form a rotationally symmetric gLoG filter. In this paper, 10 gLoG filters are used (see

Figure 5), with nine filters of different orientations and one rotationally symmetric (RS) filter. A total of 10 response maps, with one response map from each gLoG filter, are generated.

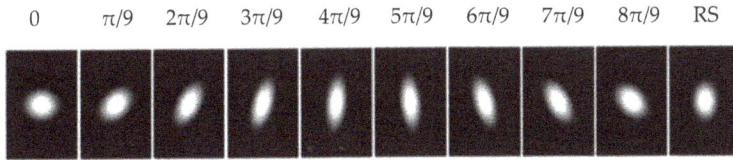

Figure 5. Ten 2-D gLoG filters with different orientations.

For hardware implementation, the architecture of the gLoG filter module is similar to that of the Gaussian filter described in the previous section, except the filter size and coefficients. In this work, the size of the gLoG filter is set to 25×25 in order to match the size of typical nuclei in the input data. As the gLoG filter coefficients are independent of the image data, they are calculated offline, converted into 16-bit precision (with 14-bit fractional value), and stored in ROM IP cores on the FPGA. The output response map (denoted by I) from each gLoG filter is stored with 8-bit precision in the block RAM on the FPGA.

2.3. Regional Maxima Calculation

Regional maxima are connected components of pixels with a constant grayscale value, t, whose external boundary pixels all have a value less than t [5,6]. As the regional maxima in a gLoG filter response map I are usually around the nuclei centers, they are detected in this module and considered as candidate pixels to calculate the nuclei centers.

The principle of regional maxima calculation used in this paper is shown in Figure 6. In Figure 6a, the response map I (denoted by dotted lines) is used as the mask image. A marker image $J = I - 1$ (shown by full lines) is generated and stored in an FPGA block RAM (if $J < 0$, it is set to 0). A *hybrid grayscale reconstruction* algorithm [6], described below, is then performed on the marker image J, and let the output be denoted by J'. After that, $I - J'$ is calculated, and where the outcome value is 1, the corresponding pixel is considered as the regional maxima. This is illustrated in Figure 6b.

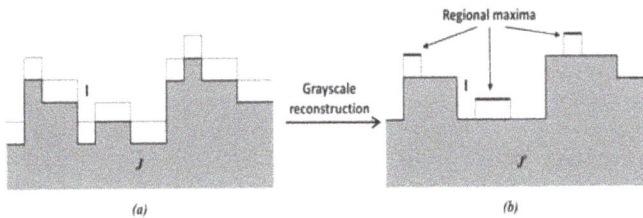

Figure 6. Principle of regional maxima calculation. (**a**) dotted lines, I, shows Mask, shaded portion shows Marker J, (**b**) J' indicates the reconstruction of J.

Figure 7 shows the block schematic of the *Regional Maxima* module, which has 3 parts: *Marker generation, Grayscale Reconstruction* and *Subtraction*. Function of *Marker Generation* ($J = I - 1$) and *Subtraction* ($I - J'$) parts are mentioned in the previous paragraph. The *Grayscale Reconstruction* of the marker image J is done in 3 steps, *Raster scan, Anti-raster scan* and *Propagation*, which are explained in the following.

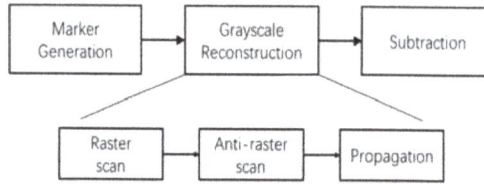

Figure 7. Block diagram of regional maxima calculation.

After generating the mask I and the marker J, a raster scan of these two images is performed. Let p denote pointer of the current pixel in the scanning, and q denote its neighbor's pixel positions.

The eight neighbors of p are denoted as $N(p)$ (see Figure 8a). The 4 neighbors reached before p in a scan order are denoted as $N^+(p)$ (see Figure 8b). The maximum value of $\{J(p), J(q), q \in N^+(p)\}$ is then calculated and denoted as s. Finally, the $J(p)$ is updated with $\min\{s, I(p)\}$. After the raster scan, an anti-raster scan (scanning from the bottom pixel) of I (i.e., the original image) and updated J is performed in a similar way. This time, it checks if for a pixel p, there exists a pixel q ($q \in N^+(p)$) such that $J(q) < J(p)$ and $J(q) < I(q)$, the q value is stored in the FIFO (First In First Out) queue.

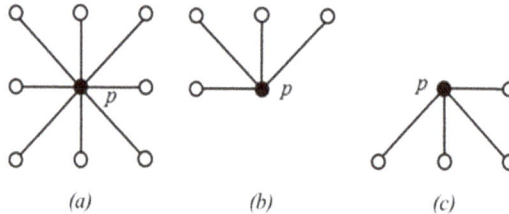

Figure 8. Illustration of neighbors of pixel p. (a) $N(p)$. (b) $N^+(p)$, (c) $N^-(p)$.

After the anti-raster scan, the propagation step is performed on the FIFO structure. In the beginning, the FIFO is checked, if it is empty, the process of grayscale reconstruction is completed; if it is not, the point which is at the beginning of the FIFO is popped out and denoted as p. The values of $I(p), J(p), J(q)$ and $I(q), q \in N(p)$ are read from images I and J. If there exist any $q \in N(p)$, such that $J(q) < J(p)$ and $J(q) \neq I(q)$, the minimum value between $J(p)$ and $I(q)$ is given to $J(q)$ and the q is put into the queue. Then another round of the loop begins. This process continues until there are no data in the queue. The updated J is the grayscale reconstructed marker image and is denoted as J'.

Finally, a binary response map $R = I - J'$ is calculated for each gLoG output, and stored in the FPGA RAM, where a binary value of 1 indicates the regional maxima.

2.4. Thresholding

The thresholding module converts the Gaussian lowpass filtered image into a binaryimage of foreground (i.e., nuclei) and background pixels. The threshold value for an input image can be calculated using any adaptive threshold methods for more effectiveness in eliminating false regional maxima in binary response map R. However, in this implementation, a global threshold value is used for simplicity. The thresholded image T is generated from the lowpass filtered image H as follows:

$$T(m,n) = \begin{cases} 1 \ (nuclei) & if \ H(m,n) < \tau \\ 0 \ (backg) & otherwise \end{cases},$$

where (m,n) is a pixel coordinate. The threshold value τ is calculated offline using Otsu's method. Implementation of above the Equation is done using a comparator, and T is stored in FPGA RAM.

2.5. Masking

A response map R_i, $1 \le i \le 10$ corresponding to 10 response maps may have false regional maxima, due to noise in the input image. The *masking* module eliminates the false maxima that are located outside nuclei masks T generated by the thresholding module. The output M of the module is calculated as follows:

$$M_i(m, n) = R_i(m, n) \,\&\, T(m, n),$$

where & is a logical AND operation. The pixel locations with $M_i(m, n) = 1$ correspond to nuclei seed candidates. The seed candidate locations from all M matrices are combined and stored in the FPGA RAM. Let the set of candidate nuclei coordinates be denoted by S.

2.6. Mean-Shift Clustering

For one nuclear region, there can be more than one candidate nuclei in S [1]. As the candidates corresponding to a nucleus are geometrically close, they can be clustered to obtain one center for each nucleus. In this paper, the nuclei candidates are clustered using a mean-shift (MS) clustering algorithm [7], and center for each nucleus is obtained by calculating the mean coordinate of members of the corresponding cluster.

The MS clustering is like a hill climbing algorithm which involves shifting a certain type of kernel iteratively to a higher density region until convergence. This is illustrated in Figure 9, where the nuclei candidates are shown with red dots. To start the algorithm, pick any unvisited candidate, let it be A and place the kernel center at A. Check if any other candidates are within the kernel (of radius r). In this example, candidate B is within the kernel (see Figure 9b). Calculate the mean of A, B and shift the kernel center to mean position (see Figure 9c). Now re-check if any new candidate is included within the kernel. Figure 9c shows that candidate C is within the kernel. The mean of {A, B, C} is calculated, and the kernel is shifted to the new mean position. The iteration continues until the kernel is settled and no new candidate is included. After convergence, all candidates within the kernel are clustered and the center of the kernel is considered as the nucleus for that cluster. The MS clustering then picks up another unvisited candidate and generates a cluster in a similar manner. The process is continued until all the candidates are clustered. The overall flowchart of the MS clustering is shown in Figure 10.

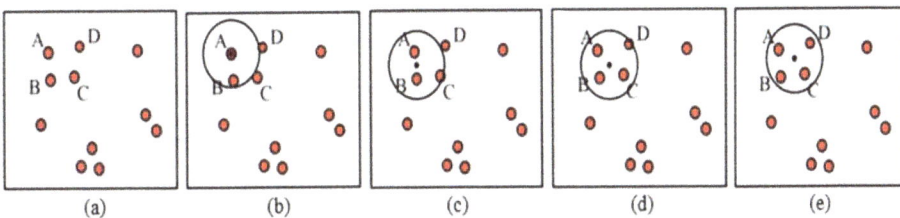

(a)   (b)   (c)   (d)   (e)

Figure 9. Mean shift clustering principles, (a) candidates in a binary image, (b) Kernel centered at A, (c) Kernel centered at mean of A and B, (d) kernel centered at mean of A, B and C, (e) kernel centered at mean of A, B, C and D. Finally, A, B, C and D clustered into one nucleus.

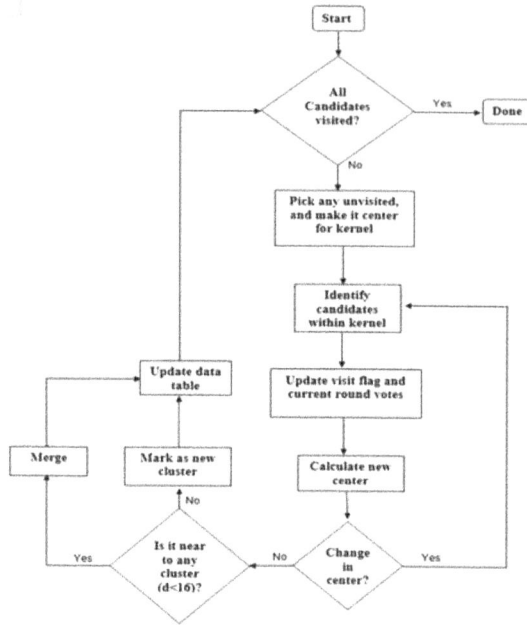

Figure 10. Flowchart of implemented mean-shift (MS) clustering.

In this paper, the MS kernel is defined as a circle with radius $r = 8$ pixels. The implemented architecture of the MS clustering is shown in Figure 11. The architecture has four modules: *Flag operator*, *Iterator*, *Merger* and *Data table*. The *Data table* structure is shown in Table 1, which stores the seed candidates, four intermediate parameters for each candidate (*visit-flag, current-round votes, maximum votes and cluster number*) and *identified Nuclei*. *Visit-Flag* identifies candidates that are visited in the clustering process (flag is set to 1 for visited candidates and 0 for unvisited candidates). *Current-round votes* V_c indicate the number of iterations done in current clustering when a candidate is within the kernel geometry. V_c is set to zero at the beginning of each cluster generation. *Maximum votes* V_M store the maximum value of *current-round votes* a candidate has achieved in all previous cluster generation and the *cluster number* (L) denotes the cluster that has obtained maximum votes for a seed candidate. The table entries are updated at the end of each cluster generation. *Identified nuclei* (N) stores the center of each converged cluster.

In the beginning, the flag operator checks the *visit-flags* table. If there are any unvisited candidates (whose visit-flag is 0), it picks one of those unvisited candidates randomly (S_i) and gives it to the *iterator*. The *iterator* places the kernel center at candidate S_i and finds all the candidates within the kernel geometry (i.e., distance < r). For those candidates (within the kernel), *visit flag* is set to 1 and *current-round vote* value is increased by 1. The iteration is repeated with the center of kernel shifted to mean position of candidates within the kernel. The process repeats until kernel center is converged (i.e., no change in mean position). The final converged point C_k is then sent to the *Merger* module.

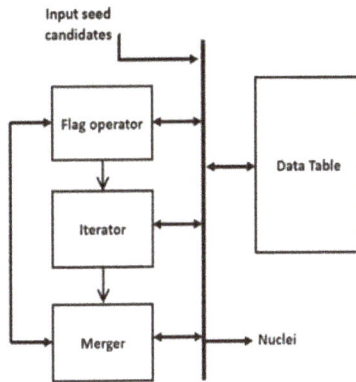

Figure 11. Architecture of MS clustering.

Table 1. Illustration of data table format. Table entry numbers are randomly filled.

Seed Candidates	Visit-Flag	Current Round Votes (V_C)	Maximum Votes (V_M)	Cluster Number (L)	Identified Nuclei (C)
(x1, y1)	1	2	2	1	(a1, b1)
(x2, y2)	1	2	3	2	(a2, b2)
(x3, y3)	0	0	0	.	(a3, b3)

The *Merger* module scans through the *Identified nuclei* column. If there exists a previously generated Nuclei $C_l (l \neq k)$ whose distance to the current convergent point C_k is smaller than a threshold (e.g., 16 pixels), then C_k should merge with C_l. The value for the merged nuclei C_l is changed to the mean coordinate of C_l and C_k. In *cluster number* column, if $L(s_i) = l$, the *maximum votes* value for corresponding candidates are changed to $V_M(S_i) = V_M(S_i) + V_C(S_i)$. If there are no *Identified nuclei* within the threshold distance to C_k, then C_k becomes a new Nuclei and added to *Identified nuclei* column. Finally, the comparison between *current round votes* and *maximum votes* are done. For a candidate $S_i \in C_k$ if $V_M(S_i) < V_C(S_i)$ then $V_M(S_i)$ is changed to $V_C(S_i)$ and $L(S_i)$ to k (indicating that candidate S_i belongs to the new cluster C_k). Example data format can be seen in Table 1.

After the operations in the *Merger* module finished, the *Flag operator* module scans through the *Visited-flags table* to check whether there are any unvisited candidates. If there are unvisited candidates, the *Iterator* is enabled again to generate a new cluster, otherwise, the *Clustering* module is disabled, and the MS clustering is done. The mean coordinate of the candidates belonging to one cluster (corresponding to a nucleus) is considered as the seed coordinate of the detected nuclei.

3. Results

The proposed architecture is implemented on DE2i-150 FPGA development board, developed by Terasic [8]. A simplified schematic of the DE2i-150 development board is shown in Figure 12 (refer to the Terasic site [8] for complete details). The board is an embedded platform with Intel N2600 Atom Dual core processor (Intel Corporation, Santa Clara, CA, USA) [9] coupled with Altera's Cyclone IV GX FPGA (Altera (Acquire by Intel), Santa Clara, CA, USA). The Atom processor has 64-bit Instruction set, 1M cache running at 1.6 GHz clock speed, and is connected to external DDR3 memory. The Atom pairs with Intel®NM10 Express Chipset through Direct Media Interface (DMI) to provide rich I/O capabilities and flexibility via high-bandwidth interfaces, such as PCI Express, Serial ATA (SATA), mSATA, and Ethernet. Cyclone IV FPGA is connected to Atom through PCI Express (PCIe) bus and NM10. The FPGA is connected to 128MB SDRAM (32 bits width), 4MB SSRAM and 64MB Flash memory with 16-bit mode. Both Atom and FPGA has a VGA connector to interface with monitor.

In this paper, the proposed architecture is implemented using only the FPGA (Atom processor is not used).

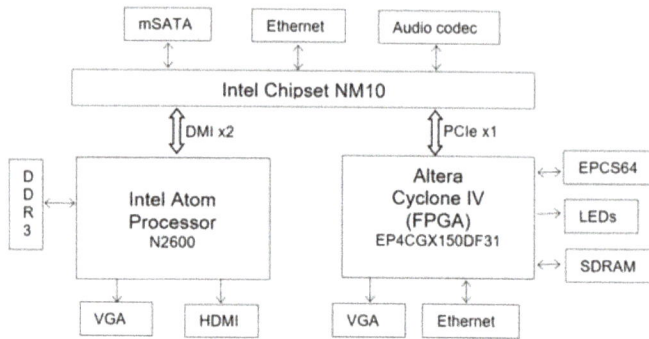

Figure 12. Simplified schematic of DE2i-150 FPGA development board Architecture (refer to [8] for more detailed schematic).

In the implementation, the block RAMs on FPGA are used to store intermediate results instead of available 128 MB SDRAM. Because, this SDRAM has a latency of four clock cycles, with a maximum allowed clock frequency of 100 MHz, which can degrade the proposed architectures performance. Because there is a lot of intermediate date generated and it should be accessible randomly. But implementing the same architectures (with block RAM replaced by available memory) on high-end FPGA boards having lower latency and higher clock frequency for memory can give a similar performance with fewer resources.

Parameter Configuration

A few parameters for the proposed architecture must be defined before generating bit file for the hardware [1]. The parameters are application dataset dependent. The Gaussian filter size M depends on the amount of noise in the input image and minimum nuclei size to detect. Filter size cannot be more than the size of smaller nuclei expect to detect, otherwise it blurs the nucleus. The rest of the parameters, like gLoG filter size, threshold value, MS clustering bandwidth are to be set according to possible nuclei size range in application dataset. In this experiment, the parameters are not fine-tuned to a dataset, but for the same parameter configuration the proposed hardware should give similar results with software (MATLAB) implementation. To check the proposed hardware flexibility with parameters across a different dataset, experiments are done on two sets of parameters. Parameter configuration of two sets are shown in Table 2. The hardware provided similar results as MATLAB [10] with respect to each set of parameters.

Table 2. Configured parameters table.

Parameter	Set 1	Set 2
Gaussian filter size	7×7	8×8
gLoG size	25×25	49×49
Threshold	155	150
MS bandwidth	8	6

The architecture performance is evaluated by comparing its execution time and accuracy with MATLAB for 256×256 size images. Before generating the bit-file for the hardware, the parameters have to be configured according to application and input image data should be initialized into ROM IP block using .hex/.mif file format. As the input is red channel data (complemented) of H&E stained images, MATLAB is used to generate the .hex/.mif file with red channel data. The resources utilized by the architecture for 256 × 256 size image on the FPGA (for set-1 parameters configuration) is presented in Table 3. MATLAB is running on AMD Athlon II CPU (Advanced Micro Devices, Inc., Austin, TX, USA) at 2.90 GHz with 4GB RAM. To compare the results, the detected nuclei coordinates in the FPGA are read out and marked on the MATLAB results. Figure 13 shows the nuclei detection results using both hardware and MATLAB.

Table 3. Resource utilization table.

Resources	Utilized
Total Logical elements	34,475
Memory Bits	4,711,338
PLLs	1
Embedded Multipliers	70

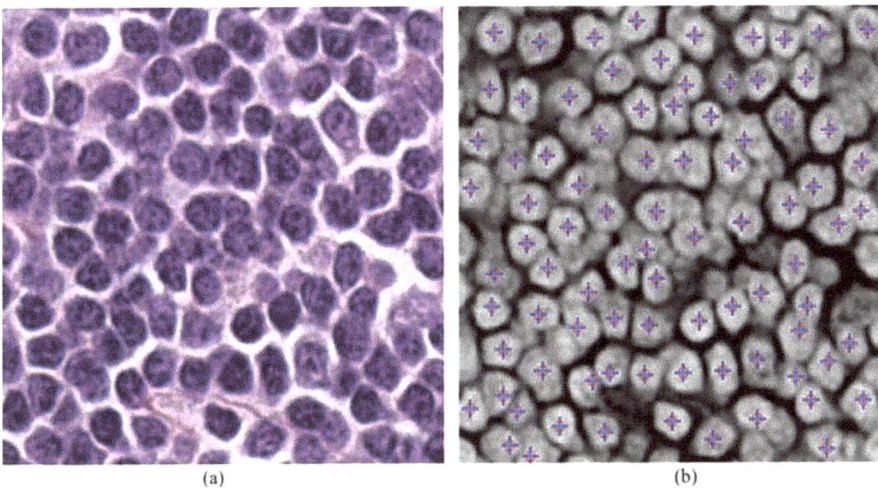

(a) (b)

Figure 13. Results of Nuclei detection with set 1 parameters configuration on both MATLAB and hardware, (**a**) input color image, (**b**) output detected nuclei indicating on complement red channel input image, blue color '+' indicates the nuclei detected using hardware, red circle 'o' indicates the nuclei detected using MATLAB.

The execution time on FPGA measured using counter register, it increments for every millisecond (i.e., the execution time is in millisecond precision) and final execution time is displayed through available 15 LEDs on the board. The average execution time over 10 different input images on both hardware and MATLAB are presented in Table 4.

Table 4. Performance comparison.

Platform	Clock Frequency	Execution Time (in sec)
MATLAB (on CPU)	2.90 GHz	1.694
Proposed implementation	100 MHz	1.108

The accurate detection of nuclei in the input image depends on the parameters mentioned above. Therefore, in this paper the accuracy of proposed hardware evaluated with respect to the results from the MATLAB (software) version (2017b, MathWorks, Natick, MA, USA) [10]. It is observed in Figure 13 that both versions give similar results for the same parameters configuration. Finding the optimized parameters to compare the accuracy of detection is beyond the scope of this paper as this paper is focused more on FPGA implementation.

4. Discussion

The proposed architecture has been implemented and tested for a small image patch of size 256×256. But the architecture can easily be extended to larger image size, as histopathology images are typically very large in size. The total processing time for a full resolution image, with a size $20{,}000 \times 20{,}000$, is expected to be in the order of hours in a regular CPU. With optimized implementation and FPGA boards with higher clock frequency, the overall processing time is expected to be in the order of minutes.

The proposed architecture shows a modest 34.5% performance improvement compared to a regular CPU, which is mainly because of the lower clock frequency (100 MHz) of the FPGA board. The speed-up factor can be improved further by exploiting the data and task parallelism in each sub module. Empirically, it can be said that smaller modules implemented on FPGA give low performance (speed up) improvement over the software (on general purpose processor) implementation as the data parallelism achieved with FPGA can be overshadowed by operating clock frequency. For larger modules, having possible data parallelism can give significant performance improvement worth of going for special hardware accelerator. Our larger goal is to design a CAD system for histopathology for which the nuclei detection is one module. It is expected that the other modules in the CAD system will have larger speed up resulting in a high overall system performance.

5. Conclusions

A software implementation of the CAD technique requires a significant amount of processing time. To assist the pathologists in real time, this processing time should be reduced. In this paper, an FPGA based hardware accelerator for the Nuclei detection has been proposed, and its performance is evaluated by implementing it on DE2i-150 FPGA development board. The hardware accelerator shows a significant performance improvement over a MATLAB, even though it is running at a lower clock frequency. Further performance improvement can be achieved by exploring the data and task parallelism exists in the algorithm. Once the nuclei are detected on the histopathology images, next step in the CAD process is to segment the nuclei and perform the diagnosis in real-time. It is the base model to develop a complete CAD accelerator for many diagnosis processes (processing of large histopathology images).

Author Contributions: Conceptualization: M.M.; Implementation: H.Z. and R.M.; Validation: R.M.; Writing—original draft preparation: H.Z.; Writing—review and editing: R.M. and M.M.

Funding: We acknowledge the support of the Natural Sciences and Engineering Research Council of Canada (NSERC) (funding reference number RGPIN-2014-05215).

Acknowledgments: We acknowledge that Haonan Zhou received Globalink Research Internship from MITACS, Canada to carry out part of this work. We also thank Hongming Xu for providing some software algorithms for nuclei detection.

Conflicts of Interest: The authors declare no conflict of interest.

References

1. Xu, H.; Lu, C.; Berendt, R.; Jha, N.; Mandal, M. Automatic Nuclei Detection based on Generalized Laplacian of Gaussian Filters. *IEEE J. Biomed. Health Inf.* **2017**, *21*, 826–837. [CrossRef] [PubMed]
2. Lu, C.; Mandal, M. Automated analysis and diagnosis of skin melanoma on whole slide histopathological images. *Pattern Recognit.* **2015**, *48*, 2738–2750. [CrossRef]
3. Al-Jobouri, L. Design of a Convolutional Two-Dimensional Filter in FPGA for Image Processing Applications. *Computers* **2017**, *6*, 19.
4. Kong, H.; Akakin, H.C.; Sarma, S.E. A generalized Laplacian of Gaussian filter for blob detection and its applications. *IEEE Trans. Cybern.* **2013**, *43*, 1719–1733. [CrossRef] [PubMed]

5. Soile, P. *Morphological Image Analysis: Principles and Applications*; Springer: Berlin, Germany, 1999.
6. Vincent, L. Morphological Grayscale Reconstruction in Image Analysis: Applications and Efficient Algorithms. *IEEE Trans. Image Process.* **1993**, *2*, 176–201. [CrossRef] [PubMed]
7. Comaniciu, D.; Meer, P. Mean shift: A robust approach toward feature space analysis. *IEEE Trans. Pattern Anal. Mach. Intell.* **2002**, *24*, 603–619. [CrossRef]
8. DE2i-150 FPGA Development Board Specifications and Architecture. Available online: https://www.terasic.com.tw/ (accessed on 15 January 2019).
9. Intel Corporation. Available online: https://www.intel.com/content/www/us/en/homepage.html (accessed on 15 January 2019).
10. Mathworks, Inc. Available online: https://www.mathworks.com/ (accessed on 15 January 2019).

Journal of
Imaging

MDPI

Article

Zig-Zag Based Single-Pass Connected Components Analysis

Donald G. Bailey [1,*,†] and Michael J. Klaiber [2,†]

1   Department of Mechanical and Electrical Engineering, School of Food and Advanced Technology,
    Massey University, Palmerston North 4442, New Zealand
2   Independent Researcher, 70176 Stuttgart, Germany; contact@michael-klaiber.de
*   Correspondence: D.G.Bailey@massey.ac.nz
†   These authors contributed equally to this work.

Received: 2 February 2019; Accepted: 29 March 2019; Published: 6 April 2019

Abstract: Single-pass connected components analysis (CCA) algorithms suffer from a time overhead to resolve labels at the end of each image row. This work demonstrates how this overhead can be eliminated by replacing the conventional raster scan by a zig-zag scan. This enables chains of labels to be correctly resolved while processing the next image row. The effect is faster processing in the worst case with no end of row overheads. CCA hardware architectures using the novel algorithm proposed in this paper are, therefore, able to process images at higher throughput than other state-of-the-art methods while reducing the hardware requirements. The latency introduced by the conversion from raster scan to zig-zag scan is compensated for by a new method of detecting object completion, which enables the feature vector for completed connected components to be output at the earliest possible opportunity.

Keywords: connected components analysis; stream processing; feature extraction; zig-zag scan; hardware architecture; FPGA; pipeline

---

1. Introduction

Connected components labelling is an important step in many image analysis and image processing algorithms. It processes a binary input image, for example after segmentation, and provides as output a labelled image where each distinct group of connected pixels has a single unique label. There are many different labelling algorithms (see for example the recent review [1]). Three main classes of algorithms are:

- Contour tracing [2,3], where the image is scanned until an object pixel is encountered. The boundary is then traced and marked, enabling all pixels to be labelled with the same label when scanning resumes.
- Label propagation algorithms [4] where labels are propagated through multiple passes through the image.
- Two pass algorithms, generally based on Rosenfeld and Pfaltz's algorithm [5]. The first pass propagates provisional labels to object pixels from adjacent pixels that have already been processed. Sets of equivalent labels are processed to derive a representative label for the connected component, usually using some form of union-find algorithm [1,6]. Finally, the image is relabelled in a second pass, changing the provisional label for each pixel to the representative label.

The different two-pass algorithms fall into three broad classes: those that process single pixels at a time (e.g., [7,8]), those that process a run of pixels at a time (e.g., [9,10]), and those that process a block of pixels at a time (1 × 2 block in [11,12], 1 × 3 block in [13], and 2 × 2 block in [14,15]). There have been several FPGA implementations of connected components labelling (e.g., [16,17]), but the key disadvantage of these two-pass algorithms is the requirement to buffer the complete image between passes.

Connected component labelling is often followed by an analysis step, where a feature vector (usually based on the shape, but can also be based on statistics of the original image pixel values) is derived for each label. These feature vectors can then be used for subsequent classification, or even directly provide output data for some image analysis applications. When the labelling and feature vector measurement are combined as a single operation, it is termed connected components analysis (CCA).

Single pass CCA algorithms, introduced by Bailey and Johnston [18,19], extract feature data for each component during the initial provisional labelling pass. The labelled image, as an intermediate data structure, is no longer required, so the second relabelling pass can be skipped, enabling the complete algorithm to operate in a single pass. This has led to efficient low-latency hardware architectures that are able to operate directly on a video stream. The basic architecture of Figure 1 works as follows: For each pixel in the input stream, provisional labels are propagated from already processed pixels (represented by the neighbourhood window). Labels assigned in the current row are cached in a row buffer to provide the neighbourhood when processing the next row. When components merge, the associated labels are equivalent. One label is selected as the representative label (usually the label that was assigned the earliest), with the equivalence between the labels recorded in the merger table. Provisional labels saved in the row buffer may have been updated as a result of subsequent mergers and may no longer be current, so the output from the row buffer is looked up in the merger table to obtain the current representative label for the neighbourhood. For a single-pass operation, feature data is accumulated for each component on-the-fly within the data table. When components merge, the associated feature data is also merged. The component data is available after the component is completed, that is after no pixels extend from that component onto the current row.

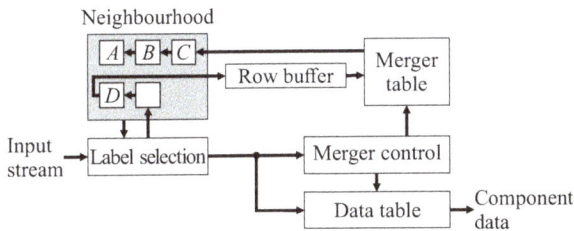

Figure 1. Basic architecture of single-pass connected components analysis.

The main limitation of the first single-pass algorithm [18] was that the data was only available at the end of the frame. In the worst case, this required resources proportional to the area of the image, preventing the use of on-chip memory for all but small images, or a restricted subset of images with a limited number of components. This was solved by Ma et al. [20], by recycling labels which requires identifying completed components, and freeing up the resources. Ma's approach aggressively relabelled each component starting from the left of each row. It, therefore, required two lookups, one to resolve mergers, and one to translate labels from the previous row to the current row.

The next improvement in this class of CCA algorithms was developed by Klaiber et al. [21]. This solved the problem of two lookups by introducing augmented labels. Labels are allocated from a pool of recycled labels, and are augmented with row number to enable correct precedence to be determined when merging.

Trein et al. [22] took an alternative approach to single-pass CCA on FPGA, and run-length encoded the binary image first. Then, each run was processed in a single clock cycle, enabling acceleration when processing typical objects. In the worst case, however, the performance of run-based processing is the same as for pixel-based processing. Trein et al.'s method also suffers from the problem of chaining, although this was not identified in their paper.

The main issue with managing mergers on-the-fly is sequences of mergers requiring multiple look-ups to identify the representative label of their connected component. Those labels that require more than one lookup to lead to their representative label are referred to as *stale labels* [6]. This can occur after two or more mergers, where a single lookup in the merger table is insufficient to determine the representative label. Bailey and Johnston [18] identified chains of mergers that occur when the rightmost branch of a sequence of mergers is selected as the representative label (as illustrated in Figure 2). Before processing the next row, it is necessary to unlink such chains so that each old label directly points to the representative label. This unlinking is called path compression in union-find parlance.

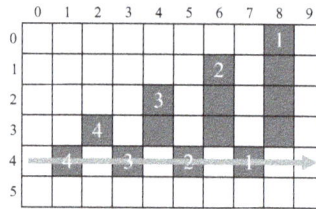

Figure 2. A chain of successive mergers: 4⇒3; 3⇒2; 2⇒1.

The labels within such chains cannot occur later in the row because the label that was allocated the earliest was selected as the representative label. therefore, chain unlinking can be deferred until the end of each row [18]. Since the representative label within such a chain is rightmost, potential chain links can be saved on a stack enabling them to be unlinked from right to left. A disadvantage of such unlinking is that it incurs overhead at the end of each row. Typically, this overhead is about 1% [18], although in the worst case is 50% for a single row, or 20% for a whole image. A further complicating factor is that the overhead is image-dependent, and cannot be predicted in advance.

To overcome the chaining problem, Jeong et al. [23] proposed to directly replace all old entries within the row buffer with the new representative label whenever a merger occurs. This removes the unlinking overhead, and also the need for the merger table. To accomplish this, the row buffer must instead be implemented as a shift register, with each stage having a comparator to detect the old label, and a multiplexer to replace it with the representative label. Since such a content addressable memory cannot easily be implemented using a block memory, the resulting logic requires considerable FPGA resources.

Zhao et al. [24] also used aggressive relabelling, similar to Ma et al. [20], but instead used pixels as the processing unit, and runs as the labelling unit. The goal of this approach is to eliminate unnecessary mergers, and avoid the overhead at the end of each row. While labelling a run at a time does significantly reduce the number of mergers required, it does not eliminate chains of mergers (the pattern is more complex than Figure 2 of course). So although Zhao et al. claim to eliminate the end-of-row processing, without correctly resolving such chains, the results for some images will be incorrect.

Finally, Tang et al. [25] optimise this approach of using runs as a labelling unit to actually eliminate the end of row processing. They assign a unique label to each run, and rather than relabel runs when they connect, the connectivity is maintained within a linked list structure for each image row. The head of the list maintains the feature vector, and whenever a run is added to the list, both the list and data are updated. Clever use of the pointers enables the pointers to be kept in order, and enable the data to be accessed with two lookups, completely avoiding the problems with chains. It also means that labels are automatically recycled, and completed components are detected with a latency of one image row. There are two limitations of this algorithm: (1) It only handles 4-connectivity, rather than 8-connectivity which is usually used; Tang et al. also propose a pre-filter to convert an 8-connected image into the required 4-connected image prior to CCA. However, the pre-filter also means that incorrect values are derived for some features (e.g., area) without additional processing, although that processing is straight forward. (2) The outermost border of the image must be set to the background before processing; Tang et al. suggest extending the image with background pixels prior to processing to guarantee this condition. However, this would reintroduce 2 clock cycles per row overhead.

The primary contributions of this paper are: a novel approach to eliminate the end-of-row overhead associated with unchaining; and a novel method to detect completed components as soon as they are completed, giving a reduction in latency. These are based on a zig-zag based scan pattern through the image, with the algorithm outlined in Section 2. An FPGA architecture for realising zig-zag based CCA is described in detail in Section 3. The algorithm and architecture are analysed in Section 4 to show correct behaviour. Finally, Section 5 compares the new algorithm with existing single-pass pixel-based approaches.

2. Proposed Approach

Unchaining within the traditional algorithms [6,18,20,21] is effectively accomplished by performing a reverse scan back through the labels merged in the current row at the end of each row. This approach comes at the cost of having to introduce additional overhead to store the sequences of mergers in a stack data structure and unchain them sequentially at the end of each image row.

This paper proposes replacing the raster scan with a zig-zag scan, with every second row processed in the reverse direction. This enables chains of mergers to be resolved on-the-fly, as part of the merger table lookup and update process. The basic architecture of Figure 1 needs to be modified for the zig-zag scan, giving the system architecture of Figure 3. Although many of the blocks have the same name and function as those in Figure 1, the detailed implementation of many of these is changed.

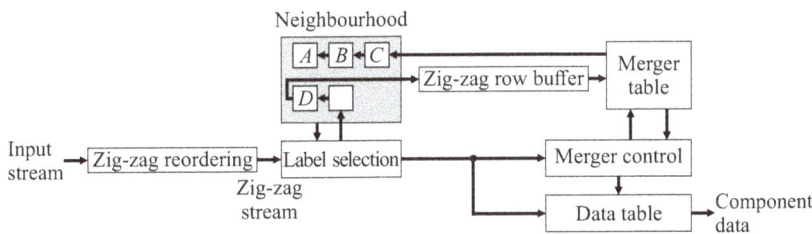

Figure 3. Basic architecture of zig-zag based single-pass connected components analysis.

First, a zig-zag reordering buffer is required in the input, to present the pixel stream in zig-zag order to the CCA unit. The row buffer also has to be modified to buffer data in zig-zag form. (Note that if the image is streamed from memory, this is unnecessary, as the pixels can directly be read from memory in zig-zag order.) Label selection is unchanged, as is the data table processing (apart from a novel extension to enable completed components to be detected earlier). The key changes are in the merger table processing for forming the neighbourhood, and merger control blocks. Zig-zag CCA is represented algorithmically in Algorithm 1. The nested **for** loops perform a zig-zag scan through the binary input image, with key steps as sub-algorithms described in the following sections.

2.1. Definitions

We first offer some definitions. The already processed pixels in the neighbourhood of the current pixel, X, are denoted A, B, C, and D as indicated in Figure 4. The labels associated with the neighbourhood pixels are designated L_A through L_D. Background pixels are assigned label 0. A logic test of L_p evaluates to true if pixel p is an object pixel and false if it is part of the background.

Even rows   Odd rows

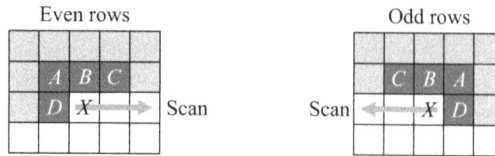

Figure 4. The neighbourhood of the current pixel, *X*, shaded dark. Shaded pixels have already been processed. Labelling is dependent on the scan direction.

Algorithm 1 Zig-zag CCA algorithm

Input: Binary image *I* of width *W* and height *H*
Output: A feature vector for each connected component in *I*
1:   $StartOfLine :=$ **False**
2:   **for** $y := 0$ **to** $H - 1$ **do**
3:      **for** $x := 0$ **to** $W - 1$ **when** y is even **else** $x := W - 1$ **downto** 0 **do**   ▷ Zig-zag scan
4:        **if** $StartOfLine$ **then**
5:          REVERSENEIGHBOURHOOD   ▷ Algorithm 3
6:          $StartOfLine :=$ **False**
7:        **else**
8:          UPDATENEIGHBOURHOOD   ▷ Algorithm 2
9:        **end if**
10:      UPDATEDATASTRUCTURES   ▷ Algorithm 4
11:     **end for**
12:    $StartOfLine :=$ **True**
13: **end for**

For the new scan order, it is convenient to define a precedence operator, $\prec$, based on the order in which pixels are encountered during processing. Given two pixels, P_1 and P_2, then

$$P_1 \prec P_2 = \begin{cases} true & \text{when } P_1.y < P_2.y \\ true & \text{when } (P_1.y = P_2.y) \wedge (P_1.y \mod 2 = 0) \wedge (P_1.x < P_2.x) \\ true & \text{when } (P_1.y = P_2.y) \wedge (P_1.y \mod 2 = 1) \wedge (P_1.x > P_2.x) \\ false & \text{otherwise.} \end{cases} \quad (1)$$

Precedence is used to select which label is the representative label during merger operations, and to determine when a connected component is completed.

Three auxiliary data structures are required for connected components analysis:

1. The row buffer, $RB[\,]$, saves the provisional labels assigned in the current row for providing the neighbourhood when processing the next row. Although the row buffer needs to manage pixels processed in a zig-zag scanned order, it is indexed within the following algorithms by logical pixel position.

2. The merger table, $MT[\,]$, indexed by label. This is to provide the current representative label for a component, given a provisional label. However, as a result of chains, more than one lookup in MT may be required.

3. The data table, $DT[\,]$, also indexed by label. This is to accumulate the feature vector extracted from each component. $IFV(X)$ is the initial feature vector to be accumulated from the current pixel, and $\circ$ is the binary operator which combines two feature vectors.

Additional variables and arrays will be defined as required in the following algorithms.

2.2. Update Neighbourhood

Since the input pixels are streamed, moving from one pixel position to the next involves shifting pixels along within the neighbourhood window. Algorithm 2 indicates how the neighbourhood is updated during normal processing. A merger can only occur between pixels A and C, or D and C [26], and if both A and D are object pixels then they will already have the same label (from processing the previous window position). Therefore, the neighbourhood can be optimised with L_{AorD} being the label L_A or L_D as required. The use of a superscript $-$, as in L_p^-, indicates the label L_p at the end of the previous iteration.

Algorithm 2 UPDATENEIGHBOURHOOD

1: **if** L_B^- **then**   ▷ Select L_{AorD} based on whether A (previous B) is an object pixel
2:   $L_{AorD} := L_B^-$ ▷ Next value of L_A
3: **else**
4:   $L_{AorD} := L_X^-$ ▷ Next value of L_D
5: **end if**
6: $L_B := L_C^-$
7: $L_{RB} := RB[C]$ ▷ Look up position C in the row buffer
8: **if** L_{RB} **then**   ▷ An object pixel is coming into neighbourhood
9:   **if** $\neg L_C^-$ **then**   ▷ It is the first object pixel after a background pixel
10:     $L_{MT} := MT[L_{RB}]$ ▷ First lookup in merger table
11:     **if** $L_{MT} = L_{RB}$ **then**   ▷ Label was representative label
12:       $L_C := L_{MT}$
13:     **else**
14:       $L_C := MT[L_{MT}]$ ▷ Second lookup in merger table to get representative label
15:       **if** $L_C \neq L_{MT}$ **then**   ▷ Label change on second lookup indicates a chain
16:         $MT[L_{RB}] := L_C$ ▷ Update merger table to unlink the chain
17:       **end if**
18:     **end if**
19:   **else**   ▷ Part of a run of consecutive pixels
20:     $L_C := L_C^-$ ▷ Repeat latest label
21:     **if** $L_{RB} \neq L_{RB}^-$ **then**   ▷ Label has changed, indicating a chain of mergers
22:       $MT[L_{RB}] := L_C$ ▷ Update merger table to unlink the chain
23:     **end if**
24:   **end if**
25: **else**
26:   $L_C := 0$ ▷ Lookup of background is unnecessary
27: **end if**

As the neighbourhood window pixels are shifted along, the new value for position C is obtained from the row buffer (line 7). If this is a background pixel, it is simply assigned label 0 (line 26). Note that if C is outside the image, for example when processing row 0 or when X is the last pixel in processing a row, then the background label (0) is used.

The row buffer provides the provisional labels assigned when processing the previous row. Although this label was the representative label for the component when it was written into the row buffer, subsequent mergers may mean that the label read from the row buffer is no longer the current representative label. It is necessary to look up the label in the merger table to obtain the current label (line 10). In a run of consecutive object pixels, all will belong to the same object, and will have the same label. The last label assigned to the run in the previous row will be the first read from the row buffer (as a result of the zig-zag scan), so only this label (see line 9) needs to be looked up in MT.

As a result of chains of mergers, a single lookup is not sufficient in the general case. Provided that the merger table is updated appropriately, two lookups may be required to give the current representative label. If the first lookup returns the same label (line 11), then that label has been unchanged (and is the representative label). However, if the first lookup returns a different label, then the provisional label may be stale and a second lookup is necessary (line 14). If the second lookup does not change the label, then this indicates that the single lookup was sufficient. If the second lookup returns a label that is different again, then this is part of a chain, and the value returned will be the current representative label.

To avoid having to lookup more than twice, it is necessary to update the merger table so that subsequent lookups of the original label produce the correct representative (line 16). This merger table update compresses the path, and performs the unchaining on-the-fly.

Within a run of consecutive object pixels, the representative label does not change. The latest label (after any merger at the previous window location, see line 20) is simply reused for C. If the row buffer output changes within a run of consecutive object pixels, this indicates that a merger occurred when processing the previous row and the provisional label from RB is out-of-date. This chain is unlinked, compressing the path by updating MT for the new label (line 22).

At the end of each row, it is necessary to reinitialise the window for the next row. As the window moves down, the pixels in the current row become pixels in the previous row. It is also necessary to flip the window to reflect the reversal of the scan direction. Algorithm 3 gives the steps required. Note that this is in place of Algorithm 2 for the first pixel of the next row.

Algorithm 3 REVERSENEIGHBOURHOOD

1: $L_{AorD} := 0$ ▷ This is now off the edge of the image
2: $L_B := L_X^-$ ▷ Moving down makes current row into previous row
3: $L_C := L_D^-$

2.3. Update Data Structures

Updating the data structures involves the following: assigning a provisional label to the incoming pixel based on the neighbourhood context; updating the merger table when a new label is assigned, or when a merger occurs; updating the feature vectors within the data table, and detecting when a connected component is completed. These are detailed in Algorithm 4.

A merger can only occur when B is a background pixel and L_{AorD} is different from L_C [26]. This condition corresponds to the block beginning line 3. The earliest assigned of L_{AorD} or L_C is selected as the representative label, and the other label is no longer used. The feature vectors associated with the two labels are merged, with the feature vector of the current pixel merged with the combination.

A new label is assigned to L_X when L_{AorD}, L_B and L_C are background (line 15). New labels are assigned from the labelling recycling first-in-first-out (FIFO) buffer. Consequently, the label numbers are not in numerical sequence, so to determine precedence under merger conditions it is necessary to augment the labels with the row number (line 17). The feature vector for the new component is initialised with the feature vector of the current pixel, $IFV(X)$.

If there is exactly one label in L_{AorD}, L_B or L_C, it is assigned to L_X and its feature vector in the data table at $DT[L_X]$ is merged with the feature vector of the current pixel $IFV(X)$, as shown in lines 26 and 30.

A connected component is finished when it is not extended into the current image row. To detect this, an active tag, AT, field is introduced within the data table, DT. For each label, AT stores the 2D coordinates on the following image row beyond which no further pixels could be added to the component. When the scan passes this point on the following row (line 34), it is determined that the component is completed, enabling the feature vector to be output and the label recycled. The initial feature vector for the active tag is

$$IFV(X).AT = \begin{cases} (y+1, x-1) & \text{when } y \text{ is even}, \\ (y+1, x+1) & \text{when } y \text{ is odd}. \end{cases} \qquad (2)$$

Algorithm 4 UPDATEDATASTRUCTURES

1: **if** $I[X]$ **then**   ▷ Object pixel
2:    **if** $\neg L_B$ **then**
3:      **if** $L_{AorD} \wedge L_C \wedge L_{AorD} \neq L_C$ **then**   ▷ Merger operation
4:        **if** $L_{AorD}.rw \leq L_C.rw$ **then**   ▷ Propagating merger
5:          $L_X := L_{AorD}$ ▷ Assign representative label
6:          $L_{old} := L_C$
7:          $L_C := L_X$ ▷ Update neighbourhood label
8:        **else**
9:          $L_X := L_C$ ▷ Assign representative label
10:          $L_{old} := L_{AorD}$
11:        **end if**
12:        $MT[L_{old}] := L_X$ ▷ Record merger in table
13:        $DT[L_X] := DT[L_X] \circ DT[L_{old}] \circ IFV(X)$ ▷ Merge data (and active tags)
14:        $L_{old} \to LabelFIFO$ ▷ Recycle the old label
15:      **else if** $\neg L_{AorD} \wedge \neg L_C$ **then**   ▷ New label operation
16:        $L_X := newLabel (\leftarrow LabelFIFO)$ ▷ From a recycle queue
17:        $L_X.rw := y$ ▷ Augment label with row number
18:        $MT[L_X] := L_X$ ▷ Initialise merger table
19:        $DT[L_X] := IFV(X)$ ▷ Start feature vector
20:      **else**
21:        **if** L_{AorD} **then**   ▷ Copy L_{AorD}
22:          $L_X := L_{AorD}$
23:        **else**   ▷ Copy L_C
24:          $L_X := L_C$
25:        **end if**
26:        $DT[L_X] := DT[L_X] \circ IFV(X)$ ▷ Add current pixel to data table
27:      **end if**
28:    **else**   ▷ Copy L_B
29:      $L_X := L_B$
30:      $DT[L_X] := DT[L_X] \circ IFV(X)$ ▷ Add current pixel to data table
31:    **end if**
32: **else**
33:    $L_X := 0$ ▷ Background pixel
34:    **if** $DT[L_A].AT = X$ **then**   ▷ Check completed object
35:      **Output:** $DT[L_A]$
36:      $L_A \to LabelFIFO$ ▷ Recycle the label
37:    **end if**
38: **end if**
39: $RB[X] := L_X$ ▷ Save label in row buffer for next row

For a label copy operation and a label merger operation, the active tag is updated along with the rest of the feature vector. The combination operator ∘ for two active tags is realised by applying precedence as defined in Equation (1) to select the later of the two active tags.

$$AT_1 \circ AT_2 = \begin{cases} AT_2 & \text{when } AT_1 \prec AT_2, \\ AT_1 & \text{otherwise.} \end{cases} \tag{3}$$

For an efficient hardware implementation, it is sufficient to store only the least-significant bit of y for each active tag entry.

Figure 5 illustrates the update of active tags and detection of completed connected components. At the start of processing row 4, there 3 components with active tags as listed. Since row 4 is even (scanning left to right), the active tags are on the right hand end of the respective components. At $(4,1)$, component 3 is extended and the active tag updated to $(5,0)$—the last possible scan position that could extend the current component 3. Similarly, at $(4,5)$ component 2 is extended. At $(4,6)$, components 1 and 2 merge with label 1 being retained as the representative label. Label 2 is recycled, and the active tags of labels 1 and 2 are combined. Further extensions of label 1 do not affect the active tag because the corresponding pixel active tags occur earlier in the scan sequence. When scanning back on row 5, label 1 is not extended, so when pixel $(5,4)$ is a background pixel, the component labelled 1 is detected as completed, the feature vector output, and the label recycled. Similarly, at $(5,0)$ component labelled 3 is detected as completed.

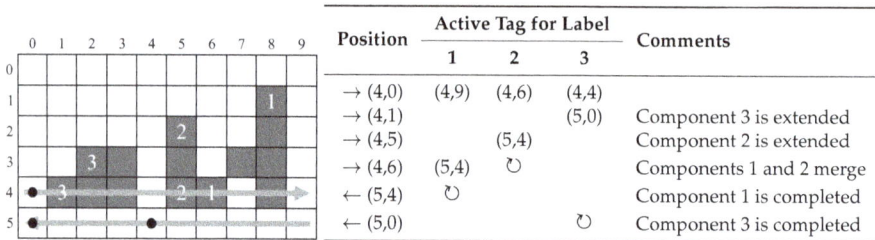

Position	Active Tag for Label			Comments
	1	**2**	**3**	
$\rightarrow (4,0)$	$(4,9)$	$(4,6)$	$(4,4)$	
$\rightarrow (4,1)$			$(5,0)$	Component 3 is extended
$\rightarrow (4,5)$		$(5,4)$		Component 2 is extended
$\rightarrow (4,6)$	$(5,4)$	↻		Components 1 and 2 merge
$\leftarrow (5,4)$	↻			Component 1 is completed
$\leftarrow (5,0)$			↻	Component 3 is completed

Figure 5. Example for detection of finished connected component at position X. ↻ indicates when the label is recycled.

3. Architecture

Within this section, the hardware architecture to realise this algorithm is described. The input pixel stream is continuous, with one 1-bit binary pixel per clock cycle. Since there are no blanking periods, a streaming protocol based on AXI4-Stream [27] (advanced extensible interface) is used throughout the design. The modified protocol shown in Figure 6 has two control bits, one indicating the last pixel in every row, and one indicating the last pixel in every frame.

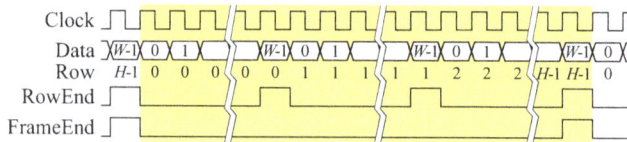

Figure 6. Continuous pixel stream protocol, with one image frame highlighted.

3.1. Zig-Zag Scan

The raster scanned input stream must be converted to a zig-zag ordered stream, where the odd numbered rows are presented in reverse order. Although this could easily be achieved with double buffering (reading the previous row from one buffer while writing the current row into a separate buffer) it can also be accomplished with a single row buffer with the access pattern shown in Figure 7.

After row 0 is initially written into the buffer, reading and writing are performed at the same address, with the raster based input stream being written into the same location that the zig-zag stream is read from. This requires switching the address sequence direction every second row. Converting the raster scan to a zig-zag scan introduces a latency of one row and one pixel.

The row buffer must also be modified to operate with a zig-zag scan pattern. Since successive rows are processed in the opposite order, the labels for each row must be read out in the reverse order that they were written. Data coming in for the new row overwrites the old data (already read out) in the buffer. As demonstrated in Figure 8, this can be accomplished by reversing the scan direction each row, effectively storing each label at the row buffer memory address corresponding to its x position.

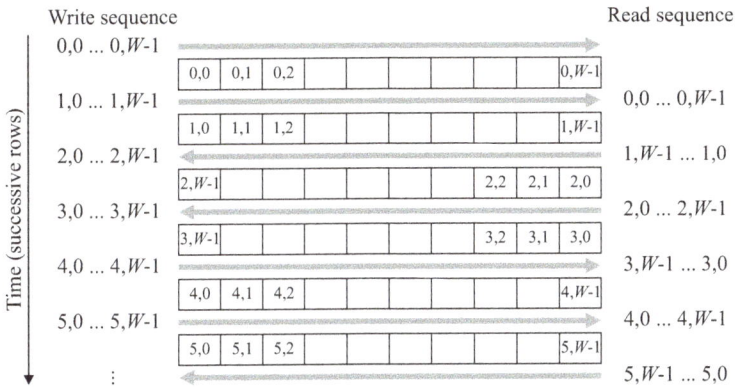

Write sequence / Read sequence

Write sequence										Read sequence
0,0 ... 0,W-1										
0,0	0,1	0,2							0,W-1	0,0 ... 0,W-1
1,0 ... 1,W-1										
1,0	1,1	1,2							1,W-1	1,W-1 ... 1,0
2,0 ... 2,W-1										
2,W-1							2,2	2,1	2,0	2,0 ... 2,W-1
3,0 ... 3,W-1										
3,W-1							3,2	3,1	3,0	3,W-1 ... 3,0
4,0 ... 4,W-1										
4,0	4,1	4,2							4,W-1	4,0 ... 4,W-1
5,0 ... 5,W-1										
5,0	5,1	5,2							5,W-1	5,W-1 ... 5,0

Figure 7. Operation of the zig-zag reordering buffer. Positions in the figure are shown in the format y, x, where y refers to the row and x to the column the pixel was assigned.

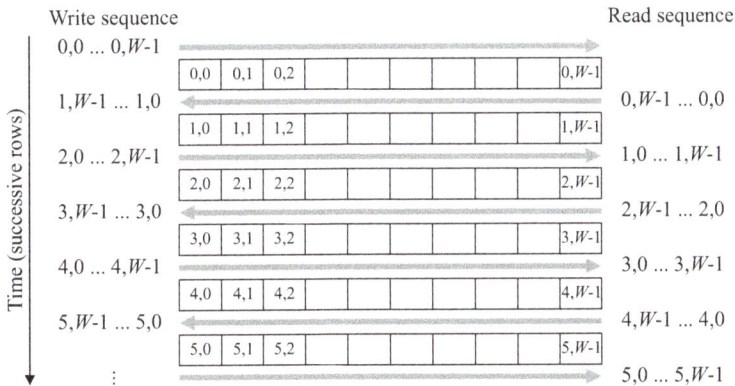

Write sequence										Read sequence
0,0 ... 0,W-1										
0,0	0,1	0,2							0,W-1	0,W-1 ... 0,0
1,W-1 ... 1,0										
1,0	1,1	1,2							1,W-1	1,0 ... 1,W-1
2,0 ... 2,W-1										
2,0	2,1	2,2							2,W-1	2,W-1 ... 2,0
3,W-1 ... 3,0										
3,0	3,1	3,2							3,W-1	3,0 ... 3,W-1
4,0 ... 4,W-1										
4,0	4,1	4,2							4,W-1	4,W-1 ... 4,0
5,W-1 ... 5,0										
5,0	5,1	5,2							5,W-1	5,0 ... 5,W-1

Figure 8. Operation of the row buffer with zig-zag ordered data.

3.2. Merger Table Processing

The label read from the row buffer may no longer be the current representative label as a result of mergers. For the look up operations performed in lines 7, 10, and 14 of Algorithm 2 it is necessary to look up the label in the merger table up to two times to obtain the current label. This is similar to the double lookup algorithm proposed in [6].

Although some labels may require two lookups, a single read port of a dual-port on-chip memory is sufficient for the merger table because it is unnecessary to look up every label from the row buffer. Labels of background pixels do not need to be looked up—all background pixels are simply labelled 0. In a sequence of consecutive object pixels, it is only necessary to look up the label of the first pixel in the sequence. An object pixel will either be followed by another object pixel or by a background pixel, neither of which need to be looked up, giving sufficient bandwidth for the two lookups.

Since each memory access requires 1 clock cycle (for synchronous memories such as the random access memory (RAM) blocks on most current FPGAs), it is necessary to pipeline the processing over 5 clock cycles as shown in Figure 9. The memory accesses are scheduled in advance so that the labels are available in the neighbourhood for assigning a label to the current pixel in stage 4.

	Stage 1	Stage 2	Stage 3	Stage 4	Stage 5
Row buffer	Row buffer read				Write to row buffer
Merger table		First read	Second read		
Neighbourhood				Assign label	
Merger table				Unlink chain	New label or merger

Figure 9. The 5 pipeline stages for processing each input pixel.

As a result of pipelining, the write to the row buffer is delayed from the read by four clock cycles. This necessitates using a dual-port memory for the row buffer. The merger table is also dual-port, with the read port used for determining the representative label in stages 2 and 3 of the pipeline. The write port for the merger table is used for initialising the merger table when a new label is assigned (line 15), and for updating the merger table during merger operations (line 3). Both new label and merger operations occur in stage 5 of the pipeline. Unchaining of stale labels is also performed as the stale labels are encountered during the neighbourhood update (Algorithm 2) in stage 4 of the pipeline. The detailed architecture for implementing this is shown in Figure 10.

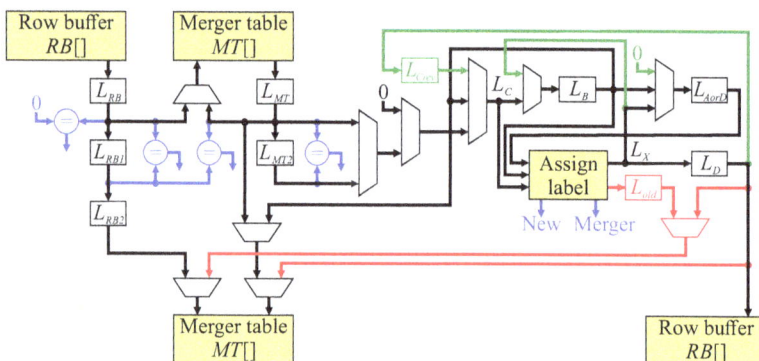

Figure 10. The detailed pipeline architecture for zig-zag connected components. Blue represents control signal generation, green indicates processing for end of row reversal, and red are the merger table updates for new label assignment and merger processing.

With synchronous memory, each read from an on-chip memory block is stored into a register; these are L_{RB} and L_{MT} for the row buffer and merger table respectively. The address for the merger table read comes either from L_{RB} for the first read, or L_{MT} for the second. Register L_{MT2} is a pipeline register to hold the data if only a single read is required, with a multiplexer selecting the output of L_{MT2} or L_{MT} as the representative label. The conditional statements in Algorithm 2 are shown in blue in Figure 10, and are used to provide control signals for selecting appropriate multiplexer inputs.

In terms of forming the neighbourhood, L_C is not directly registered, but is the output of multiplexers selecting the appropriate source register for L_C. L_B and L_{AorD} are registers. The current label output, L_X is not registered, but is the output of the combinatorial logic which assigns a label to the current input pixel. This output is registered as L_D, available in the following clock cycle for window reversal at the end of each row, and for updating the merger table in pipeline stage 5 (if required). For row reversal, L_C is assigned L_D (Algorithm 3); however, since L_C is not a register, it is necessary to insert a pipeline register, L_{Crev}.

Unchaining updates the merger table in pipeline stage 4. The data from line 16 is naturally available in that stage, but line 22 is detected at stage 2. It is necessary to delay both the address and data until stage 4. The address is delayed by pipeline registers L_{RB1} and L_{RB2}, with the data coming from L_C, which at that stage in a run of consecutive pixels, is the feedback path from L_B (line 20). For updating the merger table as a result of label assignment, for a new label, both the address and data come from L_D (line 18). In the case of a merger, L_{old} registers the old label, and is used for the address for the merger table update.

The dataflow for label assignment is shown in Figure 11. The binary input pixel is used to directly provide a control signal. The first multiplexer selects the label to propagate from the neighbourhood, with the second multiplexer selecting the background label (0), or a new label from the *LabelFIFO* (lines 16, 22, 29, 24 and 33). To reduce the logic requirements, the test for a background pixel on the row buffer output is simply pipelined through a series of registers to indicate whether L_C, L_B or L_{AorD} are object or background pixels.

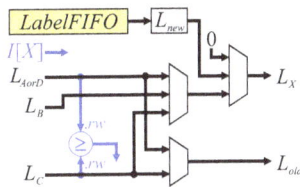

Figure 11. Architecture for label assignment. Blue represents control signal generation.

3.3. Data Table

The final key section of the architecture is that which manipulates the data table. Figure 12 shows the data flow for the update and completed object detection. The inputs come from neighbourhood processing, after registering to pipeline the processing. The current pixel label, L_X therefore, comes from the L_D register, and L_{old} in the case of mergers comes from the corresponding register in Figure 10. Data table processing is pipelined over three clock cycles, with the first cycle reading existing data from the data table when required, the second clock cycle is used to calculate the new feature vector, with the result being written to the data table (where necessary) in the third cycle. The neighbourhood position must also be registered twice before deriving the initial feature value (*IFV*) to maintain synchronisation. Control signals come from label assignment, whether it is a propagating label, a new label, a merger, or background pixel. Each of these cases will be described in turn.

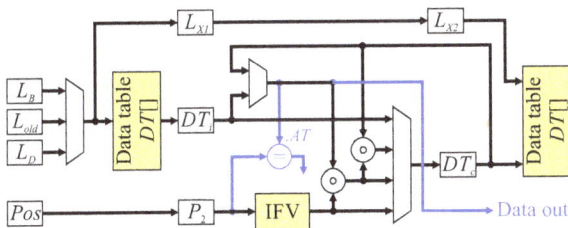

Figure 12. Architecture for data table update. Blue signals relate to detecting completed components.

For a propagating label, the neighbourhood had only a single label, which is copied to the current object pixel. If the previous pixel was a background pixel, then it is necessary to read the existing feature vector from the data table first. Otherwise, the feature vector will be available in the data table cache (DT_c) from processing the previous pixel. The initial feature vector, IFV, derived from the neighbourhood position is combined with the existing data, and the result stored in the data table cache, DT_c. The resulting feature vector is written back to the data table only when a background pixel is reached.

A new label operation has no existing data to load; the data table cache, DT_c, is simply initialised with the initial feature vector, IFV, in the second clock cycle.

A merger is a little more complex, because it may require two entries to be read from the data table. If the previous pixel was an object pixel, then the feature vector associated with L_{AorD} will be available in DT_c. However, if the previous pixel was a background pixel, then data will not be cached for L_{AorD}. To overcome this problem, when the current pixel is a background pixel, L_B is looked up in the data table. If L_B is the label of an object pixel, then on the next clock cycle, it becomes L_{AorD} and will be available in the cache. A merger will trigger the loading of L_C, so that it can be combined with L_{AorD} and IFV. During the second clock cycle, $DT[L_{old}]$ is invalidated, enabling the label to be recycled. On the third clock cycle, the merged feature vector is written back to the data table.

Preloading the data table cache also facilitates detection of completed objects. From Algorithm 4 line 34, when the active tag (AT) of a completed object is the current pixel position, the last pixel will be in neighbourhood position A. At least the last three pixels (including the current pixel) will also have been background pixels otherwise they would have extended the object. Therefore, looking up L_B when the current pixel is a background pixel gives the feature vector (containing AT) in the following clock cycle, enabling completed object detection (shown in blue in Figure 12). When the completed object is output, the data table entry is available for reuse by recycling the label.

4. Analysis

As a result of pipelining the computations, there are potentially data hazards, particularly in the use of memory for tables (the row buffer, merger table and data table), resulting from when data is expected to be in the table, but has not yet been written.

4.1. Row Buffer

For the row buffer, this can only occur at the end of the row, when the readout direction changes. The data hazards are demonstrated in Figure 13.

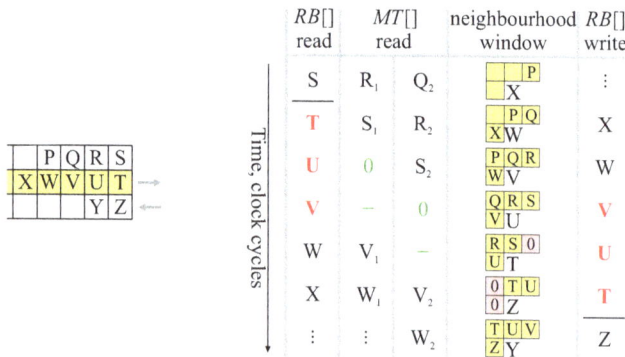

	RB[] read	MT[] read		neighbourhood window	RB[] write
	S	R₁	Q₂	·P / ·X	⋮
	T	S₁	R₂	PQ / XW	X
	U	0	S₂	PQR / WV	W
	V	—	0	QRS / VU	V
	W	V₁	—	RS0 / UT	U
	X	W₁	V₂	0TU / 0Z	T
	⋮	⋮	W₂	TUV / ZY	Z

(Left panel shows grids: PQRS / XWVUT / YZ)

Figure 13. End of row timing, showing data hazards in red. Subscripts 1 and 2 refer to the first and second reads from the merger table (if required).

The last pixel of the previous row, **S**, is read from the row buffer when the neighbourhood window is at position **X** (as a result of pipelining). In the following clock cycles, reads from the row buffer begin their backward scan of the next row. However, pixel positions **T**, **U**, and **V** have not yet been written to the row buffer (or even assigned labels in the case of **T** and **U**). At the end of the row, lookup of positions **T** and **U** in the row buffer is actually unnecessary, because their values come directly from the neighbourhood when the window moves to the next row (Algorithm 3). Rather than read position **T**, it can simply be treated as a background pixel (label 0). This ensures that when the neighbourhood is at location **T**, neighbourhood position C (which is off the edge of the image) is correctly assigned a 0 (shaded pink in Figure 13). Similarly, position **U** is copied directly from the previous neighbourhood when the neighbourhood reverses direction. The row buffer output for **U**, too, can simply be treated as a background pixel. Finally, position **V** is read in the same clock cycle as it is written. This requires that the row buffer support a write-before-read semantic, or bypass logic be added to forward the value being written to the output.

4.2. Path Compression

Since both path compression and label assignment have write access to the merger table, it is necessary to check that these will not clash by attempting to write simultaneously. The possible scenarios are illustrated in Figure 14.

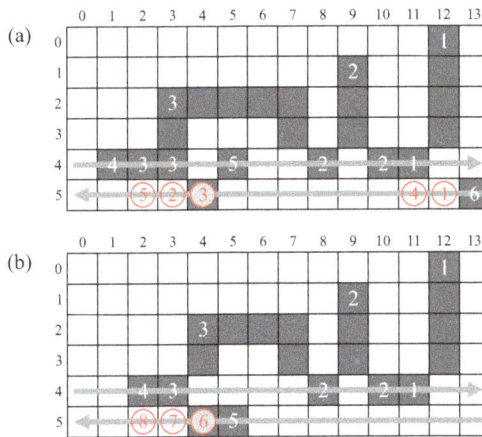

Figure 14. Accesses to update the merger table: (**a**) Scenarios with no conflicts; (**b**) Scenarios with conflicts.

A new label and merger both update the merger table in pipeline stage 5. This is the clock cycle immediately following the label assignments, as illustrated in scenarios ① and ② respectively. Unchaining is performed in pipeline stage 4, corresponding to the clock cycle when the pixel appears in the neighbourhood window. This is illustrated in scenario ③ after two lookups, and scenarios ④ and ⑤ for a changed label within a consecutive run of pixels.

There cannot be a conflict between a change within a run, and a new label, because the change would require at least one pixel within the neighbourhood, preventing a new label assignment. Similarly, there can also be no conflict between a merger and a two lookup stale label because the merger would require L_C to be non-zero, so the following pixel cannot be the first in a run. However, there can be conflicts between a new label and a two lookup stale label (scenario ⑥ in Figure 14b), and also between a merger and changed label in a run (scenario ⑦).

Where there is a conflict, the update resulting from the new label or merger should be deferred, with the stale label update taking priority. If the new label is followed by a merger (as in Figure 14b) then only the merger needs to be saved. This requires adding an additional storage register and multiplexer to the data path, and appropriate control logic. The maximum delay is two clock cycles, corresponding to ⑧, because changed labels in a run can occur at most every second pixel.

4.3. Merger Table

Potential data hazards can occur with the merger table, when data is read from the table before it is updated either as a result of merger or during the path compression.

A merger hazard is shown in Figure 15 for label 3. When scanning row 4, label 2 is read from $RB[4]$, and is determined to be a representative label after a single lookup, $MT[2]$. Two clock cycles later, when the neighbourhood window is centred on pixel $(4,3)$, component segments associated with labels 1 and 2 merge, with $MT[2] \leftarrow 1$ in the following cycle. Meanwhile, label 3 is read from $RB[6]$, and requires two lookups in MT. The second lookup occurs in the same clock cycle that the merger is being written to MT, so the second lookup would actually return the old label (2), shown in red in Figure 15, and is not recognised as a stale label. A consequence of this is that pixel $(4,6)$ would incorrectly be assigned label 2 rather than 1. To avoid this problem, the memory used for the merger table must also support the write-before-read semantic, or data forwarding be used to correctly return label (1) from the second lookup. Label 3 is then recognised as stale, and the merger table updated with $MT[3] \leftarrow 1$ as shown in green.

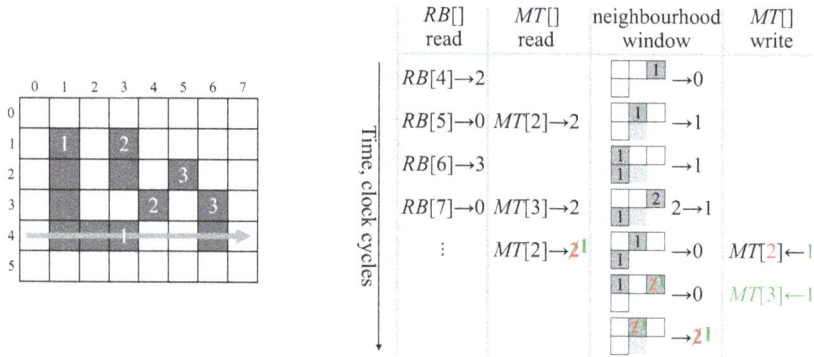

Figure 15. Timing of hazards associated with the merger table.

Delaying the merger table update after a merger (as described in the previous section) does not introduce any additional hazards because the run of pixels which induces the delay would also delay the start of the following run.

In a chain of successive mergers, such as in Figure 2, the previous merger is unlinked or compressed during the first merger table lookup, enabling the second lookup to provide the representative label. There are no data hazards associated with this process.

4.4. Data Table

Hazards within the data table can occur because the updated feature vector is written two clocks after the feature vector is read from the table. Alternating background and object pixels, with the object pixels belonging to the same connected component, can, therefore, cause a problem since the same label is being read from and written to in the same clock cycle. This can be solved if the memory supports read-before-write, or by adding bypass detection logic (the feedback data path from DT_c to DT_i is already present).

The other issue with the data table is detecting components which complete on the last pixel of a row, and on the row of the image. Equation (2) can be extended to include

$$IFV(X).AT.y = \begin{cases} H-1 & \text{when } y = H-1, \\ y+1 & \text{otherwise;} \end{cases} \qquad (4)$$

$$IFV(X).AT.x = \begin{cases} 0 & \text{when } x = 0 \text{ and } AT.y \text{ is even,} \\ x-1 & \text{when } x \neq 0 \text{ and } AT.y \text{ is even,} \\ W-1 & \text{when } x = W-1 \text{ and } AT.y \text{ is odd,} \\ x+1 & \text{when } x \neq W-1 \text{ and } AT.y \text{ is odd.} \end{cases} \qquad (5)$$

Thus, an object on the last line will be detected as complete in the clock cycle following the last pixel for that object.

5. Comparison and Discussion

In this section the proposed CCA algorithm is analysed with regards to throughput, latency and required hardware resources, and compared to other state-of-the-art CCA algorithms. For the comparison we chose the most recent CCA algorithms that are targeted for a realisation as hardware architectures [6,18–21,23,25].

5.1. Memory Requirements

The on-chip memory size and scalability with increasing image size was identified to be one of the most important criteria for a CCA hardware architecture to achieve a high-throughput for high-resolution image streams [6,18]. Therefore, the scalability of the on-chip memory is further examined in the following. As the algorithm by Jeong et al. [23] uses registers to realise the row buffer, both registers used as memory and on-chip memory (RAM blocks) are considered in the comparison of memory resources.

Table 1 compares the on-chip memory and register requirements for the algorithms presented in [6,20,21,23,25] for an image of size $W \times H$. The number of labels required, N_L, defines the number of connected components that are stored at any one time inside an architecture before their feature vectors are ultimately output. N_L is, therefore, the key factor for all architectures, as it defines the lower bound of the depth and the width for the memories of the examined CCA architectures. In their original publications the architectures extract different feature vectors. To enable a fair comparison, in Table 1 the width of a feature vector W_{FV} containing the bounding box and the area is used for comparing the required memory. Table 2 shows the number of memory bits required for each data structure of the compared CCA architectures. The total numbers of on-chip memory and register bits are shown in Figure 16.

Table 1. Comparison of on-chip memory and register requirements. For all compared architectures the feature vectors are composed of bounding box and area for each connected component, i.e., the width of the feature vector, W_{FV}, is equivalent for all architectures, $W_{FV} = 2\lceil \log_2 W \rceil + 2\lceil \log_2 H \rceil + \lceil \log_2 WH \rceil$.

	Ma et al. [20]	Klaiber et al. [6,21]	Jeong et al. [23]		Tang et al. [25]	This Work
Number of labels, N_L	$\lceil \frac{W}{2} \rceil$	$\lceil \frac{W+5}{2} \rceil$	$\lceil \frac{W}{2} \rceil$ to $\lceil \frac{W\times H}{4} \rceil$		$\lceil \frac{W}{2} \rceil$	$\lceil \frac{W}{2} \rceil$
Chain stack size, N_{CS}	$\lfloor \frac{W-1}{2} \rfloor$	$\lfloor \frac{W-1}{2} \rfloor$	—		—	—
Label width, W_L	$\lceil \log_2 N_L \rceil$	$\lceil \log_2 N_L \rceil$	$\lceil \log_2 N_L \rceil$		$\lceil \log_2 N_L \rceil$	$\lceil \log_2 N_L \rceil$
Augmented label, W_{AL}	—	$W_L + \lceil \log_2 H \rceil$	—		—	$W_L + \lceil \log_2 H \rceil$
Hardware Data Structure	**RAM**	**RAM**	**Registers**	**RAM**	**RAM**	**RAM**
Zig-zag buffer, ZZ	—	—	—	—	—	$W \times 1$
Recyle FIFO, R	—	$N_L \times W_L$	—	$N_L \times W_L$	—	$N_L \times W_L$
Row buffer, RB	$W \times W_L$	$W \times W_L$	$W \times W_L$	—	$W \times 2$	$W \times W_L$
Merger table, MT	$2N_L \times W_L$	$N_L \times W_{AL}$	—	—	—	$N_L \times W_{AL}$
Chain stack, CS	$N_{CS} \times 2W_L$	$N_{CS} \times 2W_L$	—	—	—	—
Translation table, TT	$N_L \times W_L$	—	—	—	—	—
isRoot flag, F	—	$N_L \times 1$	—	—	—	—
Active tag, AT	—	$N_L \times 2$	—	—	—	$N_L \times (\lceil \log_2 W \rceil + 1)$
Stale label stack, SLS	—	$\lceil \frac{W}{10} \rceil \times W_L$	—	—	—	—
Linked lists, LL	—	—	—	—	$3N_L \times W_L$	—
Data table, DT	$2N_L \times W_{FV}$	$N_L \times W_{FV}$	—	$N_L \times W_{FV}$	$N_L \times W_{FV}$	$N_L \times W_{FV}$

Table 2. Comparison of memory requirements of all data structures of the examined CCA architectures for different image sizes from VGA to UHD8k.

	VGA 640 × 480	DVD 720 × 576	HD720 1280 × 720	HD1080 1920 × 1080	UHD4k 3840 × 2160	UHD8k 7680 × 4320
			Ma et al. [20]			
RB	5760	6480	12,800	19,200	42,240	92,160
MT	5760	6480	12,800	19,200	42,240	92,160
CS	5742	6462	12,780	19,180	42,218	92,136
TT	2880	3240	6400	9600	21,120	46,080
DT	36,480	42,480	79,360	124,800	272,640	591,360
Total	**56,622**	**65,142**	**124,140**	**191,980**	**420,458**	**913,896**
			Klaiber et al. [6,21]			
R	2907	3267	6430	9630	21,153	46,116
RB	5760	6480	12,800	19,200	42,240	92,160
MT	5814	6897	12,860	20,223	44,229	96,075
CS	5742	6462	12,780	19,180	42,218	92,136
F	323	363	643	963	1923	3843
AT	646	726	1286	1926	3846	7686
SLS	576	648	1280	1920	4224	9216
DT	18,411	21,417	39,866	62,595	136,533	295,911
Total	**40,179**	**46,260**	**87,945**	**135,637**	**296,366**	**643,143**
			Jeong et al. [23]			
R	2880	3240	6400	9600	21,120	46,080
RB	5760	6480	12,800	19,200	42,240	92,160
AT	640	720	1280	1920	3840	7680
DT	18,240	21,240	39,680	62,400	136,320	295,680
Total	**27,520**	**31680**	**60,160**	**93,120**	**203,520**	**441,600**
			Tang et al. [25]			
RB	1280	1440	2560	3840	7680	15,360
LL	8640	9720	19,200	28,800	63,360	138,240
DT	18,240	21,240	39,680	62,400	136,320	295,680
Total	**28,160**	**32,400**	**61,440**	**95,040**	**207,360**	**449,280**
			This work			
ZZ	640	720	1280	1920	3840	7680
R	2880	3240	6400	9600	21,120	46,080
RB	5760	6480	12,800	19,200	42,240	92,160
MT	5760	6840	12,800	20,160	44,160	96,000
AT	3520	3960	7680	11,520	24,960	53,760
DT	18,240	21,240	39,680	62,400	136,320	295,680
Total	**36,800**	**42,480**	**80,640**	**124,800**	**272,640**	**591,360**

The architecture by Ma et al. [20] was the first to introduce relabelling to reduce the number of labels that are required, N_L, from $\frac{W \times H}{4}$ (in [18]) to $\frac{W}{2}$. The aggressive relabelling, however, requires two merger tables and two data tables to manage the labels changing from one row to the next. As shown in Figure 16 the architecture from [20], therefore, has the largest memory footprint among the compared CCA architectures.

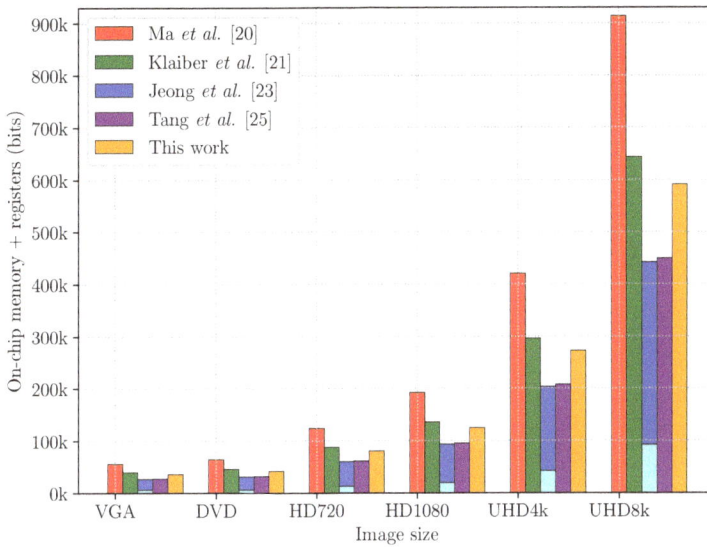

Figure 16. The bar diagram shows the number of on-memory and register bits that are required to process images of different sizes. The bars indicate on-chip memory. The cyan coloured part of [23] indicates the registers required for the row buffer.

The architectures of Klaiber et al. [6,21] use label recycling to improve memory-efficiency and, therefore, also require a maximum of $N_L \approx \frac{W}{2}$ labels. Label recycling only requires a single data table and merger table, halving their size in comparison to [20] (although the augmented labels make the merger table wider). Since the on-chip memory requirements are dominated by the data table, this results in significant savings.

The architecture described in Jeong et al. [23] would scale with the image area, i.e., a maximum of $N_L = \frac{W \times H}{4}$ would be required for a worst case image. However, if feature vectors are output before the end of the image is reached, then those labels could be reused. Such label recycling is possible for the architecture in [23], even though it is not described (only merged labels are recycled). For a fair comparison, it is, therefore, assumed that the architecture scales with the image width, i.e., $N_L = \frac{W}{2}$ and the usage of an active tag (from [21]) for label recycling is assumed, even though it is not explicitly mentioned in the original publication. Directly replacing all instances of the old label within the row buffer enables many of the auxiliary data structures to be removed. Consequently, the modified architecture from [23] requires 30% less memory than [21]. This reduction, however, is only achieved because the row buffer is designed as context-addressable memory, which has to be realised with registers on FPGAs. The cyan-coloured bar in Figure 16 shows that almost one third of the required memory is realised directly by registers. For processing large image sizes, such as UHD8k, more than 90 kbits of registers are required to realise the row buffer and around 350 kbits of on-chip memory for the other data structures. Since modern FPGAs have a register to on-chip memory ratio between 1/20 and 1/60, a significant fraction of register resources are required. Furthermore, the routing effort on an FPGA, as well as the logic for addressing a content-addressable memory as large as 90 kbits consisting of registers is significant. An analysis of the scalability of such a context-addressable memory with increasing image size is not given in [23]. It seems unlikely that a context-addressable memory scales well on FPGAs, both, with maximum frequency and area. The number of registers required by the architecture of [23] is therefore a clear disadvantage when optimising for throughput or when minimising the FPGA resources.

The architecture of Tang et al. [25] represents a significant improvement, eliminating the need for the content addressable memory of [23] with only approximately 2% additional resources. The main reductions relative to [21] (approximately 30%) come from not needing to save the labels in the row buffer, and replacing the merger table with a linked list structure. Uniquely labelling each run also automatically recycles labels, eliminating the need for the recycle FIFO and active tag. For correct operation, however, it does require the first and last row and column of the image to be background. The results in Table 2 and Figure 16 do not include the logic required to extend the image with background pixels.

The proposed CCA architecture is an advancement of [6]. Due to zig-zag scanning, an additional memory structure to reorder incoming pixels from raster-scan order to zig-zag order is required. Since zig-zag processing resolves chains on the fly, the stale label stack and chain stack are no longer required. This reduces the amount of memory required by 9% compared to the architecture presented in [21]. Compared to [23,25] approximately 20% more memory bits are required, primarily from the merger table and other auxiliary data structures. The active tag is larger than that of [6] to detect object completion at the earliest possible time; this matches the timing of [25]. The advantage over [23] is merger handling using on-chip memories, rather than a large multiplexed shift register, which is a more efficient use of resources. The advantage over [25] is the removal of the requirement for the outside row and column of pixels to be background. The proposed architecture is also able to immediately detect completed objects in the final row as they complete.

5.2. Implementation Results

Table 3 shows the results of the CCA architecture implemented using VHDL on an Intel Cyclone V 5SEMA5F31C6 (using Quartus 17.1) and a Xilinx Kintex 7 xc7k325-2L (using Vivado 2016.4). These tables show the number of lookup tables (LUTs/ALUTs), registers (FF) and on-chip memory bits (and memory blocks) each component of the CCA architecture requires for processing UHD8k images. The slightly higher memory requirements for the Cyclone V for the merger table and data table are a result of the synthesis tools rounding the memory depth up to the next power of 2.

Table 3. Synthesis results targeting a UHD8k image (7680 × 4320). ALUTs are Intel's adaptive lookup tables; FFs are the number of flip-flops or registers; M10K are the number of Intel's 10 kbit RAM blocks; BRAMs are the number of Xilinx's 36 kbit block RAMs.

Module	Intel Cyclone V 5SEMA5F31C6				Xilinx Kintex 7 xc7k325-2L			
	ALUTs	FFs	RAM (bits)	M10K	LUTs	FFs	RAM (bits)	36k BRAMs
Zig-zag buffer	28	19	7680	1	46	19	7680	0.5
Label generator	51	31	46,080	6	14	26	46,080	1.5
Row buffer	49	21	92,160	12	163	30	92,160	3
Merger table	99	103	102,400	13	219	101	96,000	3
Neighbourhood	226	252	0	0	95	217	0	0
Data table	635	275	372,736	46	470	244	322,560	10.5
Total	1088	701	621,056	78	867 [a]	637	564,480	18.5

[a] LUTs shared between multiple components are counted in both.

The scalability of the proposed CCA architecture with increasing image size is explored in Figure 17. The number of required number of LUTs/ALUTs is shown in Figure 17a. On the Intel Cyclone V the number of ALUTs increases logarithmically with the image width. On the Xilinx Kintex 7 the number of LUTs increases from VGA to HD1080 image size to almost 1400 and then drops to around 800 LUTs for UHD4k and UHD8k image size. This is a direct result of the usage of LUTs as distributed RAM to realise small memories. On Kintex 7 FPGAs this is done to prevent using valuable on-chip memory resources from being used inefficiently for small memories that only utilise a small fraction of the 18 kBit minimum size. From UHD4k all the memories are realised with RAMs. The number of LUTs from UHD4k to UHD8k image size, therefore, increases only marginally.

Figure 17b shows a small logarithmic increase in the number of registers required with image width for both FPGAs. The Cyclone V uses slightly more registers than the Kintex 7 as a result of register duplication during the place and route stage. The required on-chip memory bits scale linearly with the image width, as shown in Figure 17c. The only exception that can be observed is that for the Kintex 7 the same amount of block memory is required for the HD720 and HD1080 image sizes. This remains constant as a result of the usage of distributed RAM as indicated in Figure 17a. The small increase for the Cyclone V for the HD720 image size is simply a result of the discrete nature of the RAM blocks.

The throughput of the architecture is proportional to the maximum clock frequency. Therefore, it determines how well the throughput of the architecture scales with increasing image width. As shown in Figure 17d the maximum frequency remains almost constant for both FPGAs. A maximum frequency around 180 MHz can be reach on the Kintex 7 for all examined image sizes. For the Intel Cyclone V, the maximum frequency is around 105 MHz for all image sizes.

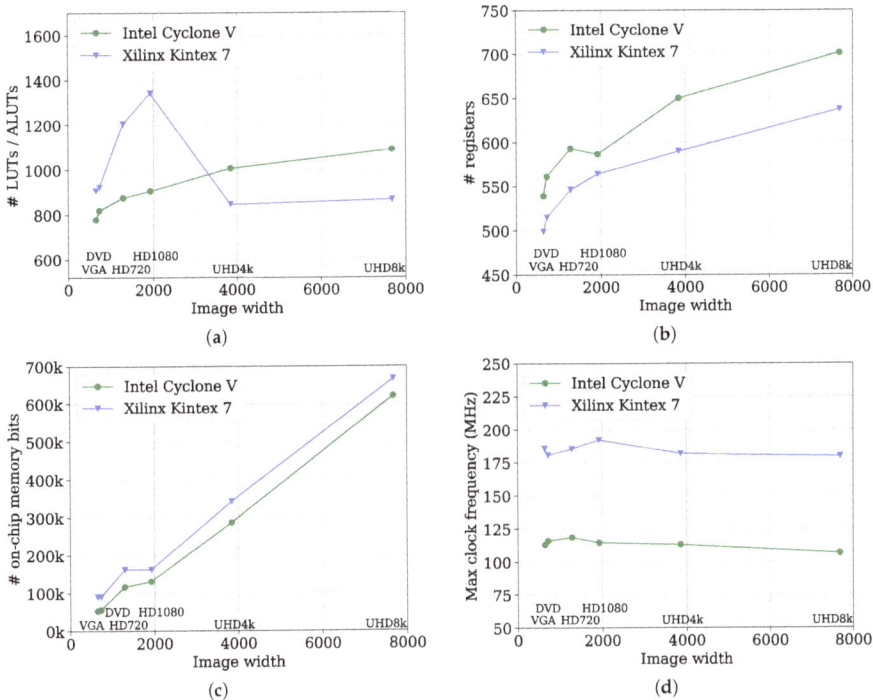

Figure 17. These diagrams that show the number of (**a**) look up tables (LUTs / ALUTs), (**b**) registers and and (**c**) on-chip memory bits for different image sizes for the implementation of the proposed CCA architecture on an Intel Cyclone V 5SEMA5F31C6 and a Xilinx Kintex 7 xc7k325-2L FPGA. In (**d**) the maximum clock frequency is shown.

5.3. Comparison of CCA Hardware Architecture

Table 4 compares the results reported by Johnston et al. [19], Ma et al. [20], Klaiber et al. [21], Jeong et al. [23], and Tang et al. [25], with the implementation results of the proposed architecture. The reported results differ in image size, extracted feature vectors, the FPGA technology used and the maximum number of labels that can be stored in the architecture. A direct comparison of the architectures from Table 4 is, therefore, not meaningful. The differences of the results of the proposed architecture are discussed for each examined architecture in the following.

Table 4. Comparison of several CCA hardware architectures. Abbreviations for the extracted feature vector are: (A) area, (C) component count, (FOM) first-order moment, (BB) bounding box.

Implementation of Architecture	Technology	Image Size (pixels)	Extracted FV	LUTs	Registers	RAM (bits)	f_{max} (MHz)
Johnston and Bailey [19] [a]	Spartan II	670 × 480	C	620	271	12 k	N/A
			A	758	299	20 k	N/A
Ma et al. [20]	Virtex II	640 × 480	A, C	1757	600	72 k	40.64
Klaiber et al [21]	Kintex 7	256 × 256	BB	493	296	108 k	185.59
		7680 × 4320		818	444	548 k	170.53
Jeong et al. [23] [b]	Cyclone IV	640 × 480	BB, FOM	36,478	N/A	18k	60.58
		1920 × 1080		57,036	N/A	29 k	58.44
Tang et al. [25]	Virtex II Cyclone IV	256 × 256	BB	543	187	72k	104.26
				489	303	7287	122.94
This work	Cyclone V	256 × 256	BB, A	682	479	22 k	122.56
		7680 × 4320		1088	701	621 k	106.52
	Kintex 7	256 × 256	BB, A	882	503	18 k	220.02
		7680 × 4320		867	637	564 k	180.47

[a] Hardware resources are for a maximum of 255 labels [19]. [b] Hardware resources are for a maximum of 127 labels [23].

Comparison to [19,20]: The proposed architecture is an advancement of these architectures. The number of memory bits was significantly reduced by the introduction of label recycling and omission of the chain stack. The required LUTs and registers are mostly used for control logic and are, therefore, similar for the proposed architecture when comparing to [19,20].

Comparison to [21]: In the proposed approach the chain stack and stale label stack are no longer required, however, the memory for storing active tag has increased compared to [21]. The required on-chip memory could, therefore, be reduced up to 10%, as shown in Table 2. There was a small increase in maximum frequency (35 MHz for 256 × 256 images and by 10 MHz for UHD8k images). This was achieved due to the simplified label assignment. The critical path was in [21] in the label assignment. For the proposed architecture it is now in the calculation of the active tag in the data table. For the 256 × 256 image size, the required on-chip memory has decreased significantly from 108 kbits to 18 kbits. In [21] most data structures on the Kintex 7 occupy full 18 kbit RAM blocks even if a significant part is unused. The proposed architecture makes use of distributed RAM for small data structures; these are realised with LUTs. This also explains why the number of required LUTs has almost doubled from [21] to the proposed architecture for small image sizes. For the UHD8k image size, the LUT and register requirements are slightly higher than in [21] reflecting the more complex control, and the improved object completion detection. It should be noted that the results in Table 4 for [21] are for extracting the bounding box only, whereas the results for the proposed architecture are for extracting bounding box and area (which requires a wider data table).

Comparison to [23]: The relatively low RAM requirement of [23] is directly a result of restricting the design to 127 labels; this would grow significantly if the design increased N_L to handle any image (the data table size is proportional to N_L). The number of registers is not directly reported in [23]. However, as the number of registers required for the row buffer is proportional to the image width (here 1920 for an HD image) and the label width (here 7 bits for 127 labels) it cannot be lower than 13,440 registers. As discussed in the analytical comparison from Table 1 and Figure 16, implementation of [23] requires significantly more registers than the other architectures while being limited to only 127 labels. The use of multiplexed registers for the row buffer would impact on the routability of the design, and this is the likely cause of the significantly lower clock frequency. The major advantage of the proposed architecture over [23] is that all of the data structures are realised as on-chip memories. This allows the proposed design to use a smaller FPGA device, as the number of registers required is much smaller and the proportion of on-chip memory and registers is closer to modern FPGAs.

Comparison to [25]: The small resource requirement comes from the simplified logic for maintaining the linked list data structures. Although the RAM requirements for the Virtex II seem anomalously large, the minimum RAM block size is 18 kbits, with the tools reporting the total size rather than just the number of bits used (the remainder of the RAM blocks are unusable). The RAM for the Cyclone IV is close to that indicated by Table 1. Again it should be noted that the results reported for Tang et al. are for extracting the bounding box only. Extracting the area as well requires a 50% wider data table, and would also require a small increase in the resources required. That said, the proposed architecture requires more resources and operates at a similar speed to [25]. It should be remembered, however, that Tang et al. requires the borders of the image to be background pixels. The logic reported does not include that required to either ensure this, or to pad the image if required.

5.4. Throughput

To compare the throughput of the architectures from Johnston and Bailey [19], Klaiber et al. [6,21], Ma et al. [20], Jeong et al. [23], Tang et al. [25] and the proposed architecture, the maximum number of clock cycles to process an image of size $W \times H$ is examined. All of the designs are capable of processing one pixel per clock cycle of the input image. The difference is the end of row processing for resolving chains, which are data-dependent.

For [6,19,21], the pattern which creates the maximum number of chain stack entries in an image is the stair pattern shown in Figure 18a. It adds an overhead of $\frac{W}{5}$ cycles to each image row to process the content stored in the chain stack and to update the merger table.

The architecture of [20] has a translation table directly connected to the output of the merger table, with many mergers managed by the translation of labels from one row to the next. This makes the pattern that creates the maximum number of chains more complicated, i.e., it repeats with a lower frequency than the pattern from [19,21]. In Figure 18b it is called the feather pattern. It adds an overhead of $\frac{W}{8}$ cycles to every second image row (giving an average of $\frac{W}{16}$ cycles per row).

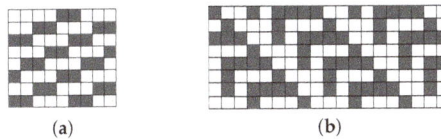

(a)   (b)

Figure 18. Image patterns that create the worst case average overhead for (a) [6,19,21] and for (b) [20].

The proposed architecture and the architectures of [23,25] are data-independent and do not have a chain stack. Therefore, they only require one clock cycle to process a pixel, with no end of row overhead for resolving chains. However, to process the complete image, [25] requires extending the image by 1 row and column on each side (i.e., to process the full image, the end of row overheads have not been completely eliminated). These results are summarised in Table 5.

Throughput also depends on the clock frequency. For each architecture and platform, the lowest clock frequency from Table 4 is selected, and scaled according to the overhead. From this, it is clearly seen in Table 5 that the proposed approach is 2 or 3 times faster than [23], primarily as a result of using memory for the row buffer rather than distributed registers. The reduction in overhead amplifies the small improvement in clock frequency over [6,21], giving a 26% improvement in throughput.

Table 5. Comparison of processing cycles for a $W \times H$ image.

Architecture	Number of Cycles	f_{max} (MHz)	Throughput (Mpix/s)
Johnston and Bailey [19]	$6/5 \times W \times H$	N/A	N/A
Klaiber et al. [6,21]	$6/5 \times W \times H$	170.53	142.11
Ma et al. [20]	$17/16 \times W \times H$	40.64	38.25
Jeong et al. [23]	$W \times H$	58.44	58.44
Tang et al. [25]	$(W+2) \times (H+2)$	104.26	102.65
This approach	$W \times H$	106.52	106.52 (Cyclone V)
		180.47	180.47 (Kintex 7)

5.5. Latency

In terms of CCA, latency can be defined as the number of clock cycles from the time when the last pixel of a connected component is received until its feature vector is output by the CCA architecture. There is a small latency (of a few clock cycles) resulting from pipelining, but the majority comes from detecting component completion, which is dependent on the image width, W. Since the width term dominates, the small pipeline latency (which is constant) will be ignored in this discussion.

The architecture of Ma et al. [20] has two data tables, one for feature vectors of connected components of the previous row and one for the current row. If a connected component is extended from the previous row to the current row, its feature vector is moved from one data table to the other. A connected component that is finished is not extended to the current row, i.e., when the end of the current row is reached the associated feature vector is still in the data table for the previous row. While processing the next row this data table scanned to detect completed components and output the feature vector. Due to aggressive relabelling, connected components are stored in the order that they appear in the current image row. Therefore, an object at the start of the row will have a latency of $2W$ cycles, while those at the end of the row will have a latency of W plus a scan time within the data table of up to $\frac{W}{2}$ (depending on the number of separate components on the row) to detect the completed object.

In the architecture of Klaiber et al. [6,21], the data table is scanned for completed objects at the start of the second row after the last pixel of the object. The latency before this scan, therefore, ranges from W to $2W$, depending on the position along the row. As a result of label recycling, the label could be anywhere within the data table, with the latency of detecting the completed component during the scan varying up to $\frac{W}{2}$. These combine to give an average latency of $1.75W$ up to a maximum of $2.5W$.

The mechanism of Tang et al. [25] detects completed objects when it encounters a hanging label, i.e., the end of a list of runs on the previous row with no connection to the current row. This is the earliest time that a component can be detected as completed, and has a latency of W clock cycles. Note that the preprocessing to convert from 4-connectivity to 8-connectivity does not introduce any significant latency. However, padding the image to ensure that the image borders are background pixels will introduce an additional row of latency (W clock cycles—not reported here).

In the proposed design, converting from a raster scan to a zig-zag scan introduces an additional latency relative to the other methods. Therefore, to minimise latency, it is essential to detect completed components at the earliest possible opportunity (on the following row), which is achieved by the new completion detection mechanism. The latency of the zig-zag conversion is W clock cycles on even numbered rows, and between 0 and $2W$ clock cycles on odd numbered rows (during the reverse scan). The latency of detection is between $2W$ at the start of a scan of a row (to scan all of the row, and back again on the next row), through to 0 at the end of a scan. These combine to give a latency of between W and $3W$, with an average latency of $2W$ clock cycles. If the zig-zag conversion is unnecessary (for example if streaming from memory in zig-zag order), then objects are detected as completed with a latency of between 0 and $2W$, with an average of W clock cycles.

The algorithm of Johnston and Bailey [18,19] does not allow completed objects to be detected before the end of the image. Similarly, Jeong et al. [23] gives no criterion for detecting a finished connected component before the end of the image. The latency is, therefore, the number of cycles from the last pixel of a connected component until the end of the image. These architectures were, therefore, not compared in terms of latency. In principle, however, although not part of the architecture of [23], there is no limitation (apart from a few more resources) against detecting and outputting the feature vector in a manner similar to that used in [21], or indeed that proposed in this paper.

Table 6 summarises the latency of the architectures considered. Although the proposed architecture introduces significant latency in the conversion of the input to a zig-zag scan, this has been mitigated by the proposed new approach to completed object detection. The slight increase in latency is the price to pay for the increase in throughput from the elimination of end of row overheads. Note that the feature vectors of any objects touching the last row of the image will be output with almost no latency (only the pipeline delay), which is significantly shorter than any of the other architectures.

Table 6. Latency (in clock cycles) for an image of width W.

Architecture	Average Latency	Maximum Latency
Ma et al. [20]	1.75 W	2 W
Klaiber et al. [6,21]	1.75 W	2.5 W
Tang et al. [25] (without padding)	W	W
This approach (with zig-zag conversion)	2 W	3 W
This approach (without zig-zag conversion)	W	2 W

6. Summary and Conclusions

Pixel based hardware CCA architectures are designed to process streamed images at one pixel per clock cycle. However, with synchronous memories within modern FPGAs, this limits the designs to one memory access per clock cycle, which can create issues with stale labels resulting from chains of mergers. Current approaches manage this by resolving stale labels at the end of each image row, although this introduces a variable, image dependent, delay.

Jeong et al. [23] solved this by replacing the memory with a multiplexed shift register, enabling all instances of old labels to be replaced immediately. However, the movement away from a memory structure comes at a cost of considerably increased logic resources and registers and a lower maximum clock frequency.

Tang et al. [25] took a different approach, and rather than relabel the pixels which have already been seen, manages merger resolution through manipulation of pointers within a linked list structure. This eliminates the overheads associated with chains, and provides an efficient mechanism for detecting completed components and recycling labels. Although it claims to have no overheads, it does require the border pixels within the image to be background. This would require padding the image before processing, and results in two clock cycles overhead for each row.

In this paper, we have demonstrated an alternative approach to resolve stale labels on-the-fly by using a zig-zag scan. This allows continuous streamed images to be processed with no data dependent overheads, while retaining the use of memory for buffering the previous row.

The cost of this approach is slightly increased control logic over prior memory based approaches. This is to handle the zig-zag scan, and to manage multiple lookups within the merger table. The memory requirements are reduced because fewer auxiliary data structures are required. The presented design also allows a slightly higher clock frequency than prior state-of-the-art designs, in addition to the improved throughput. The use of memory rather than a multiplexed shift register makes it significantly faster than the architecture of [23].

Conversion from a raster scan to a zig-zag scan does increase the latency (in terms of the number of clock cycles). This has been mitigated to some extent by a new algorithm that detects when objects are completed at the earliest possible time. Overall, the proposed changes give an improvement over current state-of-the-art methods.

Author Contributions: Conceptualization, D.G.B.; Methodology, D.G.B.; Software, D.G.B. & M.J.K.; Validation, M.J.K.; Investigation, D.G.B. & M.J.K.; Writing—Original Draft Preparation, D.G.B. & M.J.K.; Writing—Review & Editing, D.G.B. & M.J.K.

Funding: This research received no external funding.

Conflicts of Interest: The authors declare no conflict of interest.

Abbreviations

The following abbreviations are used in this manuscript:

AXI	Advanced extensible interface [27]
AT	Active tag—indicates whether a component is still active
CCA	Connected components analysis
DT	Data table—accumulates the component feature vector
FIFO	First in first out buffer
FPGA	Field programmable gate array
IFV	Initial feature vector—the feature vector of a single pixel
LUT	Look up table—the logic element on an FPGA
MT	Merger table—indicates equivalent labels, for obtaining the representative label
RAM	Random access memory
RB	Row buffer—caches labels assigned for use in the following row

References

1. He, L.; Ren, X.; Gao, Q.; Zhao, X.; Yao, B.; Chao, Y. The connected-component labeling problem: A review of state-of-the-art algorithms. *Pattern Recognit.* **2017**, *70*, 25–43, doi:10.1016/j.patcog.2017.04.018. [CrossRef]
2. Chang, F.; Chen, C.J.; Lu, C.J. A linear-time component-labeling algorithm using contour tracing technique. *Comput. Vis. Image Underst.* **2004**, *93*, 206–220, doi:10.1016/j.cviu.2003.09.002. [CrossRef]
3. AbuBaker, A.; Qahwaji, R.; Ipson, S.; Saleh, M. One scan connected component labeling technique. In Proceedings of the IEEE International Conference on Signal Processing and Communications (ICSPC 2007), Dubai, UAE, 24–27 November 2007; pp. 1283–1286, doi:10.1109/ICSPC.2007.4728561. [CrossRef]
4. Suzuki, K.; Horiba, I.; Sugie, N. Linear-time connected-component labeling based on sequential local operations. *Comput. Vis. Image Underst.* **2003**, *89*, 1–23, doi:10.1016/S1077-3142(02)00030-9. [CrossRef]
5. Rosenfeld, A.; Pfaltz, J. Sequential operations in digital picture processing. *J. Assoc. Comput. Mach.* **1966**, *13*, 471–494, doi:10.1145/321356.321357. [CrossRef]
6. Klaiber, M.; Bailey, D.G.; Simon, S. Comparative study and proof of single-pass connected components algorithms. *J. Math. Imaging Vis.* **2019**, submitted.
7. Di Stefano, L.; Bulgarelli, A. A simple and efficient connected components labeling algorithm. In Proceedings of the International Conference on Image Analysis and Processing, Venice, Italy, 27–29 September 1999; pp. 322–327, doi:10.1109/ICIAP.1999.797615. [CrossRef]
8. Wu, K.; Otoo, E.; Suzuki, K. Optimizing two-pass connected-component labeling algorithms. *Pattern Anal. Appl.* **2009**, *12*, 117–135, doi:10.1007/s10044-008-0109-y. [CrossRef]
9. Lacassagne, L.; Zavidovique, B. Light speed labeling: Efficient connected component labeling on RISC architectures. *J. Real-Time Image Process.* **2011**, *6*, 117–135, doi:10.1007/s11554-009-0134-0. [CrossRef]
10. He, L.; Chao, Y.; Suzuki, K. A run-based one-and-a-half-scan connected-component labeling algorithm. *Int. J. Pattern Recognit. Artif. Intell.* **2010**, *24*, 557–579, doi:10.1142/S0218001410008032. [CrossRef]
11. He, L.; Chao, Y.; Suzuki, K. A new two-scan algorithm for labeling connected components in binary images. In Proceedings of the World Congress on Engineering, London, UK, 4–6 July 2012; Volume II, pp. 1141–1146.
12. He, L.; Zhao, X.; Chao, Y.; Suzuki, K. Configuration-transition-based connected-component labeling. *IEEE Trans. Image Process.* **2014**, *23*, 943–951, doi:10.1109/TIP.2013.2289968. [CrossRef]
13. Zhao, X.; He, L.; Yao, B.; Chao, Y. A new connected-component labeling algorithm. *IEICE Trans. Inf. Syst.* **2015**, *98*, 2013–2016, doi:10.1587/transinf.2015EDL8135. [CrossRef]
14. Grana, C.; Borghesani, D.; Cucchiara, R. Optimized block-based connected components labeling with decision trees. *IEEE Trans. Image Process.* **2010**, *19*, 1596–1609, doi:10.1109/TIP.2010.2044963. [CrossRef] [PubMed]

15. Grana, C.; Baraldi, L.; Bolelli, F. Optimized connected components labeling with pixel prediction. In Proceedings of the International Conference on Advanced Concepts for Intelligent Vision Systems (ACIVS 2016), Lecce, Italy, 24–27 October 2016; Springer International Publishing: Cham, Switzerland, 2016; Volume 10016, pp. 431–440, doi:10.1007/978-3-319-48680-2_38. [CrossRef]

16. Schwenk, K.; Huber, F. Connected component labeling algorithm for very complex and high-resolution images on an FPGA platform. In Proceedings of the High Performance Computing in Remote Sensing V, Toulouse, France, 20–21 September 2015; Volume 9646, 14p, doi:10.1117/12.2194101. [CrossRef]

17. Appiah, K.; Hunter, A.; Dickenson, P.; Owens, J. A run-length based connected component algorithm for FPGA implementation. In Proceedings of the International Conference on Field Programmable Technology, Taipei, Taiwan, 8–10 December 2008; pp. 177–184, doi:10.1109/FPT.2008.4762381. [CrossRef]

18. Bailey, D.; Johnston, C. Single pass connected components analysis. In Proceedings of the Image and Vision Computing New Zealand (IVCNZ), Hamilton, New Zealand, 5–7 December 2007; pp. 282–287.

19. Johnston, C.T.; Bailey, D.G. FPGA implementation of a single-pass connected components algorithm. In Proceedings of the IEEE International Symposium on Electronic Design, Test and Applications (DELTA 2008), Hong Kong, China, 23–25 January 2008; pp. 228–231, doi:10.1109/DELTA.2008.21. [CrossRef]

20. Ma, N.; Bailey, D.; Johnston, C. Optimised single-pass connected components analysis. In Proceedings of the International Conference on Field Programmable Technology, Taipei, Taiwan, 8–10 December 2008; pp. 185–192, doi:10.1109/FPT.2008.4762382. [CrossRef]

21. Klaiber, M.J.; Bailey, D.G.; Baroud, Y.O.; Simon, S. A resource-efficient hardware architecture for connected component analysis. *IEEE Trans. Circuits Syst. Video Technol.* **2016**, *26*, 1334–1349. [CrossRef]

22. Trein, J.; Schwarzbacher, A.T.; Hoppe, B.; Noffz, K.H.; Trenschel, T. Development of a FPGA based real-time blob analysis circuit. In Proceedings of the Irish Signals and Systems Conference, Derry, UK, 13–14 September 2007; pp. 121–126.

23. Jeong, J.-w.; Lee, G.-b.; Lee, M.-j.; Kim, J.-G. A single-pass connected component labeler without label merging period. *J. Signal Process. Syst.* **2016**, *84*, 211–223, doi:10.1007/s11265-015-1048-7. [CrossRef]

24. Zhao, F.; Lu, H.Z.; Zhang, Z.Y. Real-time single-pass connected components analysis algorithm. *EURASIP J. Image Video Process.* **2013**, *2013*, 21, doi:10.1186/1687-5281-2013-21. [CrossRef]

25. Tang, J.W.; Shaikh-Husin, N.; Sheikh, U.U.; Marsono, M.N. A linked list run-length-based single-pass connected component analysis for real-time embedded hardware. *J. Real-Time Image Process.* **2016**, *15*, 197–215, doi:10.1007/s11554-016-0590-2. [CrossRef]

26. Wu, K.; Otoo, E.; Shoshani, A. Optimizing connected component labelling algorithms. In Proceedings of the Medical Imaging 2005: Image Processing, San Diego, CA, USA, 15–17 February 2005; Volume 5747, pp. 1965–1976, doi:10.1117/12.596105. [CrossRef]

27. ARM. *AMBA 4 AXI4-Stream Protocol Specification*; Volume IHI 0051A; ARM: Cambridge, UK, 2010.

Journal of
Imaging

MDPI

Article

A JND-Based Pixel-Domain Algorithm and Hardware Architecture for Perceptual Image Coding

Zhe Wang *, Trung-Hieu Tran , Ponnanna Kelettira Muthappa and Sven Simon

Institute of Parallel and Distributed Systems, University of Stuttgart, 70569 Stuttgart, Germany;
trung.hieu.tran@ipvs.uni-stuttgart.de (T.-H.T.); st152915@stud.uni-stuttgart.de (P.K.M.);
sven.simon@ipvs.uni-stuttgart.de (S.S.)
* Correspondence: zhe.wang@ipvs.uni-stuttgart.de; Tel.: +49-711-68588403

Received: 29 March 2019; Accepted: 16 April 2019; Published: 26 April 2019

Abstract: This paper presents a hardware efficient pixel-domain just-noticeable difference (JND) model and its hardware architecture implemented on an FPGA. This JND model architecture is further proposed to be part of a low complexity pixel-domain perceptual image coding architecture, which is based on downsampling and predictive coding. The downsampling is performed adaptively on the input image based on regions-of-interest (ROIs) identified by measuring the downsampling distortions against the visibility thresholds given by the JND model. The coding error at any pixel location can be guaranteed to be within the corresponding JND threshold in order to obtain excellent visual quality. Experimental results show the improved accuracy of the proposed JND model in estimating visual redundancies compared with classic JND models published earlier. Compression experiments demonstrate improved rate-distortion performance and visual quality over JPEG-LS as well as reduced compressed bit rates compared with other standard codecs such as JPEG 2000 at the same peak signal-to-perceptible-noise ratio (PSPNR). FPGA synthesis results targeting a mid-range device show very moderate hardware resource requirements and over 100 Megapixel/s throughput of both the JND model and the perceptual encoder.

Keywords: just-noticeable difference (JND); luminance masking; contrast masking; texture detection; perceptual coding; JPEG-LS; downsampling; FPGA

1. Introduction

Advances in sensor and display technologies have led to rapid growth in data bandwidth in high-performance imaging systems. Compression is becoming imperative for such systems to address the bandwidth issue in a cost-efficient way. Moreover, in many real-time applications, there is a growing need for a compression algorithm to meet several competing requirements such as decent coding efficiency, low complexity, low latency and high visual quality [1]. It has been realized that algorithms specifically designed to meet such requirements could be desirable [2–4]. Compared with off-line processing systems, the computational power and memory resources in real-time high-bandwidth systems are much more limited due to the relatively tight constraints on latency, power dissipation and cost, especially in embedded systems such as display panels for ultra high definition contents and remote monitoring cameras with high temporal and spatial resolutions.

The use of existing transform-domain codecs such as JPEG 2000 and HEVC has been limited in real-time high-bandwidth systems, since such codecs typically require storing multiple image lines or frames. Especially when the spatial resolution of the image is high, the line or frame buffers result in both expensive on-chip memories and non-negligible latency, which are disadvantages for a cost-efficient hardware implementation of the codec, e.g., on FPGAs. While JPEG-LS is considered to have created a reasonable balance between complexity and compression ratio for lossless coding, its use in lossy coding is much less widespread due to the inferior coding efficiency compared with transform-domain codecs and stripe-like artifacts in smooth image regions. It is desirable to investigate the feasibility of a lightweight and hardware-friendly pixel-domain codec with improved compression performance as well as significantly improved visual quality over that of the lossy JPEG-LS.

One possibility is to exploit the visual redundancy associated with properties of the human visual system (HVS) in the pixel domain. Features and effects of the HVS can be modeled either in the pixel domain or in the transform domain. While effects such as the Contrast Sensitivity Function (CSF) are best described in the Fourier, DCT or Wavelet domain and hence can be exploited by compression algorithms operating in these domains [5–7], other effects such as visual masking can be well modeled in the pixel domain [8,9]. The term visual masking is used to describe the phenomenon that a stimulus (such as an intensity difference in the pixel domain) is rendered invisible to the HVS by local image activities nearby, hence allowing a coarser quantization for the input image without impacting the visual quality. The masking effects of the HVS can be estimated by a visibility threshold measurement model, which ideally provides a threshold level under which the difference between the original signal and the target signal is invisible. Such a difference threshold is referred to as just-noticeable difference (JND) [10]. Compression algorithms like JPEG-LS operating in the pixel domain can be adapted to exploit the pixel-domain JND models, e.g., by setting the quantization step size adaptively based on the JND thresholds. One problem with such a straightforward approach, however, is that the JND thresholds must be made available to the decoder, incurring a relatively large overhead.

A classic pixel-domain JND model was proposed by Chou and Li [9]. This model serves as a basis for various further JND models proposed in research work on perceptual image/video compression, such as Yang et al.'s model [11] and Liu et al.'s model [12], which achieve improved accuracy in estimating visual redundancies at the cost of higher complexity. A good review of JND models as well as approaches to exploit JND models in perceptual image coding was given by Wu et al. [13].

In this work, a new region-adaptive pixel-domain JND model based on efficient local operations is proposed for a more accurate detection of visibility thresholds compared with the classic JND model [9] and for a reduced complexity compared with more recent ones [11,12]. A low complexity pixel-domain perceptual image coder [14] is then used to exploit the visibility thresholds given by the proposed JND model. The coding algorithm addresses both coding efficiency and visual quality issues in conventional pixel-domain coders in a framework of adaptive downsampling guided by perceptual regions-of-interest (ROIs) based on JND thresholds. In addition, hardware architecture for both the proposed JND model and the perceptual encoder is presented. Experimental results including hardware resource utilization of FPGA-based implementations show reasonable performance and moderate hardware complexity for both the proposed JND model and the perceptual encoder. The remainder of the paper is organized as follows. Section 2 reviews background and existing work on pixel-domain JND modeling. The proposed JND model and its FPGA hardware architecture are presented in Sections 3 and 4, respectively. Section 5 discusses the hardware architecture for the JND-based perceptual image coding algorithm [14]. Experimental results based on standard test images as well as FPGA synthesis results are presented in Section 6, which show the effectiveness of both the proposed JND model and the perceptual encoder. Section 7 summarizes this work.

2. Background in Pixel-Domain JND Modeling

In 1995, Chou and Li proposed a pixel-domain JND model [9] based on experimental results of psychophysical studies. Figure 1 illustrates Chou and Li's model. For each pixel location, two visual masking effects are considered, namely luminance masking and contrast masking, and visibility thresholds due to such effects are estimated based on functions of local pixel intensity levels. The two resulting quantities, luminance masking threshold LM and contrast masking threshold CM, are then combined by an integration function into the final JND threshold. In Chou and Li's model, the integration takes the form of the MAX($\cdot$) function, i.e., the JND threshold is modeled as the dominating effect between luminance masking and contrast masking. Basic algorithmic parts of JND modeling described in the rest of this section are mainly based on Chou and Li's model.

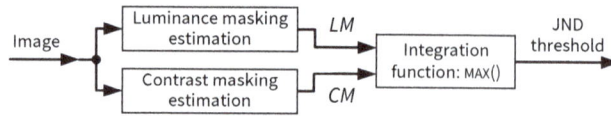

Figure 1. Chou and Li's pixel-domain just-noticeable difference (JND) model (1995).

2.1. Luminance Masking Estimation

The luminance masking effect is modeled in [9] based on the average grey level within a 5×5 window centered at the current pixel location, as depicted in Figure 2a. Let $BL(i,j)$ denote the background luminance at pixel location (i,j), with $0 \le i < H$ and $0 \le j < W$ for an image of size $W \times H$. Let $B(m,n)$ be a 5×5 matrix of weighing factors ($m, n = 0, 1, 2, 3, 4$). As shown in Figure 2b, a relatively larger weight (2) is given to the eight inner pixels surrounding the current pixel, since such pixels have stronger influences on the average luminance at the current pixel location. The sum of all weighting factors in matrix B is 32. While other weighting factors can be considered for evaluating the average background luminance, the matrix B used in Chou and Li's JND model [9] results in highly efficient computation and has been used in many subsequent models (see, e.g., [11,12]). Further, let $p(i,j)$ denote the pixel grey level at (i,j). The average background luminance BL is then given by

$$BL(i,j) = \frac{1}{32} \sum_{m=0}^{4} \sum_{n=0}^{4} p(i-2+m, j-2+n) \cdot B(m,n) \tag{1}$$

Obviously, Equation (1) can be implemented in hardware by additions and shifts only. It can be readily verified that 23 additions are required. Chou and Li examined the relationship between the background luminance and distortion visibility due to luminance masking based on results of subjective experiments [9,15], and concluded that the distortion visibility threshold decreases in a nonlinear manner as the background luminance changes from completely dark to middle grey (around 127 on an intensity scale from 0 to 255) and increases approximately linearly as the background luminance changes from grey to completely bright. Specifically, a square root function is used in [9] to approximate the visibility thresholds due to luminance masking for low background luminance (below 127), whereas and a linear function was used for high background luminance (above 127):

$$LM(i,j) = \begin{cases} T_0 \cdot \left(1 - \sqrt{\frac{BL(i,j)}{127}}\right) + 3, & \text{if } BL(i,j) \le 127 \\ \gamma \cdot (BL(i,j) - 127) + 3, & \text{otherwise,} \end{cases} \tag{2}$$

where T_0 denotes the visibility threshold when the background luminance is 0 in the nonlinear region when $BL(i,j) \le 127$, while γ is the slope of the growth of the visibility threshold in the linear region when the background luminance is greater than 127. The values of parameters T_0 and γ depend on the specific application scenario, such as viewing conditions and properties of the display. Both T_0 and γ increase as the viewing distance increases, leading to higher visibility thresholds. Default values of $T_0 = 17$ and $\gamma = \frac{3}{128}$ are used in [9], and these are also used for the JND model in this paper.

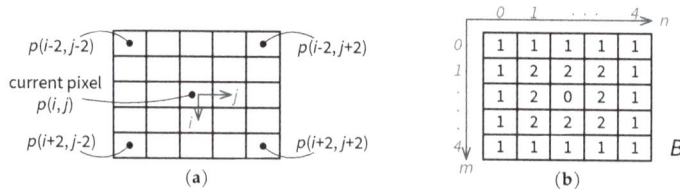

Figure 2. Pixel window for JND estimation and weighing factors for the background luminance: (**a**) JND estimation window of 5×5; and (**b**) weighing factor matrix B.

2.2. Contrast Masking Estimation

The contrast masking effect is modeled in [9] based on: (1) the background luminance at the current pixel; and (2) luminance variations across the current pixel in the 5×5 JND estimation window. Luminance variations, e.g., due to edges are measured by four spatial operators, G_1–G_4, as depicted in Figure 3. The result from an operator G_k is the weighted luminance intensity difference across the current pixel in the direction corresponding to k, with $k = 1, 2, 3, 4$ for vertical, diagonal 135°, diagonal 45° and horizontal difference, respectively. The kth weighted luminance intensity difference ID_k is calculated by 2D correlation, and the maximum weighted luminance difference MG is obtained as:

$$ID_k(i,j) = \frac{1}{16} \sum_{m=0}^{4} \sum_{n=0}^{4} p(i-2+m, j-2+n) \cdot G_k(m,n) \tag{3}$$

$$MG(i,j) = \max_{k=1,2,3,4} \{|ID_k(i,j)|\} \tag{4}$$

In Chou and Li's model, for a fixed average background luminance, the visibility threshold due to contrast masking is a linear function of MG (also called luminance edge height in [9]) by

$$CM(i,j) = \alpha(i,j) \cdot MG(i,j) + \beta(i,j) \tag{5}$$

Both the slope α and intercept β of such a linear function depend on the background luminance BL. The relationship between α, β and BL was modeled by Chou and Li as

$$\alpha(i,j) = BL(i,j) \cdot 0.0001 + 0.115 \tag{6}$$

$$\beta(i,j) = \lambda - BL(i,j) \cdot 0.01 \tag{7}$$

Parameter λ in Equation (7) depends on the viewing condition. The value of λ increases as the viewing distance becomes larger, leading to higher visibility thresholds. A default value of $\lambda = 0.5$ is used in [9].

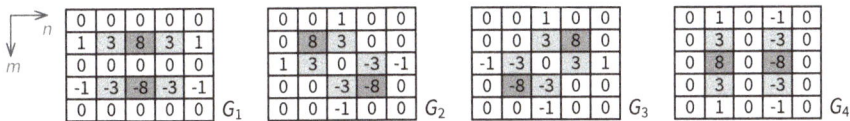

Figure 3. Directional intensity difference measurement operators G_1–G_4.

2.3. Formulation of JND Threshold

In Chou and Li's model, the final JND threshold is considered to be the dominating effect between luminance masking and contrast masking:

$$JND(i,j) = \max\{LM(i,j), CM(i,j)\} \tag{8}$$

Since in real-world visual signals there often exist multiple masking effects simultaneously, such as luminance masking and contrast masking, the integration of multiple masking effects into a final visibility threshold for the HVS is a fundamental part of a JND model [11]. Contrary to Chou and Li, who considered only the dominating effect among different masking effects, Yang et al. [11,16] proposed that: (1) in terms of the visibility threshold, the combined effect T in the presence of multiple masking effects $T^1, T^2, ..., T^N$ is greater than that of a single masking source T^i ($i = 1, 2, ..., N$); and (2) the combined effect T can be modeled by a certain form of addition of individual masking effects, whereas T is smaller than a simple linear summation of the individual effects $T^i, i = 1, 2, ..., N$, i.e.,

$$\max\{T^1, T^2, ..., T^N\} < T < \sum_{i=1}^{N} T^i \tag{9}$$

Yang et al. [11] further proposed that the right-hand side of the above inequality is due to the overlapping of individual effects. A pair-wise overlap $O^{i,j}$ is hence modeled for the combination of two individual masking factors T^i, T^j $(i < j)$ by a nonlinear function $\gamma(T^i, T^j)$, weighted by an empirically determined gain reduction coefficient $C^{i,j}$ $(0 < C < 1)$, i.e.,

$$O^{i,j} = C^{i,j} \cdot \gamma(T^i, T^j) \tag{10}$$

The total overlap is modeled as the sum of overlaps between any pair of masking factors. The combined visibility threshold is given by the difference between the sum of all thresholds due to individual masking effects and the total overlap, called the nonlinear-additivity model for masking (NAMM) [11]:

$$T = \sum_{i=1}^{N} T^i - \sum_{i=1}^{N} \sum_{j=i+1}^{N} O^{i,j} = \sum_{i=1}^{N} T^i - \sum_{i=1}^{N} \sum_{j=i+1}^{N} C^{i,j} \cdot \gamma\left(T^i, T^j\right) \tag{11}$$

For simplicity and the compatibility with existing models including Chou and Li's, in Yang et al.'s model [11] the nonlinear function γ is approximated as the minimum function $\text{MIN}(\cdot)$, and only luminance masking and contrast masking effects are considered. The result is therefore an approximation of the general model given by Equation (11). In Yang et al.'s model, the final visibility threshold at pixel location (i, j) in component θ $(\theta = Y, Cb, Cr)$ of the input image is a nonlinear combination of the luminance masking threshold T^L and an edge-weighted contrast masking threshold T_θ^C given by

$$JND_\theta(i, j) = T^L(i, j) + T_\theta^C(i, j) - C_\theta^{L,C} \cdot \text{MIN}\{T^L(i, j), T_\theta^C(i, j)\} \tag{12}$$

Yang et al. selected default values of gain reduction coefficients as $C_Y^{L,C} = 0.3$, $C_{Cb}^{L,C} = 0.25$ and $C_{Cr}^{L,C} = 0.2$ based on subjective tests in [16]. The compatibility with Chou and Li's model can be seen by letting $\theta = Y$ and $C_Y^{L,C} = 1$ in Equation (12), i.e., considering the luminance image only and assuming maximum overlapping between the luminance and contrast masking effects.

3. Proposed JND Model

In the proposed JND model, each input pixel is assumed to belong to one of three basic types of image regions: edge (e), texture (t) and smoothness (s). The weighting of the contrast masking effect, as well as the combination of the basic luminance masking threshold (LM) and contrast masking threshold (CM) into the final JND threshold, is dependent on the region type of the current pixel. Figure 4 illustrates the proposed JND model, where W_e, W_t and W_s are factors used for weighting the contrast masking effect in edge, texture and smooth regions, respectively. As shown in Figure 4, to combine LM and weighted CM values, the $\text{MAX}()$ function is used for edge and NAMM is used for texture and smooth regions. Depending on the region type of a current pixel, the final output, i.e., JND threshold for the current pixel, is selected from three candidates JND_e, JND_t and JND_s, corresponding to the visibility threshold evaluated for the edge, texture and smooth region, respectively.

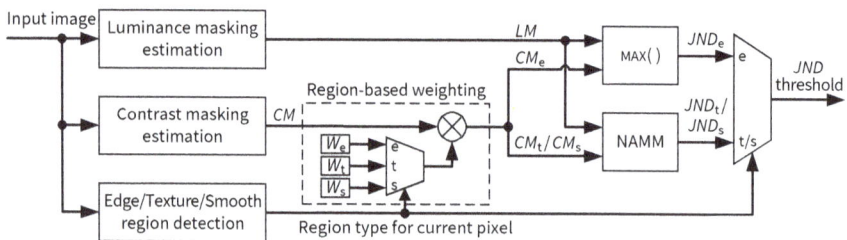

Figure 4. Block diagram of the proposed JND model.

The individual treatment of edge regions in a JND model was first proposed by Yang et al. [16]. Clear edges such as object boundaries are familiar to the human brain, since they typically have simple structures and draw immediate attention from an observer. Hence, even a non-expert observer can be considered as relatively "experienced" in viewing edge regions of an image. As a result, distortions, e.g., due to lossy compression, are more easily identified at edges than in other regions with luminance non-uniformity [11,17,18]. In Yang et al.'s work [11], visibility thresholds due to contrast masking are reduced for edge regions (detected by the Canny operator) compared with non-edge regions. Weighting factors of 0.1 and 1.0 are used for edge and non-edge pixels, respectively, such that edges are preserved in a subsequent compression encoder exploiting the JND thresholds.

Textures, on the other hand, are intensity level variations usually occurring on surfaces, e.g., due to non-smoothness of objects such as wood and bricks. Since textures have a rich variety and generally exhibit a mixture of both regularity (e.g., repeated patterns) and randomness (e.g., noise-like scatterings) [19], the structure of a texture is much more difficult to predict than that of an edge for the human brain. Eckert and Bradley [18] indicated that about three times the quantization noise can be hidden in a texture image compared with an image of simple edges with similar spectral contents. To adequately estimate the contrast masking effects in texture regions, Liu et al. [12] proposed to decompose the image into a textural component and a structural one. Both components are processed independently for contrast masking in Liu et al's model [12], with the masking effects computed for the textural and structural components weighted by factors of 3 and 1, respectively. The masking effects of both components are added up to obtain the final contrast making in Liu et al.'s JND model.

The main differences of our JND model to the works by Chou and Li [9], Yang et al. [11] and Liu et al. [12] are: (1) marking pixels in an input image as edge, texture or smooth regions, instead of decomposing the image into multiple components processed separately; (2) combination of *LM* and *CM* into the final JND threshold using the maximum operator for edge regions and NAMM [11] for non-edge regions; (3) alternative weighting of the contrast masking effect compared with [11,12]; and (4) less complex edge and texture detection schemes more suitable for FPGA implementation compared with [11,12]. The following subsections provide details on our JND model.

3.1. Edge and Texture Detection

Each input pixel is assigned one out of three possible regions in the input image, i.e., edge, texture and smoothness. Different regions are detected by lightweight local operations such as 2D filtering, which can be implemented efficiently on FPGAs (see Section 4). Figure 5 illustrates the detection scheme, where the input is the original image while the outputs are three binary maps corresponding to edge, texture and smooth regions, respectively. Edges are detected by the Sobel operator [20] which uses two 3×3 kernels. It is well known that the Sobel operator requires less computation and memory compared with the Canny operator [21], which is used in the JND models in [11,12]. To reduce the impact of noise in the input image, Gaussian low-pass filtering is performed prior to edge detection. A two-dimensional 3×5 Gaussian kernel with standard deviation $\sigma = 0.83$ is used by default in the proposed JND model. The vertical size of the Gaussian kernel is chosen as 3 for a low memory requirement as well as a low latency of an FPGA implementation. For computational efficiency, an integer approximation of the Gaussian kernel discussed in Section 6.1 is used, which can be implemented efficiently by shifts and additions. Figure 6 presents edges detected in different JND models for the BARB test image. Edges obtained by the proposed lightweight scheme (i.e., Gaussian smoothing followed by Sobel) are depicted in Figure 6b. The four panels in the middle and right columns of Figure 6 show outputs of the Canny edge detector in Yang et al.'s model [11] with sensitivity thresholds of 0.5 (default [11], middle panels) and 0.25 (right panels). Morphological operations have been used in Yang et al.'s software implementation [22] of their JND model to expand the edges given by the original Canny operator (see Figure 6d,f). Such operations result in bigger regions around the edges having reduced visibility thresholds to protect edge structures.

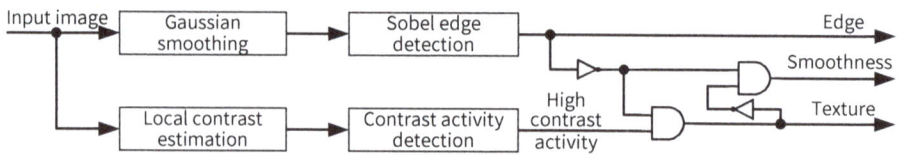

Figure 5. Edge, texture and smooth region detection scheme.

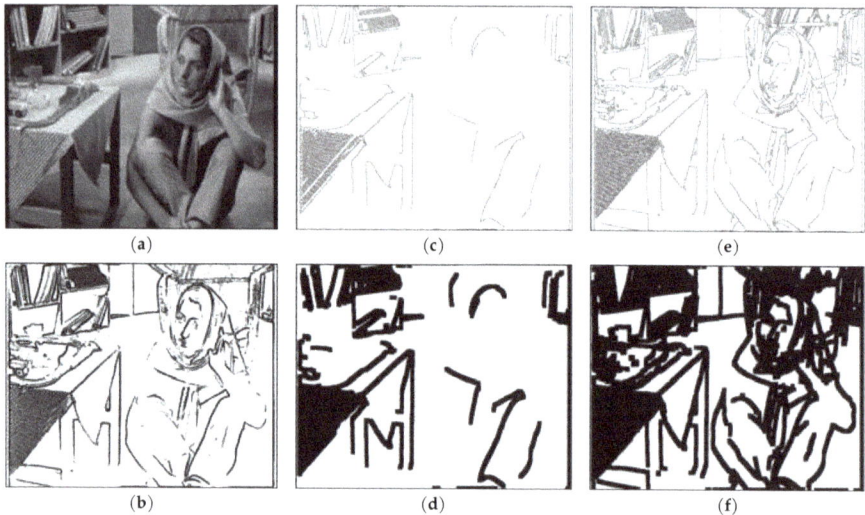

Figure 6. Edges (black) obtained in the proposed and Yang et al.'s JND model: (**a**) original BARB image; (**b**) edges detected by the proposed scheme with default edge-magnitude threshold 11; (**c**) output of original Canny with edge sensitivity threshold 0.5 (default in [11]); (**d**) actual edge regions from Yang et al.'s implementation [22] with threshold 0.5; (**e**) original Canny with edge sensitivity threshold 0.25; and (**f**) actual edge regions from Yang et al.'s implementation [22] with edge sensitivity threshold 0.25.

Many of the well-known texture analysis techniques (e.g., [23]) focus on distinguishing between different types of textures. While such techniques achieve promising results for image segmentation, they typically require larger blocks and computationally-intensive statistical analysis such as multi-dimensional histograms, and their complexity/performance trade-offs are not well-suited for JND modeling especially in resource-constrained scenarios. As discussed earlier, a desirable property of a JND model is to distinguish textures as opposed to structural edges and smooth regions, and a reasonable complexity/quality trade-off is an advantage especially for FPGA applications. Even if some texture regions were not picked up by a lightweight texture detection scheme compared with a sophisticated one, the visibility thresholds in such regions computed by the JND model would still be valid, e.g., for a visually lossless compression of the input image, since weighting factors for contrast masking are generally smaller in non-texture regions than in texture ones. For the reasons above, a low complexity local operator is used for texture detection in our JND model.

The proposed texture detection scheme works as follows. Firstly, a local contrast value is calculated for every pixel location. Figure 7a shows a 3×3 neighborhood for evaluating the local contrast, where p_0 is the intensity value at the current pixel location and p_1–p_8 are intensity values of the eight immediate neighbors of p_0. Let μ be the average of all intensity values in the 3×3 neighborhood. Then, the local contrast C can be measured for the current pixel location in terms of mean absolute deviation (MAD):

$$C^{\mathrm{MAD}} = \frac{1}{9} \sum_{i=0}^{8} |p_i - \mu|, \quad \text{where } \mu = \frac{1}{9} \sum_{j=0}^{8} p_j \tag{13}$$

Obviously, C^{MAD} is invariant to image rotation and intensity-level shifts. In an implementation, e.g., based on FPGA, the divisions in Equation (13) can be avoided since such divisions can be canceled by multiplications on both sides of the equation. A division-free implementation of the local contrast calculation equivalent to that in Equation (13) is used in the proposed hardware architecture for the JND model, as discussed in Section 4.4.2.

Next, the total contrast activity in the neighborhood is estimated based on local contrasts. Figure 7b presents an example of computed local contrasts, the thresholding of such local contrasts into a contrast significance map, the computation of a contrast activity value and finally the derivation of a binary high-contrast-activity decision. Let C_i be the local contrast at pixel location i in the 3×3 neighborhood centered about the current pixel. Then, contrast significance s_i is given by

$$s_i = \begin{cases} 1, & \text{if } C_i \geq T_C \\ 0, & \text{otherwise}, \end{cases} \tag{14}$$

where T_C is a threshold for local contrast. A higher value of T_C corresponds to a smaller number of local contrasts detected as significant. In this paper, $T_C = 8$ is used. Contrast activity CA at the current pixel location is estimated as the total number of significant local contrasts in the 3×3 neighborhood:

$$CA = \sum_{i=0}^{8} s_i \tag{15}$$

The presence of a texture is typically characterized by a high contrast activity (HA):

$$HA = \begin{cases} 1, & \text{if } CA \geq T_A \\ 0, & \text{otherwise}, \end{cases} \tag{16}$$

where T_A is a threshold for contrast activity. A lower value of T_A corresponds to a higher sensitivity to local contrast activities. In this paper, $T_A = 5$ is used. Figure 8a plots the contrast activities computed for the BARB image (cf. Figure 6a). The HA map after thresholding is shown in Figure 8b.

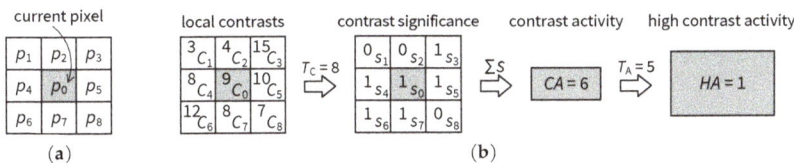

Figure 7. Illustration of contrast activity detection: (**a**) neighborhood for local contrast estimation; and (**b**) example of local contrasts, contrast significance and derivation of the high-contrast-activity decision.

Finally, denoting the binary output of the edge detector by E, a pixel is considered to be in a texture region (T) if it has a high contrast activity and is not an edge, as indicated in Figure 5:

$$T = HA \wedge \overline{E} \tag{17}$$

and a pixel is considered to be in a smooth region (S) if it is neither an edge nor a texture:

$$S = \overline{E} \wedge \overline{T} \tag{18}$$

The final edge, texture and smooth regions obtained for the BARB image are depicted in Figure 8c. While it is possible to achieve a better separation of the image into different regions using more sophisticated texture analysis and segmentation algorithms such as in Liu et al.'s model [12], the proposed lightweight edge and texture detection scheme has achieved quite reasonable results, as shown in Figure 8c, which provides a firm basis for a region-based weighting of contrast masking discussed in the next subsection. Comparisons of different JND models are given in Sections 6.2 and 6.3.

Figure 8. Texture information of the BARB image in the proposed scheme; (**a**) visualization of contrast activity (treated as grey values and multiplied by 20 for visibility); (**b**) high contrast activity (black) regions after thresholding with $T_A = 5$; and (**c**) final edge, texture and smooth regions.

3.2. Region-Based Weighting of Visibility Thresholds due to Contrast Masking

In the proposed JND model, each basic contrast masking threshold estimated using Equation (5) is multiplied by a weighting factor based on the region in which the current pixel is located. Let W_e, W_t and W_s be the weighting factors for edge (e), texture (t) and smooth (s) regions, respectively. Then, the adaptively weighted contrast masking effect CM_κ is given by

$$CM_\kappa(i,j) = W_\kappa \cdot CM(i,j), \quad \kappa = \{e, t, s\} \tag{19}$$

where κ denotes the region type of the current pixel. In Yang et al.'s JND model [11], a weighting factor equivalent to $W_e = 0.1$ is used to preserve visual quality in edge regions, while in Liu et al.'s JND model [12] a weighting factor equivalent to $W_t = 3$ is used to avoid underestimating visibility thresholds in texture regions. From Equation (19), it is obvious that larger values of W_e, W_t and W_s correspond to larger results for the contrast masking effects (and hence the final JND thresholds) in edge, texture and smooth regions, respectively. Values for weighting factors W_e, W_t and W_s may vary, for example depending on different viewing conditions and applications. Based on our experiments as well as for reasons discussed in the following subsection, values for the weighting factors are selected as $W_e = 1$, $W_t = 1.75$ and $W_s = 1$ in this work as default for the proposed JND model for normal viewing conditions and general purpose test images. More details about the test images and viewing conditions in our experiments are provided in Section 6.2.

3.3. Final JND Threshold

In the proposed JND model, the luminance masking and weighted contrast masking effects are combined using the NAMM model in texture (t) and smooth (s) regions, whereas, in edge (e) regions, the masking effects are combined using the maximum operator $\text{MAX}(\cdot)$, as shown in Equation (20).

$$JND(i,j) = \begin{cases} LM(i,j) + CM_\kappa(i,j) - C_\gamma^{L,C} \cdot \text{MIN}\{LM(i,j), CM_\kappa(i,j)\}, & \text{if } \kappa = \{t, s\} \\ \text{MAX}\{LM(i,j), CM_e(i,j)\}, & \text{otherwise.} \end{cases} \tag{20}$$

The individual treatment of edge regions is based on the similarity between simple edge regions and scenarios in classical psychophysical experiments to determine distortion visibility thresholds in the presence of luminance edges, where simple edges are studied under different background luminance conditions [8]. Hence, for well-defined edges, the visibility thresholds modeled by Chou and Li based on such experiments should be considered as suitable. For the same reason, we selected $W_e = 1$.

4. Hardware Architecture for the Proposed JND Model

4.1. Overview of Proposed JND Hardware Architecture

Figure 9 depicts the overall hardware architecture of proposed JND estimation core implemented on FPGA. The core includes four main parts (names of functional modules of the architecture are indicated in italics): *Luminance Masking Function*, *Contrast Masking Function*, *Edge-texture-smooth Function*, and *JND Calculation Function*. The streaming input pixel ($p(i, j)$) is first buffered in row buffers which are needed for the filtering operations applied in our JND model. From the row buffers, pixels are grouped as a column of 3 pixels ($\{p(i, j)\}_1$) or a column of 5 pixels ($\{p(i, j)\}_2$). The 3-pixel column is sent to the *Edge-texture-smooth Function*, while the 5-pixel column is sent to both *Luminance Masking Function* and *Contrast Masking Function*. From these three functions, region mask $M_{ec}(i, j)$, luminance masking threshold $LM(i, j)$ and contrast masking threshold $CM(i, j)$ are calculated, respectively. The *JND Calculation Function* combines these masks together and generates the final JND value ($JND(i, j)$) for each pixel in the input image.

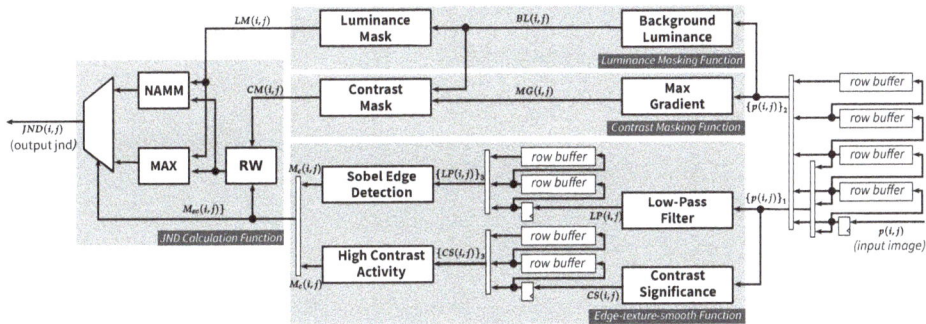

Figure 9. Overall architecture of the proposed JND model.

4.1.1. Row Buffer

The proposed JND architecture employs a common row buffer design [24], which includes registers for the current row pixel and several FIFOs for previous row pixels. Suppose r is the vertical window radius of a filter kernel, the number of required FIFOs for this design is $2 \cdot r - 1$. The row buffers are needed before every filtering operation. In our implementation, there are three places where row buffers are deployed: after the input, before the calculation of high contrast activity and after low-pass filtering. The latter two row buffers are for $r = 1$ and the first row buffer is for $r = 1$ and $r = 2$.

As shown in Figure 9, the rightmost row buffers contain four FIFOs to support a filter kernel with a maximum size of 5 ($r = 2$). The output of the row buffer forms a pixel-array denoted as $\{p(i, j)\}_2$ (see Equation (21)) which is fed to *Background Luminance* module and *Max Gradient* module where 5×5 filter kernels are applied. A subset of this row buffer output, $\{p(i, j)\}_1$, is sent to *Low-Pass Filter* module and *Contrast Significance* module which consist of 3×5 and 3×3 kernel filtering operations, respectively.

$$\{p(i, j)\}_r = \{p(i - r, j), p(i - r + 1, j), ..., p(i + r - 1, j), p(i + r, j)\} \tag{21}$$

4.1.2. Pipelined Weighted-Sum Module

For filtering operations, which are employed in several parts of proposed JND model, a common design to perform weighted-sum is introduced, as illustrated in Figure 10. The block representation of a *Pipelined Weighted-Sum* (PWS) module is depicted in Figure 10a. The input to this module is an array of column pixel denoted as $\{p(i, j)\}_{rm}$, and the output is a weighted-sum value calculated as

$$\hat{p}(i,j) = w_s \cdot \left(\sum_{m=0}^{2 \cdot r_m - 1} \sum_{n=0}^{2 \cdot r_n - 1} \left(w_{mn} \cdot p(i+m-r_m, j+n-r_n) \right) \right). \tag{22}$$

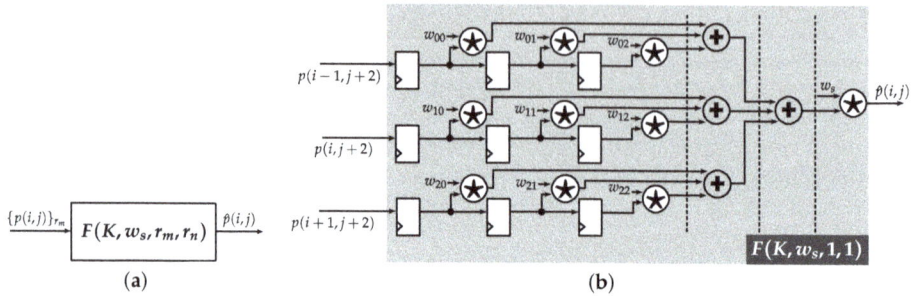

Figure 10. Pipelined Weighted-Sum (PWS) module. (**a**) Block representation. (**b**) PWS for 3×3 kernel. Dotted lines indicate possible pipeline cuts. The $\star$ operator indicates customized shift-based multiplier.

The *PWS* module is parameterized as a function $F(K, w_s, r_m, r_n)$, where K is a 2D array of coefficients, w_s is an output scaling factor, and r_m, r_n are vertical and horizontal kernel window radius, respectively. Figure 10b presents a zoom-in sample design for $F(K, w_s, 1, 1)$ with K defined as

$$K = \begin{bmatrix} w_{00} & w_{01} & w_{02} \\ w_{10} & w_{11} & w_{12} \\ w_{20} & w_{21} & w_{22} \end{bmatrix} \tag{23}$$

The operator denoted as $\star$ is a *Customized Shift-based Multiplier* (CSM), which generally consists of sum and shift operators. The actual content of this operator will be defined according to the value of a given coefficient. For example, considering the coefficient -3 in kernel G_1 (see Figure 3), the multiplication of this coefficient with a pixel value p can be rewritten as: $-3 \cdot p = -(p \ll 1 + p)$, which now consists of one left shift operator, one adder and one sign-change operator. Since all the coefficients are known, this customized multiplier strategy allows us to optimize for both timing and hardware resource.

4.2. Luminance Masking Function

As discussed in Section 2.1, the calculation of the luminance masking threshold (LM) includes two steps. The first step is finding the background luminance (BL), which can be realized by a *PWS* module $F(B, \frac{1}{32}, 2, 2)$. The second step is calculating LM based on the value of BL. Since the value of BL belongs to the same range as of input pixel value, which is an 8-bit integer in our implementation, the latter step can be simply realized as a look-up operation (see Figure 11). The *LM ROM* is implemented by Block RAM and has 256 entries, each with $5 + \sigma$ bits where 5 and σ are implicitly the number of bits for integer part and fractional part of LM, respectively. The output of this function is indeed 2^σ larger than the actual value of LM ($\widehat{LM}(i,j) = 2^\sigma \cdot LM(i,j)$). The scaling factor 2^σ is discussed further in Section 4.3.

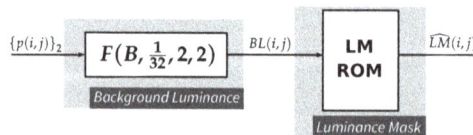

Figure 11. Luminance masking function.

4.3. Contrast Masking Function

Contrast masking function consists of two modules: the first module (*Max Gradient*) calculates *MG* based on input pixels from the row buffer. The second module (*Contrast Mask*) computes *CM* from *MG* and *BL*, which is the output of *Background Luminance* module (see Figure 12). For each of the directional gradient operations (G_i, $i = 1, 2, 3, 4$), *PWS* module is deployed with output scaling factor $w_s = \frac{1}{16}$ and the two radii are set to 2. Absolute values of these modules' outputs are then calculated, by *Abs* functions, and compared to each other to find the maximum value (*MG*). The absolute function can be simply realized by a multiplexer with *select* signal being the most significant bit of the input.

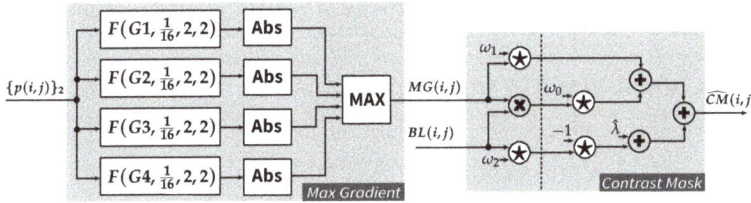

Figure 12. Contrast masking function.

The contrast masking threshold (*CM*) is calculated for each pixel location based on the value of *MG* and *BL*. This calculation requires multiplications by several real numbers which cannot be accurately converted to shift-based operators. To keep the implementation resource-efficient, without using floating point operations, a fixed-point based approximation strategy is proposed as in Equation (24). A scaling factor 2^σ is applied to the overall approximation of the given real numbers for providing more accuracy adjustment.

$$\begin{aligned}
\omega_0 &= 2^\sigma \cdot (2^{-14} + 2^{-15} + 2^{-17}) \approx 2^\sigma \cdot 0.0001 & \omega_2 &= 2^\sigma \cdot (2^{-7} + 2^{-9}) \approx 2^\sigma \cdot 0.01 \\
\omega_1 &= 2^\sigma \cdot (2^{-3} - 2^{-7} - 2^{-9}) \approx 2^\sigma \cdot 0.115 & \hat{\lambda} &= 2^\sigma \cdot 2^{-1}
\end{aligned} \tag{24}$$

With the above approximations, Equations (5)–(7) are then rewritten as Equation (25) and implemented as *Contrast Mask* module shown in Figure 12. In this implementation, σ is empirically set to 5, since it provides a reasonable trade-off between accuracy and resource consumption.

$$\widehat{CM}(i,j) = BL(i,j) \cdot MG(i,j) \cdot \omega_0 + MG(i,j) \cdot \omega_1 + \hat{\lambda} - BL(i,j) \cdot \omega_2 \tag{25}$$

4.4. Edge-Texture-Smooth Function

This function consists of two separate modules: *Edge Detection* and *High Contrast Activity* which, respectively, mark pixel location belonging to edge region and high contrast activity region. These modules receive the same 3-pixel column as an input and output a binary value for each pixel location. The output of *Edge Detection* module ($M_e(i,j)$) and *High Contrast Activity* module ($M_c(i,j)$) are combined into a two-bit signal ($M_{ec}(i,j)$), which has $M_e(i,j)$ as the most significant bit (MSb) and $M_c(i,j)$ as the least significant bit (LSb). $M_{ec}(i,j)$ is then used as the *select* signal for multiplexers in *JND Calculation Function*. The following subsections discuss each of these modules in detail.

4.4.1. Edge Detection

The edge detection algorithm applied in the proposed JND model requires three filtering operations: one for Gaussian filtering and the other two for finding the Sobel gradients in horizontal and vertical directions. These filters are realized by *PWS* modules, as depicted in Figure 13a,b. The coefficient array G can be found in Section 6.1, and the kernels S_x, S_y are as follows:

$$S_x = \begin{bmatrix} -1 & 0 & 1 \\ -2 & 0 & 2 \\ -1 & 0 & 1 \end{bmatrix} \quad S_y = \begin{bmatrix} -1 & -2 & -1 \\ 0 & 0 & 0 \\ 1 & 2 & 1 \end{bmatrix} \tag{26}$$

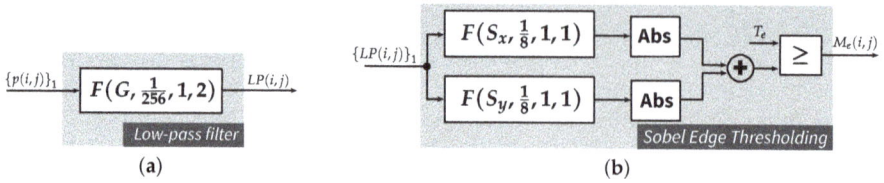

Figure 13. Edge detection module: (**a**) low-pass filter; and (**b**) Sobel edge thresholding module.

4.4.2. High Contrast Activity

To detect high contrast activity regions, the contrast significance CS needs to be calculated for each pixel location. The proposed architecture for this task is illustrated in Figure 14. Considering Equation (13), two divisions by 9 are required for finding C^{MAD}. This can actually introduce some errors to the implementation using fixed-point dividers. Therefore, the following modification is done to find CS:

$$\hat{C}^{\mathrm{MAD}} = \sum_{j=0}^{8} \left| 9 \cdot p_j + \hat{\mu} \right|, \qquad \text{where } \hat{\mu} = -\sum_{j=0}^{8} p_j \qquad (27)$$

It is obvious that the value of $\hat{C}^{\mathrm{MAD}}$ is 81 times as large as C^{MAD}. Therefore, instead of comparing C^{MAD} to the threshold T_C as in Equation (14), the modified $\hat{C}^{\mathrm{MAD}}$ is now compared to the new threshold $T_{\mathrm{hc}} = 81 \cdot T_C$. This strategy indeed requires extra hardware resources if T_C is not implemented as a constant but can guarantee the accuracy of CS without using floating-point operation.

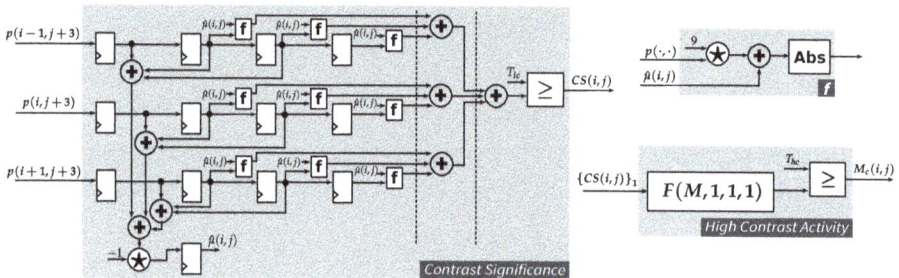

Figure 14. High-contrast activity module: (**Left**) contrast significance estimation module; (**Top-right**) function f; and (**Bottom-right**) high contrast activity thresholding module.

Considering the implementation of *Contrast Significance* module depicted in Figure 14, the input 3-pixel column is registered four times: the first three register columns are for calculating $\hat{\mu}$ and the last three register columns are for calculating $\hat{C}^{\mathrm{MAD}}$. There is one clock cycle delay between these two calculations, which is resolved by inserting a register, as shown in the bottom-left side of the module.

4.5. JND Calculation Function

Figure 15 presents the implementation of Equations (19) and (20), which calculate the final value of JND based on the contrast masking threshold ($\widehat{CM}$), the luminance masking threshold ($\widehat{LM}$) and the region mask (M_{ec}). The *Region-based Weighting* module (RW) applies a weighting factor to the incoming contrast mask. The weighting factors, which depend on the region type for the current pixel, are $W_e = 1$, $W_t = 1.75$ and $W_s = 1$ for edge, texture and smooth regions, respectively. The texture weight can be rewritten as $W_t = 2^1 - 2^{-2}$, which results in two shift operations and one adder in our customized shift-based multiplier. The other two weights can be simply realized as wires connecting the input and the output. The region mask is used as the *select* signal of a multiplexer in order to choose correct weighted value for the next calculation phase.

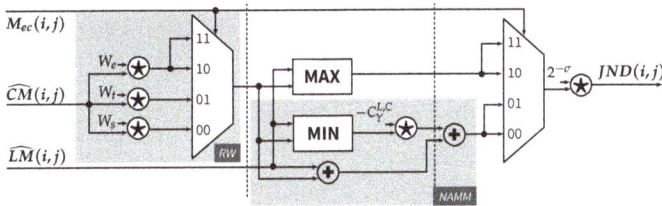

Figure 15. JND calculation function.

In the next calculation phase, the weighted contrast masking threshold ($\widehat{CM}_\kappa$) is fed to the *MAX* module and *NAMM* module, which compute the JND value for the edge region and non-edge regions, respectively. For the *CSM* module in *NAMM*, an approximation is done for $C_Y^{L,C}$, as shown in Equation (28). The final value of JND is then computed by removing the scaling factor 2^σ applied to the input contrast masking and luminance masking thresholds.

$$\hat{C}_Y^{L,C} = 2^{-2} + 2^{-5} + 2^{-6} + 2^{-8} \approx 0.3 \tag{28}$$

5. JND-Based Pixel-Domain Perceptual Image Coding Hardware Architecture

A low complexity pixel-domain perceptual image coding algorithm based on JND modeling has been proposed in our earlier work [14]. Its principle is briefly described in what follows, before addressing architectural aspects. The perceptual coding algorithm is based on predictive coding of either the downsampled pixel value or the original pixels according to the encoder's decision about whether the downsampled pixel is sufficient to represent the corresponding original pixels at visually lossless (or at least visually optimized in the case of suprathreshold coding) quality. Figure 16 illustrates the algorithm of the perceptual encoder. The *Visual ROI determination* block compares local distortions due to downsampling against the distortion visibility thresholds at corresponding pixel locations given by the pixel-domain JND model. If any downsampling distortion crosses the JND threshold, the current downsampling proximity (a 2 × 2 block in [14]) is considered to be a region-of-interest, and all pixels therein are encoded. In non-ROI blocks, only the downsampled mean value is encoded. In both cases, the encoder ensures that the difference from a decoded pixel to the original pixel does not exceed the corresponding JND threshold, fulfilling a necessary condition on visually lossless coding from the perspective of the JND model. The predictive coder exploits existing low complexity algorithmic tools from JPEG-LS [25] such as pixel prediction, context modeling and limited-length Golomb coding but uses a novel scan order so that coherent context modeling for ROI and non-ROI pixels is possible. The ROI information and the predictive coder's outputs are combined to form the output bitstream. More detailed information on the coding algorithm can be found in [14]. The remainder of this section provides information on the hardware architecture for such a perceptual encoder.

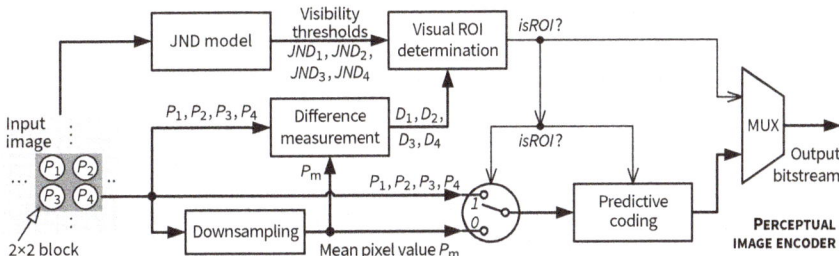

Figure 16. JND-based pixel-domain perceptual image coding algorithm proposed in [14].

5.1. Top-Level Architecture of the JND-Based Pixel-Domain Perceptual Encoder

The overall proposed architecture for the perceptual encoder is depicted in Figure 17. On the top level, apart from the JND module discussed in Section 4, the proposed encoder architecture can be divided into two main parts: an *Encoder front end* module and a *Predictive coding* module. As shown in Figure 17, pixels encoded by the predictive coding path are provided by the *Encoder front end*, which performs the following tasks:

- Generate the skewed pixel processing order described in [14].
- Downsample the current 2×2 input block.
- Determine whether the current input 2×2 block is an ROI based on the JND thresholds.
- Select the pixel to be encoded by the predictive coding path based on the ROI status.

For clarity, the JND module, as well as the delay element for synchronizing the JND module outputs with the input pixel stream for the encoder, is omitted from the discussions on the encoder architecture in the rest of the paper. In addition, since existing works (e.g., [26]) have well covered architectural aspects of fundamental pixel-domain predictive coding algorithms such as JPEG-LS, the following discussion focuses mainly on the aspects of the proposed encoder architecture that enable the skewed pixel processing, the JND-based adaptive downsampling and the ROI-based pixel selection [14].

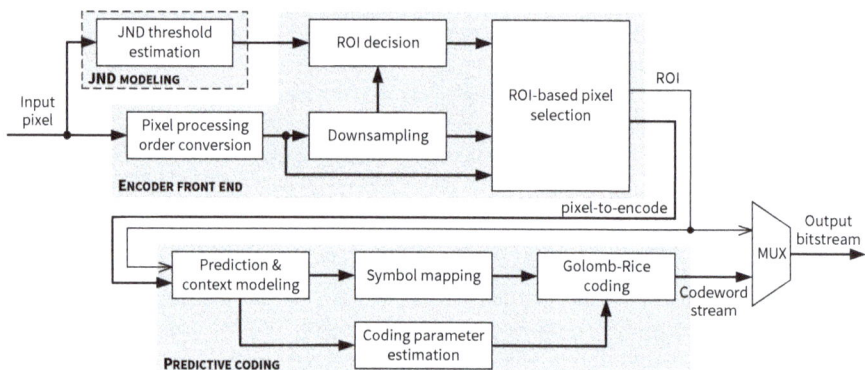

Figure 17. Overview of the proposed JND-based perceptual encoder architecture.

5.2. Input Scan Order vs. Pixel Processing Order

The raster scan order represents a common sequence in which pixels in an image are produced or visited, for example at the output interface of a sensor or at the input interface of an encoder. The encoder architecture in this paper assumes that pixels of an input image are streamed sequentially into the encoder in a raster scan order, with the source of the input image being arbitrary, such as a camera sensor, e.g., when the encoder is directly connected to the sensor to compress raw pixels, or an external memory, e.g., when the whole image needs to be temporarily buffered for denoising before compression. Inside the encoder, pixels do not have to be processed in the same order as they have been received. Figure 18 shows an example in which the input pixels are received in a raster scan order whereas the actual encoding of the pixels follows a skewed scan order [14]. Obviously, internal pixel buffers such as block RAMs on FPGAs are required, if an encoder's internal pixel processing order differs from its input pixel scan order. An architecture for implementing the skewed pixel processing order is presented in Section 5.4.

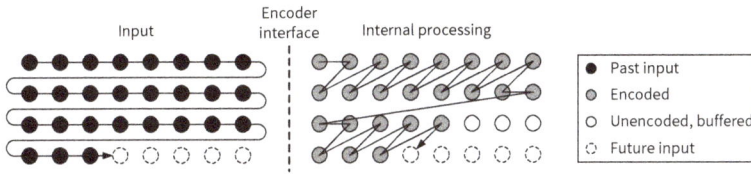

Figure 18. Input pixel scan order (raster scan) vs. internal pixel processing order (skewed scan [14]).

5.3. Encoder Front End

A high-level architecture for the *Encoder front end* is presented in Figure 19. Input pixel buffering and skewed pixel output are performed in the *Pixel processing order conversion* module, which is composed mainly of shift registers and FIFOs as row buffers. When enough pixels are buffered so that the skewed processing can be started, pixels from the same columns in a pair of rows (called an upper row and a lower row in this paper) are outputted by the row buffers. After a full 2×2 pixel block is stored in the *Downsampling window*, the mean value of the block is computed by the *Downsampling* module. A *Lower row delay* block is used to delay the output of pixels on the lower row, as required by the skewed scan order. Figure 19 shows that all four original pixels in the *Downsampling window* and the output of the *Downsampling* module are sent to the *ROI decision* module, as well as the JND thresholds. Depending on whether the current 2×2 block is an ROI, either an original pixel or the downsampled mean value is adaptively selected by the *ROI-based pixel selection* module and forwarded to the predictive coding path. Different components of the encoder front end are connected by pipeline registers and their operation is controlled by a state machine. More details and architectural aspects of this module are examined in the following subsections.

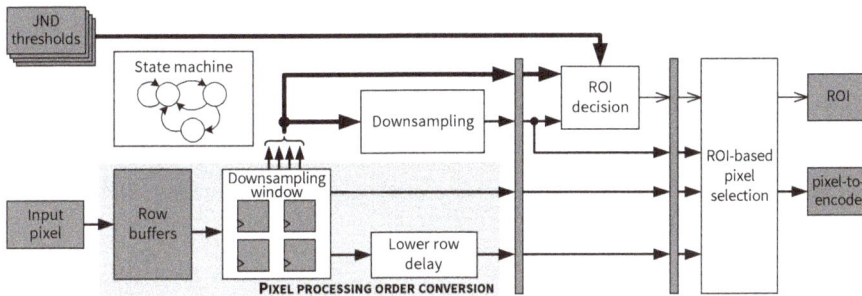

Figure 19. Encoder front end module.

5.4. Pixel Processing Order Conversion

The architecture of the *Pixel processing order conversion* module is shown in Figure 20. At the input side, pixels of the input image arrive sequentially (i.e., streaming scenario), as indicated in the waveform in the top-left side of Figure 20. According to the skewed scan order (cf. Figure 18), pixels in a pair of rows shall be interleaved with a delay in the lower row. As depicted in Figure 20, two different row buffers (dual-port RAMs) are used to store input pixels depending on the current row index. The modulo-2 operation on the *row_index* signal is implemented by taking the least significant bit (LSb) of *row_index*. The conversion process is as follows. Firstly, all pixels in an upper row (e.g., first row of the input image) are stored in the *Upper row buffer*. Next, pixels in a lower row (e.g., second row of the image) begin to be received and stored in the *Lower row buffer*. As long as neither row buffer is empty, both buffers are read simultaneously every two clock cycles, as illustrated in the waveform in the top-right side of Figure 20. Outputs of both row buffers are then fed into the *Downsampling window* consisting of two two-stage shift registers. Downsampling as well as ROI detection is performed once all 4 pixels of a 2×2 block are in the *Downsampling window*. Finally, by inserting an offset into the data path for the lower row pixels using the *Lower row delay* block, the skewed scan order [14] is obtained at the output of the *Pixel processing order conversion* module. The two output pixel values from the upper and lower rows are denoted as p_U and p_L, respectively. Both p_U and p_L are candidates for the final pixel to be encoded, which is determined later by the *ROI-based pixel selection* module.

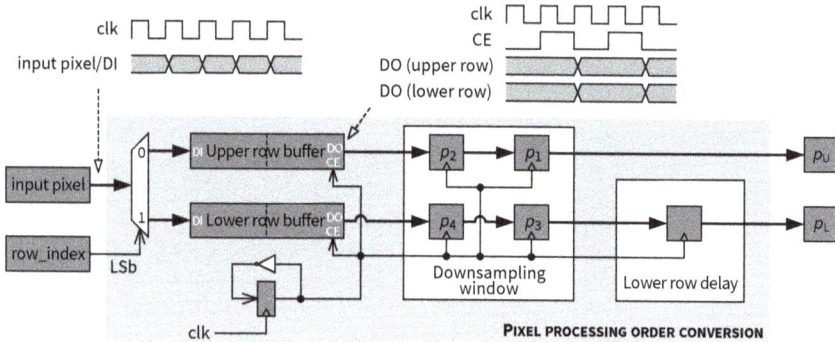

Figure 20. Pixel processing order conversion module.

5.5. Downsampling and ROI Decision

The architecture of the *Downsampling* and *ROI decision* modules is presented in Figure 21. Let p_1, p_2, p_3, p_4 be the four pixels of a 2×2 block in the downsampling window and p_m be the downsampled mean value. The *Downsampling* module implements the following operation:

$$p_m = \text{ROUND} \left(\frac{p_1 + p_2 + p_3 + p_4}{4} \right) \tag{29}$$

As shown in Figure 21, downsampling is performed by first adding up all 4 pixel values in an adder tree and then shifting right by 2 bits. The extra addition by 2 before the right shift is used to implement the rounding function in Equation (29). Such a downsampling scheme is straightforward and computationally efficient. When higher compression ratio is desired, the downsampling module and the corresponding register window and can be extended to deal with larger block sizes, and a low-pass filtering can be optionally employed before the downsampling to reduce aliasing.

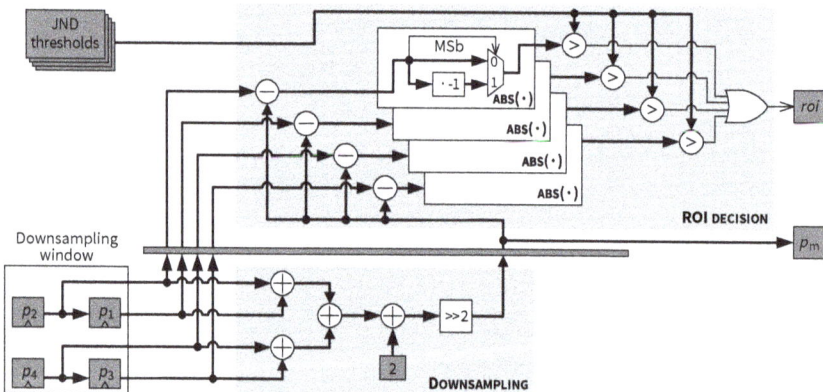

Figure 21. Downsampling and ROI decision modules.

The exploitation of the JND thresholds in the *ROI decision* module is illustrated in the upper part of Figure 21. The downsampled value p_m is first subtracted from each of the original pixels p_1–p_4.

The magnitude of a resulting difference value $|p_i - p_m|, i = \{1, 2, 3, 4\}$ is the downsampling error at the ith pixel location in the current 2×2 block. Such a downsampling error is then compared with the corresponding difference visibility threshold JND_i. The current block is considered as an ROI ($roi = 1$) if any downsampling error is greater than the corresponding JND threshold. Conversely, a non-ROI block ($roi = 0$) is identified if all four downsampling errors are within the corresponding four JND thresholds. Downsampling can be applied to all non-ROI blocks without causing visual artifacts, since all pixels in a non-ROI block have visually "no difference" to the downsampled value of that block from a JND perspective.

5.6. ROI-Based Pixel Selection

The final pixels to be encoded are chosen by the *ROI-based pixel selection* module. Architecture of this module is depicted in Figure 22. The *new_block* signal is a binary control flag which is asserted when the upper row pixel register p_U contains the first pixel of a new 2×2 block (see p_1 in Figure 16). Figures 19–21 indicate that p_m, p_U and *roi* signals are based on the same 2×2 block, i.e., these signals are synchronized with each other, whereas p_L is delayed by one column compared with p_U. The *ROI delay* block generates an ROI status signal synchronized with p_L. The selection criteria are as follows.

(1)   If the current 2×2 block is a non-ROI block ($roi=0$) and p_U contains the first pixel of the block (*new_block*=1), then the downsampled pixel value p_m is selected to replace p_U.
(2)   If the current block is a non-ROI block ($roi=0$) and p_U contains the second pixel of the block (see p_2 in Figure 16, *new_block*=0), then p_U is skipped (i.e., *pixel-to-encode* is marked as invalid).
(3)   A lower row pixel contained in p_L is skipped if it is in a non-ROI block as indicated by the corresponding delayed ROI status signal.
(4)   For any pixel, if the 2×2 block containing that pixel is an ROI block, then that pixel is selected for encoding, as shown in Figure 22.

Finally, the selected pixels, as well as the corresponding ROI flags, are transferred to the subsequent *Predictive coding* module, as indicated in Figure 17.

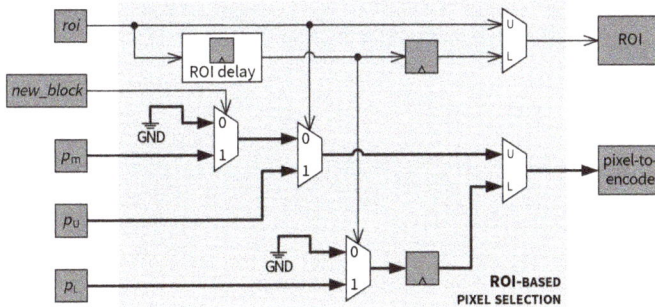

Figure 22. ROI-based pixel selection module.

5.7. Predictive Coding and Output Bitstream

Pixels from the *Encoder front end* are compressed along the predictive coding path which comprises four main modules: *Prediction and context modeling, Symbol mapping, Coding parameter estimation* and *Golomb-Rice coding*, as depicted in the lower part of Figure 17. These blocks are implemented in a high throughput and resource efficient architecture for the classic context-based pixel-domain predictive coding, which is fully pipelined without stall. The throughput is 1 pixel/clock cycle. Architectural details here are similar to those in existing publications, e.g., on the hardware architecture for the regular mode of JPEG-LS [26]. The variable-length codeword streams from the predictive coding path are combined with the ROI (in raw binary representation) at the output multiplexing (*MUX*) module, where a barrel shifter is used to formulate fixed-length final output bitstreams. Detailed architecture for the predictive coding path and bitstream multiplexing is omitted due to space limitations.

6. Experimental Results

6.1. Analysis of Integer Approximation of the Gaussian Kernel

As discussed in Section 3.1, a 3 × 5 Gaussian kernel with standard deviation $\sigma = 0.83$ is employed in the proposed JND model. Figure 23a shows the original kernel coefficients with a precision of four digits after the decimal point, whereas an integer approximation of the same kernel is presented in Figure 23b. In total, 15 multiplications and 14 additions are required in a straightforward implementation of the filtering with the original kernel, whereas the integer kernel can be implemented with 25 integer additions plus several shift operations (for instance, multiplying x by 15 can be implemented by a shift-add operation as $(x << 4) - x$, where $<<$ is the left shift operator). The impact of using the integer kernel on the accuracy of results is analyzed in Table 1. The results using the integer kernel after both Gaussian smoothing and Sobel edge detection (cf. Figure 5) have been compared with those using the original kernel for various test images (see Section 6.2). Table 1 indicates that on average 97% of the results based on the integer version of the kernel matches those of the floating-point version after the smoothing step, whereas over 99% of the results based on the integer version of the kernel are the same as those based on the floating-point version after the edge detection step. Since the performance of the integer Gaussian kernel is closely comparable to that of the floating-point one, it is reasonable to use the integer kernel for the improved resource efficiency.

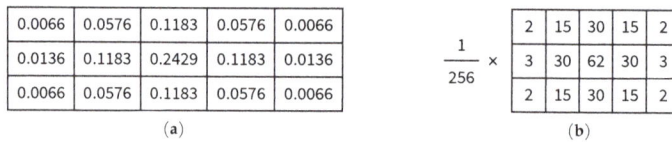

0.0066	0.0576	0.1183	0.0576	0.0066
0.0136	0.1183	0.2429	0.1183	0.0136
0.0066	0.0576	0.1183	0.0576	0.0066

(a)

$$\frac{1}{256} \times$$

2	15	30	15	2
3	30	62	30	3
2	15	30	15	2

(b)

Figure 23. Coefficients of 3 × 5 Gaussian kernel in Section 3.1: (**a**) original; and (**b**) integer approximation.

Table 1. Influence of the integer Gaussian kernel on the accuracy of smoothing and edge detection results in comparison with the original kernel in floating-point double precision.

Average Ratio of Pixel Locations with Same Results Using the Integer Kernel and the Original One	
After Gaussian Smoothing	After Sobel Edge Detection
97.00%	99.89%

6.2. Performance of the Proposed JND Model

The proposed JND model was implemented in software and experimented with widely used standard test images. The performance of the proposed JND model was tested in terms of both the distortion visibility of JND-contaminated images and the amount of imperceptible noise that can be shaped into the images, i.e., visual redundancies in the images. To reveal or compare visual redundancies given by the JND models, the well-known PSNR metric is often used with a particular interpretation in the literature on JND models. For example, it is pointed out in [9] that, if the JND profile is accurate, the perceptual quality of the corresponding JND-contaminated image should be "as good as the original" while the PSNR of the JND-contaminated image should be "as low as possible". Chou and Li believed that PSNR can be used to quantify the amount of imperceptible distortion allowed for transparent coding of images [9]. With this interpretation, a lower PSNR value corresponds to a larger potential coding gain. Other examples of work in which the PSNR metric is used in a similar way to analyze the performance of JND models include [11,12,27,28].

Multiple greyscale 8 bit/pixel test images [29,30] of different sizes and contents were used in our experiments. For each test image, four sets of JND profiles were computed using Chou and Li's original model [9], Yang et al.'s model [11,22], Liu et al.'s model [12,31] and the proposed one. A JND-contaminated image was then obtained by injecting the JND profile as a noise signal to the original image. As described in [9], noise injection works by adding each original pixel with the corresponding visibility threshold multiplied by a random sign $\{-1,1\}$. The resulting JND-contaminated image can be used in both objective tests such as PSNR measurement to reveal the JND model's capability for estimating the visual redundancy and subjective tests to validate the model by comparing the original image with the JND-contaminated one. Since each sign is generated independently, the above random-sign noise injection scheme may occasionally cause most injected noise samples in a small neighborhood to have the same sign, which often shows a correlation to distortion visibility even when the noise injection is guided by a high quality JND profile (see [13] for an example). An alternative is to ensure additionally a zero-mean of the randomly-generated signs of noise samples in every $M \times N$ block, which is referred to as zero-mean random-sign noise injection in this work. A neighborhood size of 2×2 in the zero-mean random-sign scheme was used in our experiments. The distortion visibility experiment on the proposed JND model was conducted on a 31.1″ EIZO CG318-4K monitor with 100 cd/m^2 luminance and with viewing conditions specified in [32]. The original test image is temporal-interleaved with the JND-contaminated image at a frequency of 5 Hz, and a noise signal is invisible if no flickering can be seen. In our experiments, hardly any flickering could be noticed at a normal viewing distance corresponding to 60 pixels/degree. Figure 24 presents a test image and various noise-contaminated images. An original section of the BALLOON image is in Figure 24a, and a white-Gaussian-noise-contaminated image (PSNR = 31.98) is shown in Figure 24b. A JND-contaminated image (PSNR = 31.97) based on Chou and Li's JND model is in Figure 24c, whereas the JND-contaminated image based on the proposed model is in Figure 24d. While the noise in Figure 24b is quite obvious, the same amount of noise injected based on Chou and Li's JND model is much less visible (see Figure 24c), and an even higher amount (0.23 dB more) of noise based on the proposed model and the zero-mean random-sign injection scheme is almost completely invisible, as shown in Figure 24d.

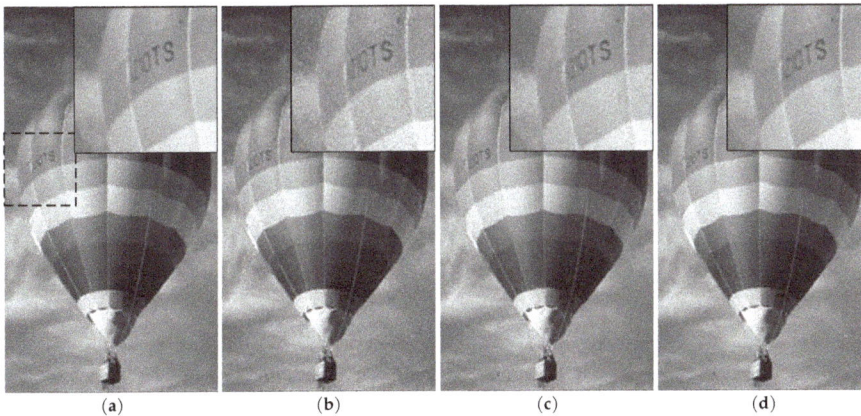

Figure 24. Visualization of JND-contaminated images: (**a**) original section of the BALLOON image; (**b**) contaminated with white noise, PSNR = 31.98; (**c**) contaminated with JND profile given by Chou and Li's model [9] with random-sign injection, PSNR = 31.97; and (**d**) contaminated with JND profile given by the proposed JND model with zero-mean random-sign injection, PSNR = 31.74.

Table 2 shows a comparison of PSNR values of JND-contaminated images based on different JND models. As discussed above, the PSNR metric was used as an indication of visual redundancy measured by a JND model, which can be removed without impairing the visual quality. A lower PSNR value is preferable since it corresponds to a more accurate estimation of the visual redundancy, which can be used to guide a visually lossless image coding or watermarking. Table 2 indicates that the proposed JND model on average improved the accuracy of visual redundancy estimation by 0.69 dB and 0.47 dB compared to Chou and Li's model and Yang et al.'s model, respectively. Compared with Liu et al.'s model, which applies on top of Yang et al.'s model an additional total-variation-based textural image decomposition [12], the average accuracy of the proposed model was lower by 0.6 dB. Such a gap could be justified by the relatively low computational complexity of the proposed model, especially for resource-constrained embedded systems.

Table 2. Performance comparison of different JND models for measuring the visual redundancy in test images based on PSNR values of JND-contaminated images.

Image	PSNR [dB]			
	Chou & Li [9]	Yang et al. [11]	Proposed	Liu et al. [12]
AERIAL2	33.11	32.23	32.01	31.52
BALLOON	31.97	31.89	31.74	31.57
CHART	30.91	31.92	30.65	30.35
FINGER	32.69	33.49	31.50	29.24
GOLD	30.93	30.32	30.18	29.81
HOTEL	29.92	29.96	29.44	28.85
MAT	32.22	32.40	31.87	31.46
SEISMIC	37.84	36.35	36.83	36.46
TXTUR2	32.06	31.05	30.60	30.04
WATER	34.18	34.44	34.06	34.01
WOMAN	30.94	30.22	30.22	29.25
Average	32.43	32.21	31.74	31.14
Improvement vs. Chou & Li	–	0.22	0.69	1.29

6.3. Complexity Comparison of Proposed JND Model and Existing JND Models

Table 3 lists the number of operations required by Chou and Li's JND model, which is the basis for the other pixel-domain JND models discussed in this paper. The complexity of two JND models extending Chou and Li's model, including Yang et al.'s model and the proposed one, are compared in Table 4 in terms of the number additional operations required in the main algorithmic parts of these JND models. Compared with Chou and Li's JND model, Yang et al.'s model additionally performs edge-based weighting of the contrast masking effect using a Canny edge detector followed by a 7×7 Gaussian filter [9]. From the upper part of Table 4, it can be seen that Yang et al.'s model required approximately 162 additions, one multiplications, one division and a look-up table (LUT) in addition to the basic operations required in Chou and Li's model (Table 3). It can be seen from the lower part of Table 4 that compared to Yang et al.'s model, the proposed model required about half the number of extra additions and required neither additional LUTs nor division operations.

Table 3. Basic operations required for computing a visibility threshold by Chou and Li's JND model.

Algorithmic Step	Addition	Multiplication	LUT	Remark
BL	24	–	–	Equation (1)
ID	44	–	–	Equation (3)
MG	3	–	–	Equation (4)
α	1	1	–	Equation (6)
β	1	1	–	Equation (7)
final *CM*	1	1	–	Equation (5)
LM ($BL \leq 127$)	–	–	1	Equation (2)
LM ($BL > 127$)	3	–	–	Equation (2)
Final *JND*	1	–	–	Equation (8)
Total	78	3	1	

Table 4. Approximate number of additional operations per pixel required for computing a visibility threshold by Yang et al.'s JND model and the proposed model.

Model	Algorithmic Step	Addition	Multiply	LUT	Division	Remark
	C: smoothing	37	–	–	1	$\sigma = 1.4$ [33]
	C: gradients	10	–	–	–	Sobel
	C: gradient-magnitude	1	–	–	–	[24]
	C: gradient-direction	3	–	1	–	[24]
	C: non-max suppression	2	–	–	–	[24]
Yang's	C: gradient-histogram	2	–	–	–	[34]
	C: 2-thresholding & hysteresis	2	–	–	–	[35]
C: Canny	7×7 Gaussian	102	–	–	–	$\sigma = 0.8$ [11]
	Edge-weighting	–	1	–	–	[11]
	NAMM	3	1	–	–	Equation (12)
	Total	162	2	1	1	
	E: 3×5 smoothing	25	–	–	–	Figure 23b
	E: Sobel gradients	10	–	–	–	Equation (26)
	E: magnitude	1	–	–	–	Figure 13b
	E: thresholding	1	–	–	–	Figure 13b
Proposed	T: local contrast	26	–	–	–	Equation (27)
	T: contrast significance	1	–	–	–	Equation (14)
E: edge	T: contrast activity	8	–	–	–	Equation (15)
T: texture	T: high activity	1	–	–	–	Equation (16)
	CM_t weighting	1	–	–	–	$W_t = 1.75$
	Final *JND*	6	2	–	–	Equation (20)
	Total	80	2	–	–	

A comparison of software complexity in terms of CPU time was made for different JND models. The comparison was based on the original authors' implementation of Yang et al.'s model [22] and Liu et al.'s model [31], as well as our own implementation of Chou and Li's model and the proposed one. All models were implemented in MATLAB. The software models were run on a desktop computer with Intel Core i7-4820K (3.70 GHz) CPU and 32 GB of RAM. The operating system was Windows 7 64-bit. The test image used was BARB with a resolution of 720×576. The time need by each model to evaluate the JND profile was obtained as the least CPU time measured from running each JND model 30 times on the test image. The results are presented in Table 5. It can be seen that the CPU time required by the proposed model to evaluate the JND profile was 68 ms, which was less than twice of that (37 ms) required by Chou and Li's model. By contrast, the CPU time required by Yang et al.'s model was 88 ms, which was more than twice of that required by Chou and Li's model. In the case of Liu et al.'s model, the CPU time was 474 ms, which was over an order of magnitude more than that of Chou and Li's model.

Table 5. CPU time used by MATLAB implementations of different JND models for evaluating the JND profile of the BARB test image.

	Chou & Li	Yang et al.	Liu et al.	Proposed
CPU time (ms):	37	88	474	68
Increase vs. Chou & Li:	–	138%	1181%	84%

To compare the JND models in terms of hardware resource requirement and speed, we implemented hardware models of three JND models in VHDL, including Chou and Li's original model, Yang et al.'s model and the proposed one. The hardware models were simulated and synthesized using Xilinx Vivado Design Suite 2018.2. The target device was selected as Xilinx Kintex-7 XC7K160T with a speed grade of −2. For the FPGA implementation of the proposed JND model, the input image was assumed to be greyscale with 8 bits/pixel and with a horizontal size of up to 1024 pixels. Table 6 presents the FPGA resource utilization of the synthesized models and their maximum clock frequency. The pixel throughput was one pixel per clock cycle. Table 6 shows that, compared with Chou and Li's JND model, the amount of required FPGA hardware resource was increased by over 200% for Yang et al.'s JND model, while for the proposed model the resource increase was less than 100%. In terms of the maximum clock frequency, the proposed model achieved the same performance as Chou and Li's model, i.e., 190 MHz, which was about 35% faster than the 140 MHz achieved by Yang et al.'s model.

Table 6. FPGA resource utilization and clock frequency comparison of three JND models: Chou and Li's model, Yang et al.'s model and the proposed one.

Resource Type	Available	Chou & Li	Yang et al.	Proposed
Slice LUTs	101,400	1414 (1.39%)	4128 (4.07%)	2621 (2.58%)
Slice Registers	202,800	839 (0.41%)	2482 (1.22%)	1543 (0.76%)
Block RAM 36Kbits	325	2.5 (0.77%)	10.5 (3.23%)	4.5 (1.38%)
Clock frequency (MHz)		190	140	190

6.4. Compression Performance of the Perceptual Codec Based on the Proposed JND Model

The proposed JND model was implemented in combination with the perceptual encoder described in Section 5. Parameter values for the JND model are as discussed in Section 3. Compressed image quality of the perceptual codec was compared with that of JPEG-LS for a range of rates corresponding to approximately 2:1 to 6:1 compression. Objective metrics used to evaluate the compressed image quality included PSNR, MS-SSIM [36,37] and HDR-VDP score [38,39]. Compressed data rates of the perceptual codec based on the proposed JND model were additionally compared with those of JPEG, JPEG 2000 and JPEG XR at the same perceptual quality given by PSPNR [9]. The compression experiments were based on widely used standard test images, as described in Section 6.2.

Figure 25 presents comparisons of rate-distortion performance between the perceptual codec based on the proposed JND model and JPEG-LS for test image GOLD, TXTUR2 and WOMAN. It can be seen from the MS-SSIM and HDR-VDP curves that the perceptual codec exhibited a clear gain in perceptual quality over JPEG-LS in a rate range between 1 and 3.5 bits-per-pixel (bpp). In terms of PSNR, which is not a perceptual quality metric, the perceptual codec delivered an improved coding performance of about 10–15% over JPEG-LS at rates below approximately 1.5–2 bpp. Figure 26 provides visual comparisons of images compressed to approximately the same rate by JPEG-LS and the perceptual codec combined with the proposed JND model. Selected parts of two different types of images are shown. From this figure, it is evident that the proposed scheme achieved improved visual quality by avoiding the stripe-like artifacts of JPEG-LS.

Towards the goal of visually transparent coding, a codec's performance can be related to its ability to keep coding distortions within the visibility thresholds provided by the JND model. As discussed in [9], the peak signal-to-perceptible-noise ratio (PSPNR) is a metric taking visual redundancy into account based on the JND model.

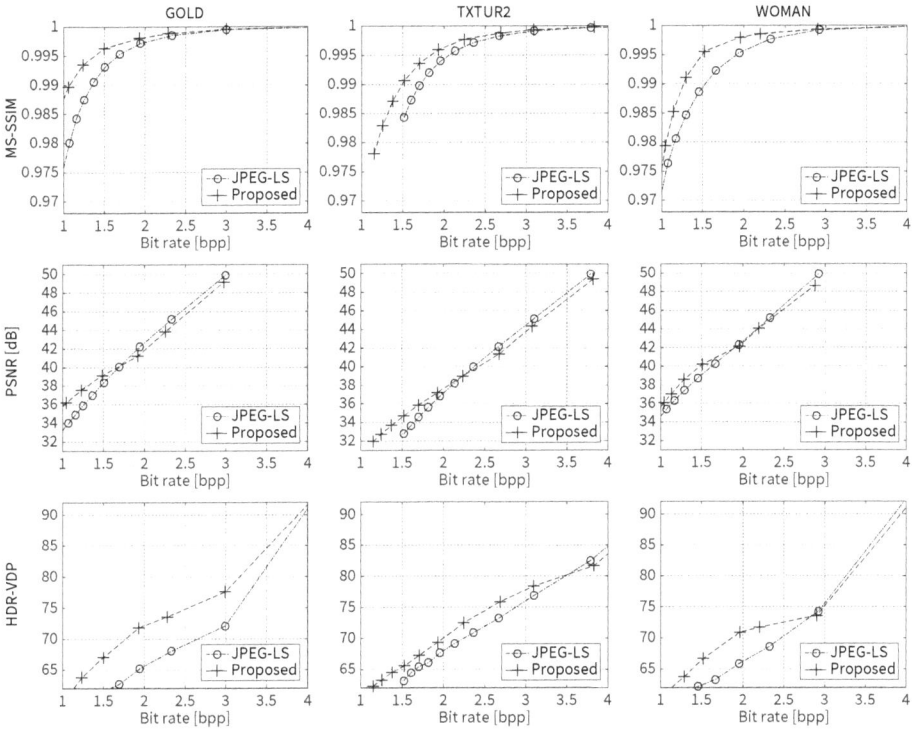

Figure 25. Objective rate-distortion plots of the proposed codec and JPEG-LS: top to bottom, MS-SSIM, PSNR and HDR-VDP values; and left to right, results for test images GOLD, TXTUR2 and WOMAN.

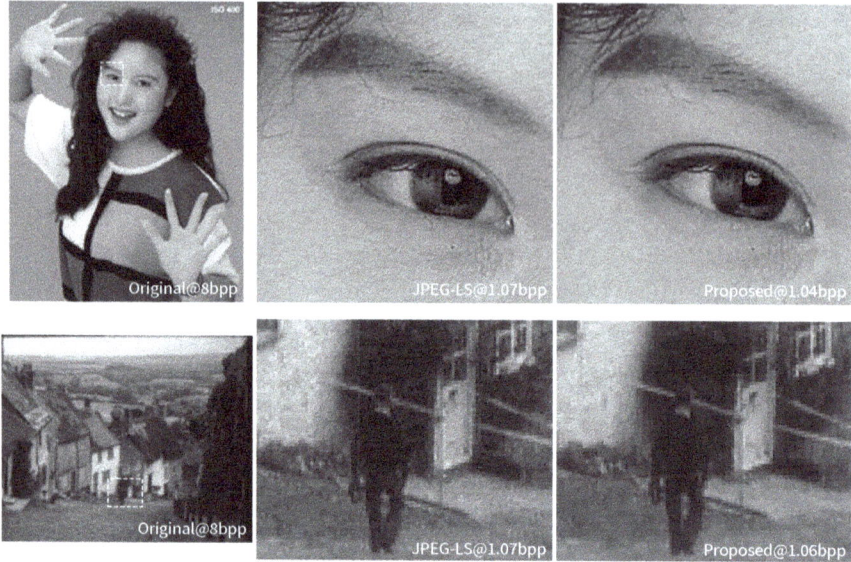

Figure 26. Visual quality of images compressed by JPEG-LS and the proposed JND-based perceptual codec at closely comparable bit rates: top and bottom, WOMAN and GOLD image; and left to right, original image, selected section compressed by JPEG-LS, and same section compressed by the perceptual codec.

While transform-domain codecs such as JPEG, JPEG 2000 and JPEG XR have higher complexity and latency than a pixel-domain codec such as the proposed JND-based one or JPEG-LS, it is possible to find out experimentally the bit rates at which any coding distortion in the compressed image is kept below the corresponding visibility threshold given by the proposed JND model. Table 7 shows the minimum compressed bit rates for JPEG, JPEG 2000, JPEG XR and the proposed JND-based perceptual codec at which the PSPNR reaches the upper bound, i.e., none of the coding errors exceed the JND thresholds, which can be considered as a necessary condition given by the JND model on perceptually lossless coding. For this experiment, the proposed JND model, the baseline JPEG, Kakadu implementation [40] of JPEG 2000 (with visual weights) and the ITU-T reference implementation [41] of JPEG XR were used. Table 7 indicates that, at the same visual quality given by PSPNR, the perceptual codec required on average about 58%, 48% and 41% fewer bits compared with JPEG, JPEG 2000 and JPEG XR, respectively.

Table 7. Compressed data rates of JPEG, JPEG 2000, JPEG XR and the proposed JND-based perceptual encoder at the same quality in terms of peak signal-to-perceptible-noise ratio (PSPNR).

Image	Bit Rate (bpp)			
	JPEG	**JPEG 2000**	**JPEG XR**	**Proposed**
AERIAL2	6.04	5.10	4.44	2.68
BABOON	7.03	5.50	4.91	3.37
BALLOON	2.60	2.19	1.58	0.97
BARB	4.37	3.89	3.31	2.14
BOATS	4.11	3.70	3.19	1.75
CAFE	6.29	4.81	4.51	2.54
CATS	2.88	2.20	2.06	1.45
CHART	3.58	2.80	2.53	1.37
EDUC	4.50	3.96	3.53	2.21
FINGER	5.91	4.70	4.40	3.01
GOLD	5.00	4.00	3.42	1.93
HOTEL	4.98	3.90	3.46	1.74
LENNAGREY	4.64	3.70	3.34	1.69
MAT	3.61	2.50	2.44	1.23
PEPPERS	4.93	4.10	3.54	1.85
SEISMIC	2.11	1.88	1.46	1.30
TOOLS	6.26	5.09	4.58	2.68
TXTUR2	6.31	5.20	4.47	2.68
WATER	3.55	2.89	2.55	1.03
WOMAN	5.01	4.19	3.56	1.96
Average	4.69	3.82	3.36	1.98
Saving by perceptual encoder	57.8%	48.1%	41.2%	–

6.5. FPGA Resource Utilization and Throughput of the Proposed Perceptual Encoder Architecture

The architecture for the proposed JND model and perceptual encoder was implemented in hardware using VHDL hardware description language. The hardware model for the perceptual encoder was simulated and synthesized using Xilinx Vivado Design Suite 2016.4. The target device was selected as Xilinx Kintex-7 XC7K160T, a popular mid-range FPGA, with a speed grade of −2. Since the proposed perceptual encoder is compatible with different JND models (and vice-versa for the proposed JND model), the proposed JND model and perceptual encoder were implemented as separate modules, and their synthesis results are reported separately for clarity. An integration of these two modules is straightforward, as is obvious from Section 5. Synthesis results for the proposed JND model as well as two other JND models are presented in Section 6.3.

Table 8 shows the FPGA resource utilization of the proposed perceptual encoder architecture for 8–16 bits/pixel input greyscale images with a horizontal size of up to 2048 pixels. It can be seen that the proposed encoder architecture required 5.85% of logic resource and 2% of the BRAM resource on the target FPGA, and a pixel throughput of about 140 Megapixel/s (1 pixel/clock cycle) was achieved. For both the proposed JND model and the perceptual encoder architecture, the logic and BRAM resources used were well below 10% of all the available resources of each type on the target FPGA, which, on the one hand, provides abundant hardware resources for the other image processing tasks running on the FPGA such as noise cancellation, and, on the other hand, leaves ample room for using multiple parallel encoding instances on a single FPGA when higher pixel throughput is demanded.

Table 8. FPGA resource utilization of the proposed perceptual encoder architecture.

Resource Type	Used	Available	Percentage
Slice LUTs	5934	101,400	5.85%
Slice Registers	2300	202,800	1.13%
Block RAM 36Kbits	6.5	325	2%
Clock frequency (MHz)	140		

7. Conclusions

A new pixel-domain JND model and a perceptual image coding architecture exploiting the JND model are presented. In the proposed JND model, lightweight and hardware-efficient operators are used to identify edge, texture and smooth regions in the input image. Different weighting factors for the contrast masking effects are applied to pixels in different regions. The contrast masking and luminance masking effects are combined into the final JND value in the new approach, i.e., using the nonlinear additivity model for masking (NAMM) operator for texture/smooth regions and the maximum operator for edge regions. The proposed JND model and architecture are suitable for implementation on FPGAs for real-time and low complexity embedded systems. In the proposed architecture for a low complexity pixel-domain perceptual codec, the input image is adaptively downsampled based on the visual ROI map identified by measuring the downsampling distortion against the JND thresholds. The proposed JND model provides a more accurate estimation of visual redundancies compared with Chou and Li's model and Yang et al.'s model. Since the computational complexity of the proposed model is significantly less than that of Liu et al.'s model based on image decomposition with total variation, the proposed JND mode achieves a new balance between the accuracy of JND profile and the computational complexity. Experimental results further show that the proposed JND-based pixel-domain perceptual coder achieved improved rate-distortion performance as well as visual quality compared with JPEG-LS. At the same perceptual quality in terms of PSPNR, the proposed coder generated fewer bits compared with JPEG, JPEG 2000 and JPEG XR. Finally, FPGA synthesis results indicate that both the proposed JND model and the perceptual coder required a very moderate amount of hardware resources to implement in terms of both logic and block memory resources. On a mid-range FPGA, the hardware architecture of the proposed JND model required about 2.6% of logic and 1.4% of block memory resources and achieved a throughput of 190 Megapixel/s, while the hardware architecture of the perceptual encoder required about 6% of logic and 2% of block memory resources and achieved a throughput of 140 Megapixel/s.

Author Contributions: Conceptualization, Z.W. and S.S.; Methodology, Z.W.; Software, Z.W., T.-H.T. and P.K.M.; Validation, Z.W., T.-H.T. and P.K.M.; Investigation, Z.W., T.-H.T. and P.K.M.; Writing–original draft preparation, Z.W.; Writing–review and editing, Z.W., T.-H.T., P.K.M. and S.S.; Visualization, Z.W. and T.-H.T.; Supervision, S.S.; Project administration, S.S.

Funding: This research received no external funding.

Conflicts of Interest: The authors declare no conflict of interest.

References

1. Stolitzka, D. Developing Requirements for a Visually Lossless Display Stream Coding System Open Standard. In Proceedings of the Annual Technical Conference Exhibition, SMPTE 2013, Hollywood, CA, USA, 22–24 October 2013; pp. 1–12.
2. The Video Electronics Standards Association. Display Stream Compression Standard v1.1. Available online: http://www.vesa.org/vesa-standards/ (accessed on 30 November 2018).
3. VESA Display Stream Compression Task Group. *Call for Technology: Advanced Display Stream Compression*; Video Electronics Standards Association: San Jose, CA, USA, 2015.
4. Joint Photographic Experts Group committee (ISO/IEC JTC1/SC29/WG1). Call for Proposals for a low-latency lightweight image coding system. *News & Press*, 11 March 2016.

5. Watson, A. DCTune: A technique for visual optimization of DCT quantization matrices for individual images. *Soc. Inf. Displ. Dig. Tech. Pap.* **1993**, *XXIV*, 946–949.
6. Ramos, M.; Hemami, S. Suprathreshold wavelet coefficient quantization in complex stimuli: Psychophysical evaluation and analysis. *J. Opt. Soc. Am.* **2001**, *18*, 2385–2397. [CrossRef]
7. Liu, Z.; Karam, L.; Watson, A. JPEG2000 encoding with perceptual distortion control. *Image Process. IEEE Trans.* **2006**, *15*, 1763–1778.
8. Netravali, A.; Haskell, B. *Digital Pictures: Representation, Compression, and Standards*, 2nd ed.; Springer Science+Business Media: New York, NY, USA, 1995.
9. Chou, C.H.; Li, Y.C. A perceptually tuned subband image coder based on the measure of just-noticeable-distortion profile. *IEEE Trans. Circuits Syst. Video Technol.* **1995**, *5*, 467–476. [CrossRef]
10. Jayant, N.; Johnston, J.; Safranek, R. Signal compression based on models of human perception. *Proc. IEEE* **1993**, *81*, 1385–1422. [CrossRef]
11. Yang, X.; Ling, W.; Lu, Z.; Ong, E.; Yao, S. Just noticeable distortion model and its applications in video coding. *Signal Process. Image Commun.* **2005**, *20*, 662–680. [CrossRef]
12. Liu, A.; Lin, W.; Paul, M.; Deng, C.; Zhang, F. Just Noticeable Difference for Images With Decomposition Model for Separating Edge and Textured Regions. *IEEE Trans. Circuits Syst. Video Technol.* **2010**, *20*, 1648–1652. [CrossRef]
13. Wu, H.R.; Reibman, A.R.; Lin, W.; Pereira, F.; Hemami, S.S. Perceptual Visual Signal Compression and Transmission. *Proc. IEEE* **2013**, *101*, 2025–2043. [CrossRef]
14. Wang, Z.; Baroud, Y.; Najmabadi, S.M.; Simon, S. Low complexity perceptual image coding by just-noticeable difference model based adaptive downsampling. In Proceedings of the 2016 Picture Coding Symposium (PCS 2016), Nuremberg, Germany, 4–7 December 2016; pp. 1–5.
15. Safranek, R.J.; Johnston, J.D. A perceptually tuned sub-band image coder with image dependent quantization and post-quantization data compression. In Proceedings of the 1989 International Conference on Acoustics, Speech, and Signal Processing (ICASSP '89), Glasgow, UK, 23-26 May 1989; Volume 3, pp. 1945–1948.
16. Yang, X.K.; Lin, W.S.; Lu, Z.; Ong, E.P.; Yao, S. Just-noticeable-distortion profile with nonlinear additivity model for perceptual masking in color images. In Proceedings of the 2003 IEEE International Conference on Acoustics, Speech, and Signal Processing (ICASSP '03), Hong Kong, China, 6–10 April 2003; Volume 3, pp. 609–612.
17. Girod, B. What's Wrong with Mean-squared Error? In *Digital Images and Human Vision*; Watson, A.B., Ed.; MIT Press: Cambridge, MA, USA, 1993; pp. 207–220.
18. Eckert, M.P.; Bradley, A.P. Perceptual quality metrics applied to still image compression. *Signal Process.* **1998**, *70*, 177–200. [CrossRef]
19. Mirmehdi, M.; Xie, X.; Suri, J. *Handbook of Texture Analysis*; Imperial College Press: London, UK, 2009.
20. Danielsson, P.E.; Seger, O. Generalized and Separable Sobel Operators. In *Machine Vision for Three-Dimensional Scenes*; Freeman, H., Ed.; Academic Press: San Diego, CA, USA, 1990; pp. 347–379.
21. Canny, J. A Computational Approach to Edge Detection. *IEEE Trans. Pattern Anal. Mach. Intell.* **1986**, *PAMI-8*, 679–698. [CrossRef]
22. Yang, X. Matlab Codes for Pixel-Based JND (Just-Noticeable Difference) Model. Available online: http://www.ntu.edu.sg/home/wslin/JND_img.rar (accessed on 30 November 2018).
23. Ojala, T.; Pietikainen, M.; Maenpaa, T. Multiresolution gray-scale and rotation invariant texture classification with local binary patterns. *IEEE Trans. Pattern Anal. Mach. Intell.* **2002**, *24*, 971–987. [CrossRef]
24. Bailey, D.G. *Design for Embedded Image Processing on FPGAs*; John Wiley & Sons (Asia) Pte Ltd.: Singapore, 2011.
25. Weinberger, M.J.; Seroussi, G.; Sapiro, G. The LOCO-I lossless image compression algorithm: Principles and standardization into JPEG-LS. *IEEE Trans. Image Process.* **2000**, *9*, 1309–1324. [CrossRef] [PubMed]
26. Merlino, P.; Abramo, A. A Fully Pipelined Architecture for the LOCO-I Compression Algorithm. *IEEE Trans. Very Large Scale Integr. Syst.* **2009**, *17*, 967–971. [CrossRef]
27. Jia, Y.; Lin, W.; Kassim, A.A. Estimating Just-Noticeable Distortion for Video. *IEEE Trans. Circuits Syst. Video Technol.* **2006**, *16*, 820–829. [CrossRef]
28. Wei, Z.; Ngan, K.N. Spatio-Temporal Just Noticeable Distortion Profile for Grey Scale Image/Video in DCT Domain. *IEEE Trans. Circuits Syst. Video Technol.* **2009**, *19*, 337–346.

29. The USC-SIPI Image Database. Available online: http://sipi.usc.edu/database/database.php (accessed on 30 November 2018).

30. ITU-T T.24. *Standardized Digitized Image Set*; ITU: Geneva, Switzerland, 1998.

31. Liu, A. Matlab Codes for Image Pixel Domain JND (Just-Noticeable Difference) Model with Edge and Texture Separation. Available online: http://www.ntu.edu.sg/home/wslin/JND_codes.rar (accessed on 30 November 2018).

32. ISO/IEC 29170-2 Draft Amendment 2. *Information Technology—Advanced Image Coding and Evaluation—Part 2: Evaluation Procedure for Visually Lossless Coding*; ISO/IEC JTC1/SC29/WG1 output Document N72029; International Organization for Standardization: Geneva, Switzerland, 2015.

33. Malepati, H. *Digital Media Processing: DSP Algorithms Using C*; Newnes: Oxford, UK, 2010; Chapter 11.

34. Varadarajan, S.; Chakrabarti, C.; Karam, L.J.; Bauza, J.M. A distributed psycho-visually motivated Canny edge detector. In Proceedings of the 2010 IEEE International Conference on Acoustics, Speech and Signal Processing (ICASSP '10), Dallas, TX, USA, 14–19 March 2010; pp. 822–825.

35. Xu, Q.; Varadarajan, S.; Chakrabarti, C.; Karam, L.J. A Distributed Canny Edge Detector: Algorithm and FPGA Implementation. *IEEE Trans. Image Process.* **2014**, *23*, 2944–2960. [CrossRef] [PubMed]

36. Wang, Z.; Simoncelli, E.P.; Bovik, A.C. Multiscale structural similarity for image quality assessment. In Proceedings of the Thirty-Seventh Asilomar Conference on Signals, Systems Computers, Pacific Grove, CA, USA, 9–12 November 2003; Volume 2, pp. 1398–1402.

37. Wang, Z. Multi-Scale Structural Similarity (Matlab Code). Available online: https://ece.uwaterloo.ca/~z70wang/research/iwssim/msssim.zip (accessed on 30 November 2018).

38. Mantiuk, R.; Kim, K.J.; Rempel, A.G.; Heidrich, W. HDR-VDP-2: A Calibrated Visual Metric for Visibility and Quality Predictions in All Luminance Conditions. *ACM Trans. Graph.* **2011**, *30*, 40:1–40:14. [CrossRef]

39. Mantiuk, R.; Kim, K.J.; Rempel, A.G.; Heidrich, W. HDR-VDP-2 (Ver. 2.2.1). Available online: http://hdrvdp.sourceforge.net/ (accessed on 30 November 2018).

40. Taubman, D. Kakadu Software (Ver. 7). Available online: http://kakadusoftware.com/software/ (accessed on 30 November 2018).

41. ISO/IEC 29199-5 | ITU-T T.835. *Information Technology—JPEG XR Image Coding System—Reference Software*; ITU: Geneva, Switzerland, 2012.

MDPI
St. Alban-Anlage 66
4052 Basel
Switzerland
Tel. +41 61 683 77 34
Fax +41 61 302 89 18
www.mdpi.com

Journal of Imaging Editorial Office
E-mail: jimaging@mdpi.com
www.mdpi.com/journal/jimaging

www.ingramcontent.com/pod-product-compliance
Lightning Source LLC
Chambersburg PA
CBHW051849210326
41597CB00033B/5837